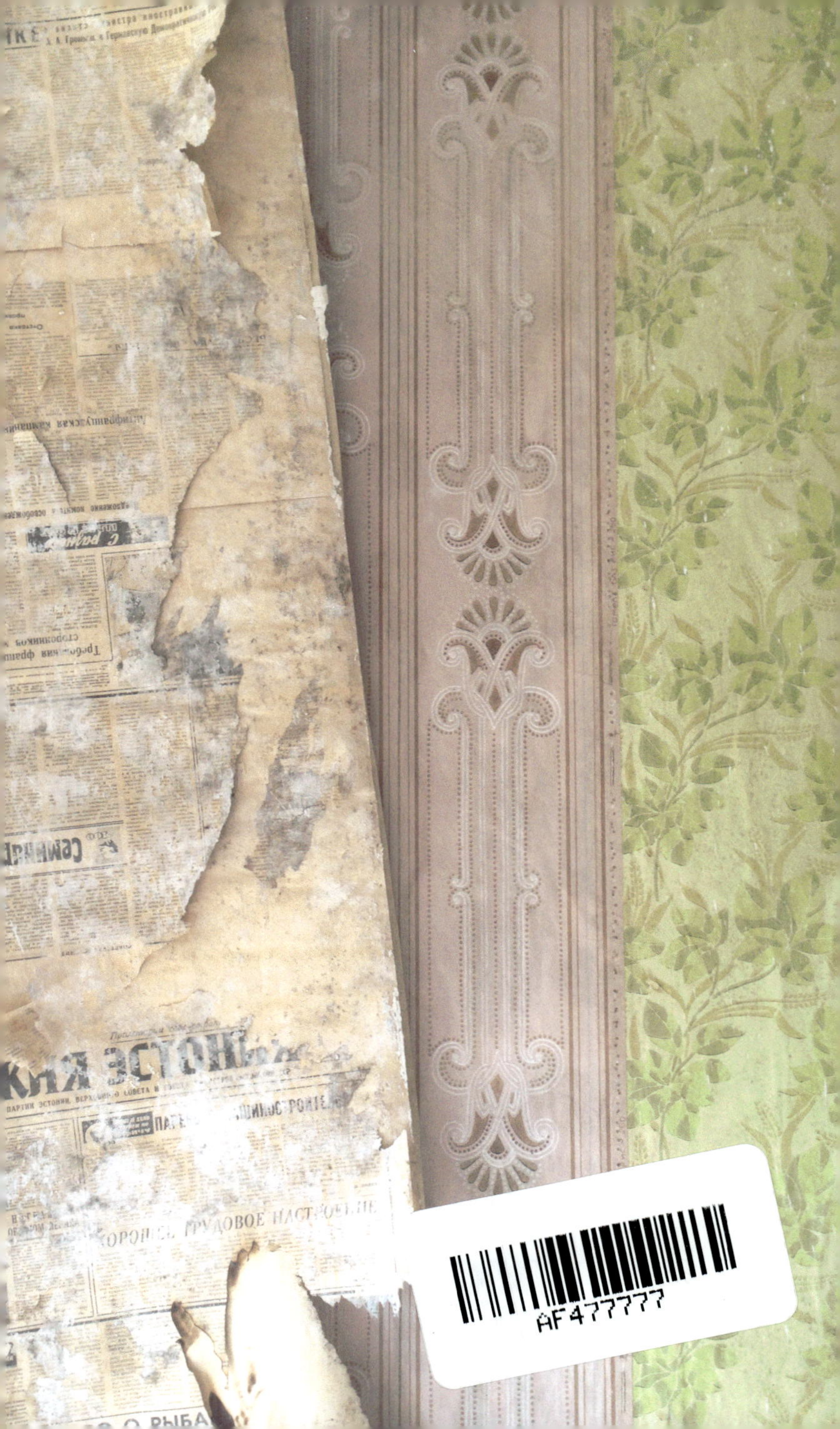
AF477777

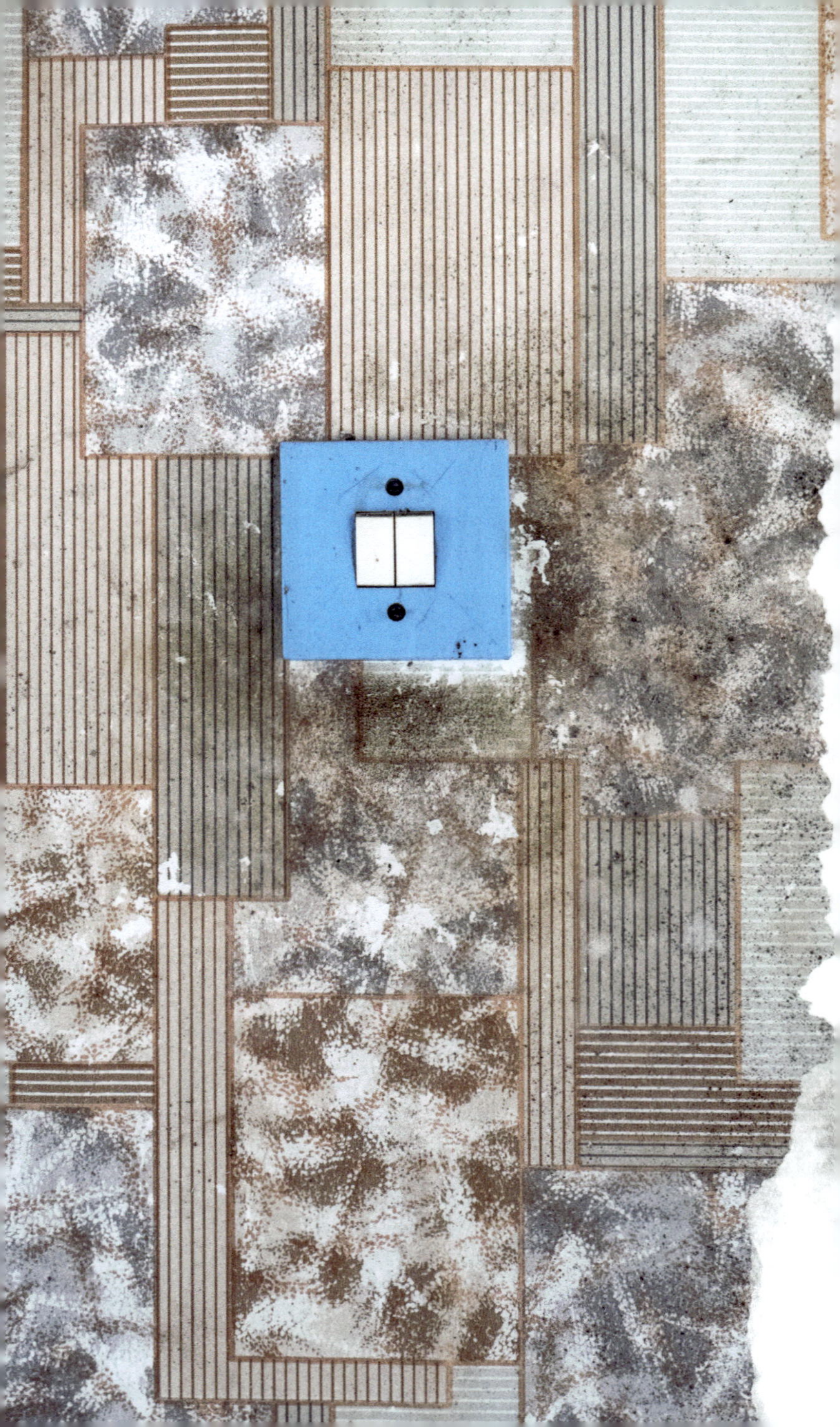

# HOME MADE RUSSIA

PHOTOGRAPHY  Mikhail Akhmatov, Valerii Rodin
TEXT  Vladimir Arkhipov, Susan B. Glasser

DESIGN AND EDIT  Murray & Sorrell FUEL
TRANSLATOR  Andrew Bromfield
CO-ORDINATOR  Julia Goumen

# HOME MADE RUSSIA

### Post-Soviet

### Folk Artefacts

## Vladimir Arkhipov

FUEL

# Introduction

Vladimir Arkhipov

This book makes no claims to being a piece of serious research, although, it goes without saying, it did not come about as a result of nothing. The folk phenomenon of the home-made production of functional everyday items is wide scale, spontaneous, and largely unknown. Such things have always been with us, and can be found today in any country in the world. This book, however, deals only with the Russian part of this phenomenon.

In 1994 I saw, at an acquaintance's dacha, an unusual hook on which clothes were hanging. It was made from an old toothbrush, without bristles, and had obviously been bent over a fire. There was something strange in that moment of recognition. I immediately saw the light, as it were, and recalled similar things that I knew, belonging to my relatives, friends, acquaintances, or acquaintances of acquaintances. Before then I hadn't really noticed them. Now it seemed to me that it would be an interesting task to gather them all together and look at them in large numbers – a gathering of equals. The first on the list of candidates to approach was my father who, I remembered, had several strange 'thingamyjigs'. I started my collection with them. Then I set to work on my cousins, aunts and uncles. Then it was the turn of friends, acquaintances and non-acquaintances. After that things started to seek me out themselves. People who liked the idea called me, and continue to call, in order to inform me when, what, and where they had seen something similar. It's clear that the process of searching for things has its own momentum, its own internal logic, and is of a highly accidental nature. It is this reason that the items discovered are listed randomly in this book.

Here you will only get acquainted with a fraction of my collection. In almost all cases, my interest in some or other item led to the spontaneous desire of the author of that item to begin to tell me how it had all come about. I realised that it would be a good idea to record all of this, so I bought myself a dictaphone and a camera and began to document these stories and processes. Sometimes they gave me old photographs of themselves – where they, of course, looked a lot younger. Because of this, the styles of the authors' or witnesses' photographs vary. In some cases there are no photos because, like many people, they didn't want to have their photos published. Apart from this a few people refused to give, or asked me not to publish their names, surnames, professions, work places or places of residence. The interviews which I recorded with the authors of the objects appear in an edited form. My questions have been omitted in order to print monologues from the authors, which, in my opinion, have more value.

During the eleven years this project, which I call 'The People's Museum of Home-Made Objects', has taken, I have got into some unusual situations: in 1998 in the city of Orel I was set upon by drunk police officers who

confiscated my camera and dictaphone, exposed the film in the camera, and beat me up. (This is the reason why there are no photographs from Orel.) In 1999, in the Ryazan region, drunk youths wanted to interrupt my interview, but they paid the price for this when they were nearly cut to shreds by the man I was interviewing. In 1996, while recording an interview with a trader near the University metro station, some 'brothers', market heavies, came up to me without my noticing and asked me, in none too polite a manner, what I was doing. I could think of nothing better than to answer the question honestly. My answer made quite a strong impression on them; their distrust and threatening behaviour changed into friendliness. 'That was pretty cool how you thought that up – if you want, record all the traders, then you can come with us, we'll sort you out with a slapper, and then you can eat and drink like a man.'

In Berlin in 1995, through bad translation and my own stupidity, I lost the chance to acquire a 5-metre mummy crocodile that a famous Egyptologist/ archeologist wanted to present me with. He had been jumping with joy at my exhibition because, standing next to home-made Russian things, he had seen analogies with, and understood the functional purpose of, certain mysterious ancient Egyptian items.

There are over a thousand items in my collection today, and they all have three characteristics in common: functionality, a visual uniqueness and the testimony of the author, who is both the creator and the user. They represent an astonishing part of modern folk-material culture but, unfortunately, are under the constant threat of ruin, because I do not have the means at my disposal for their proper storage. I have never once, in the eleven years I've been collecting them, received any help, support, or even interest from the state. However, I have some people to thank for their moral support and practical help. They are, above all, Andrei Arkhipov, Mikhail Akhmatov, Martin Barlow, Konstantin Batinkov, Dmitrii Bragin, Nikolai Brizgov, Vasilii Bichkov, Maria Chekmenyova, Andrei Drozhdov, Vladimir Dukelskii, Irina Fadeeva, Bart Goldhorn, Jan Kalnberzin, Deborah Kermoud, Vitalii Khitrov, Vladimir Krichevskii, Andrei Lazarev, Valentina Lopatina, Kirill Medvedev, Viktor Miziano, Georgii Mnatsakanov, Georgii Nikich, Aleksei Orekhov, Adrian Plant, Nikolai Poliskii, Olga Potapova, Valerii Rodin, the Ruchkins, Natalya Saltikova, Vladislav Sofronov, Marina Starush, Aleksandr Tarasov, Vitalii Khitrov, Lidiya Vasileva, Yulia Vainzof, Jonathon Watkins, Irina Yurna, Aleksandr Zaitsev, Ksenia Zorina, Natalia Zublotskite.

Susan B. Glasser
*Washington Post*

For as long as Vladimir Arkhipov could remember, he lived surrounded by his father's home-made contraptions: blinking Christmas tree lights, when there weren't any to be bought in the 1960s; a jury-rigged radio receiver, around which the family would huddle, listening to the forbidden *Voice of America*. There was even a television aerial made out of unwanted forks, purchased only because his grandmother was at the store, the Soviet Union was about to collapse and there was nothing else for sale.

But it took Arkhipov decades to realise that his father's ingenious solutions were in fact invaluable artefacts of Soviet culture; the private side of life in a country where consumer shortages were an everyday occurance. Today, he is Russia's leading – in fact, as far as he knows, only – collector of these unique inventions, having assembled over one thousand. Ranging from a home-made tractor to a tiny bath plug made from a boot-heel, each one is a small essay in adaptation.

As Russia tentatively enters the world of global consumerism, Arkhipov's 'thingamyjigs' tell the story of its Soviet past – and of the wrenching years since the Soviet collapse, when the items of capitalist commerce started to become available in Russia, but were still largely unobtainable by the country's impoverished millions. The art critic Yekaterina Dyogot calls them, 'fragments of the sunken, non-market civilization of Soviet socialism.' They are also just plain clever, in the quirky personalised way of inventions meant to serve their maker and not a marketing department.

'This is a completely unique phenomenon – things that were never meant to be goods for sale. People made them for themselves,' says Arkhipov. 'In the 21st century, it seems somehow unreal.' It is not just individual quirks but political realities that his objects document. He connects his collection directly to the individual Russian experience in an oppressive state. He argues that in such a place, 'each person who can make something with his hands prefers to make something small and concrete rather than uniting with others to change their lives. Everyone still struggles with their own problems alone.'

In Soviet times, the centrally planned economy begat chronic shortages and perpetual consumer angst – a situation where a missing spare part could become a crisis for a factory and individual needs never registered in the deep recesses of bureaucracy. With no obvious way to change the system, individuals did what they could to live within it, at-home inventors creating a thousand items missing from the stores.

Take the tiny device known as a 'Conman' that Arkhipov pulls from one of the dusty bins in his studio. It is, in effect, a home-made plug, that converts

a light-bulb socket into an electrical outlet. 'Everything,' Arkhipov says, 'relates to the history of the country.' After the destruction of World War II, there were chronic power shortages. In villages, electrical outlets were forbidden. People were allowed just one light bulb per house, to be turned on a few hours a day. Dictator Joseph Stalin even decreed jail terms for installing banned outlets: 'but still people needed electrical sockets.'

Arkhipov's collection has now grown to include toys, tools, mechanical and electronic devices, even improvised forms of transportation. A few items defy classification, 'because there is nothing else like them in existence'. Some are whimsical, like the briefcase-shaped gasoline can made by a driver after years of ferrying bosses and their attaché cases to work. 'I don't think even he knew why it turned out this way,' Arkhipov muses. 'He must have dreamed of becoming a boss himself.'

Arkhipov says he often knows at a glance whether objects were made before or after the Soviet fall. 'This could not appear now,' he says as he cradles a toy Kalashnikov assault rifle wrapped in scrap metal. In Soviet times, such metal was a staple of home-made inventions; today it is a commodity, bought and sold for precious roubles by poor people who would no longer think of wasting it on a child's toy.

A brightly coloured carrying basket, in contrast, is a product of more recent times. It is woven, Arkhipov says, from the colour-coded bands used by European banks to separate denominations of cash. The basket-weaver worked in a Moscow bank. 'He just collected them from the garbage bins'.

Arkhipov is sure that sooner or later Russia will stop producing objects that reflect its communist past. Maybe then, he says with a laugh, he will go ahead and create his own hand-made 'utopia' – only living with the creations he has collected. After all, he says, 'I already have a home-made refrigerator, a washing machine, a telephone, different kinds of furniture. A home-made paraglider, a boat, a car, a tractor... Toys you can play with, instruments, tools, a hammer, a drill, a screwdriver. Everything one needs to live with.'

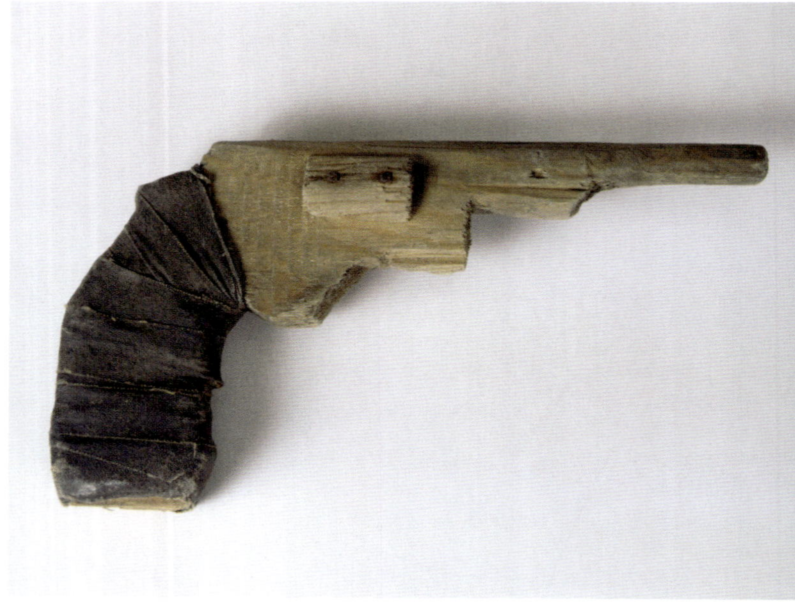

**Aleksandr Sigutin**                    Rostov-on-Don, 1968

Well, I'm thirty-eight now, but when I was nine or ten, we made such pistols. Since then progress has made a great leap forward and now they've got all kinds of metal and plastic pistols that you can hardly tell apart from the real thing. What can I say about the technology used? We made it according to the template of an older guy's imitation one. It was cut out of pine, with God's help. The older guys even made revolving chambers for their pistols. That was a bit hard for me to do. Then we got hold of a handle, from a shovel or a rake for example, and cut off about 5 centimeters, split it carefully into two parts with an axe or a knife and then attached it with nails.

We didn't play cowboys, but war games. Not far from us there was a factory that produced building materials. They used to load sand there. We used to run and play war there. Well, after a few years we all got into 'The Three Musketeers' and we started to make sabres. And the toy pistol got lost somewhere in some shed. And it stayed there for about twenty years. During that time I'd got married and had a kid. And then when my daughter was about six, we were cleaning out the shed and we came across this pistol. I was reading Greek myths to her, about Aphrodite, Zeus, and Athena the warrior. And then she got hold of that pistol and all summer played at being the warrior with it.

Wood, insulating tape

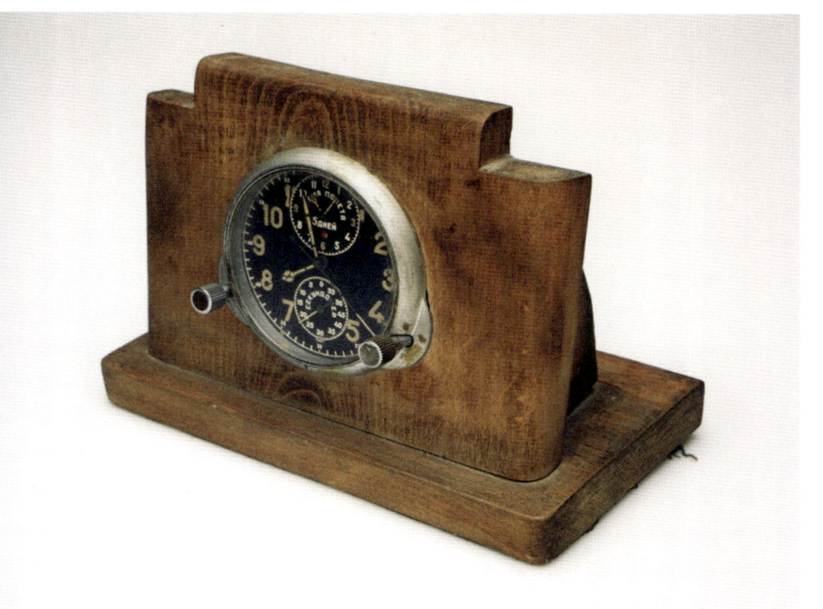

**Yefim Liberman** Armavir, c.1946

*As recounted by his granddaughter Vera Khlebnikhova:* This is what was left to me by my grandfather, my mother's stepfather, who was a pilot during the war. This is a kind of souvenir of his time as a pilot. It's likely that the clock was just taken from an aircraft and the rest built around it. Here you can find out the flight time and here the days are counted, up to five. These are for those long-distance flights. This clock also glows in the dark. Flannel has been thoughtfully stuck to the base so as not to scratch the furniture. And the front panel is then fitted onto it. It's slightly inclined and fastened on with supports and propped up from the back with utilitarian wooden bits. Then all this is attached to a short wooden plank. It's a simple device, with no frills, the only decorative thing about it are these sculpted corners on the front panel. I think it's from the end of the 1940s when he had already left the army. At the beginning of the war, in 1942 or 1943, he was an instructor in the Armavir flying school and was in Armavir after the evacuation. It was about 1946 or 1947 because after that they left there and they couldn't have got hold of such a thing. So, more than likely this is a kind of farewell from his military post, from that military city.

Aircraft clock, wood, glue, flannel, screws

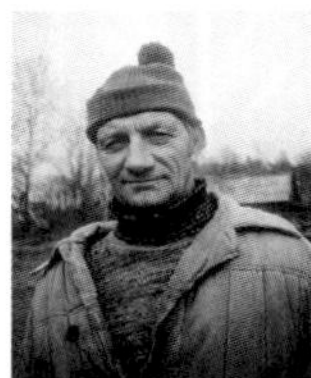

**Ivan Sokolv**                    Nikola-Lenivets, Kaluga region, 1975

I was still studying at the Technical Institute then, it was, fuck, sometime in the 1970s. There was a pond here, but now it's very small, it's been overgrown. Back then it was an OK pond. Shit, I came here on my holidays when I was studying. So, what could you make it from, so that it was suitable? You go into the forest, for fuck's sake, and carve it out of something. Out of wood, from a fucking bird cherry tree. It was fucking cool wood, from bird cherry. It's a soggy kinda tree, fucking out of this world. I battered the puck with it and, fuck, nothing. I only changed the insulating tape once, or twice... it's fucking cool. Even the old tape is probably still left on it. Then I didn't have any time, I got married, went into the army... It's almost thirty years old, I made it in the autumn, just before the pond was frozen over. The guys, a bit younger than me, used to ride out to visit me on holidays and at weekends. The guys from Koltsovo used to come round and we'd take each other on, three against three. I used to study in Kaluga and took the puck from there sometimes. Usually the sticks were home-made, they were shit. You'd give the puck a good fucking bash and it'd fall apart. Is it a hockey stick if you play once with it and it turns into a piece of shit? We used to bash the puck about from morning to evening. We'd play for a rouble, everyone'd put in a rouble and you'd put on your skates and you'd bring a rouble or two with you and it was team against team. Three periods of twenty minutes each. If you lost, that was it, the cunts, but if you won they'd have to pay up, you'd get a case of booze and we'd all get pissed... ha, ha, ha.

Bird cherry stick, insulating tape

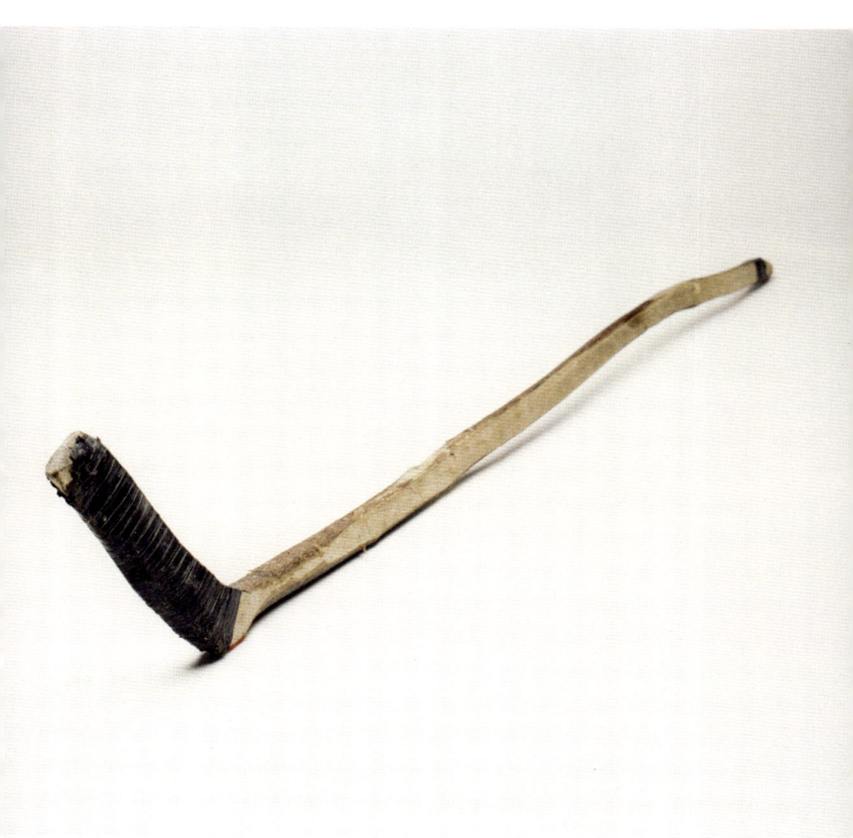

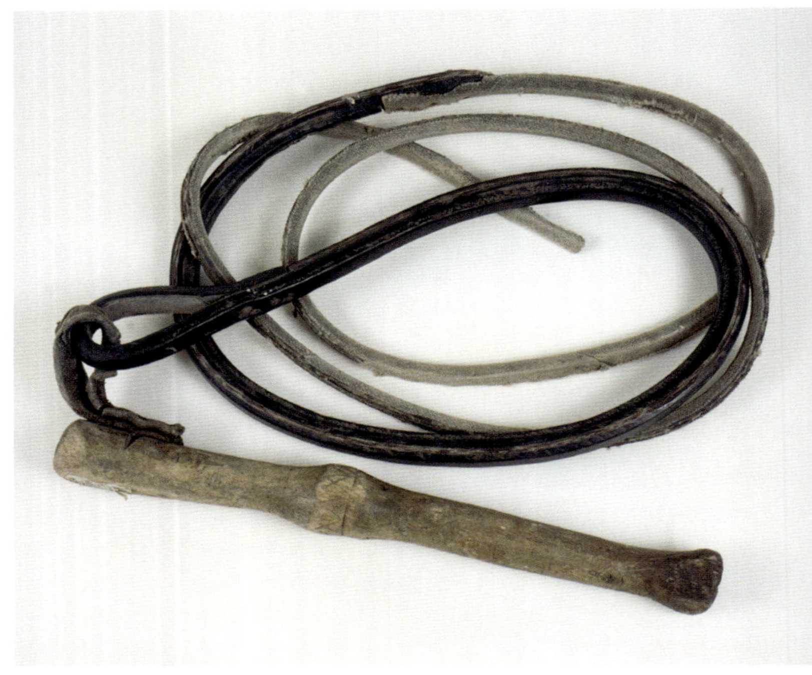

**Ivan Sokolov**                                             Kaluga region, c.1990

A whip, that's what it is, fuck it. I've got to graze the cattle, don't I? Yes, I do.
And where can I get a whip from? Who's going to give me one? I need one
that cracks good and loud. To put a real fucking scare into the cows, how
else can I control them? So I made this whip.

Stick, leather

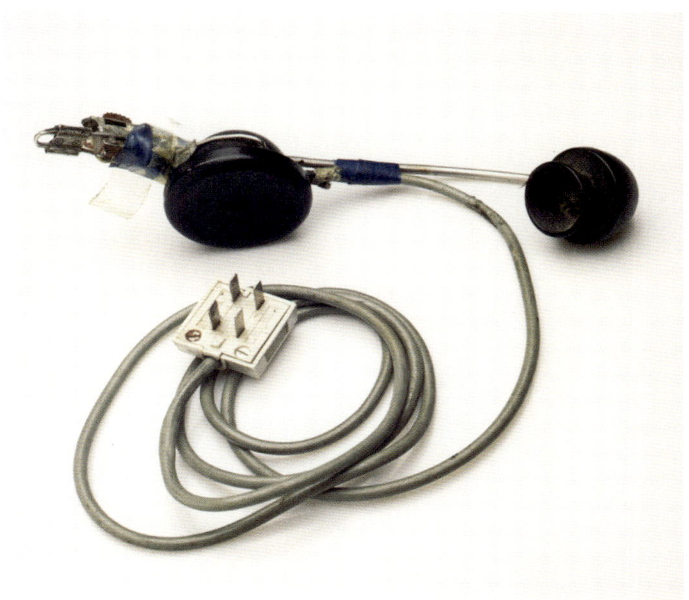

**Sergei**                                                   Moscow, c.1980

*As recounted by Vera Khlebnikova:* This is a telephone receiver that was made by my niece's husband for someone I know. It was made a long, long time ago as the answer to their problem regarding having a telephone in the kitchen. The receiver has an ordinary plug, which goes into the telephone socket. Then the wire was led into the kitchen and on the other end was attached quite a long lead, and a receiver made from old headphones – they look like those pilot's headphones with a microphone attached so that the pilot would have his hands free. Or maybe they were some kind of dispatcher's headphones used at a telephone exchange centre. This is all connected to the lead with the help of some kind of strange black glue, like chewing gum, and isolation tape. When a ring was heard from the main room, it would be connected to the telephone (I wouldn't even call it a telephone), with the help of a part which had been added on. And so it turned out that you could chat away on this phone while, at the same time, doing something with your right or left hand, like stirring something in a saucepan, for example.

Earphones, microphone, switch, wire, telephone plug

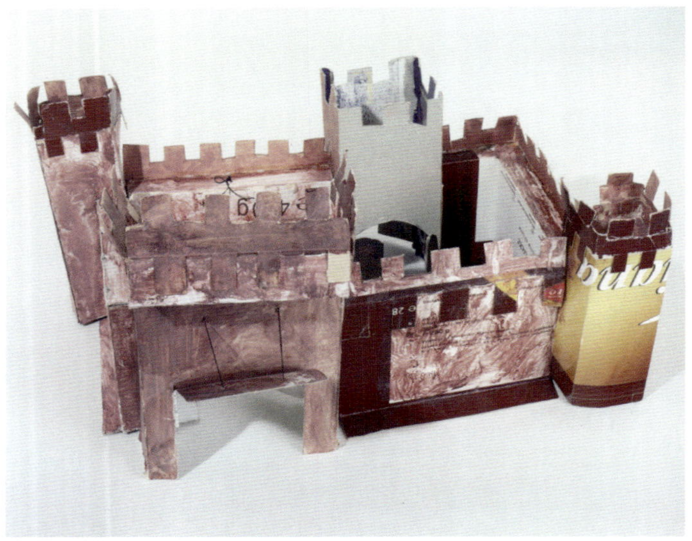

**Ivan Lopatin**                                            Michurinsk, 1995

A lot of chocolate boxes had piled up and like a typical Russian – a hoarder – I couldn't bring myself to throw them away. I looked at them and thought, why not make a fortress? To begin with I made one tower, as it was almost ready-made from an empty cognac box. I cut it off, looked at it and then started to build around that tower. Then from other chocolate boxes I started to build walls. My imagination started to grow, and I made these fortress wall defences. After Senka had played with it a little bit, we wanted to chuck it out because, well, it had only taken a day or two to make. It'd been so simple. But he fell in love with it and kept it, although there wasn't anything particularly interesting about it. There were lots of toy soldiers, very small ones, which me and Senka played with. It was fun when you put them in the fortress, we started to shoot at them with elastic bands. We flicked the elastic bands and shot at the soldiers hiding behind those defences. Then we invented a drawbridge and then a second gate was needed.

There were different kinds of boxes, from Cognac, left over from a birthday, to all kinds of 'magarichi'. I'm a surgeon by profession, and we get small salaries. Well, it's not even interesting to get into that. But 'magarichi' are payment for good work by our citizens who think that surgeons need to be fed – as they're starving here.

Boxes, glue, paint

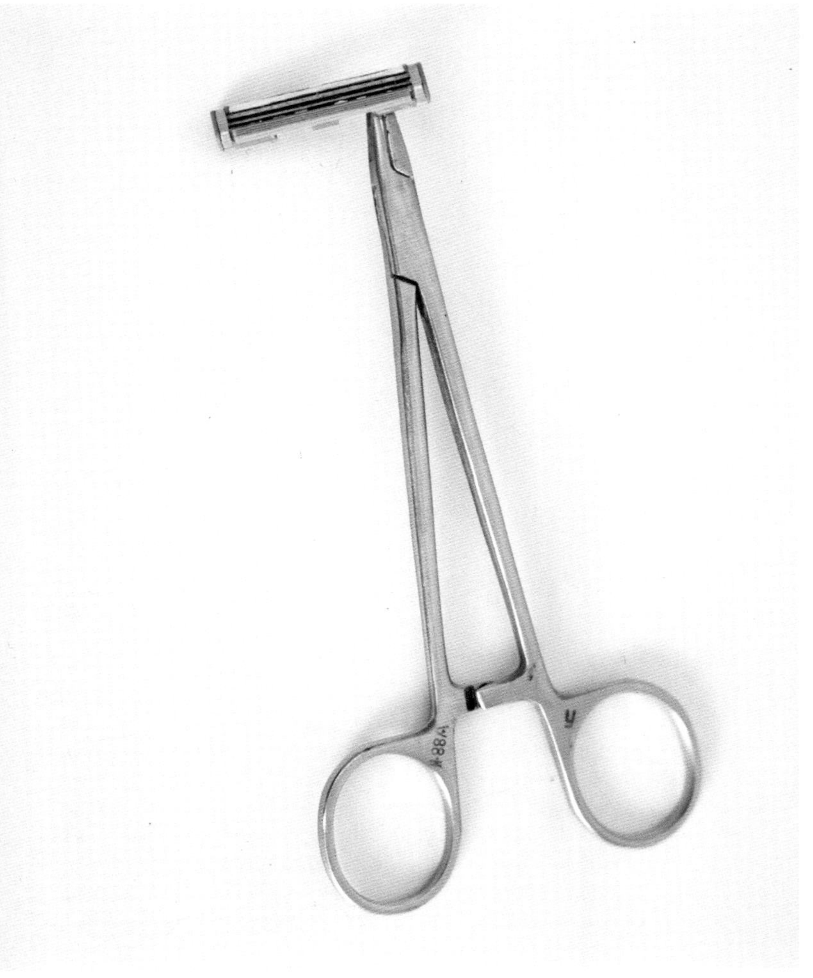

**Ivan Lopatin**                                    Michurinsk, 1997

I just shave with it. It's my financial situation and I'm simply too lazy to buy a blade, it's too inconvenient and I'm reluctant to do it. This is the sort of needle holder we sew with during operations. I've got two or even three 'Shicks', one at work, one here and one at her place.

Surgical clamp, disposable blade

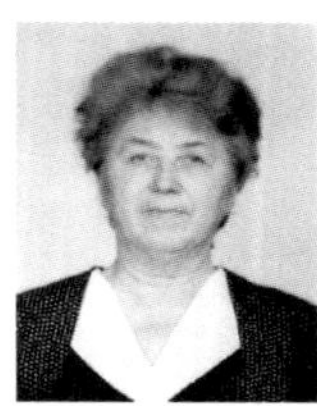

**Lubov Arkhipova**                    Kolomna, 1991

The hat had to be quite light, not a warm winter one made from fur. More for the autumn cold. It had to cover up the kid's head and ears. I took a bit of a skirt made from checked material, then I got an old hat made out of warm fur. It was a bit easier to make the pattern along the lines of that old hat. I made the middle quite flat, from the forehead to the back of the head. The ear part was cut so that the ears would be snugly covered, so that the wind wouldn't get in. Then I put in some lining cut from an old flannelette shirt. I did it very carefully, and everything was smoothed out. I made one for my grandson Nikita. The boys run about all over the place and they can get very sweaty. But in this hat it was easier because it's not so heavy. They don't sell such hats in the shops now. They used to sell them, those 'budyonovki', hats with peaks, ear muffs and a red star at the front. They don't send them to us from abroad either and Russian firms don't produce them, so you have to make everything yourself at home. You have to try to think things up, to try to make them along the lines of the old patterns. And so the hat turned out OK, in fact quite good. I'm pleased with it. It's soft and warm, just like I wanted.

Skirt and shirt material, thread, cord

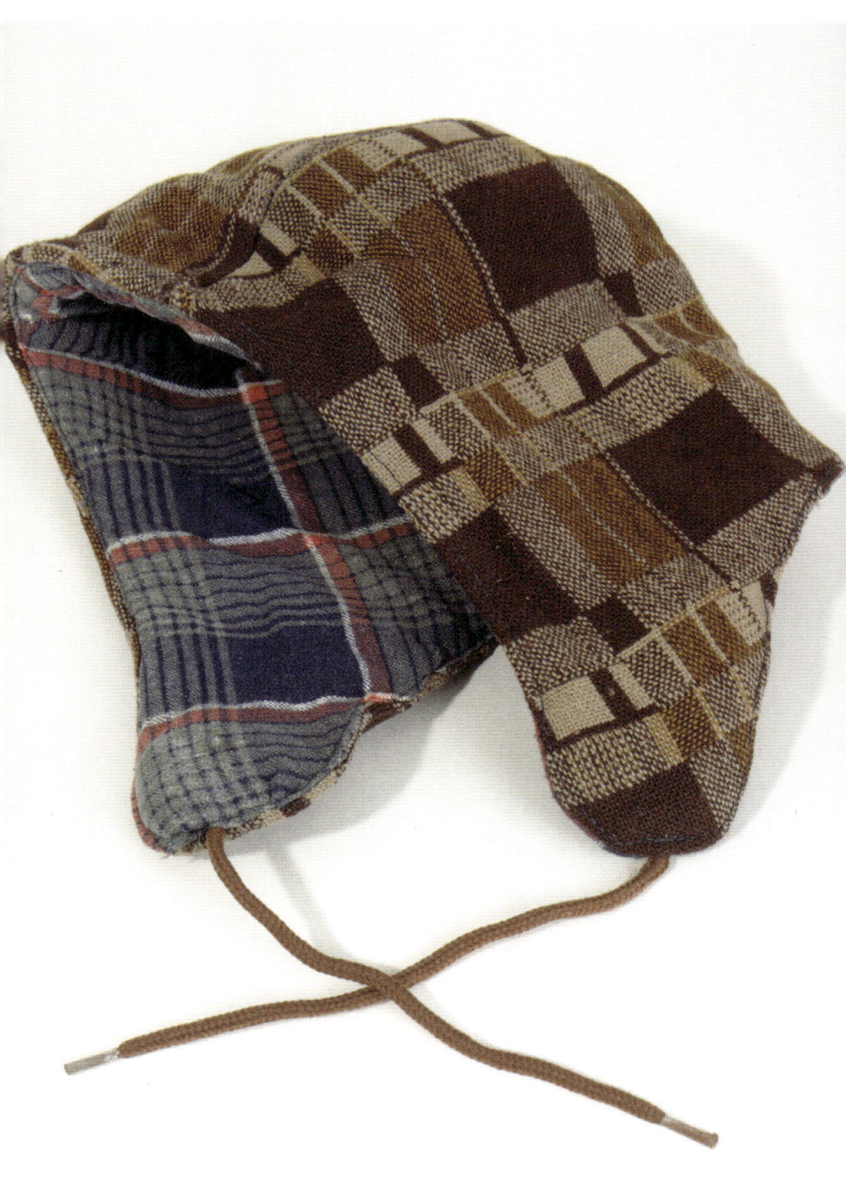

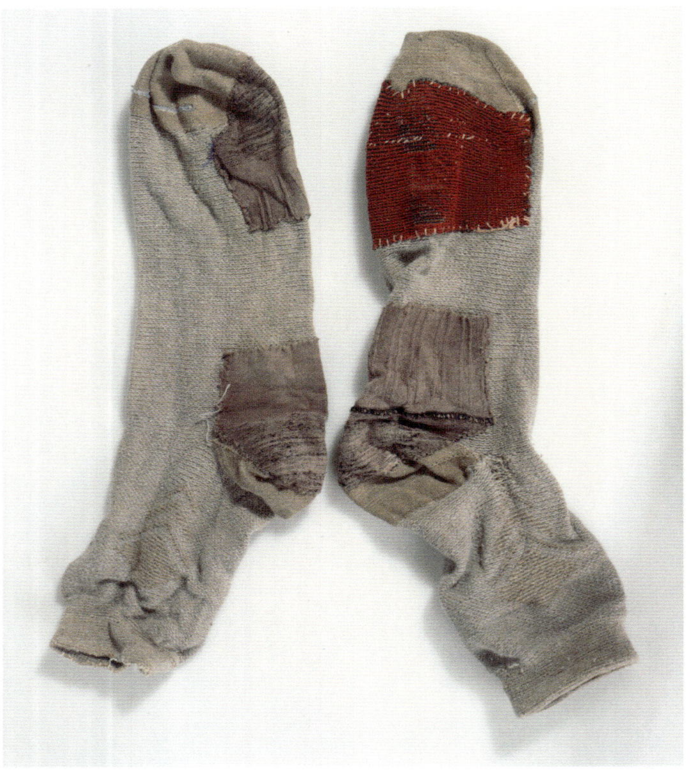

**Lubov Arkhipova**                                    Kolomna, 1995

I'm forced to try to make ends meet, something I've been taught from childhood. In the environment we grew up in, one of constant need, we were forced to patch up clothes and to darn socks to make them last longer. We patch up clothes and treat everything with care, because this extends their lives, and in turn helps the family budget. When you darn some personal item, such as socks or some shirt or T-shirt, you experience a feeling of warmth and love towards the person who owns it. I try to do it well, so that it looks smart, and I get a lot of satisfaction from it myself, all the time hoping that my work will be liked and appreciated. Of course, if it was possible just to get rid of old clothes and buy new ones in their place, I'm sure nobody would object. But, as these materials are hard to come by, we're forced to patch up stuff.

Socks, darning thread

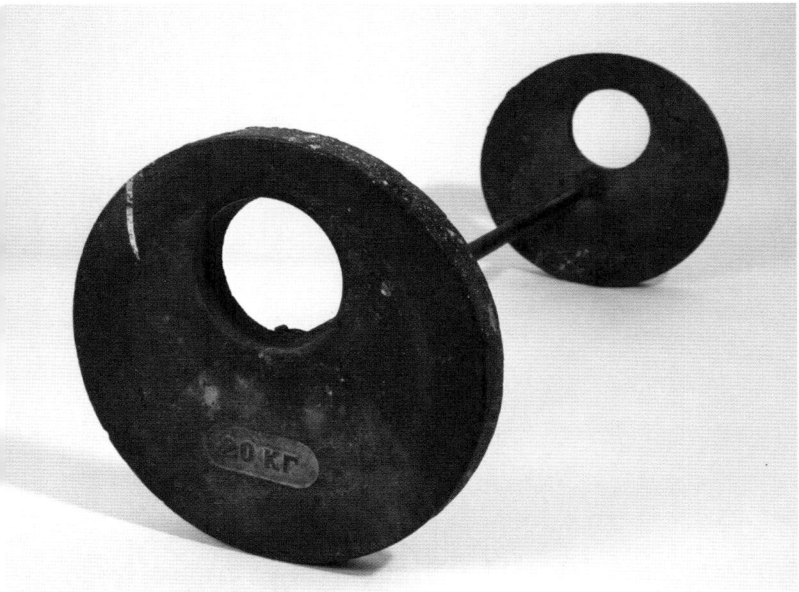

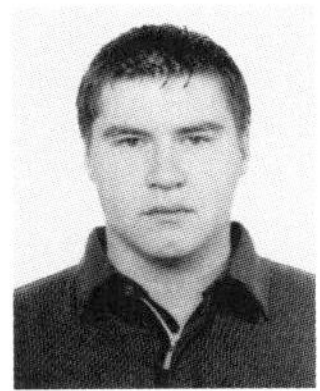

**Nikolai Korolyov**  Moscow, 1996

In 1996, while I was living in student halls, I was studying and kind of trying to keep in shape by working out. In our small sports hall there were two rooms. The first had all the metal stuff, and in the second were mats, punch bags and so on. In the first room, apart from the metal stuff, there were dumb-bells but no weights. We looked for weights but there wasn't any money to buy them – they are very expensive. At the time they were undertaking repairs on our sports hall and there was a builders' pulley around which was attached to the roof by ropes. And under this were counterweights, of 20kg – we called them pancakes. So we decided to, as it were, borrow these from the builders and we asked them for two. Then we found a kind of metal handle that went with the weights. We asked one of the builders to weld this handle onto the weights.

Cast iron counterweights, steel rod

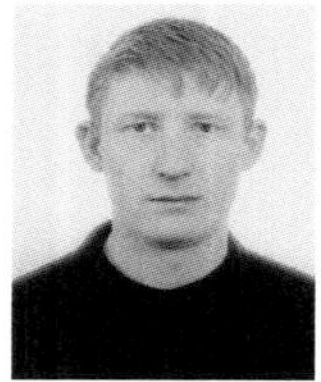

**Aleksei Solomkin**                                        Vladimir region, 1995

I've got a neighbour, his name's Nikolai, who is very kind and jolly and we like to drink beer together. It worked out that how we drink beer is very interesting. We open our bottles, each of us sitting on his own porch, and flick our bottle tops onto the other's lawn. After a while quite a lot of those bottle tops had accumulated there, so the grass in front of my house had become very messed up, full of all the tops. From time to time this caused some problems between me and my wife. Naturally enough, she didn't like all that mess. And so, after a row, I started to clear away those tops. I filled up two pockets with them. And as I was picking them up, walking around our house, I started to think of how I could put them to some use. It would've been a shame just to chuck them all away. But I couldn't think of anything so I just stuck them all in the shed.

Then, suddenly, the idea came to me. I'd seen those tops flattened out on someone's porch. They'd served two functions. They stopped you slipping in winter and they got rid of mud from your boots so that you didn't drag a load of dirt into the house. The problem was though that I've got a brick porch and so there was no way I was going to be able to hammer bottle tops into it. I thought and thought but nothing sprang to mind. Then my brother came to stay. When we were in the shed he asked me, 'Why have you got all these bottle tops hanging about?' I told him and as he worked in a factory he said that he'd help me do something with them. So a week later he brought me some plastic Textolite with openings in it. I had some material left over, some improvised stuff, where the screws are and where the home-made rivets fix into these bottle tops. Well, that's basically how it all came about.

Beer bottle tops, Textolite, screws, rivets

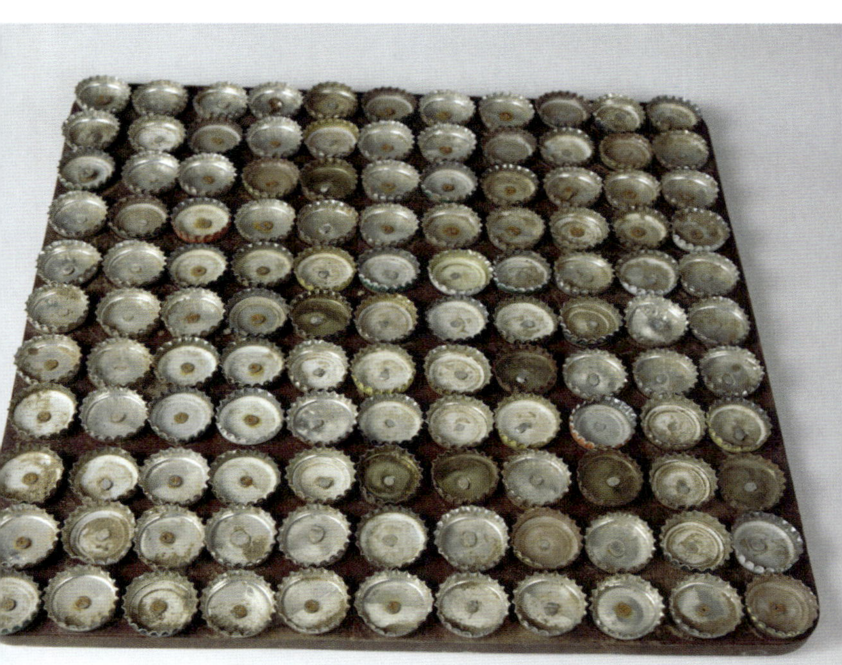

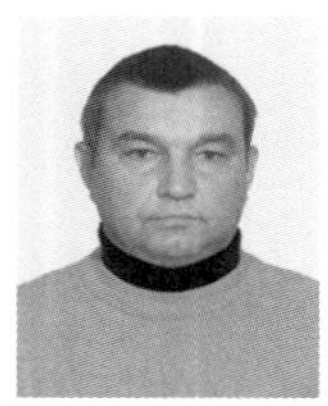

**Andrei Smirnov**                                        Moscow, 1994

When we lived in a communal apartment everyone had their own pans, dishes, table and cupboard in the kitchen. It was a big apartment for eight families. At first we all got on well, like good neighbours. Nothing disappeared, we all knew each other. Then, when they started breaking up the communal apartments, our neighbours moved away and they started moving other temporary people in. Soldiers, refugees – all sorts. The dishes, the matches, all kinds of little bits and pieces started disappearing. My wife was getting nervous and suggested I put a lock on the cupboard, so I did – to stop all the riff-raff helping themselves.

Cupboard, lock

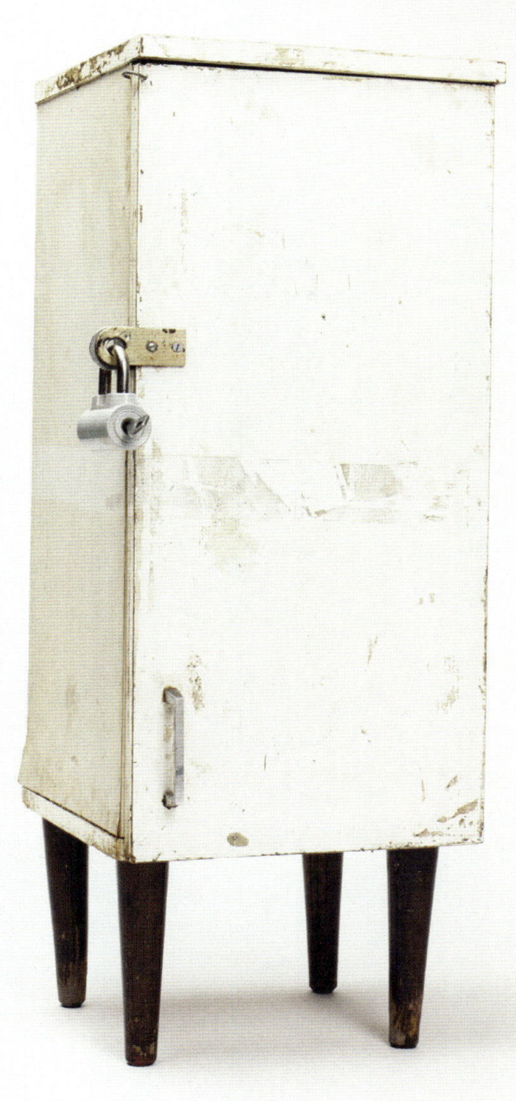

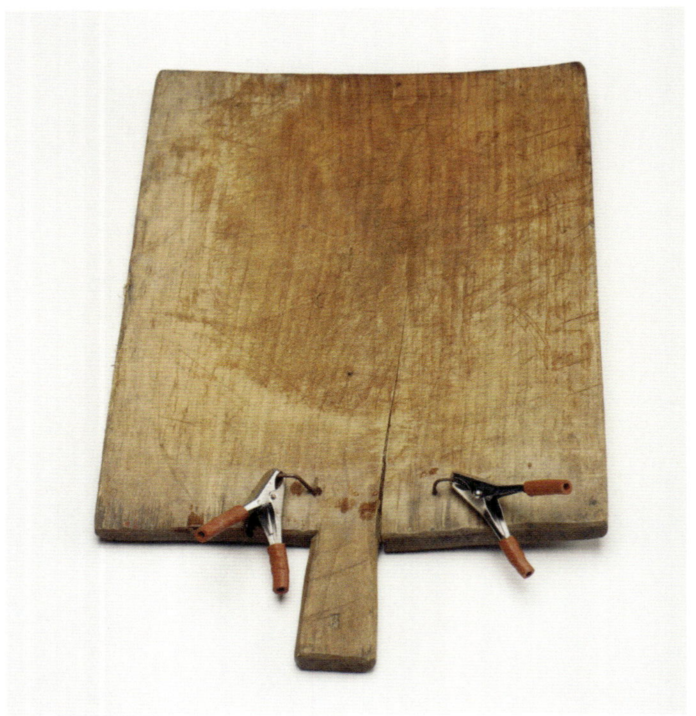

**Andrei Smirnov**                                                    Moscow, 1995

Who cuts up the meat in your house? You do eat meat, don't you? Then you must know that when you're cutting up meat, you always need an extra hand. Isn't that right? Cutting out the tendons, you always pull on a piece and then wonder how you can stretch that spot. Well, it's very easy. You just fix a pair of crocodile clips to your cutting board, or maybe just one – and the problem's solved. You grab one edge with a crocodile clip and pull away. Then you cut the stretched meat any way you like – cut pieces out or trim the edge, for instance. That's all there is to it.

Wooden board, crocodile clips, wire

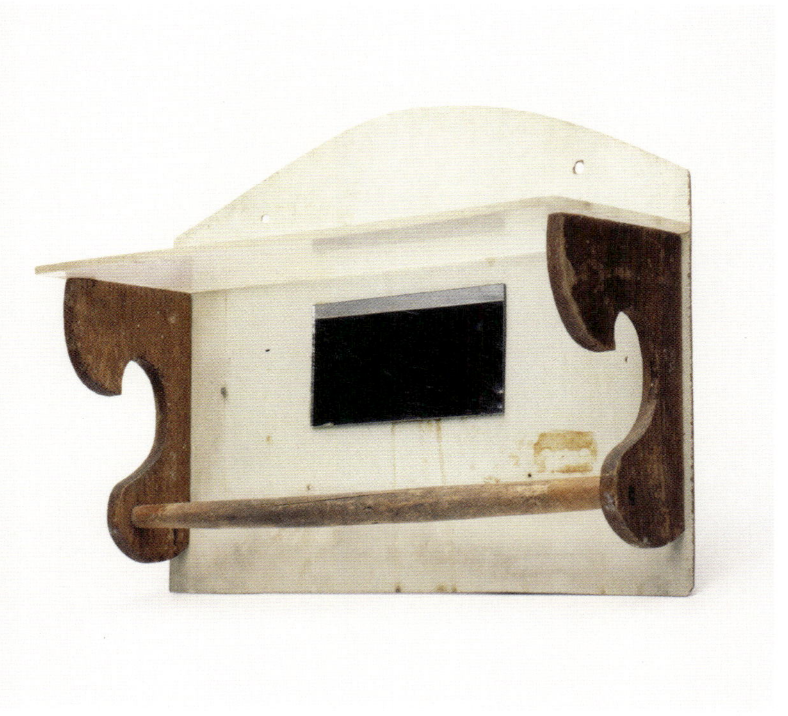

**Andrei Smirnov**                                    Moscow, 1984

It goes back to the time when we used to live in a communal apartment. There was one bathroom for everyone, and everyone had their own shelves and mirrors. And when we moved in there, we had to put up our own too. We weren't planning on staying there very long – we were hoping to get an apartment of our own. But we ended up living there for fifteen years. I couldn't find any small shelves in the shops, and so I made one myself. I thought it would be temporary, but things turned out differently.

Wood, perspex, mirror, screws

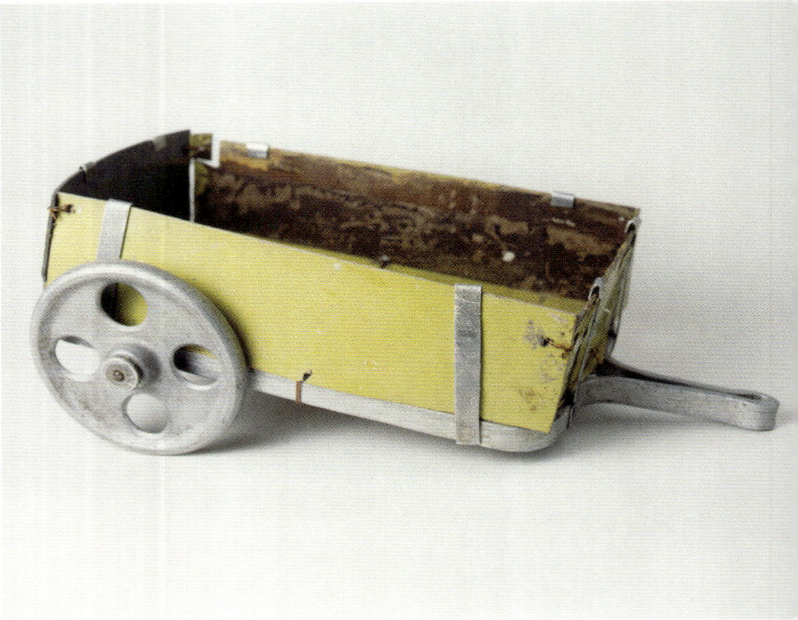

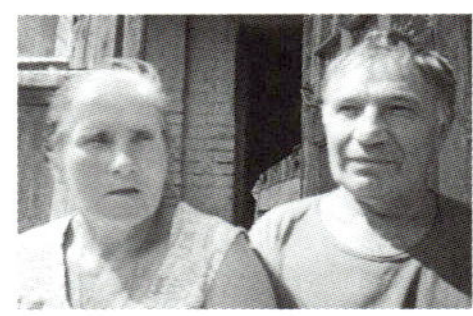

**Aleksandr Buligin**                    Ryazan, 1997

So, do you like this wagon? Well, I'll tell you how it was made. Grandad made it because this big toy tractor we had should have had a trailer but it didn't. Vanya said, 'Grandad, make me a wagon.' And he said, 'OK Vanya, I'll make you one.' The back has been made from linoleum and the framework we bought for the greenhouse. Well, we didn't buy it really, we got hold of it. This is some kind of aluminium tape. He made the wagon's framework from it. The wheels are from a child's wagon. Vanya put sand in it. Then his friend came round and they broke it, so Grandad started to make it again. It's called a 'farkop'. 'Grandad, my farkop is broken.' Well, he put together a lot of stuff. And his grandson was pleased and used this toy to cart sand about. Everyone was happy.

Aluminium strip and bar, pushchair wheels, linoleum, rivets

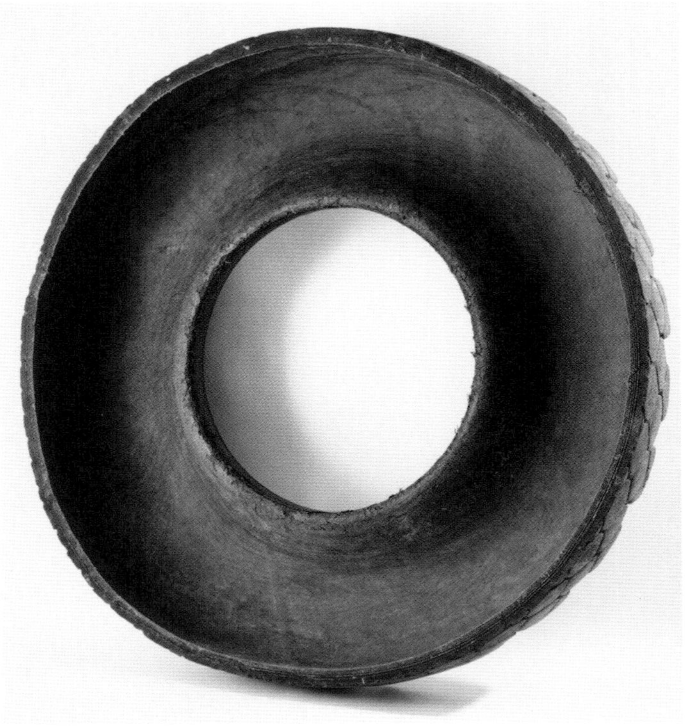

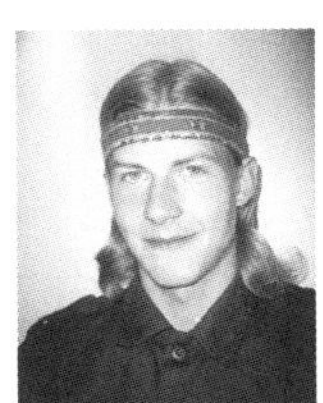

**Artyom Vasiliev**          Ryazan region, 1995

It happened that I ended up with a couple of ducks. I needed to find some kind of dish from which they could drink in peace. As there was nothing suitable around, my neighbours came up with the idea that I could make something from a wheel. That's how the idea was born. Thanks to the fact that there was a maintenance station nearby I was able to find an old tractor tyre, which my father and I cut into two parts.

Tractor tyre

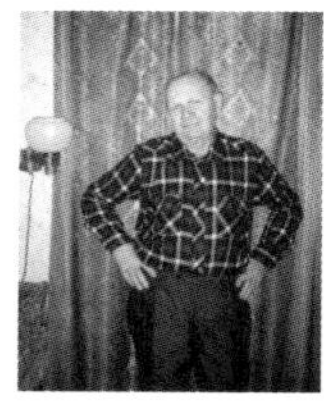

**Nikolai Ruchkin**                                    Ryazan, 1995

It's usually not so easy to open your ordinary bottle of beer or vodka with a knife, or against the edge of something. And so we set a challenge – to make a bottle opener. There are bigger openers, but they're not so convenient – more like souvenirs. And so we started to think about how to make a real opener that was also kind of nice to look at. It became almost like a competition – who was the cleverest. At the time, the end of the 1970s, high boots for women were very popular. We had Russian boots at one time, but everyone had forgotten about them until suddenly they came back into fashion. So we came to the conclusion that the best bottle opener would have to be in the shape of a woman's boot. It wasn't too big, so whoever carried keys with them could add it to their key ring. So, you could have everything with you on that key ring. The shape is also nice. Well, you know, boots can be different colours. We did it like this – we got hold of some foil – you can find all types of different coloured foil. You put this foil between the metal and this part. And when it's made from plexiglass, it's transparent and you get a kind of pattern from the foil. It turns out that the shape and the colour are nice.

Steel strip, plexiglass, rivets

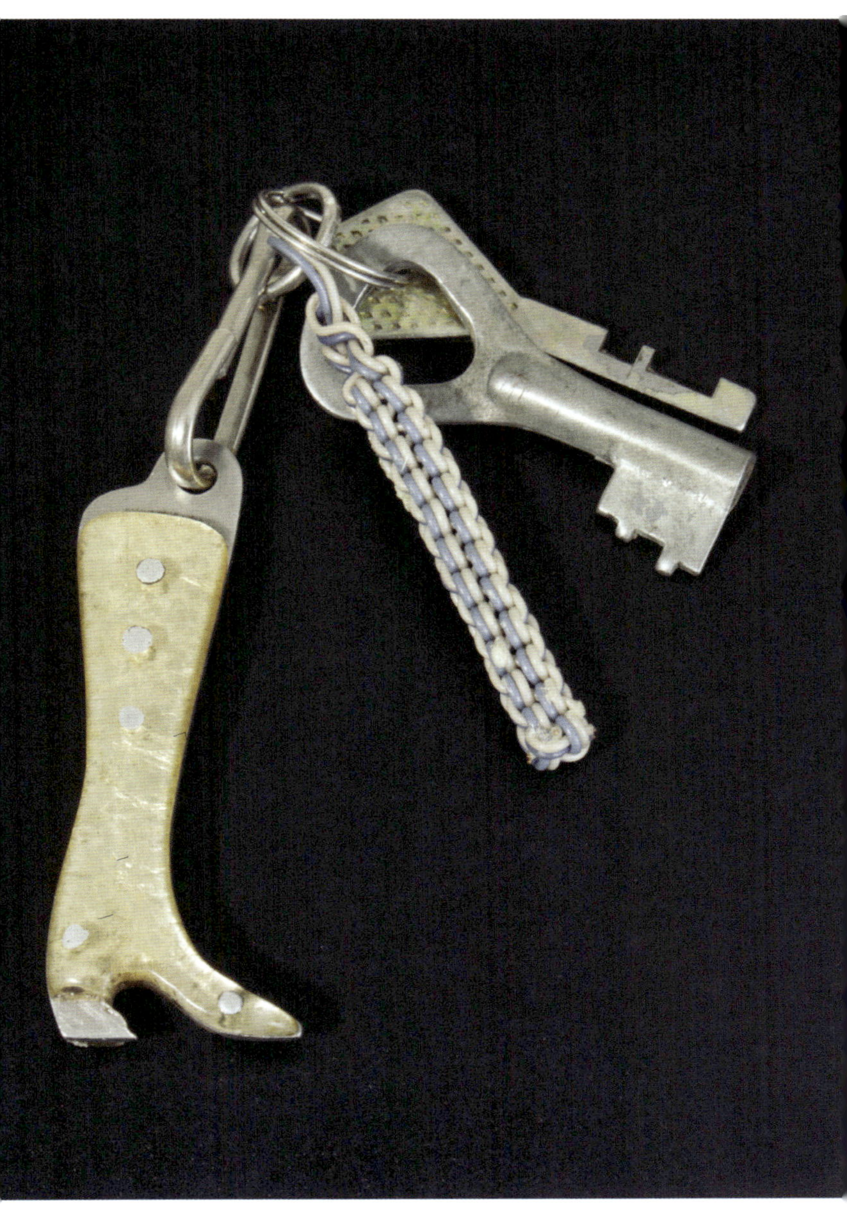

**Nikolai Ruchkin**                                        Ryazan, 1970–2000

These are ordinary knives although the points are not very sharp, as they weren't forged too well. If you sharpen them too much then they wear out quickly. I selected the steel. I didn't have any special equipment, so I chose a steel which I would be able to forge. This kind of steel they usually chuck out so I chose the strips I needed, according to length and width. Then, if it was suitable, I shaped it. I drew out the shape on a sheet of paper, and then I fixed it to the steel and cut around it. I didn't make it during work hours but rather during lunch breaks. I used to go and see the lathe operators to cut out the shape. When the basic shape was ready, I then used to come to some agreement with the forgers. We had very good specialists at our factory, good guys, so I'd get a bit of steel and go and see them. And they'd tell me, 'There's nothing doing with this bit, you can't forge it, but this bit – we'll do it'. They'd forge it how I wanted, as it was important not only that they forged it, but that it was malleable too. When they'd done me a strip, I set to work on it. I got all the grime off it, and polished it up like a mirror. Then I chose the pad. I went to another workshop, where the guys sorted me out and I made the handle. I fixed the handle on myself. I stuck two strips on and I had myself a knife. And so that this fastening wasn't visible, I stuck some more stuff on, on top of it, held on with glue. Or you get hold of some bearing, and you can make an excellent knife like that. It's solid, doesn't rust, and stays sharp for a long time, but sometimes you can forge it too much, and then it breaks easily.

Steel, rivets, plastic

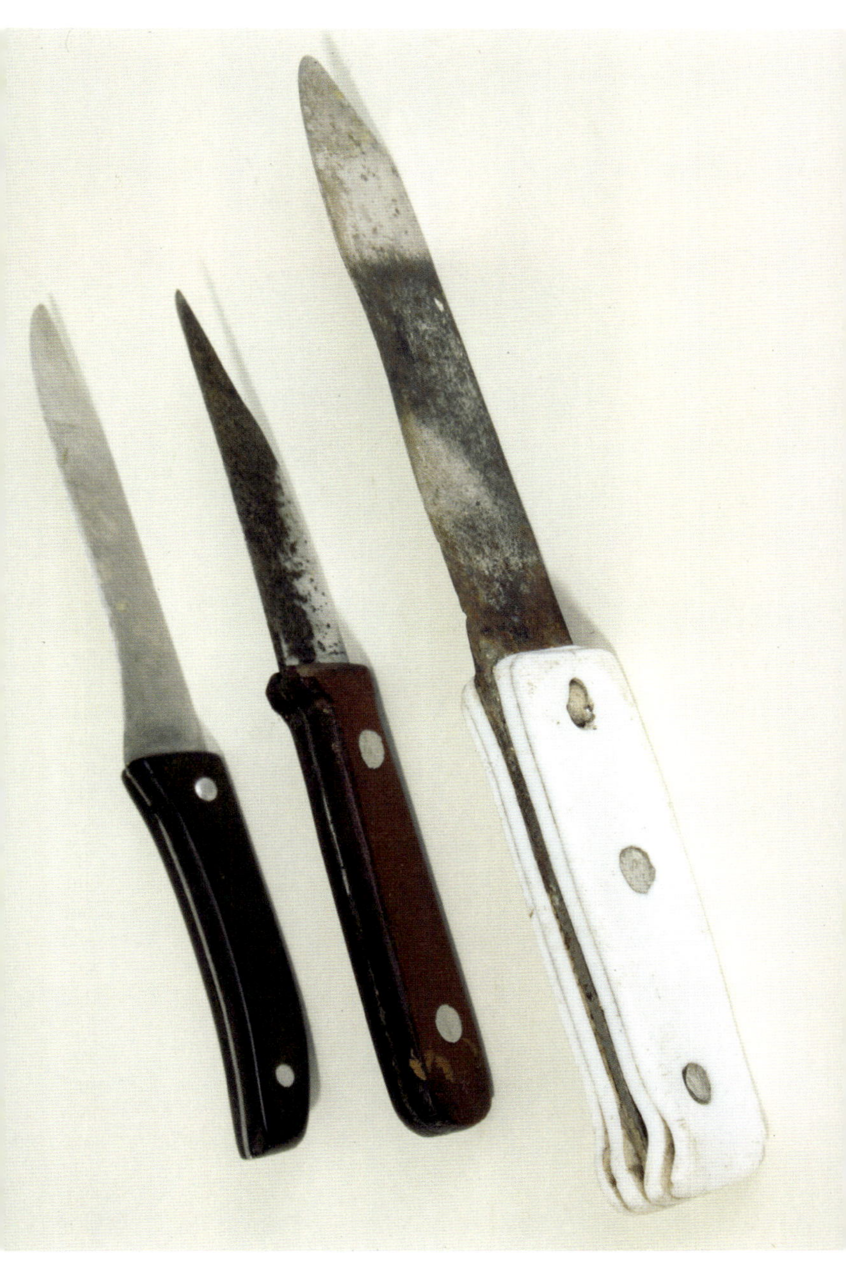

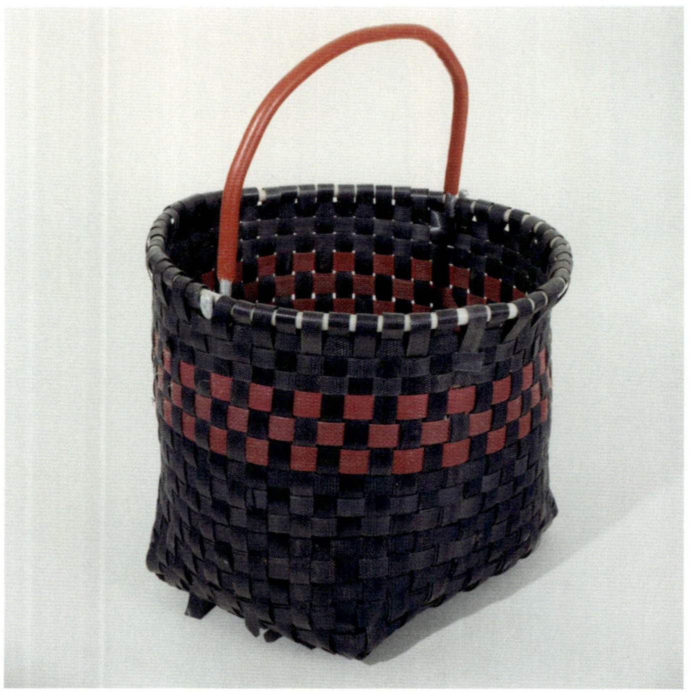

**Nikolai Ruchkin**                                    Ryazan, 1993

It was difficult to get hold of a basket around 1993. I remembered life in the countryside, and how they wove them there, but I didn't have any vine. I saw these ribbons for wrapping stuff up, and wondered if it would be possible to weave baskets from them. When we used to weave with vine we started from the top – it's fixed around the rim – but here I had some problems. I got a bit lost. So I decided to try the other way round – to start weaving from the bottom – but this didn't work either. Then I took a square board and separated out these ribbons and started to weave across. And this is how I got the base. I started to fold, but the shape didn't turn out so well, so I got hold of a bucket and put it on the square, and started to fold the ribbons inside it. But they wouldn't stay still. So I got some rope to fix it on with, and then it held like I needed it to. Finally I needed to do the rim. I got stuck here too. I decided to use insulating tape, and I did the rim with that and started to braid. When I'd finished braiding, they turned out kind of like bars. It wasn't level at all. So I flattened everything, and there was nothing left over.

Wrapping ribbon, wicker, aluminium wire, insulating tape

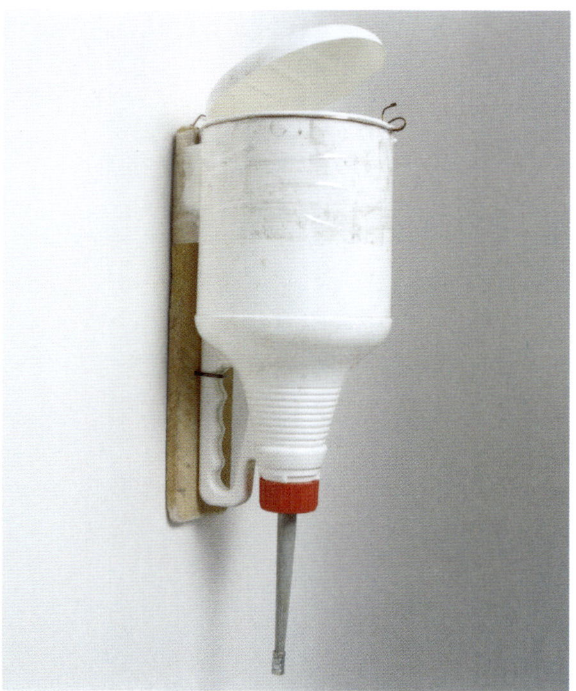

## Aleksandr Mnatsakanov

Moscow, 1993

*As recounted by his daughter Lena:* This is the washstand that my dad made, to my specifications, from an empty 2-litre syrup bottle with a narrow neck. It was because I needed a washstand where I lived, out of the city, where the water pipes had stopped working. I'd been in the shop and discovered that a new one cost 40 thousand roubles ($8). I wasn't too pleased to find this out, I can tell you. From my salary of 100 thousand ($20), I would have had to pay the state 40 thousand for a washstand. No way! I could make one myself and it'd turn out better! So that's how this thing came about. The idea was mine – I saw that canister and realised that it was the same size as a washstand. It was only necessary to make a kind of tap where the top was, cut off the bottom and pour the water out from there. But, I have to say that my dad brilliantly carries out all my ideas. When I had explained it all to him he followed my instructions, not just in a simple way, but artistically. It all turned out beautifully. He was searching and selecting the materials for a long time.

Plastic bottle, wood, screws, nuts, ballpoint pen

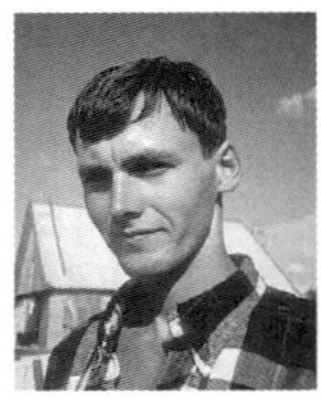

**Sergei Kharitonov**                                                    Voronezh, 1996

*As recounted by his sister Larisa:* This is a house for a queen bee, to protect her and to keep her safe from attacks by other bees – like when we want to put a new queen bee into a hive. And so for this it's necessary to have a house like this for her, for the new bee – you know, temporarily. And so when the bees are used to her and this house isn't necessary, we can free her from it. It's like a little prison and she's a temporary prisoner. I'm not sure if they sell these kind of things or not – if they exist at all.

He appropriated one of Granny's haircurlers and found a bottle top, then put them together and made this original house for a queen bee. This elastic band is to hang the house inside the hive so that the bees are able to get at it. They have to feed her and, basically, make love to this queen bee, and continue their activities and keep up the life of the hive.

We call it a little house. Simply, a little house for a queen bee. Some years ago, maybe three or five years ago, Granny used to curl her hair to look nice. But now Granny doesn't need her curlers, so she gladly donated them to us for the hive's structure. My brother made it – well it's basically not that much work. Both my father and my brother keep bees, and I help with the honey eating more than anything else.

Hair curler, bottle top, elastic band

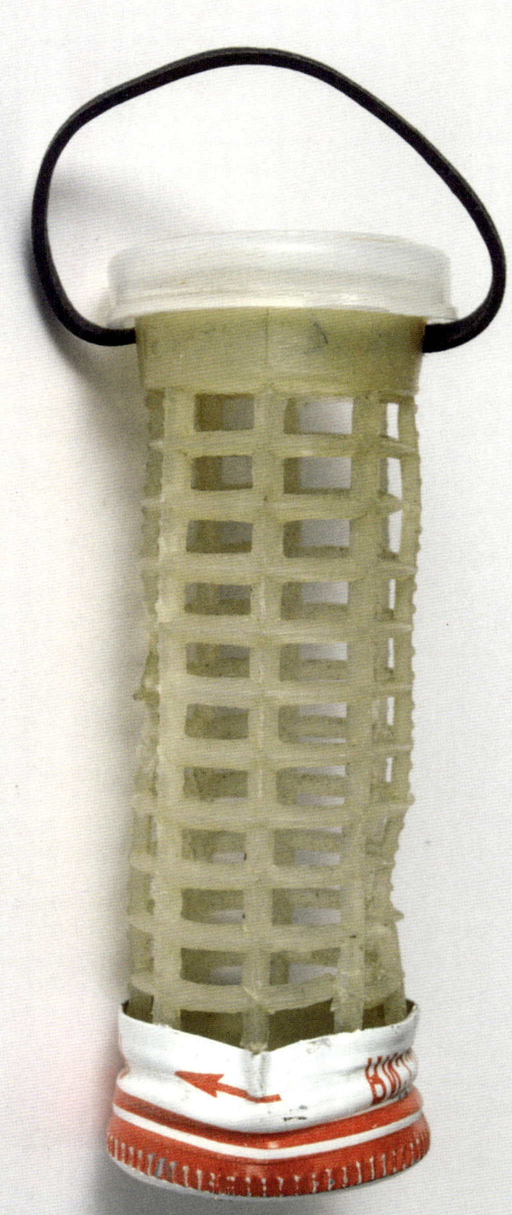

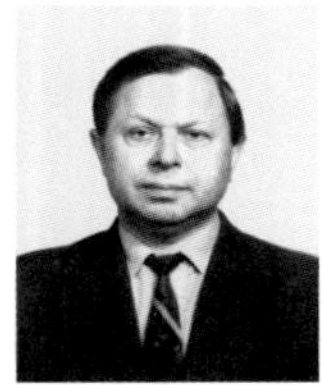

**Aleksandr Tarasov**                    Ramenskoye, Moscow region, 1980

This is a television aerial, for the 33rd channel, which in the period between 1978 and 1980 was transmitted in Leningrad. There weren't any antennas for sale and the magazine *Radio* published some different plans for making them. Basically this antenna was made using a sketch from this magazine. Instead of cutting it out of a sheet of metal I took a piece of fibreglass laminate, which is plastic with foil on one side. And the tracks were cut out from foil according to the sizes published in *Radio*. As for the base, I used a base from a table lamp – it was necessary to fix it on with something. There's nothing miraculous about this construction, I was more amazed that Arkhipov saw something in it. I consider it to be a very simple thing, made for a purpose, between other jobs. The signal from the antenna is received through this cable and then sent to the TV. The cable has to correspond with the elements of the antenna in order to effectively transmit the signal coming from the antenna. Apart from that, this cable has to go around the antenna in a certain way so that the wave resistance in the current of the cable connecting the antenna matches the 'line'. Well, here you need to use your wits. How can you lay this cable around the antenna? Around the edges some openings were drilled and thread was put into them and then with the method they use in radio electronic equipment it was tied on. They bind sausages up like that. And because of this it reminds some people of plaits, or a sausage.

Table lamp base, Textolite, a conductor, screws

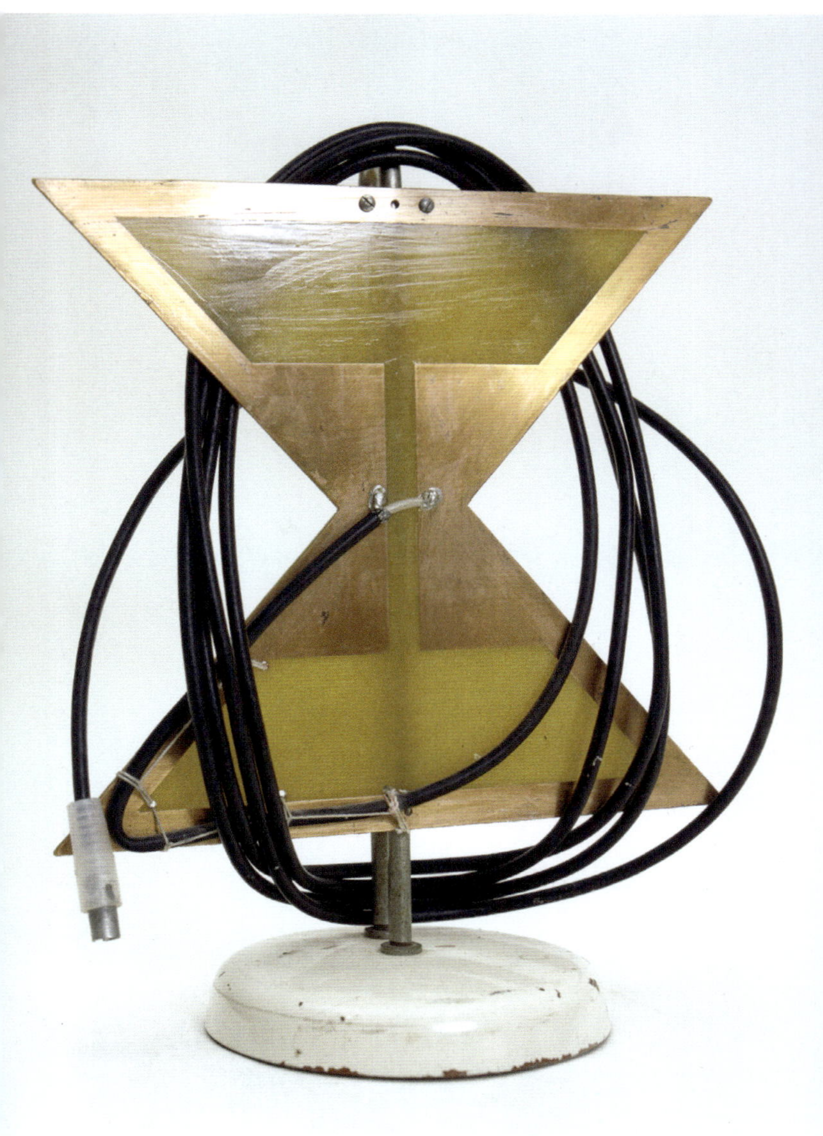

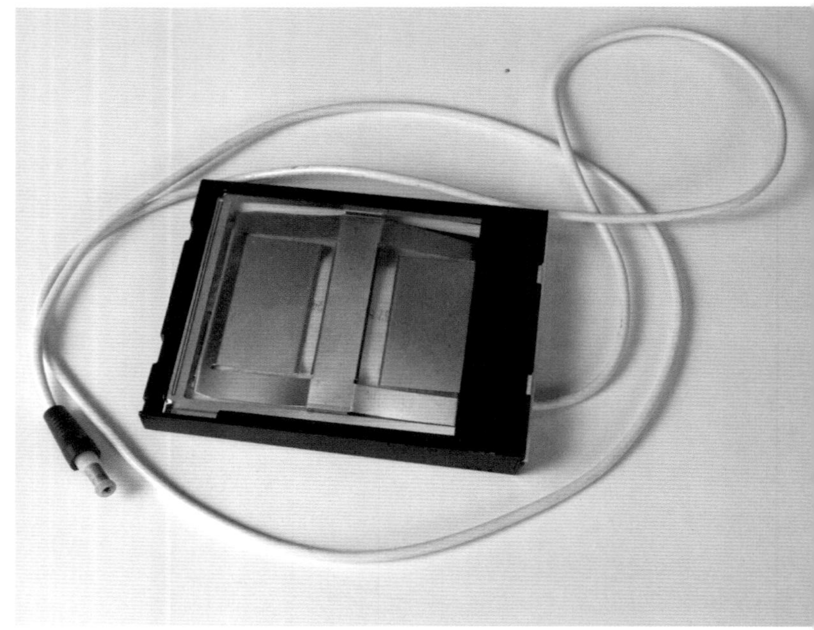

**Aleksandr Tarasov**                    Ramenskoye, Moscow region, 1990

I have a transistor radio and a Polaroid camera. After you've taken ten pictures with a Polaroid, the cartridge, which contains a good source of power in the form of a dry element, has to be thrown away. On the cartridge it's written 'do not open' because there are alkaline elements inside and the 'Greens' would naturally get worked up if you break it apart and throw it out with the rubbish. I decided that it's better to use them before you throw them away. But how to use them? Better for my transistor radio to get two to three hours a day use from those batteries than for me to go to the shop just for new ones. I just took a piece of Textolite, and worked out where the Polaroid contacts go on it in order to connect with the camera. Under these contacts I put in two metal contacts, cut off from the battery, and soldered on some wires. Onto the ends of these wires I soldered on a standard socket – and turned the radio on. The radio works wonderfully, but not for a month, more like a day or two. But I get a lot of satisfaction from the fact that when I throw the battery away it's been used 100% and not 50%. It's only lazy people who can bring themselves to chuck away stuff that's only been 50% used up.

Polaroid cartridge, wire, printed circuit board

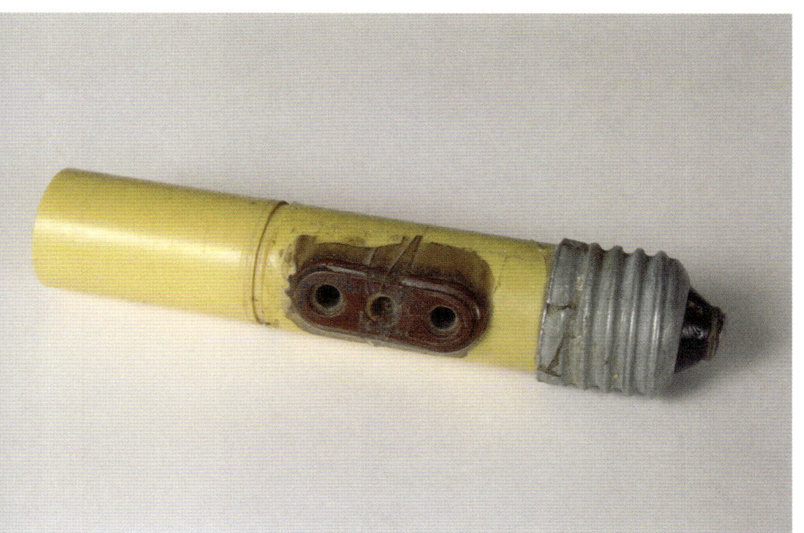

**Aleksandr Tarasov**        Ramenskoye, Moscow region, 1993

It all started a couple of years ago when I got a garage in which the only electricity was a light socket, without any plug sockets. But I needed plugs for my drill and other tools. And then I remembered the old, old stagnant years when there existed an item called 'Conman'. Why did they call it 'Conman'? In those long ago times plug sockets were banned in villages. The people there were only allowed to have light sockets. But clever people had the 'Conman'. They screwed them into the light socket and then plugged electronic devices into them. I made this one with my own hands. I took a base from an electric lamp and a plug from an electrical device, then joined them together with the plastic shell of a deodorant bottle. This was so I could hold this plastic shell and screw things into the light socket without getting a 220-volt shock. In this way I made use of an old method of getting access to the electrical supply when you don't have any plugs at hand.

Deodorant bottle, epoxy glue, electric lamp socket, plug, wire conductor

**Aleksandr Tarasov**  Ramenskoye, Moscow region, 1984

In the depths of those stagnant times, when there were shortages of everything, I had to work out some kind of method for evenly spreading paint or varnish on the surface of a board. In order to solve this problem I took the foam-rubber cylinder used in women's hair curlers. This was the basic idea which made it possible to turn, to revolve and to apply the paint in a flat layer.

I passed this steel part through its axis and bent it into shape. That's all really. A very simple solution. I varnished several surfaces with it, and it was very convenient as it was possible to use just a small jar's worth of varnish, you didn't need a bucketful. It was about 1983 or 1984. I still use it now. Everything is dependent on how long the foam rubber lasts. If it disintegrates then you need to replace it. If the curlers work then everything is OK, but if they give out then the item ceases to be of use. I painted a cabinet with it, which I made myself. It's coated with varnish in the tone of the other furniture so that it all goes well together. You can check out the results of my activities.

Steel wire, hair curler

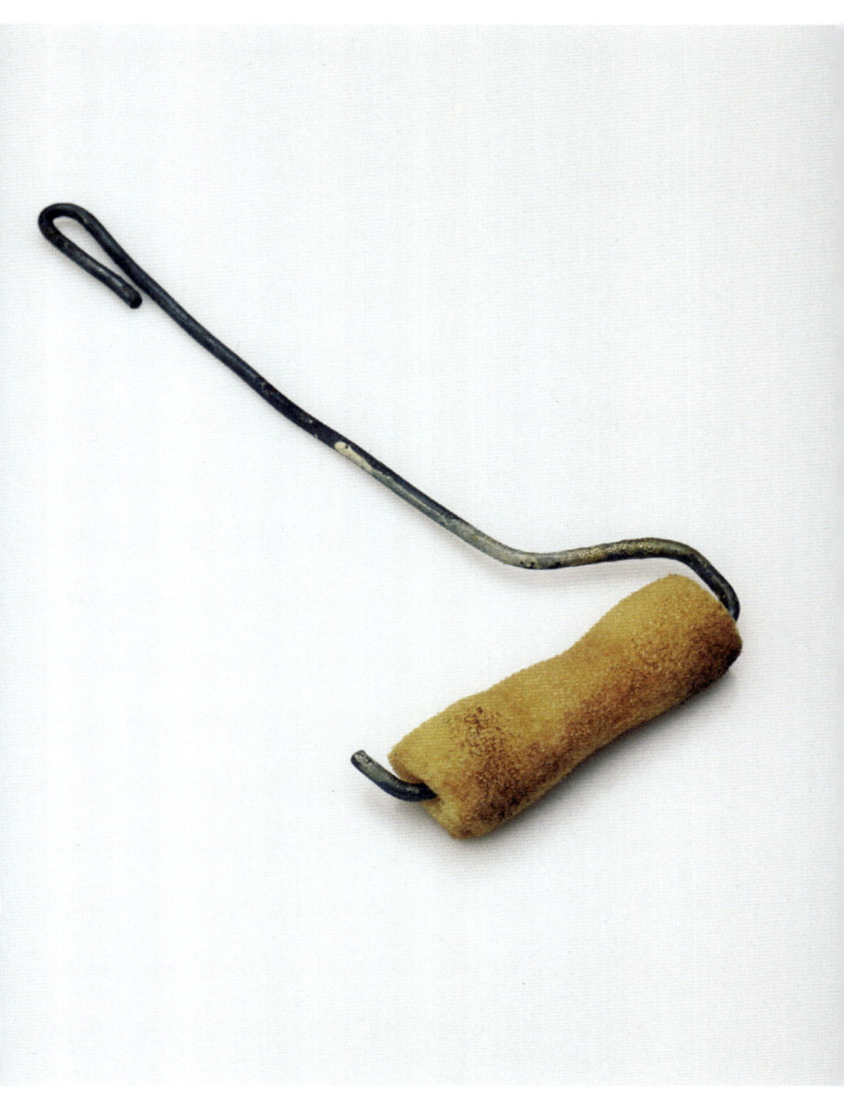

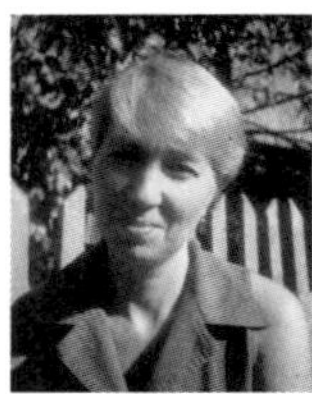

**Evgenii Vasiliev**                              Stolptsi, Ryazan region, 1979

*As recounted by his daughter (pictured):* So I'll tell you about this object. If you look at it you'll never guess what it is. As a matter of fact, it's a very simple thing. It's a bath plug. It's just a rubber bath plug made from micropore. They used to make soles for shoes from this kind of stuff. Well, it's like that, you know. It's very stretchy and solid enough. And an ordinary table fork has been stuck into it.

It all came about quite accidentally. We needed a plug for the bath and they didn't sell them in the village. We'd got hold of a bath but without a plug, and so we had to think of something. We didn't want to go to the city especially for one, so we got hold of some micropore and cut a plug out of it. At first it looked completely different. There was a metal ring like you can find on any ordinary plug. But it hadn't been made very well and kept coming off the plug. At that time, the person who'd made the bath was busy working in the building trade, repairing houses, that kind of stuff, so he didn't remake the plug straight away, and we had to use the plug as it was for a while. Well, what was at hand was a fork. It was very convenient. You'd insert the fork in, raise it up and pull it out, just like an ordinary plug. That's it really. They've been with us now for a long time, the micropore and the fork together, like part of the family almost.

Boot heel, fork

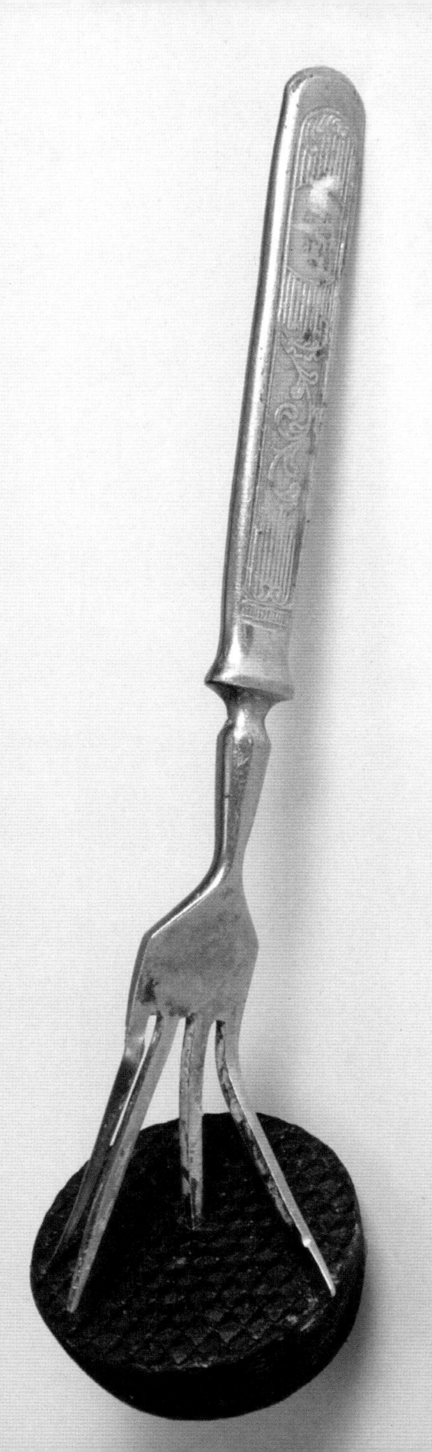

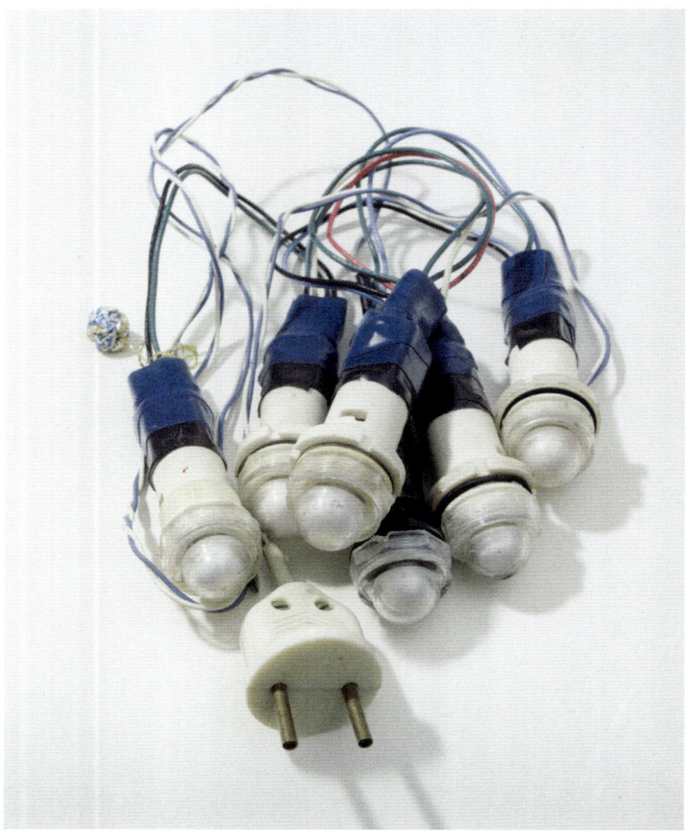

**Aleksei Galkin**                                        Baikonur, 1983

*As recounted by his wife:* In the winter of 1983 in Baikonur, in the very cold of winter, a young lieutenant, gazing at his young daughter, thought to himself that he should do something to really get the festive season going. He remembered that at the 'Buran' rocket base there was a multitude of beautiful lamps that burnt with different coloured lights. So he gathered them together and made them into a garland. What's more, these lamps were for rockets, for flights to the Moon – everything was from the 'Buran' rocket base. The wires, judging by appearances, were from here and there. Well, this garland served our family loyally for ten years and now, when it's reached its twelfth year, we want to present it to Volodya, for the museum.

Lamps, wire, insulating tape, plug

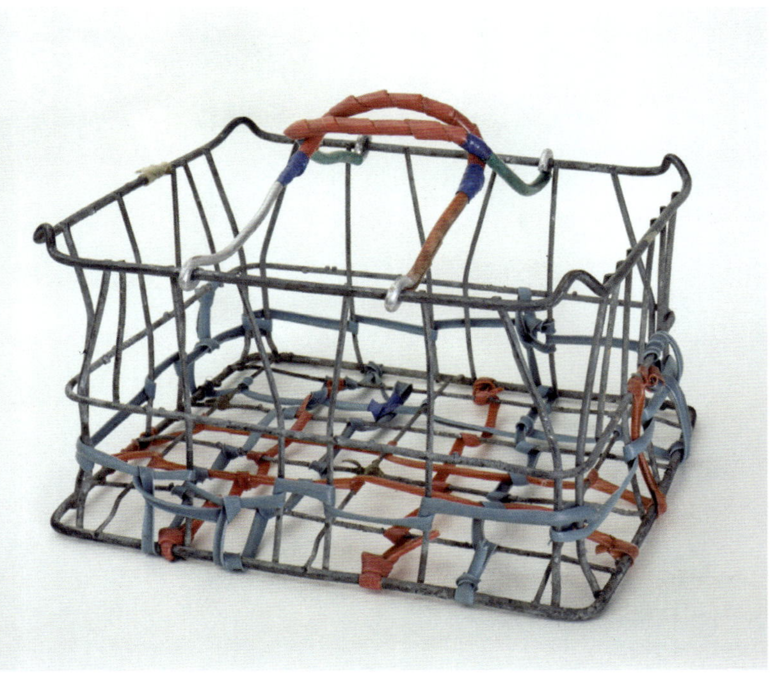

**Nikolai Kozhin**                                                    Orel, 1997

This is from our dacha life – it's for carrying potatoes so that they don't fall out all over the place, so as not to waste so much energy. The metal crate had been replaced with a plastic one; there was a load of iron just lying around and I began thinking how to put it to use. It's a sturdy construction that is very solid. It's made from a milk-bottle crate. It was broken off and this mesh stuck in there. So that nothing falls out during the journey this tourniquet has been wrapped round it. This is so that nothing is blown out by the wind, as sometimes happens. A fishing rod can be kept here – it also won't fall out. It's functional but not very aesthetic. Well, these things are functional but not so interesting. The milk crates have been cut to size. Your usual bottles go in here, there were a whole lot here. I put the grid inside – it's a lot easier to use now for one thing. These bar-type struts have been welded on. The carrier is easy to take off plus it holds on well too. It's very convenient.

Steel milk crate, insulating tape, aluminium cable, tourniquet

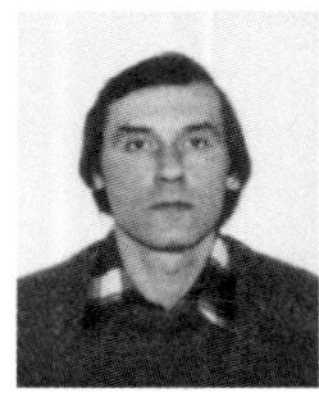

**Aleksandr**                                                    Moscow, 1985-8

It was probably about ten years ago – sometime between 1985 and 1988. I got hold of a lamp, a quartz lamp, and, as I often had the 'flu, I decided to somehow heat up the flat with this quartz lamp.

I started to try to work out how to make it. Its working voltage, 100 volts, was lower than the voltage of the electrical current, which was 220 volts. And then I had the idea to use an old reflector, where the reflector's spiral acts as extra resistance to the lamp, and at the same time to use the reflector like the reflector of a heating device. The components were made and it wasn't bad that it was under the heating element, as the flow of air acts as an extra cooler. It turned out to be an interesting construction and quite efficient. Then the spiral was connected to the lamp, so that if the spiral heated up, the lamp turned itself off. I've never seen a lamp like this; I just know that they exist. They're used in medicine for operations, during surgery, where there are lots of bacteria. They also use them in the restoration of cars. These lamps ionise the air around them and they kill off any microbes through radiation. The gauze itself shines when the lamp has heated up enough. You see, there's mercury in there, little balls of it rolling around. There aren't any lamps like this one in the shops; they've got different ones. But when I made this one, there was nothing at all in the shops.

Heater, reflector, quartz lamp

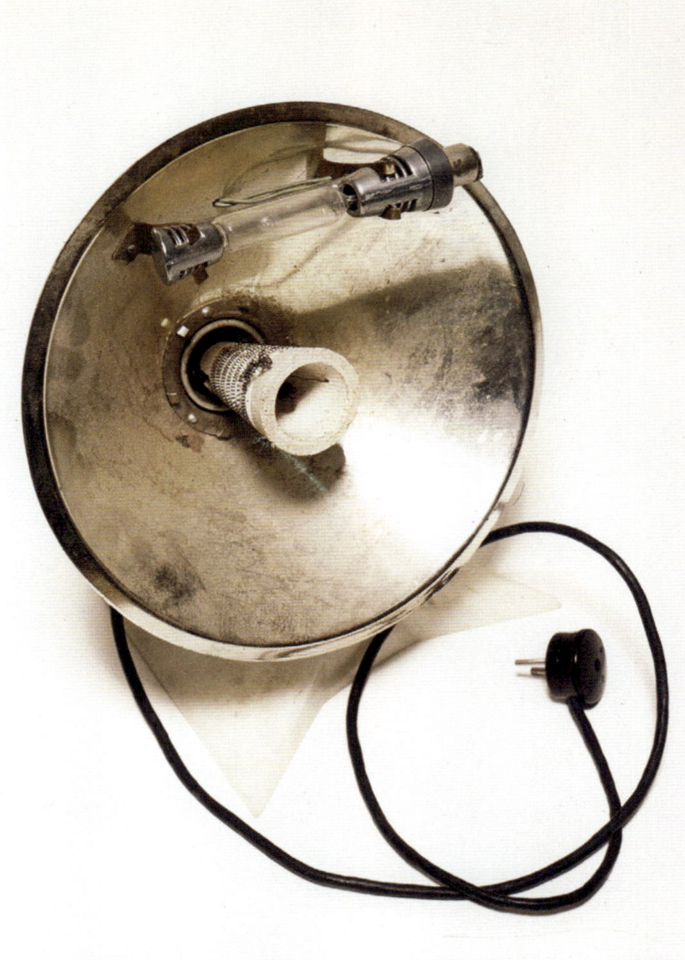

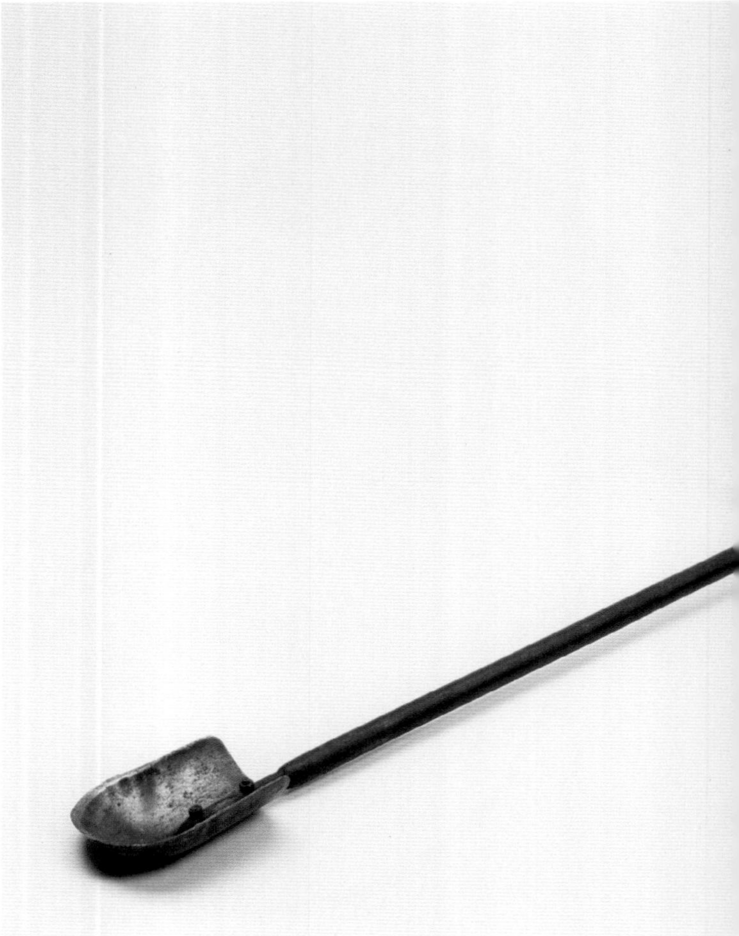

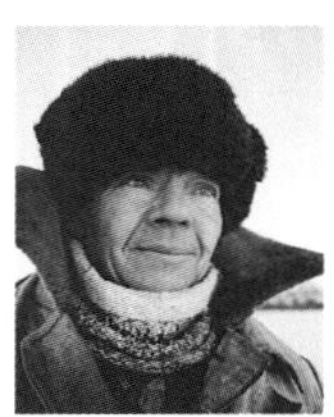

**Aleksandr Piskaryov**     Nizhny Novgorod, 1990

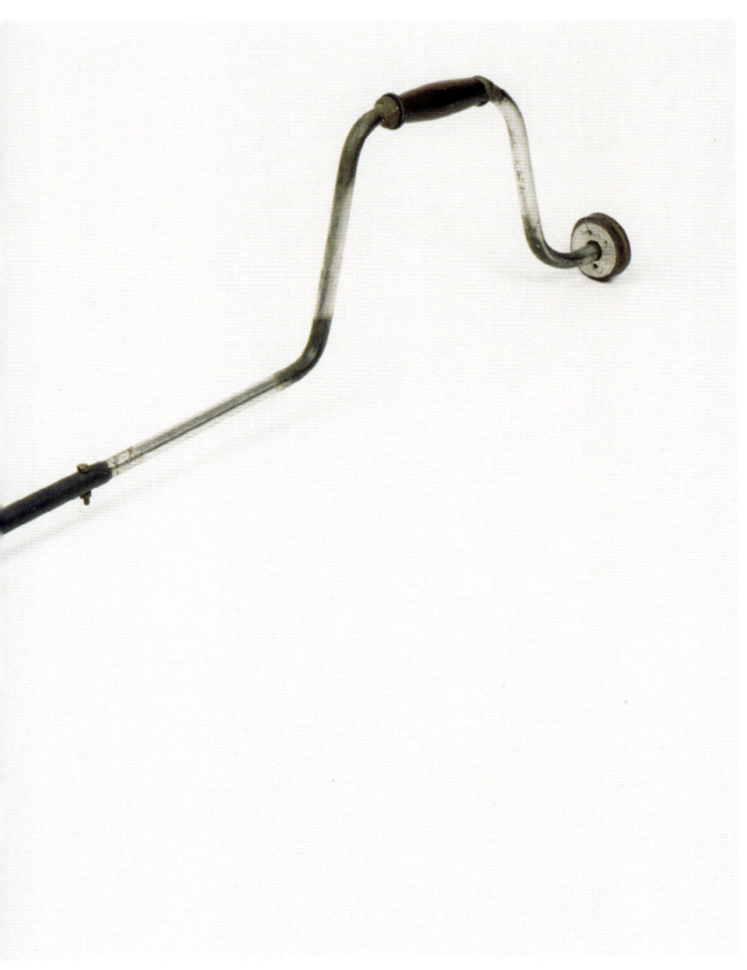

The bore is home-made. I like the fact that it has round spiral edges, that are sharp like knives. It makes big holes in the ice, only you don't need any screws, bolts or anything else to use it. You just pull off the stopper and put it together. Very convenient. You go to the pond specially to catch small fish, and you need to know when they're biting, and when they're not. Last time I caught five pikes and a perch.

Steel tube, Textolite, steel plate

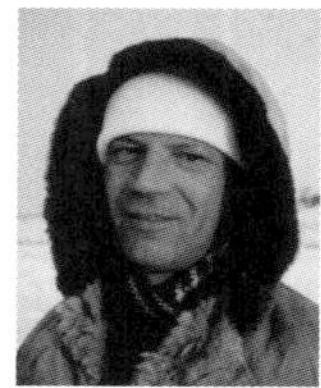

**Aleksandr Pogodin**                                              Nizhny Novgorod, 1995

There are various ways of making fish feeders. I made one like this so that it would go through a hole in the ice, for winter fishing. In the summer I fish from a boat or from the bank, usually with a rod – I don't like all those predatory methods, they're not my style. But controlling the rod, toying with the line – there's a whole subtle process to that, it takes skill. In the summer you use summer feeders, and in the winter you use winter ones. I've got a few of them for different conditions. I made this one just recently – in my opinion it's the most successful design. And it takes the most work to make as well. The body is made of brass: I soldered it and made holes in it to let the boiled grain through. The bottom's made of lead. I had an old battery from a Moskvich and it started to leak so I broke it up, took out the lead plates, melted them down and poured the lead into a mould to make a thick round slab. That formed the sinker – it holds the feeder in the right position. The feeder can be filled quickly – there's a spring along the central axis. You pull it up and put in boiled grain, for instance. Well, naturally the dimensions are designed so it will fit through a hole in the ice. I usually make the holes with this breast drill, and the diameter of the blades is 14 or 15 centimetres, so the size of the feeder can't be any bigger than that.

Brass, lead, spring

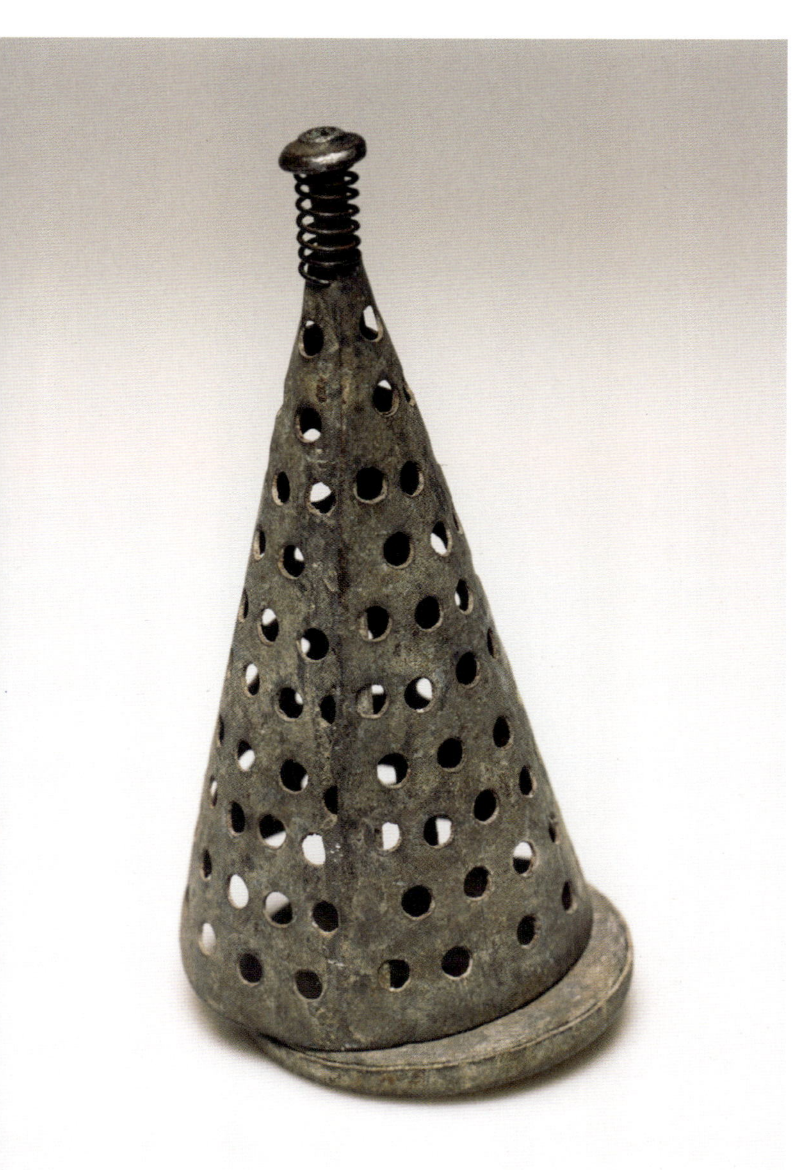

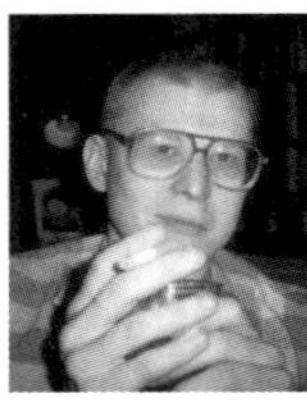

**Andrei Lazarev**                                    Moscow, 1996

Well, I made a paintbrush. I wanted to paint and I didn't have one, so I got the stuff together and made it. And when I'd gone and made it, you came round, took it off me and brought me a new one – conned me I'd say. At first I made it for painting and then it became impossible to paint with it because it got all shredded up.

The wooden part is just a bit of wood, a bit of wood that was hanging around. I had the hairs for the brush already – they're from the hide of a pony, which used to be on the table. I cut it up, tied them together with thread and stuck them on with glue – some resin.

A paintbrush has to be like this. How else? I tied them up into a bunch and then glued them onto the wooden handle. But it's impossible to paint with it. How can you paint with it? It's shit. I dipped it into the paint pot, painted with it and then put it aside. You came round and brought me a new paintbrush. Cool. But the one I made doesn't fit into your plan. It falls apart. A paintbrush has to come together at the ends, or be hard, but this one is neither, it's not hard and the ends don't come together. I've cut it down ten times – it used to be twice as long.

Yeah, I made a unique fucking piece of shit.

Wood, glue, thread, pony hair

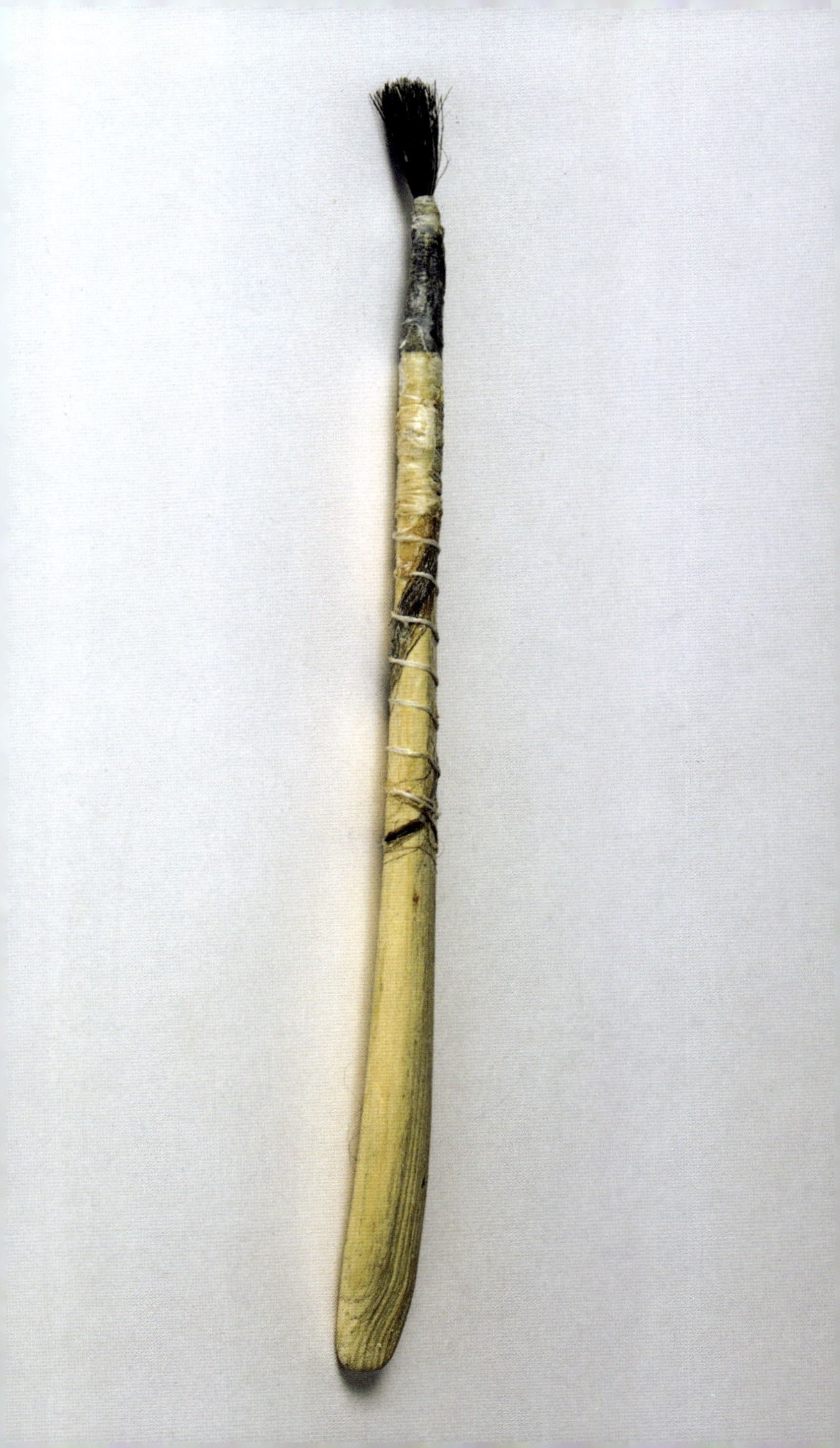

**Anonymous** Moscow, 1994

*As recounted by Aleksandr Sigutin:* This shovel has been around for a long time. I've been working here for almost three years – it's been here all that time. I should say that I work for an organisation that provides social and medical assistance to people who have fallen on hard times. They've lost everything, and our organisation tries to help them out a bit.

A lot of people gather here each morning for appointments. I should point out that the cleaners don't service our plot because they're afraid of getting infected with something, because among our patients there are people suffering from tuberculosis, cholera, hepatitis and dysentery. So, because of this, the visitors have to clean the area themselves. Our workers ask them to do this, and they do the work with pleasure because, for them, it's a chance to receive extra care and attention, and to get fitted out with a uniform and receive some further medical assistance. Sometimes there aren't enough tools for everyone, and so some enthusiasts cobbled together this shovel from a metal crutch and the scoop of a broken spade. And they use it here to sweep up rubbish and to clean up stuff lying in the snow. So, it's strange and a little bit absurd, this cobbled-together object which was the result of their labour and their illnesses.

Spade scoop, crutch

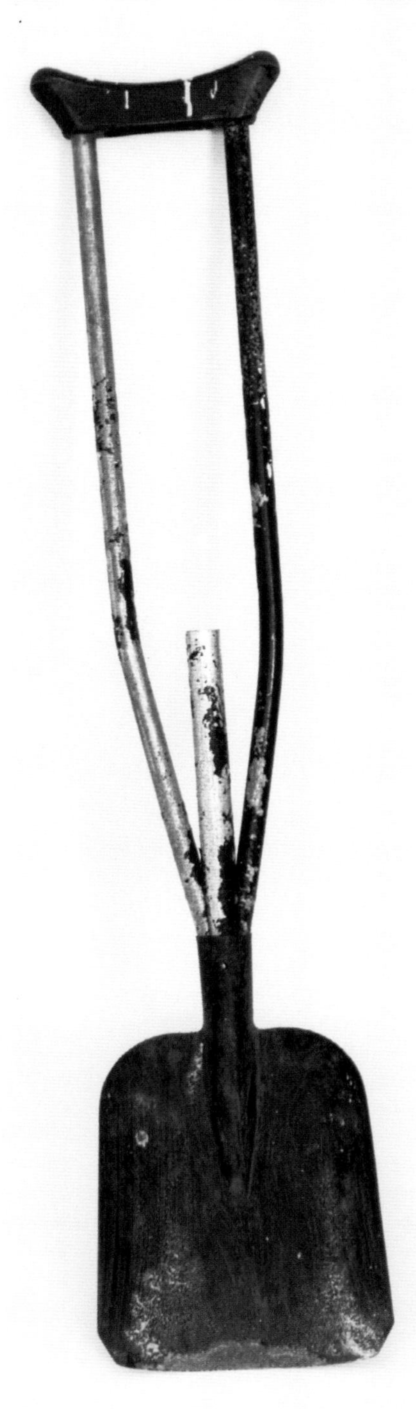

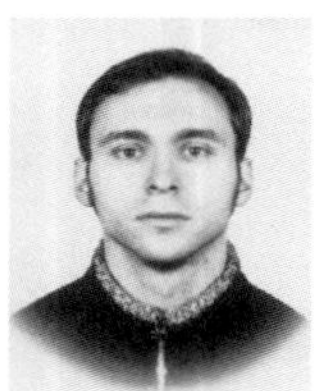

**Aleksei Orekhov**                                      Ryazan region, 1997

There aren't so many streetlights. There's one in front of the village administration building, there's one at the bus stop and there's one near the shop. In winter, especially, you can't walk around in the streets. I hung a lamp on a post right opposite my house and screwed in a light bulb. But, what d'ya know? It only lasted there a few days. I went up again and put in another bulb and I remember that everything was OK and that it shouldn't have burnt out. When I was putting it in, Manya, my neighbour, came up and admitted that her grandchildren, who had come up from Moscow, had been entertaining themselves by chucking pebbles at the lamp when there was no one about, and broke the lamp. Well, you're not going to tear their heads off for that.

In the cattle shed we've got a load of different bits of metal, so I hung that lamp there, but this time behind bars. I got hold of some aluminium wire and wound it round the lamp so that pebbles couldn't get through, and I went up there again, put another bulb in and everything was OK. It hangs there and doesn't get smashed. At the beginning they were running around of course, but it's so quiet here you can hear everything, especially stones bouncing off metal. Well, everything's OK now. The light bulbs don't get smashed and I've got a light in front of my house. It's all free too.

Aluminium and copper wire

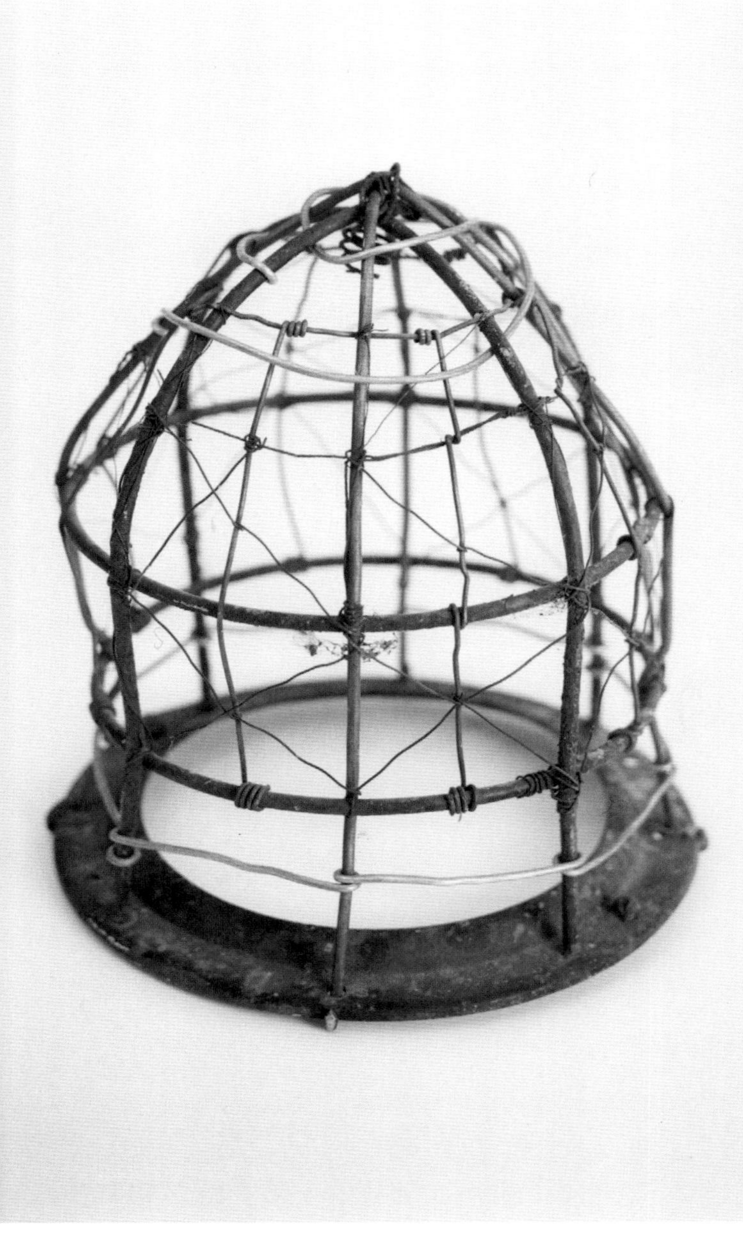

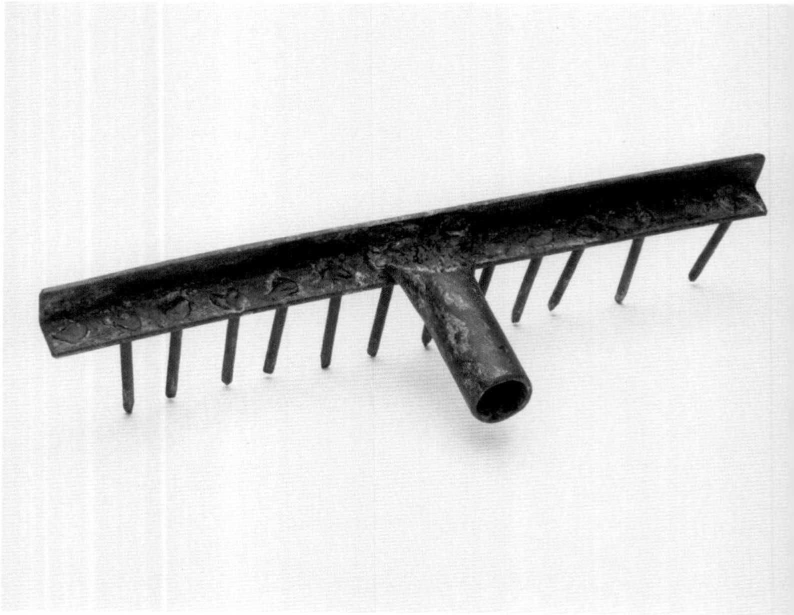

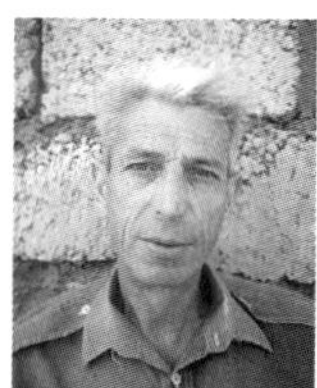

**Aleksei Kleshchyov**                                        Kolomna, 1995

I'm a welder who's been working with a welding machine since 1953. I can
weld anything at all, without exception. I do all kinds of stuff at the allotment:
I make spades, redo stuff, the lot. If you want to become a welder, I'll teach
you how. You can seize the moment, if the desire's there. Ah, that's not welding,
Valod. It's just a rake – a rake is just a rake. Well, everything here is my own, I
made them all myself. All these shovels. That's not welding either, that's just
modelling. Welding is when it's under some pressure – yeah, that's welding!
Fifty atmosphere pipes – who can weld them? Volodya – where they did all
the welding stuff, there's no one there now. Well, I'm off to do some welding.

Steel tube, bracket, nails

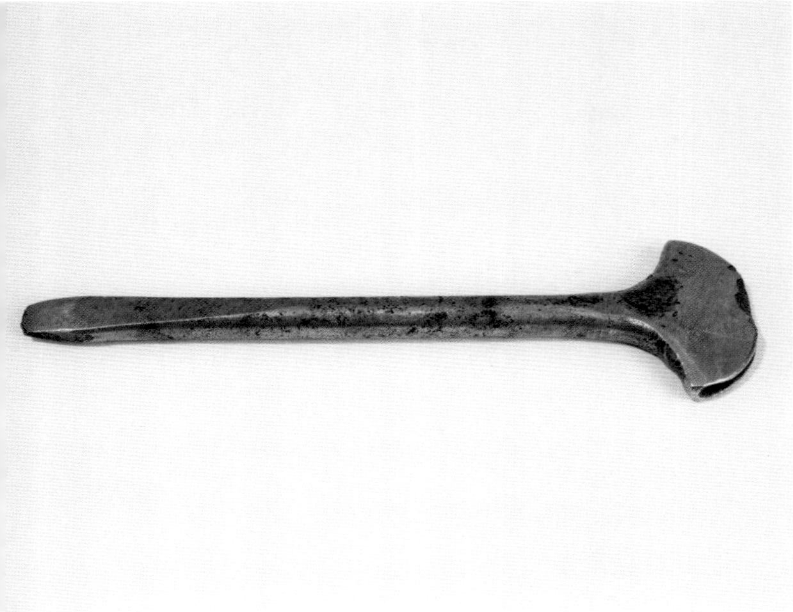

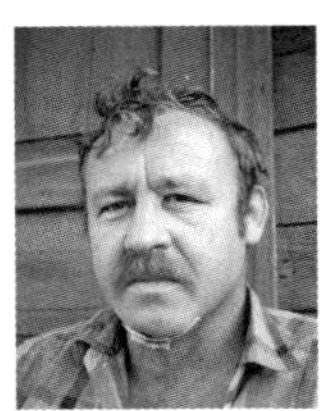

**Nikolai Barsukov**                    Ryazan, 1997

About eight years ago I got a car, a ZIL, for working on the collective farm as a driver. At first there weren't any tools, and I needed a screwdriver. To make it was quite simple. You get hold of a valve from any car or tractor, with the cap, of course. Then you go to the blacksmith and heat the cap to flatten it, so you get a kind of formed end with a handle. It's very convenient for turning and it doesn't pull. Finally you flatten the other end and sharpen as necessary. That's about it. You can temper it in water. You don't have to heat it. It depends on what kind of valve you've got – if it's an exhaust, you don't need to. That's it, your screwdriver is ready. The work takes exactly fifteen minutes. It's very practical and it'll serve you well. If you don't lose it, it'll serve you all your life, you just have to sharpen it once in a while.

Engine valve

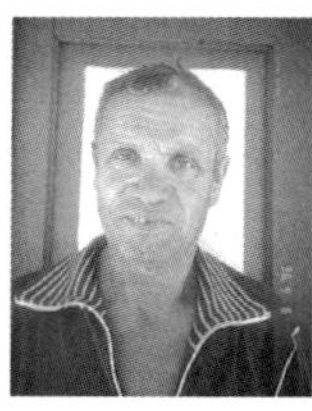

**Nikolai Egorov**                              Moscow, 1994

*As recounted by his daughter Nastya:* Well, this is a home-made thread spooler, with eight spools – two spools in each row. It's made from a plastic mineral water bottle. The bottle doesn't have a bottom; instead of a cork another spool, without thread, has been inserted; and it has sixteen holes in it. The holes have been made with something metal, or so it appears, with something hot used to burn through, maybe with nails or a knitting needle, I don't know. In the holes cocktail straws have been inserted, cut according to the size of the spools. Well, that's pretty much it really. The spools go into the straws, the ends are thrust into these holes. It also has holes for thread, in order to pull them out of there, so that they don't get tangled up. Well, it's very simple. If you need a thread of a certain colour, you pull it out through the holes, then you can cut it off. It's very convenient, because, when you sew, the threads usually lie in some kind of box, or in a jar, and they always get tangled up in there and you have to waste a lot of time and energy untangling them. This way is very convenient and economical. This object is very functional and useful.

Plastic water bottle, cocktail straws

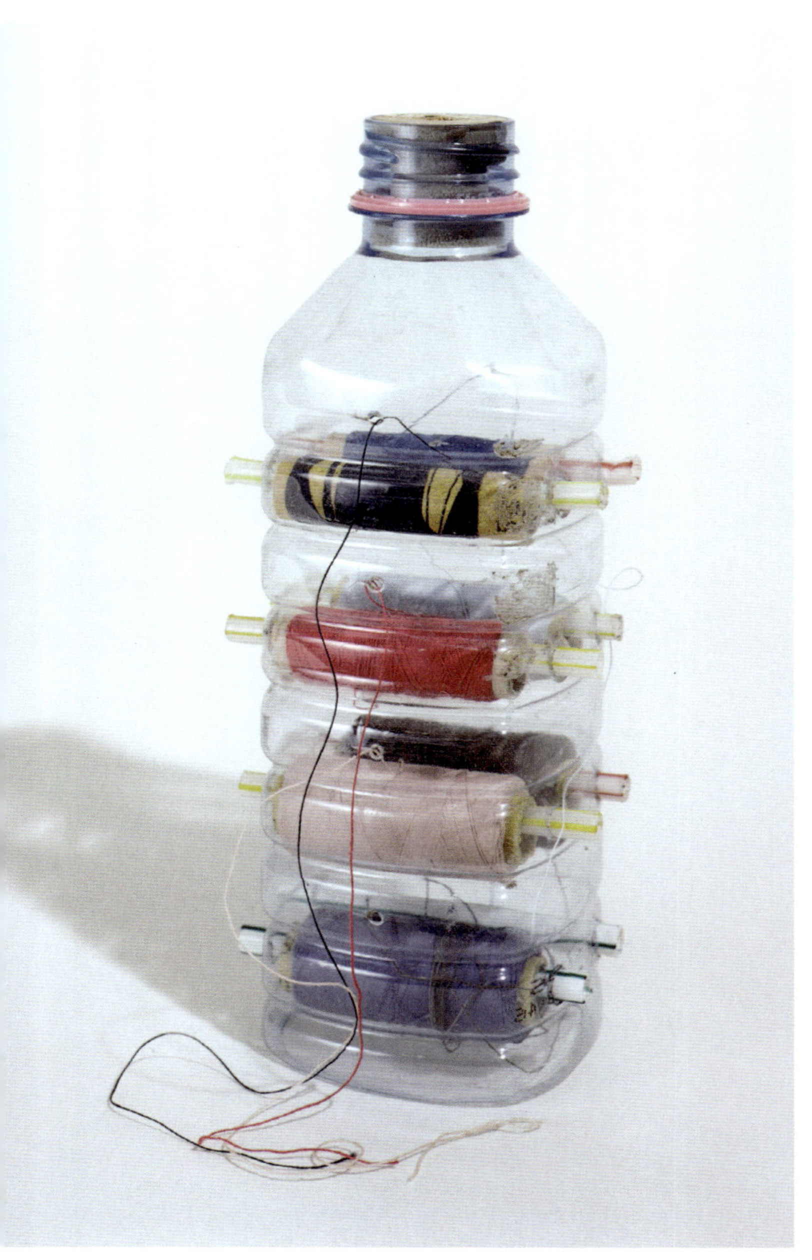

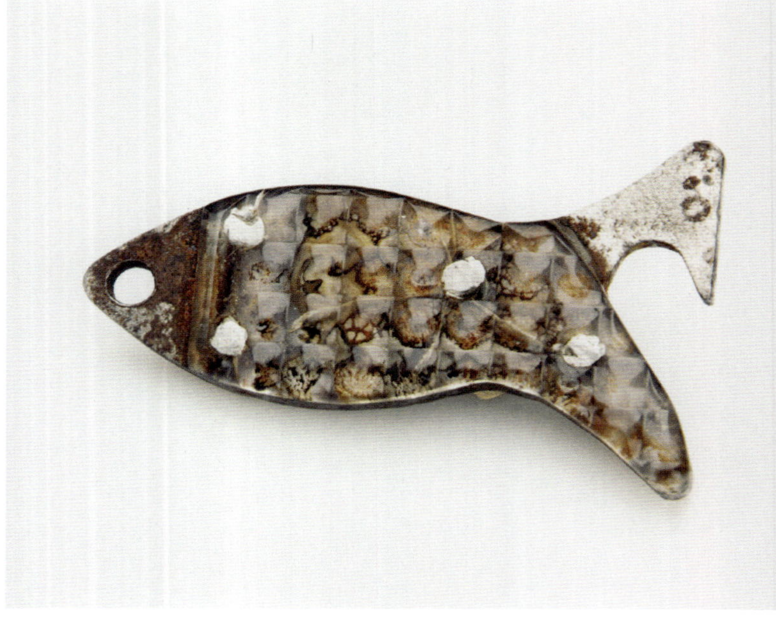

**Sergei Vasiliev**                                                  Ryazan, 1988

It's a kind of fish. I made it. But it's not a very good opener. It was just a trial
run. I made it from a lamp. I glued some plastic, from a lamp, a worktop
lamp I think. It's already about fifteen years old. My mother's got a smaller
one. It was made as a pendant for keys and to open stuff. So you've got your
opener right there. There weren't any such pendants for sale, a pendant and
an opener at the same time. There are all kinds now, but then you couldn't
get hold of anything you could carry with you to open bottles. It opens beer
bottles OK, by the way. Ha, ha, ha.

Steel plate, plexiglass, rivets

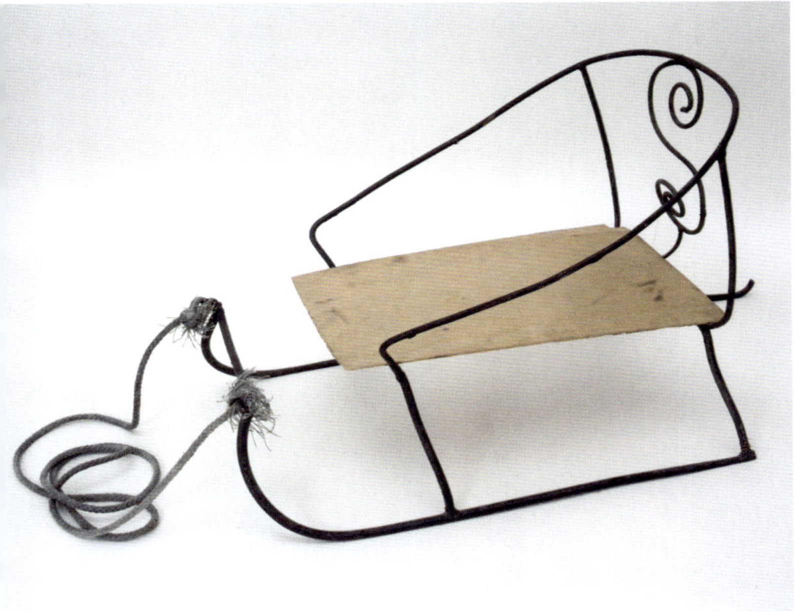

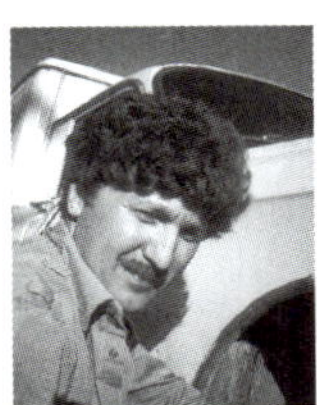

**Nikolai Medvedev**                                    Torzhok, 1977

*As recounted by his son Andrei:* As far as I remember, it was made during my first year at school, and my father used to drag stuff on it. It was a pretty good sledge. You could get up a pretty good speed on it. We used to go to the garage in winter to get potatoes, cucumbers and tomatoes that were stored there, and used the sledge so that we didn't have to carry them all back ourselves. When I was little my father used to drag me there on the sledge and then I would walk back on foot, with my father dragging something behind him on the sledge. We've got a snow-cat for that now, and the sledge has rusted up. When my father used to work at the factory, it was easy to get hold of metal from here and there. It wasn't difficult getting hold of a bar or two to stick in there and welding wasn't a problem. He just got hold of it and welded it.

Steel bar, plywood, rope

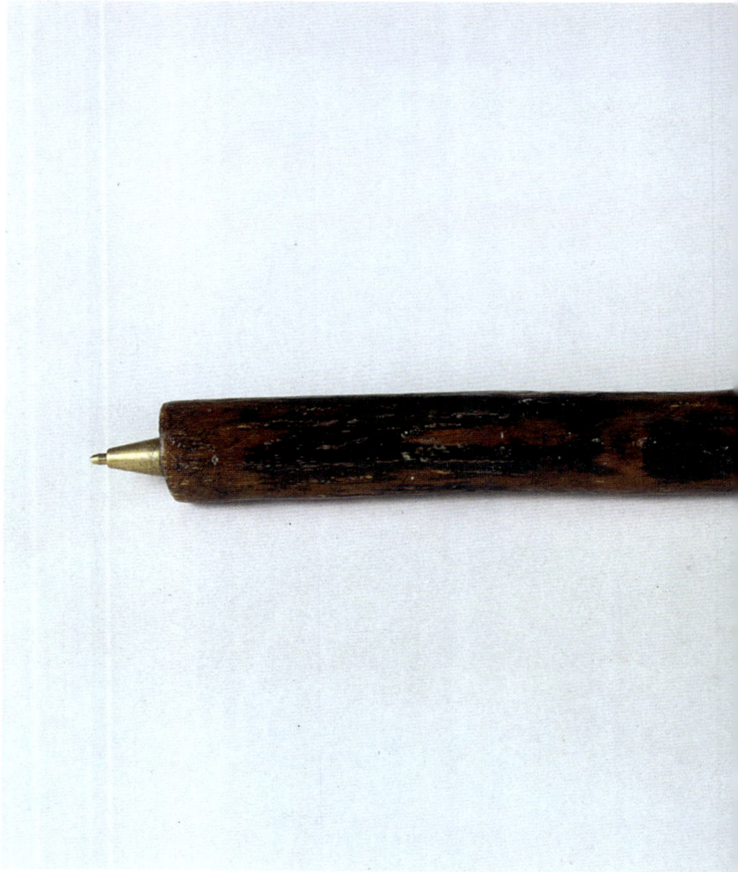

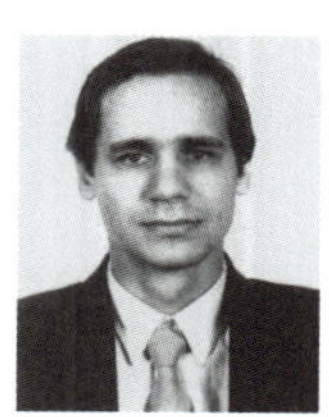

**Andrei Drozdov**                    Moscow region, 1988

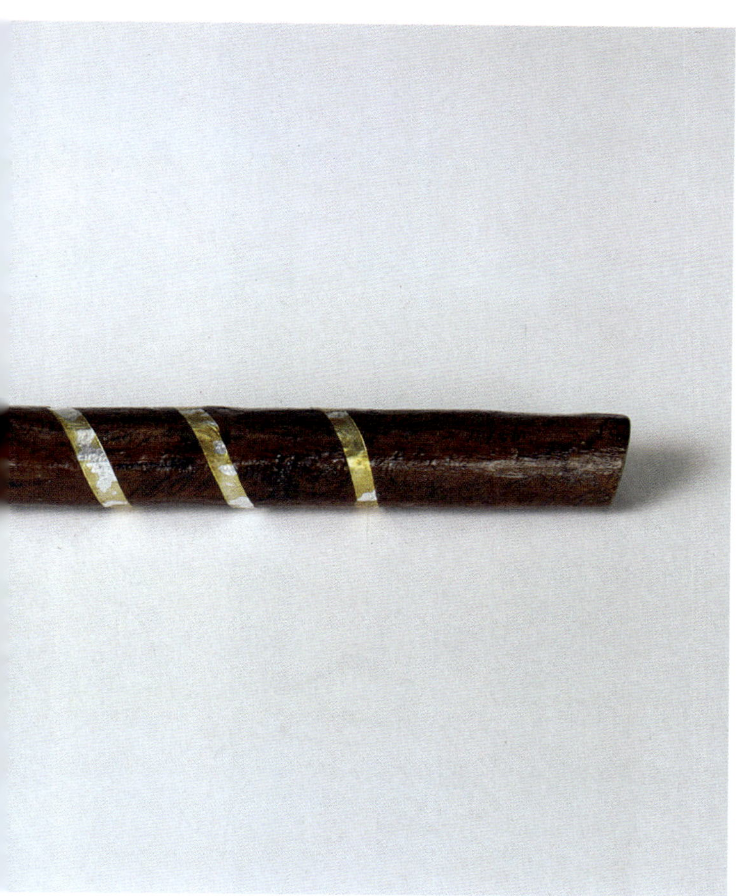

I was at the dacha, in the village. There aren't any shops there. The nearest shop is in the next village. There was nothing there except what people brought with them, mostly food, and I think that was rationed too. Remember, there was nothing at all then – everything had just suddenly disappeared. It was called perestroika. Anyway, there wasn't any point in making an extra trip to the shop, so when we needed a ballpoint pen, I went and made one. I had the inside of a pen, but the cover, the pen itself, was broken. I must have broken it in my bag by accident when we were driving to the village. I found a twig, I think it was lime, and dug the pith out of it – it's soft in lime twigs. I lacquered it with nail polish that I got from Marinka and added this decorative stripe.

Lime twig, nail varnish

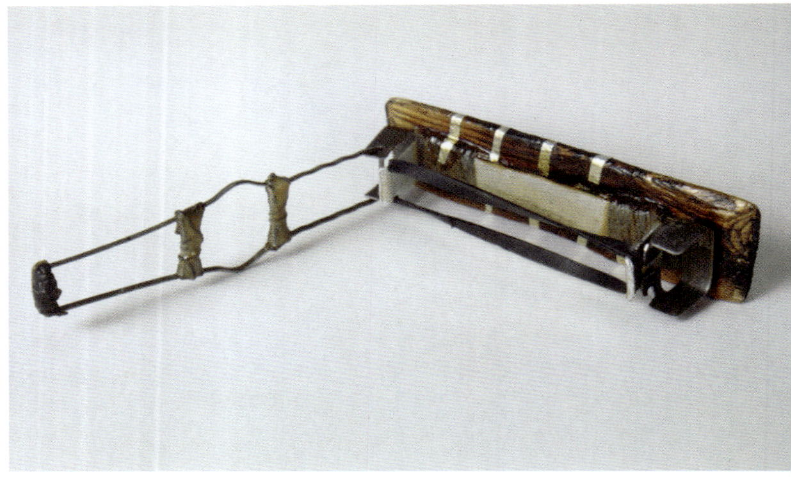

**Andrei Drozdov**                    Moscow, 1991

I've got a hair grip made from wood. The wood is rectangular, 10 by 13 centimetres, covered in varnish and foil and dipped in lacquer. On one side the grip, a complex construction, has been stuck on with epoxy resin. It consists of an aluminium U-shaped holder, which was bent out of transformer steel and grooved out with a needle file. The arc is made from two pins, also glued together with epoxy resin. Several like this were made, and the design was improved each time. The purpose of making this was also to satisfy an aesthetic need. The first hair grip was made for my wife, you could say she inspired me. The rest were made simply because of my desire to improve the design, some kind of aspiration towards perfection.

*As recounted by his wife:* I had long hair and I couldn't buy a hair grip anywhere. I had one but it was broken, and after suffering with this for some time I asked my husband to make me one. He didn't have anything to do during the summer holidays as he was a student then, and needed to do something to keep himself busy. And also of course, there was the desire to make his wife a present using his own hands, as a kind of expression of his love.

Wood, hairpin, epoxy glue, tin strip

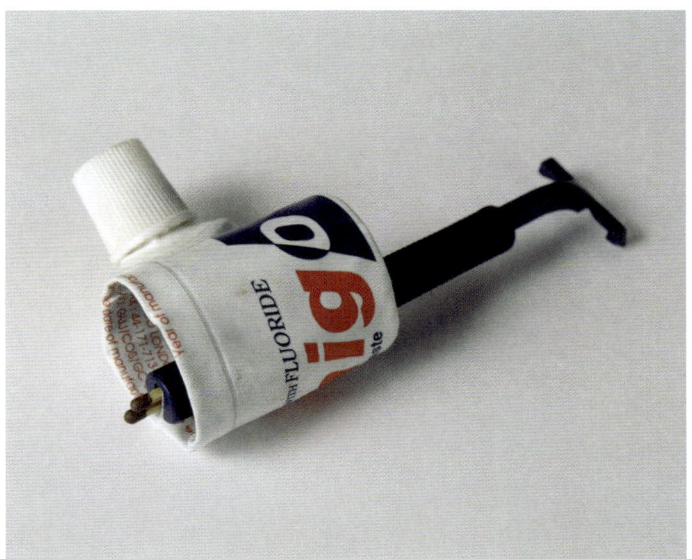

**Andrei Drozdov**                                        Moscow, c.1991

This is a paste squeezer or a paste presser. The first time I saw this type of object was probably some old industrial device slipped over a tube that had paste at the end and, by turning it, it was possible to squeeze all the paste out from even the very end. Well, this is an old disposable razor with the blade taken out. There was already a hole in the razor, probably for plastic producers to save money, so I carefully hollowed it out up to the end of the razor. It was then possible to slip it onto the edge of the tube.

I thought about it, and had a look around. It's like anything that you make, you look for stuff. When I turned this razor over in my hands, it'd been hanging about somewhere and I realised what I could make from it. Or maybe, the other way around, I wanted to make this thing and I looked for the razor. But these ideas almost always occur simultaneously. I made it in about five minutes. There was no particular purpose behind it, I just realised the use I could put the razor to and well, naturally, I wanted to squeeze out all the paste. It was when I was studying at university, 1991 or maybe 1993, but no later. Well, my wife says that we only used it once, but well, even for one tube it was worth it: an old razor and five minutes' work. It was better than trying to squeeze the tube on the edge of the sink. That's a real hassle.

Disposable razor, matches

**Andrei Drozdov**                                        Moscow, 1990

It was necessary to make a record box as there were records but no box. And records get everywhere without a box. Well, I have this aesthetic and ethical principle – don't waste money, especially on such nonsense. The need to make it arose from this principle. And when the need arose, the action automatically followed. It's all very simple. In Russia, that is to say, in the Soviet Union, there were a lot of boxes made from thick cardboard, more than likely it was cardboard used for electronic stuff, which is very solid and doesn't go soggy. The cardboard was folded to the necessary size and stuck together at the edges with epoxy resin. It was then flattened down as it was very springy. Then holes were made in it and it was held together with clips so that the resin dried in place. And then it came into being and got used. A collection of records was kept in it and what's more you could fit more records in it than in a standard box.

My mum worked in the Ministry, and they had those boxes there. It's the solidness of this cardboard that is really amazing. And the story of the clips is also quite interesting. I used to take sofas apart and repair them and the separate parts were held together with those clips. We kept the clips, and still have a whole box of them in the house. They were just usual common clips, but in a sense, quite amazing really.

Cardboard, epoxy glue, clips

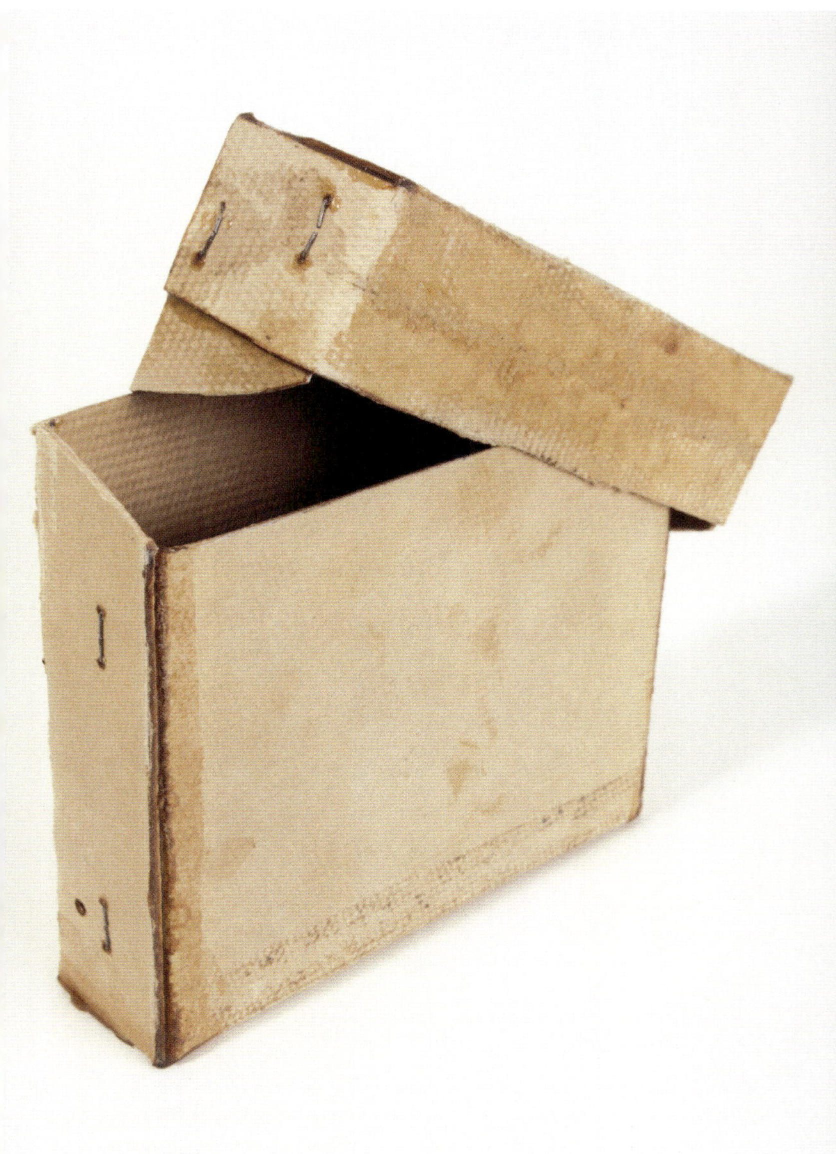

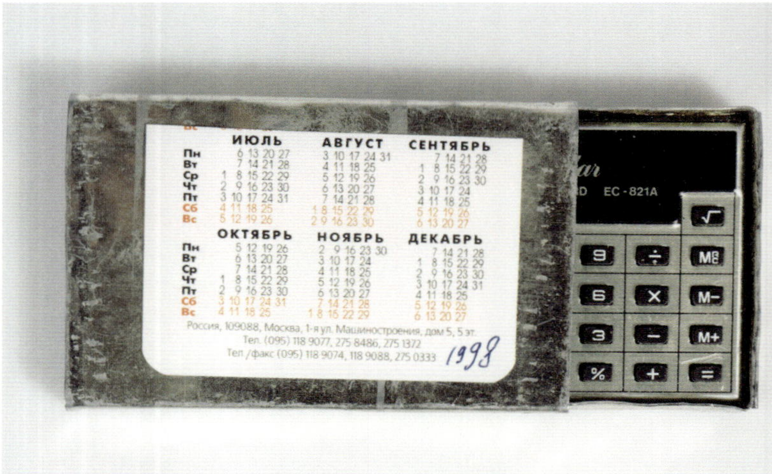

**Andrei Drozdov**                                                    Moscow, 1991

This old thing – it's not a top model, just a common calculator from China. Its iron case was made during my student days when there were loads of cheap calculators. But they were disposable, you couldn't change the batteries. And that was the reason for the appearance of such heavy iron cases for them. They stopped the buttons getting pressed accidentally and turning the calculator on. And, you know, my calculator is still running on those batteries today. In 1991 my wife started university and it's her calculator now.

The iron is from a tin for conserved food, some sprats in tomato sauce or something. It was a tin with paper wrapping, and we peeled the paper off because it was better without any pictures on it. What was the coolest though was that we folded the edges over twice, and because of this you can't cut yourself on it. I had known for a long time that you need to do that with iron. Then I flattened them down with pliers on an anvil so that they were flat and didn't fold back into shape. But it wasn't my anvil, it was my father-in-law's. The hammer was his as well.

Food tin, glue, pocket calculator

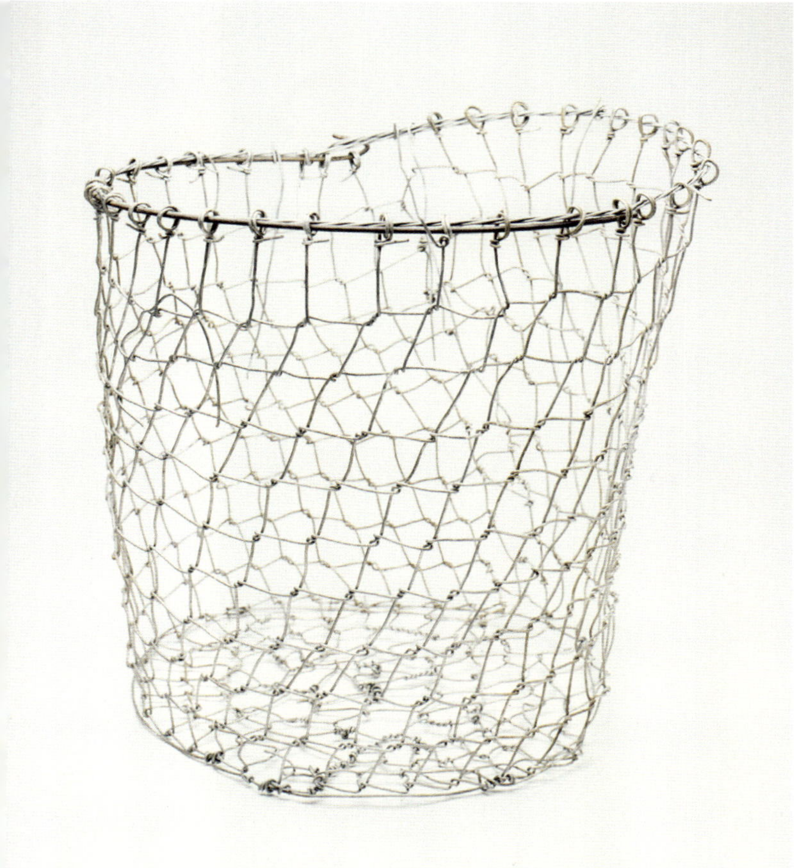

**Nikolai Babinov**                              Kaluga region, 1991

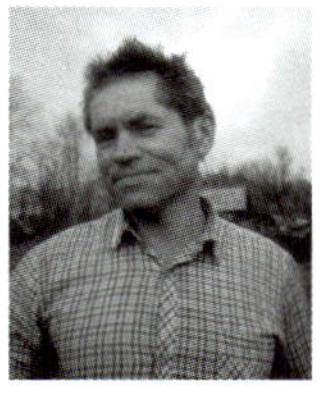

It's made from a hay basket. What's bad about it is that it gets deformed when you carry heavy stuff in it. But then you can only carry large stuff in it, like hay, as the openings are so big anything small will just fall out. It's not even really suitable for wood chippings either. But, I suppose, all the same, it makes things easier.

Aluminium wire

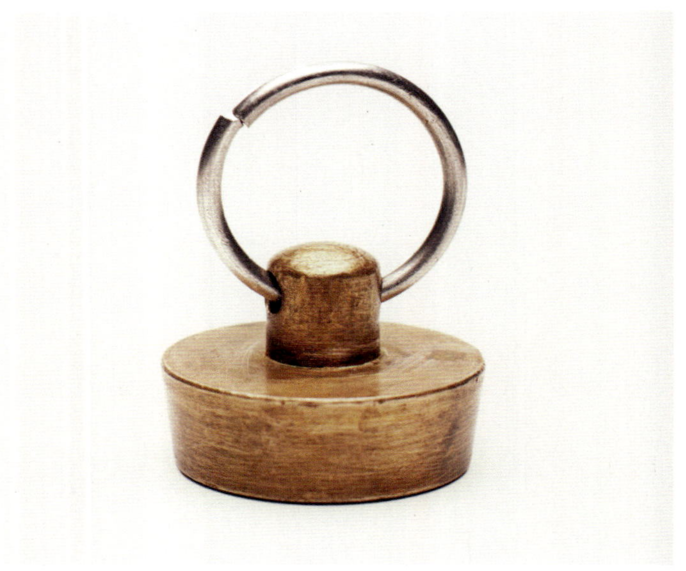

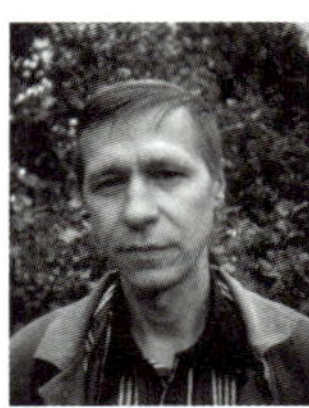

**Sergei Fedorishchenko**                    Kolomna, c.1990

It came about that I had to make a plug for a bath. It's moulded from plastic. My mate Volodka asked me to make one out of bronze. It's bulkier and, supposedly, more reliable. He brought me a model of the plug and I found a part and measured out the dimensions. I carved out the cone from the old plug, catching this angle, into the undercut. You really need to drill into the undercut here. I did the boring with a cutter, because everything here is connected. Then I went to see the drillers, because I had to make some opening in order to put the chain through it. The driller, Peter, said, 'I'll do the drilling for you and you make me one.' Everything was ready and in place and so I made a second plug. 'I'll do the ring now,' he said. But, you understand, bronze is a heavy material. A plastic plug can come out easily, let water through. That's quite easy. If you can get hold of some stainless steel, you can make it from that as well.

Bronze, steel ring

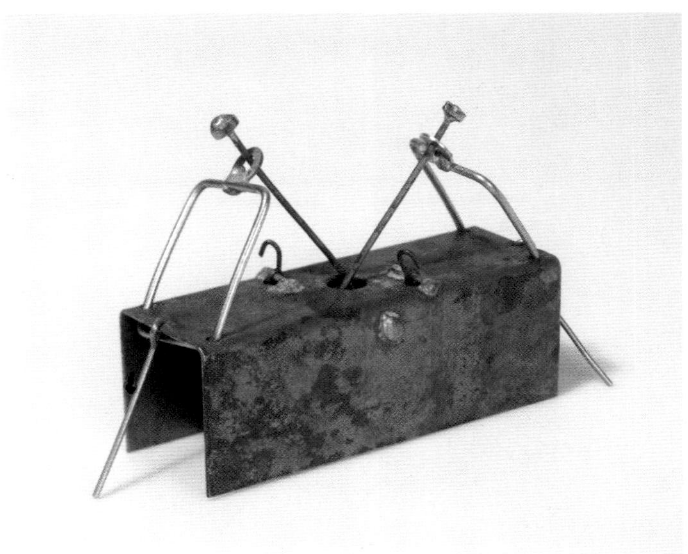

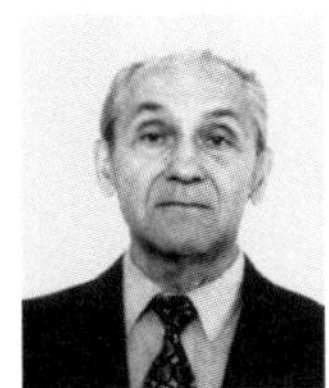

**Nikolai Kotov**  Orel, 1998

This is a mousetrap with two traps. For two mice. Let's say, you rarely get to your dacha or something. An ordinary mousetrap kills one mouse and that's all, but this one gets a couple. The principle is that your usual mousetrap comes down from above onto the mouse and this, from below. You load it with a bit of bread, and the mouse crawls, crawls, pulls at it and... The second one is exactly the same. Even though the mouse can see the first one there, it still goes for it – they're so stupid. And this winter I even caught a rat in this. Everyone was amazed – but a fact is a fact. It stuck its nose in here and this ring came up under its nose. It looks like it struggled here for a long time but couldn't get free. It's a necessary domestic thing. I only get to the dacha about once a week, you know. When you have mice running about the place – it's not so nice. Bit by bit you catch them.

Steel sheet, wire, springs

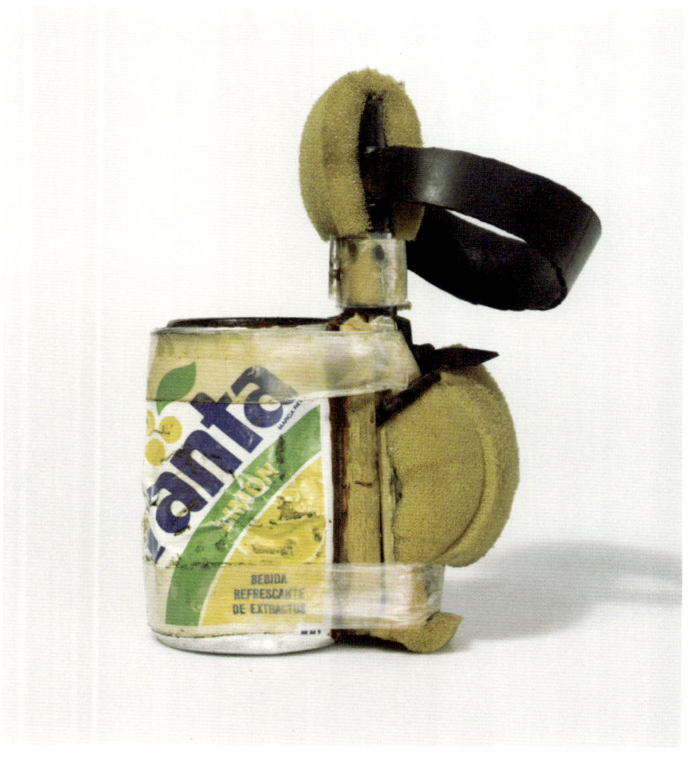

**Igor Kachan**                                          Leningrad, 1990

The maracas are made from Fanta cans. The container is small, very small, stuck onto this wooden thing with insulating tape and two elastic bands. And one big elastic band is wrapped around your foot, and the small one around your finger. But like this, it turns out, it's impossible to play in your socks. You have to take off your socks or play with socks full of holes.

This can was given to me by a friend who had gone to Spain for a competition, and he brought it back from there. There weren't any here then. It was in 1990. Look, it's dented, 'cos I often put it down, stepped on it – it got dented. Now I never see such small ones. If you use a big can, it's too heavy to swing. The inside is filled with... what's it called? Groats? No, millet, millet!

Fanta can, sellotape, wood, foam, elastic bands

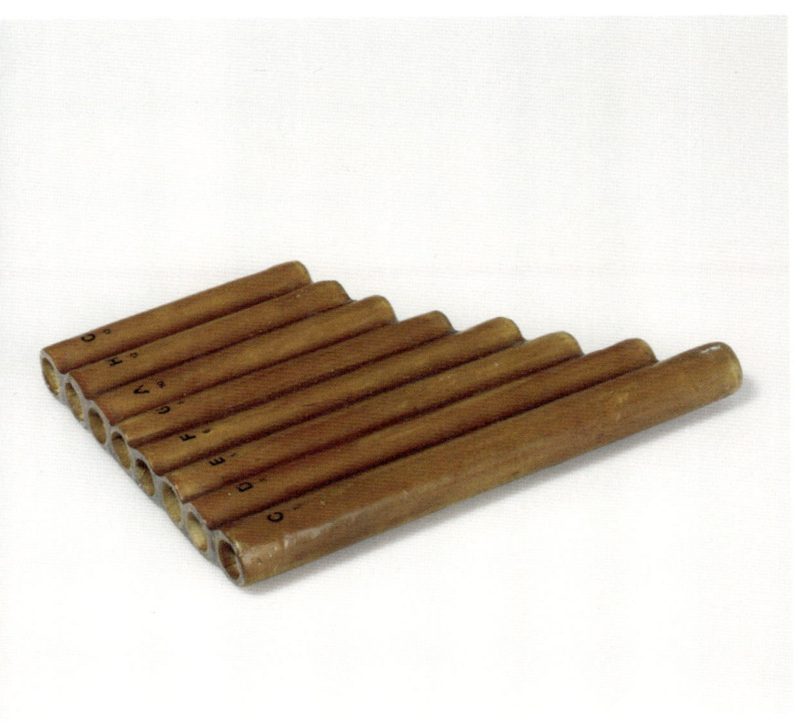

## Igor Kachan

Saint Petersburg, 1993

It was 1993, I was working as a watchman and I had loads of free time. And as I was a musician at the time, I wanted to get hold of some new sounds to go with my guitar. I really like the sound of pan pipes. But there weren't any for sale, nor any harmonicas. They were banned, considered anti-Soviet instruments. And then I saw that they were selling kugikli – a Kursk folk instrument. It was just five pipes and you could get a melody from them. And I thought: if I pour in epoxy resin it'll be a pan pipe. I bought two packs of those pipes and cut them down in size in order to get a half-tone at a certain level. The higher the sound frequency of the pipes, the harder they are to tune. Tuning was very simple: you just cut it to size very roughly, light a candle and drip in drops of wax and the drops reduce the internal volume and make the sound higher. And so you drip in drops of wax until you get the right note. Once I could even play a melody on it... But I forget how to now.

Kugikli, epoxy glue, wax

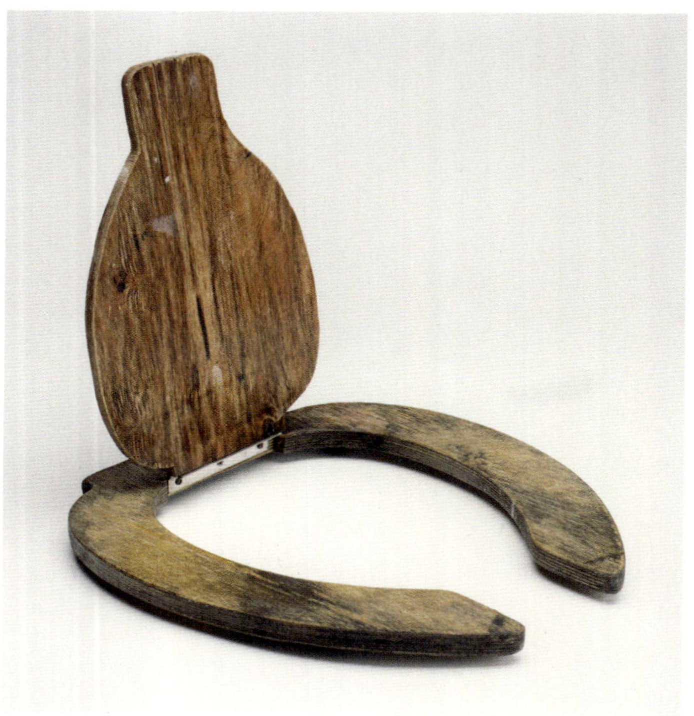

**Igor Kochan**                                                Leningrad, 1991

Well, to cut a long story short, I made this because I was too mean to buy one. The thing is that recently we've become used to always having water, and we haven't been storing it up. And so, if someone goes to the toilet, and there isn't any water, you need to cover the toilet up with something. But the toilet pan was broken. One of the rods from the seat had broken. I went to the shop to buy a new one but they cost twenty-five roubles! Twenty-five roubles – there's no way I was going to pay that. So I took two brackets and fixed them onto the seat with bolts. Then I took the inside of a lamp, bored holes in it and attached it. So I had a kind of double seat. I guess I just didn't think about covering it up. Well, it's not such a disgrace, to hell with it. Although it's not too late and I could still fix something on the top.

We never really appreciate our own labour. If I can do something myself, then I'll do it – I don't have the means to do otherwise. Now it's difficult to earn money, it's better to waste it only on stuff you can't do yourself.

Toilet seat, plywood, brackets, metal hinge, screws

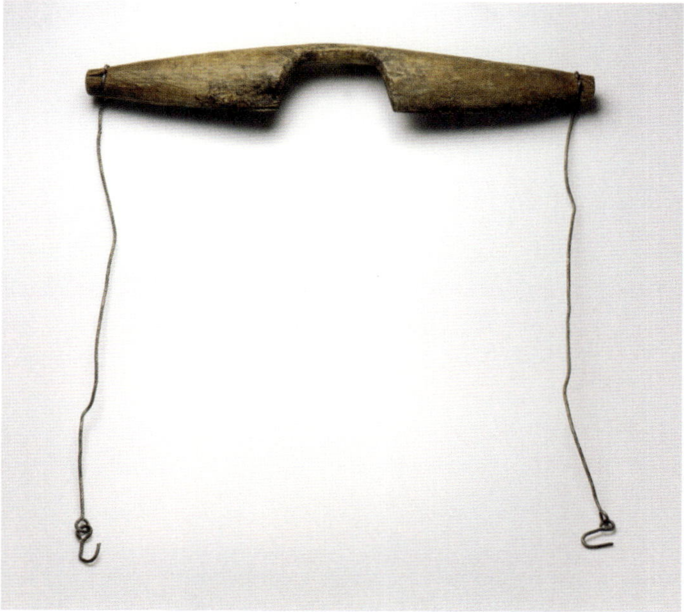

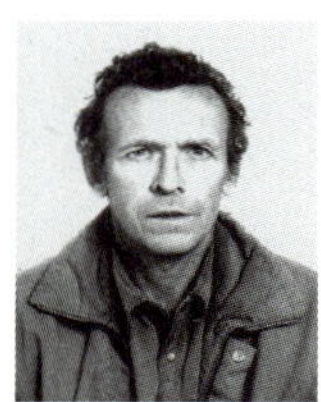

**Pechonkin**                    Arkhangelsk region, c.1988

To start you choose a piece of aspen that is a bit wider than your shoulders, and then you cut it out with an axe or a chisel. You choose a piece that's going to rest well on your shoulders, like this one. You can carry water in the damp, because if you get caught in the rain, it just blackens and that's all. It's made from aspen poles, from the allotment, fence poles, well, mostly stakes, and the studs are from willow. The old folks say that the allotment has been here for fifty years and I've seen that there are lots of water carriers here. You know, a bucket on your shoulders, carried on your shoulders, is less convenient than this, by the way: you go along, and water splashes everywhere. But here you just hold onto the steel wire, or some people make small chains – if you're rich.

Aspen wood, steel wire

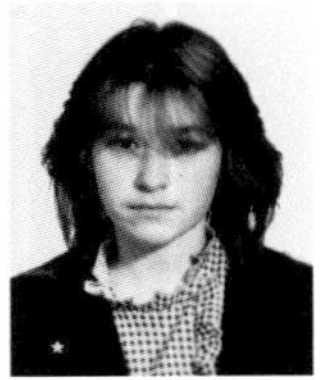

**Viktor Kuzmichyov**                                     Moscow, 1992

*As recounted by his daughter Masha (pictured):* One of the first great blows to my soul happened when I inadvertently smashed mum's favourite teapot. Well... to be more precise I didn't completely smash it, I just knocked off the handle. I dropped it and the handle came off. It had probably been cracked before. I was in complete shock. Mum was coming and I thought I would die right there on the spot. What could I do? I just curled up somewhere in the corner of the kitchen and started crying. But then dad unexpectedly came home first, discovered me sitting in the corner, in tears. 'What's the matter. What's happened?' he asked. I showed him the teapot. He said, 'Calm down, calm down. Everything will be OK.' And he promised to take it to the factory and think of something, but I didn't think it was possible to do anything and I didn't stop crying. Even so, he took the teapot to the factory and in a couple of days he brought it home with a strange handle fixed onto the neck and tightened on with a bolt from the side of the spout. It was a solid handle made from good stainless steel. Mum of course looked upon all of this with scepticism. She said it wasn't aesthetically pleasing and that basically it would be impossible to use it, that the handle would get hot and things like that. But it turned out that the handle didn't get so hot, and that it was even a little bit more solid than the previous one. As a result mum calmed down and we continued to use that teapot.

Teapot, steel, screw

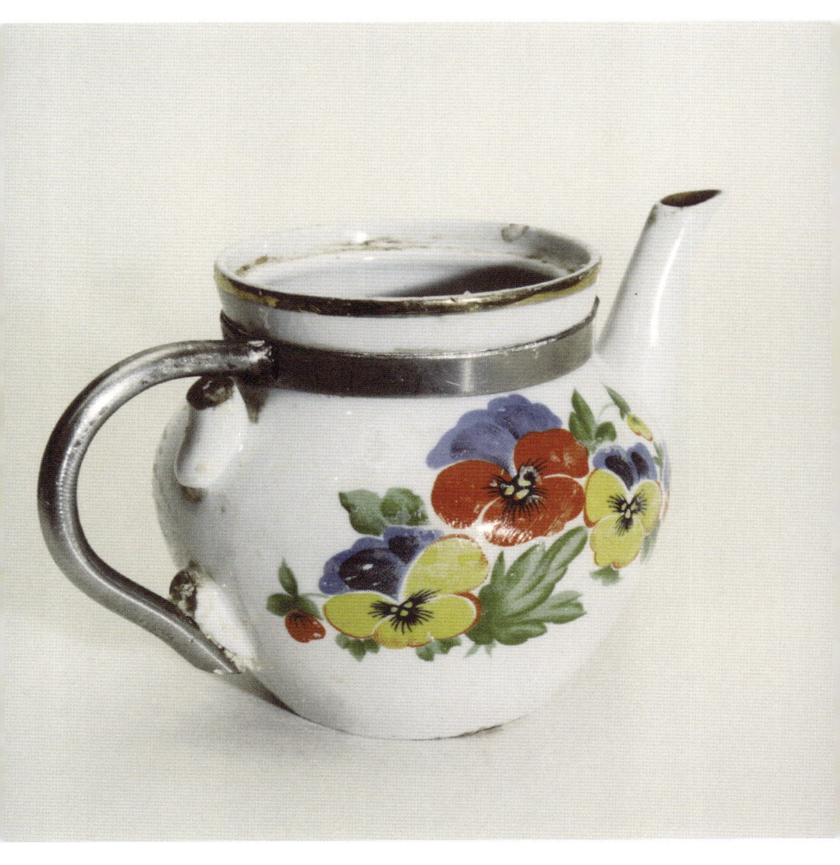

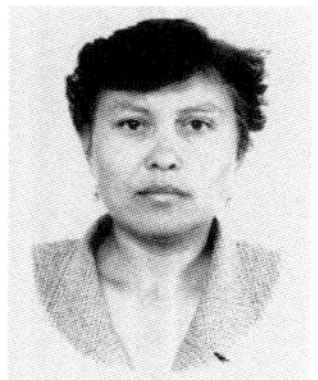

**Tatiana Semak**                                                    Moscow region, 1993

*As recounted by her daughter Ksenia:* This bag was made by my mother some time ago. The situation was like this: she was a chemist working in an institute when, at the beginning of the 1990s, they stopped paying her. So my mum and me left our jobs and I started to study at university. She's not such a social person but once she got chatting to one of our neighbours in the lift. The neighbour worked in a freezer factory and suggested that they try to set up a business out of selling ice cream. They put their money together and did just that. They bought ice cream in bulk at the factory and sold it on intercity trains. The neighbour took my mum to the factory and showed her everything. In winter it was all very simple – you just got hold of an ordinary bag and put the ice cream in that. But in the summer there was nothing doing, even with money it would have been difficult, but the money had been spent on something else and without cash it was impossible. In summer the ice cream would melt and so it became necessary to think of something. We found a box made of polystyrene on the dump, and we had the leatherette at home, which at one time had been used for the balcony doors. We sewed it from that leatherette, put polystyrene inside and on the top we put a bit of that stuff that you use to seal the windows in winter, and then made a handle. And that was it. All the same the ice cream still melted. Thank god that's all over with now. Best to forget it.

Polystyrene, imitation leather, foam, thread, elastic

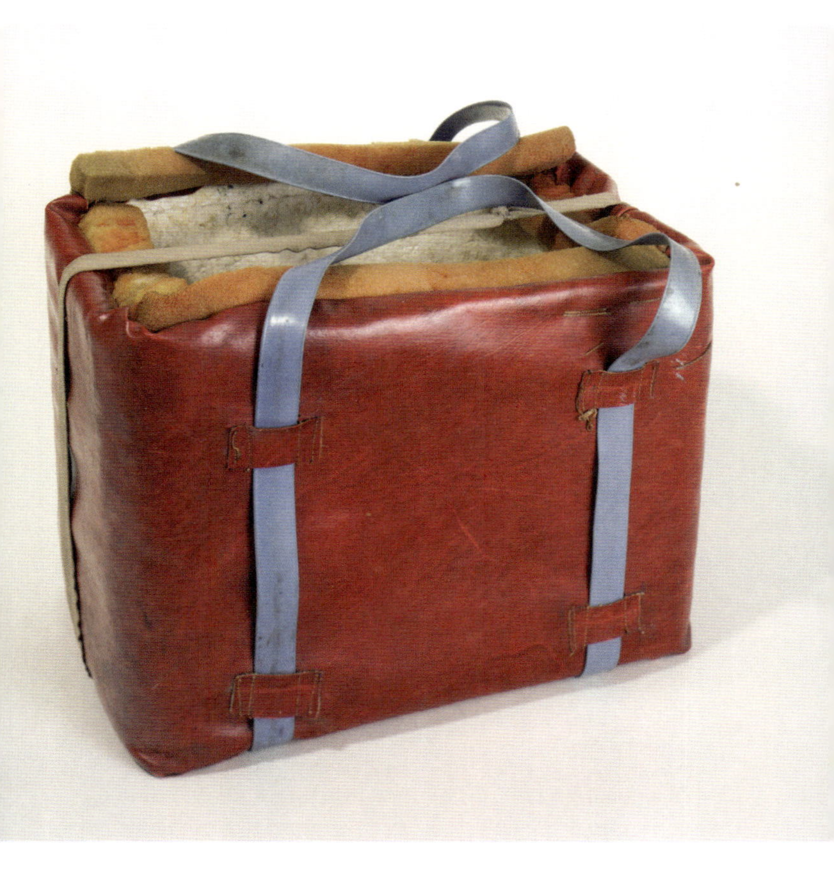

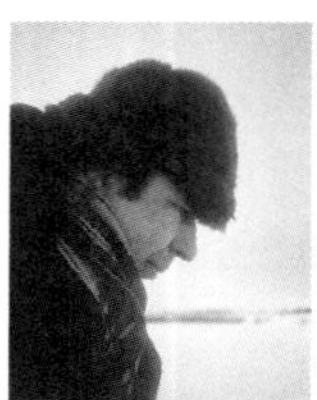

**Nikolai Pimenov**                                   Moscow region, c.1996

Well, these 'goat's legs' were published about eight or ten years ago in the magazine *Fisherman-Sportsman*. It's a convenient thing for fishermen who go ice fishing, and have to change their holes in the ice a lot, to find fish. It's not like those fishermen who just stand with their rods and fish: they don't have to change position at all, they just set the bait, sit down and catch fish. The ice fishermen have to run about from place to place dragging their stool or box with them. This stool is fixed onto a belt and is always with you – wherever I want to go, I go and sit there.

You get hold of a pipe, and at the end of it some threading is carved. Then a holder is made which is fixed directly onto the stool, and it's also got threading. The tube is screwed into the holder, and the strap is attached to the belt. The seat – well, this is the back of a chair. You can construct it differently, but why make it from scratch when the material is lying around? If a chair had been chucked out why not take its back, the foam rubber, and the upholstered material.

Chair back, chain, screws, metal shank

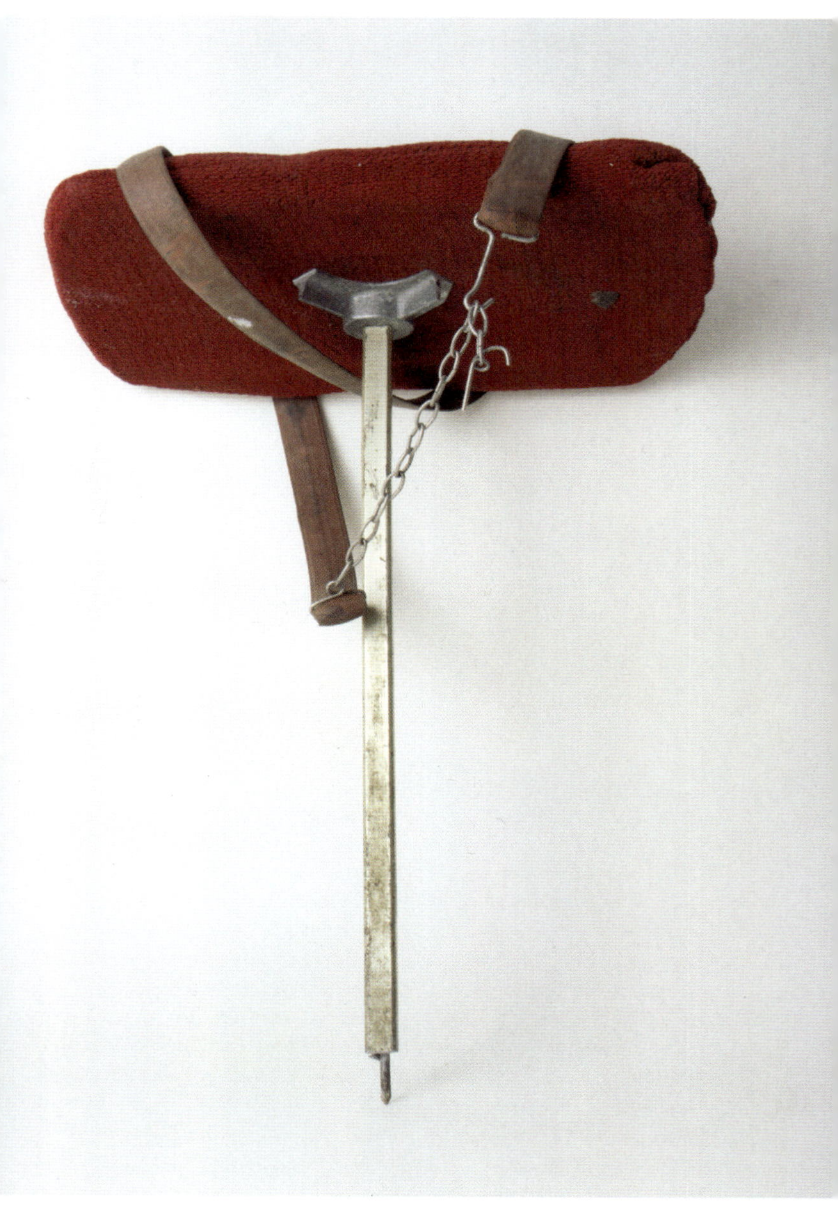

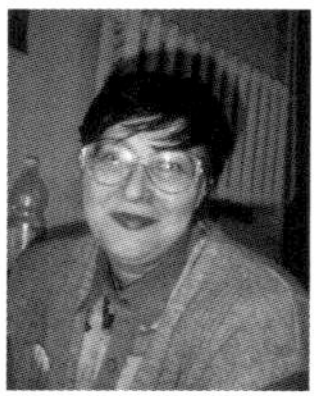

**Gennadii** Tolyatti, c.1980

*As recounted by his wife Natasha (pictured):* They say that the Volga used to swarm with fish, and people used to catch them with the help of this device. It's a harpoon. I have the feeling that you could only catch crocodiles in Africa with this now. There used to be more fish, and people mainly used to catch sturgeon, but now it's probably not possible to use this as the Volga is sick and there aren't many valuable breeds of fish in it. I reckon this was made about thirty years ago. It was considered a poacher's tool, that is you could get heavily fined for using such a thing for catching fish. Officially, they didn't exist, but fishermen had them and used to use them whenever they could. Fifteen years ago sterlet soup was a common thing. My husband even brought sterlet home to his family, and you could make everyone happy with such tasty things. Now, unfortunately, the best you can hope for is pike, or some other kind of fish that are basically good for nothing, too bony. Also, fishing has become a lot harder now, and the fishing inspectors have got laws governing how many kilos of fish you can catch.

Steel, wood

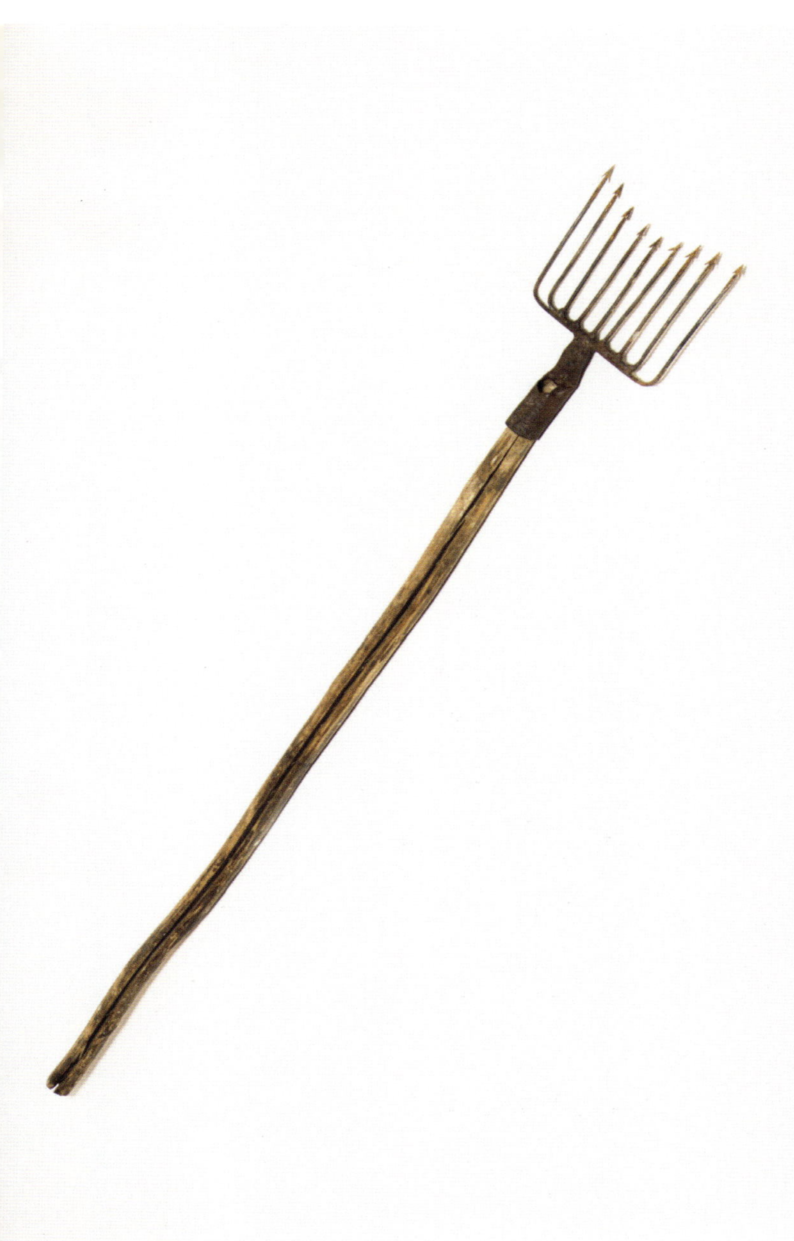

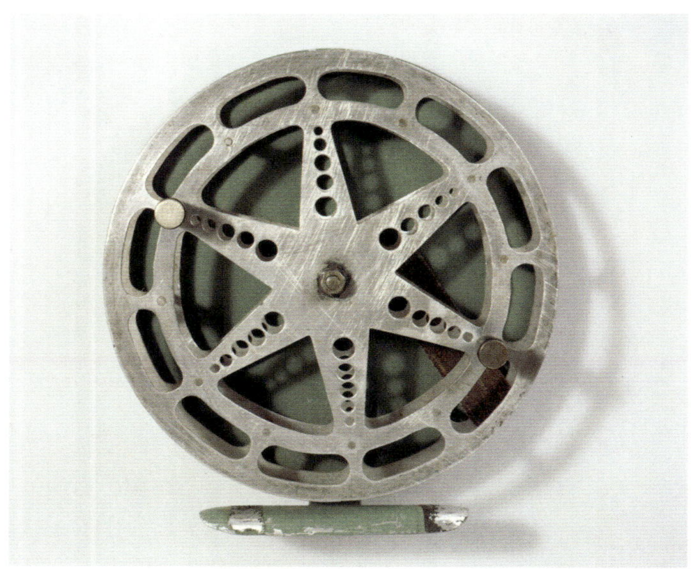

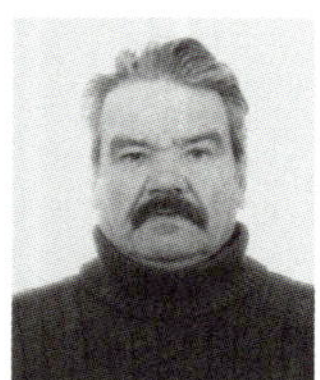

**Yurii Ilyushenko**                                                    Yaroslavl, 1994

Ah, fuck it. Well, over there is a shell. What do you need to buy stuff for when you can make it yourself? I'm a lathe operator, for fuck's sake. The lathe's not far off. Do you think it takes long, or what? I cut just it in two, they made it with cracks but I bent it into shape, that's all. They don't manufacture those spools, everyone makes them for themselves. Whoever is a fisherman can do it for himself of course. That shell, y'know. My grandson's got a videocamera. He'll show you straight off.

Duralumin plates, steel pivot, rivets

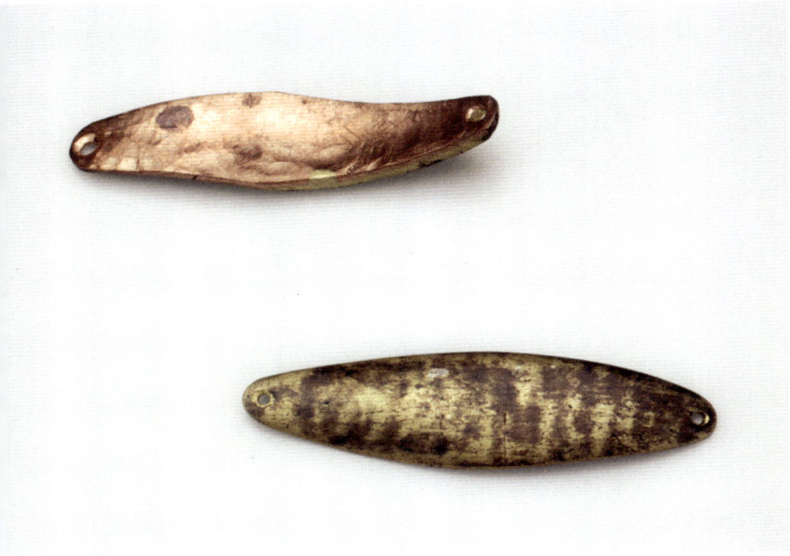

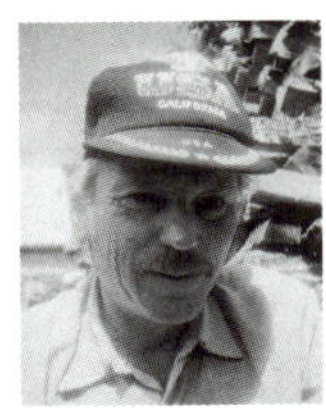

**Nikolai Karpov**  Onega, Arkhangelsk region, 1998

I made these from brass. This bit goes on the pike, like they write about in magazines. Mostly, the diameter is 191, and here two radii of 51. I've loved metal my whole life, and I've always worked as a welder. Without counting the army, I've been welding for thirty years. I've welded with argon, the lot. My speciality is metal. Anything that you put your whole soul into is cool. You can get large fish. I made the die. The rest the guys made, at the factory. I'm more into the hooks, I don't do nets. I couldn't really give a shit about nets.

Brass

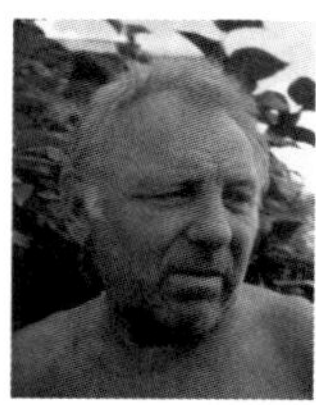

**Vasilii Bobrov**    Voronezh region, 1995

What can I tell you? If you're not a fisherman yourself, it'll take ages. It just looks like it's all simple, but there's an awful lot to it. Which hook to choose, which line, which rod, which bait – all sorts of things. Take the bait for instance, there's millet, oats, maize, peas, lentils, various kinds of dough, worms, mosquito grubs, ants' eggs, dragonfly larvae, mayfly larvae and caddis flies, not to mention all sorts of artificial baits and spinners. So you see, there's something for every fish. Also it depends on the season, what the weather's like, what depth you're fishing at. Usually each fisherman knows his own spot – what the depth is, what the bottom's like, what kind of fish to catch when. And if you want fish there all the time you have to feed them a bit.

I'll tell you about this can – I think it was a can of Chinese corned beef. But I made a fish feeder out of it. I cut off the lid, put on a mesh top, and fastened the edges down with wire. The loops are made of wire, and the catch too. I made lots of holes so the bait would wash out through them. For example, you take some bran and mix it with clay and make a ball. Then you put it in the feeder and lower it to the right depth for when you're fishing from a boat.

Tin can, wire, metal mesh

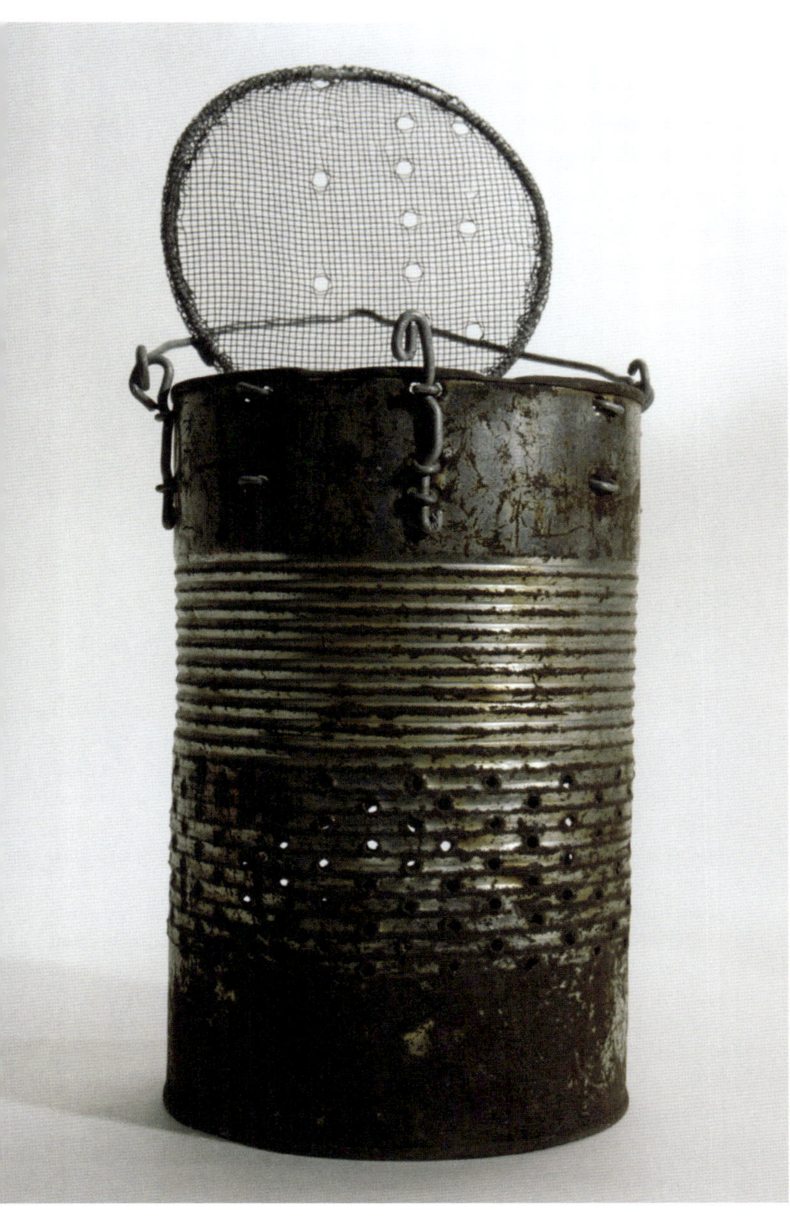

**Vasilii Bobrov**                                        Voronezh region, 1997

It's just an absolutely primitive boot hanger. If you were a hunter or fisherman like anyone else, you'd have understood me straight away. Have you seen those long boots? Waders? Well, I often walk through the village in them when I'm on my way to go fishing, although I turn them down of course. They're grand boots, the only problem is – how can you store them? They're really long and the tops crack. Somehow they always crack in the same place if you stand them like ordinary boots – they get a hole in the same spot. I've glued on patches but it's no good. They just leak in the same place again. Pashka and me sometimes go to the lakes furthest away. Every time we take our boots off, his feet are dry and there are no patches on his boots, so I asked him, 'Out with it, come on'. He said, 'How do you keep your boots?' and I said, 'The usual way, the same way everyone does'. Ah, but not everyone does! He did me a drawing of how to make a hanger and hang up my boots so they wouldn't crack. So I had a go and I made this thing. Pashka's a welder, he invented this entire industrial design version, but I just bent mine out of odd bits of wire that came to hand. It suits me and I've been wearing these boots more than four years now. Take a look. It looks simple enough – you just keep the boots upside-down, but who would ever guess that?

Copper wire, aluminium wire

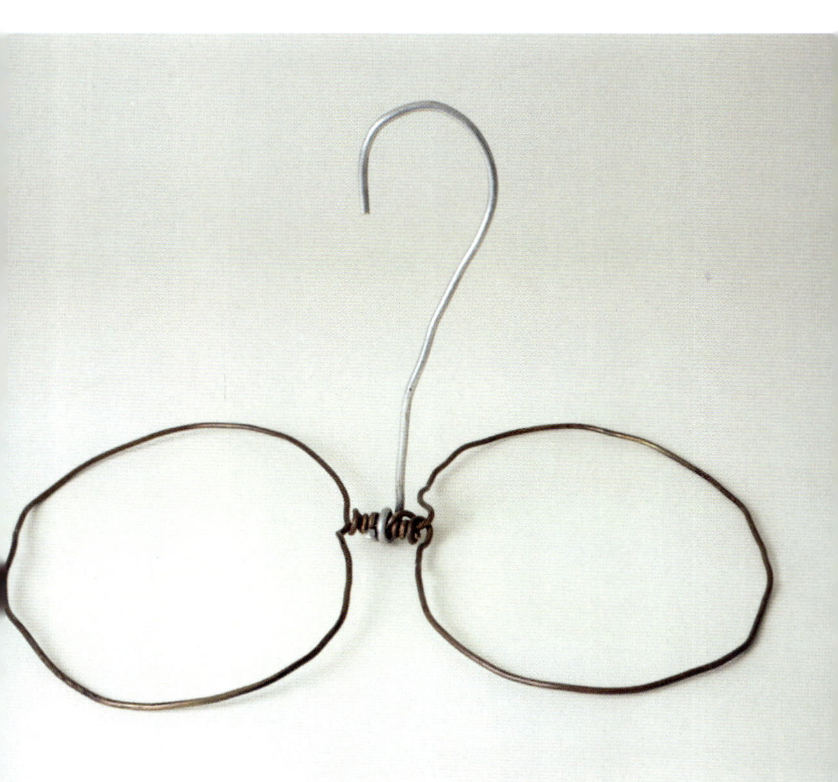

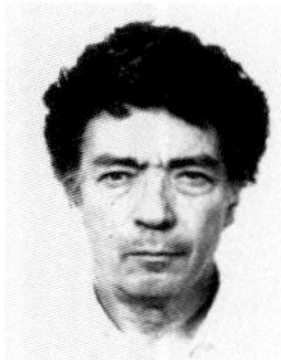

**Aleksandr Konychev**                    Kolentsym, Ryazan region, 1988

I have a childhood friend called Genka Konychev. We used to go out to visit our grannies in the village for the summer, where there's a river called the Pronya. That was where we met, by the river, when we were fishing. We were still little kids, and mostly we used a rod and a line with weights. When Genka and I got to know each other, we started going fishing together. Genka's granny kept animals – a cow, a sheep, a piglet – and so, of course, she had big feed baskets for feeding them. I suggested to Genka we should try catching fish with the baskets, but Genka wouldn't at first, because he was a feeble specimen. I was stronger than him and he was afraid he wouldn't be able to lift the soaking-wet basket. But I persuaded him, and we started trying to catch fish in the reeds with a basket. You have to tread quietly, so as not to frighten the fish away, and a few times we saw really big fish in among the reeds, although we never caught one. That was when I got the idea of making a fish-spear. If the basket didn't work, then we'd get them with a harpoon. We used files to sharpen some old forks, or old bits of metal – there were lots of different versions. But we still didn't manage to catch anything with our spears all summer long.

Next year we met up again during the summer holidays and Genka said, 'I know why we don't catch any fish. It's because the spears are all wrong. A harpoon has to be made properly. My uncle always brings fish home with his harpoon. We should go and talk to him.' We walked to the next village where his uncle lived, and when we saw his spear we were gob-smacked. Genka started asking him to make some like that for us. He promised. But when he'd made one, he said that one would be enough for both of us.

Steel, aluminium

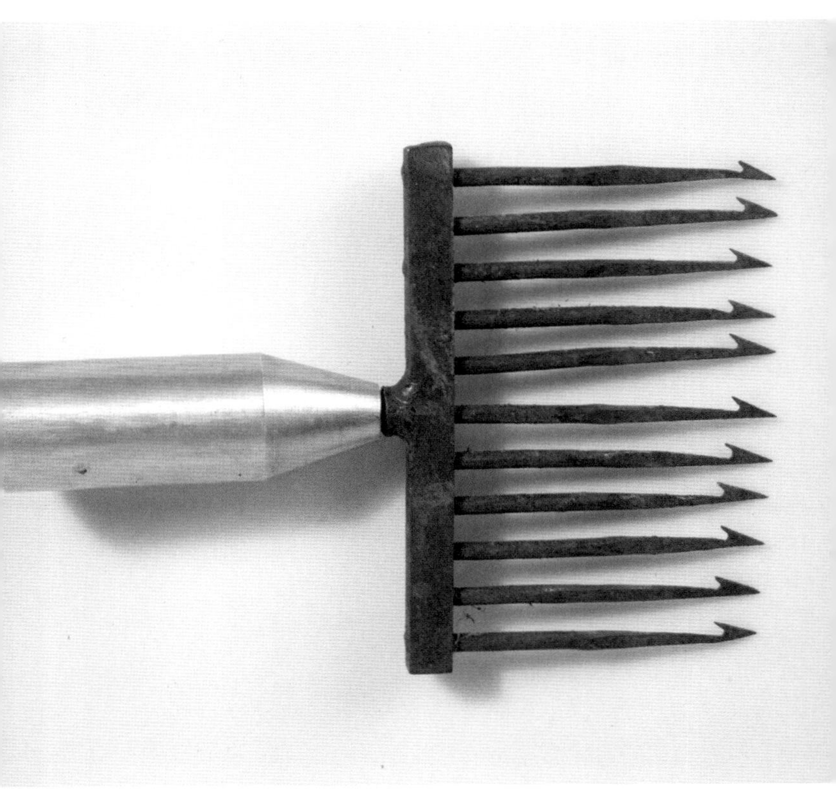

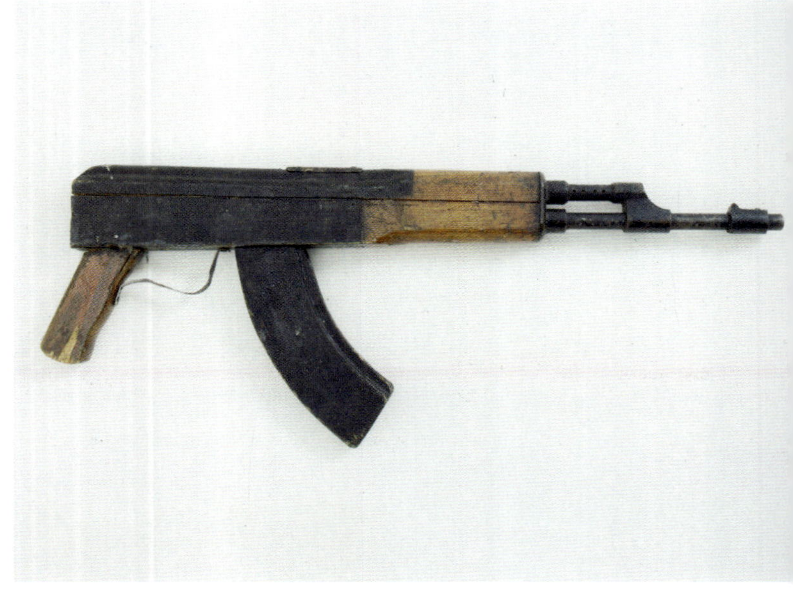

**Aleksandr Konychev**                                    Ryazan, c.1985

I made this once upon a time. It was when Mishka was still little, and he liked to play at war. There was nothing you could buy for the kid, so I made it for him. There were some fake looking submachine guns in the shops, but he wanted his to be 'like a real one'. I don't remember how I made it or what I used – it was a long time ago. I must have done a good job though, as it's still in one piece and later my grandchildren played with it.

Wood, metal

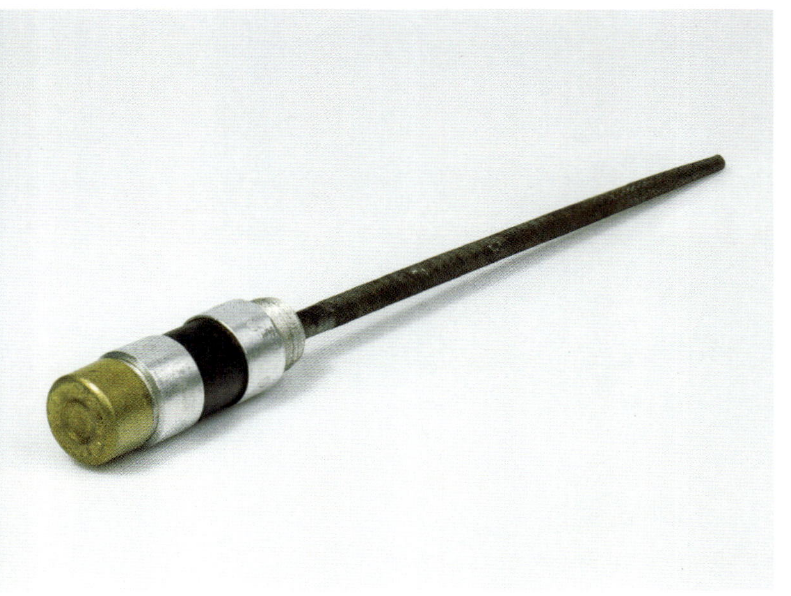

## Aleksandr Konychev

Ryan, 1990

In the factory they gave us these files without any handles. We still had to get the work done, so we had to look around for something that would fit. This handle's made from one of the circuit-breaker fuses in our switchboard room. I went to see the lads in the power section who were friends of mine, and they had these fuses, a whole heap of them just lying there. From their shape and size they looked like handles, so I took one. They told me to take more and now we've got nowhere to put them all.

Circuit-breaker fuse, file

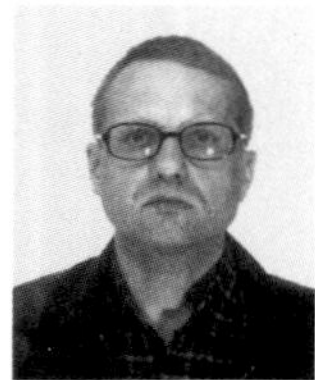

**Konstantin Bokhorov**                                    Moscow, c.1980

This card library, by my reckoning, contains more than 2,000 English words set out according to the following principle: the English word was written with a passage and an indication of the word in speech; on the other side the word was translated with its Russian equivalent. It kept growing for a long time. Really, it was very convenient, as the cards were such an easy shape to hold and carry with you. You could keep them in your pocket and check them when you were riding on the Metro, for example, or on other forms of public transport. They were cut out of thick cardboard and because of this they didn't get all bent up. Basically, they were very convenient things. Naturally, over time, I grew out of those cards and didn't need them anymore. Here there's no basic English, just words which present a certain amount of difficulty as regards memorising them, and also words which you can encounter in special situations. The words are explained according to their use in a sentence, like in a dictionary. But in a dictionary you just look up the word and that's all. With this method of study you can work with those words which you're bad at remembering, or create a whole new set of variants, of uses for them. That way they really get into your head. In the box they are organised alphabetically, like in a dictionary, for convenience. I was too lazy, unfortunately, to make index cards for them. It's far from a masterpiece. I just gathered the words that start with the same letter together, ordered them according to the alphabet and kept them together with rubber bands.

Cardboard box, glue, newspaper, card, bicycle-tyre rubber

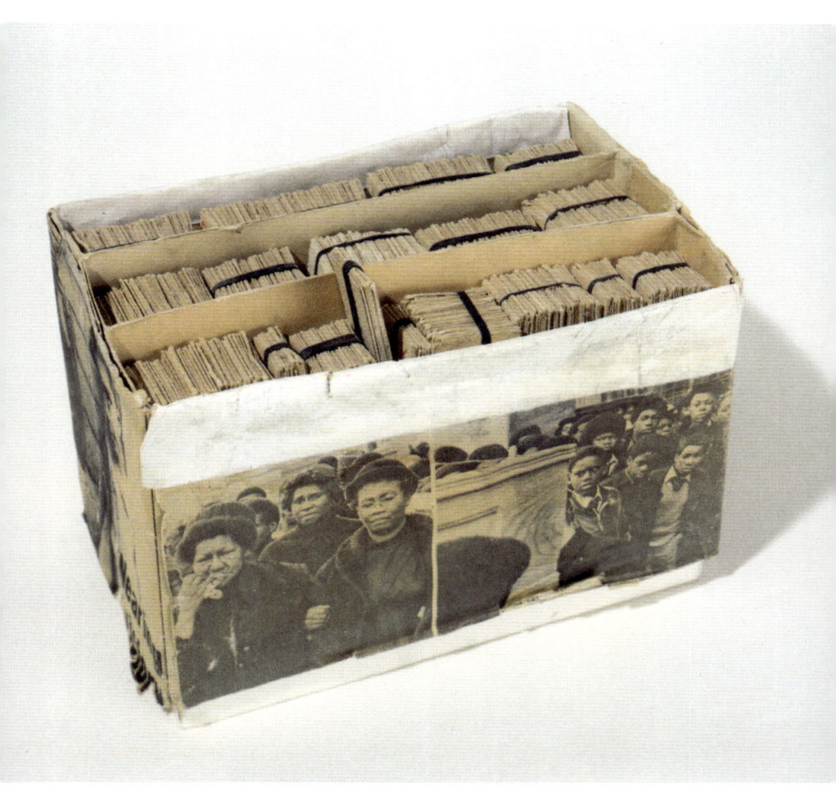

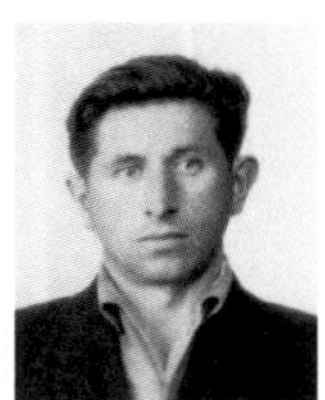

**Aleksandr Chebureev**                                        Kolomna, 1965

If you get hold of a TV then you need some sort of table for it. There weren't many tables in the shops for TVs at that time. First, for a comrade, I made a kind of primitive TV cabinet base. It consisted of a frame of the right size so that the TV sat right on it. The legs were carved – we've got a lathe in the workshop, and I brought this part home for the TV base.

A bit later Vasilii added the record player. Between the legs we made another frame, and on the frame we made a kind of box that would cover the record player. So we worked it all out and did it. It wasn't like it was absolutely impossible to obtain this kind of thing in the shops – it wasn't so expensive at the time, so we could have done it. But, I'll say it again, there wasn't all that much actually for sale, and so we got by on our wits. We made our own fridges, TV bases, and a bit later I made myself a much improved TV base. Well, that's how it was: we adapted stuff, worked out how to put stuff to good use.

Wood, screws

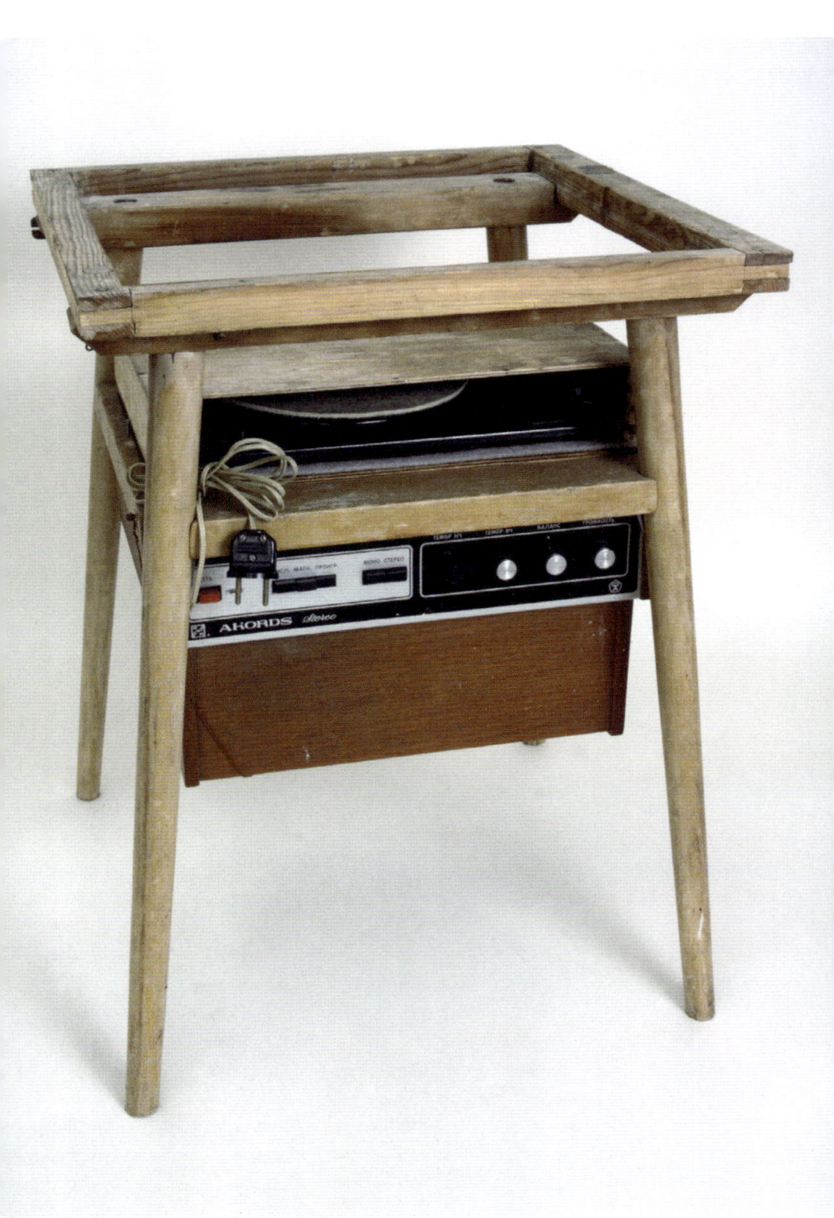
AKORDS stereo

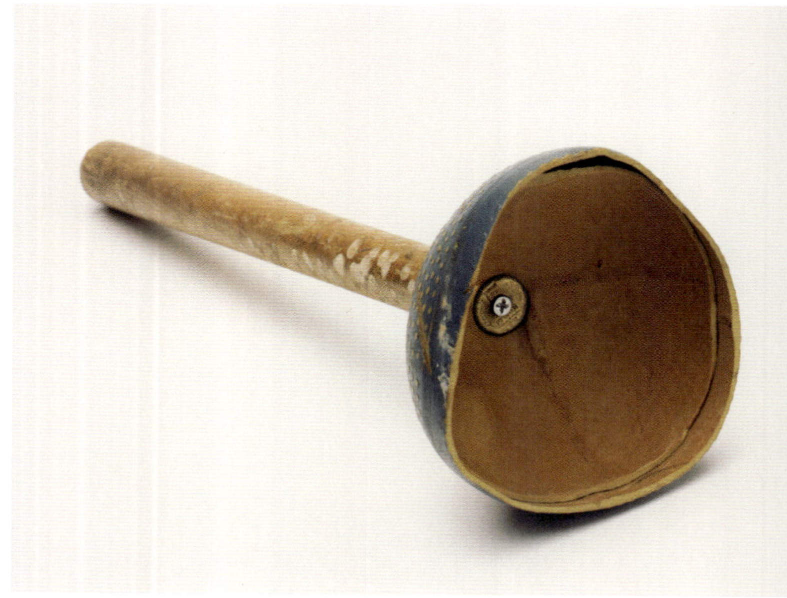

**Aleksandr Chebureev**                    Kolomna, 1990

It goes back to the time when the shops were all empty, when perestroika started. The late 1980s and early 1990s. My old plunger split, and I needed one for something or other. I went to the shop and there was nothing there. Fat chance of finding any plungers! I borrowed one from the neighbours once, but then I felt ashamed to bother them again about something so petty. Surely I could make one myself, couldn't I? My daughter had a rubber ball that was punctured, which I cut in half and fixed onto the leg of a stool. There used to be those stools with legs that screwed on – they were always breaking, and I came across one of those legs somewhere. I only used it a couple of times, and then I bought one.

Rubber ball, chair leg, screw

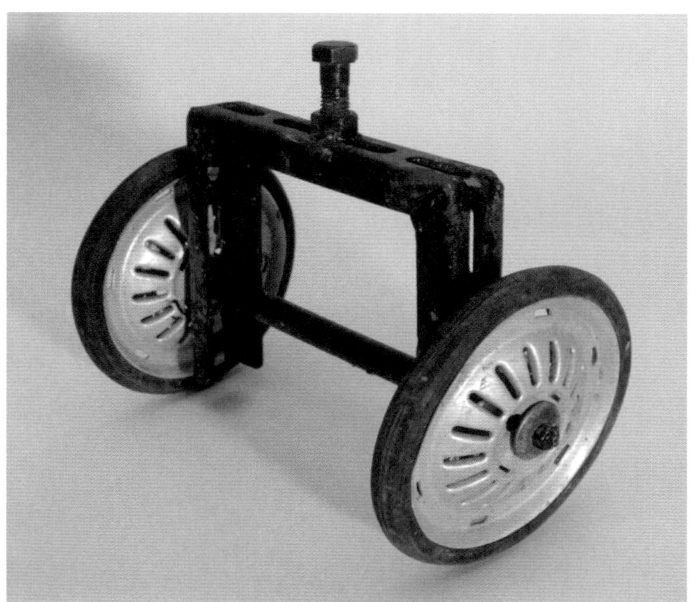

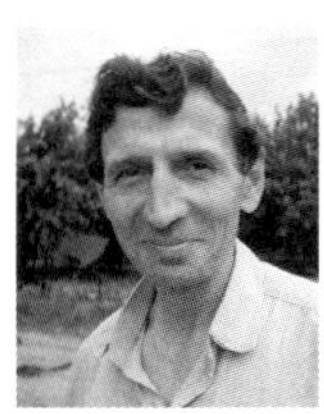

**Aleksei**                                              Kolomna, 1995

I needed some posts to make an enclosure for my allotment but there was no material around here – no pipes, not even a tree trunk. The size needed to be 2 or 3 metres. I thought up something to put the material on so I didn't have to transport it here myself. These wheels – they're a transport device with a motor. You have two wheels, an axis and a clamp. You take one end of a pipe, for example, and fix it with a rope. Then you fix the other end. These are just ordinary pipes left over from some heating repairs I made at home. So I used the pipes to make a fence – I made a cut, bent them 90 degrees and that was all. It's like they say, everything's to hand if you look hard enough.

Toy-carriage wheels, steel bracket, bolts

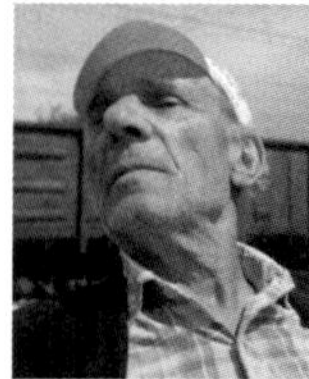

**Oleg Petrischev**                                                    Perm, 1994

*As recounted by his granddaughter Marina:* This is grandad's aluminium spoon; he cut the hole himself in order to let soap bubbles through when my brother Dima was small. He did it with some kind of saw, I'm not sure what it's called – I didn't even understand why he had done it. This is his favourite spoon, it's the only one like it we have, not made of tin but aluminium. The rest of it is completely ordinary. Mum had decided a long time ago to chuck it out, but Dima loved it. I don't know if he'd broken another spoon if my mum would have told him off, but this one maybe was easier to cut, I don't know. There were always tools in a special box in the corridor, which he always kept tidy, and was very careful with. He always yelled at us if we took something from it and then put it back in the wrong place. But mum was in charge, at the helm – our mum's that kind of woman. She's a theatre director – well, not actually in a theatre, more working with kids. But anyway, she's a talented person. She told Dima fairy tales, growled, barked, mewed, made strange faces, and he laughed and so of course ate with pleasure and mostly it was easy to feed him. But at other times, there was nothing doing, it dragged on for hours and everyone was fed up. Grandpa came in with a mug and banged on it with a spoon, and started stirring stuff in there. This immediately attracted the kid's attention. He stirred and stirred, then pulled out the spoon and started blowing soap bubbles with it. Little Dima was completely taken aback as he'd never seen any cutlery like that before.

Teaspoon

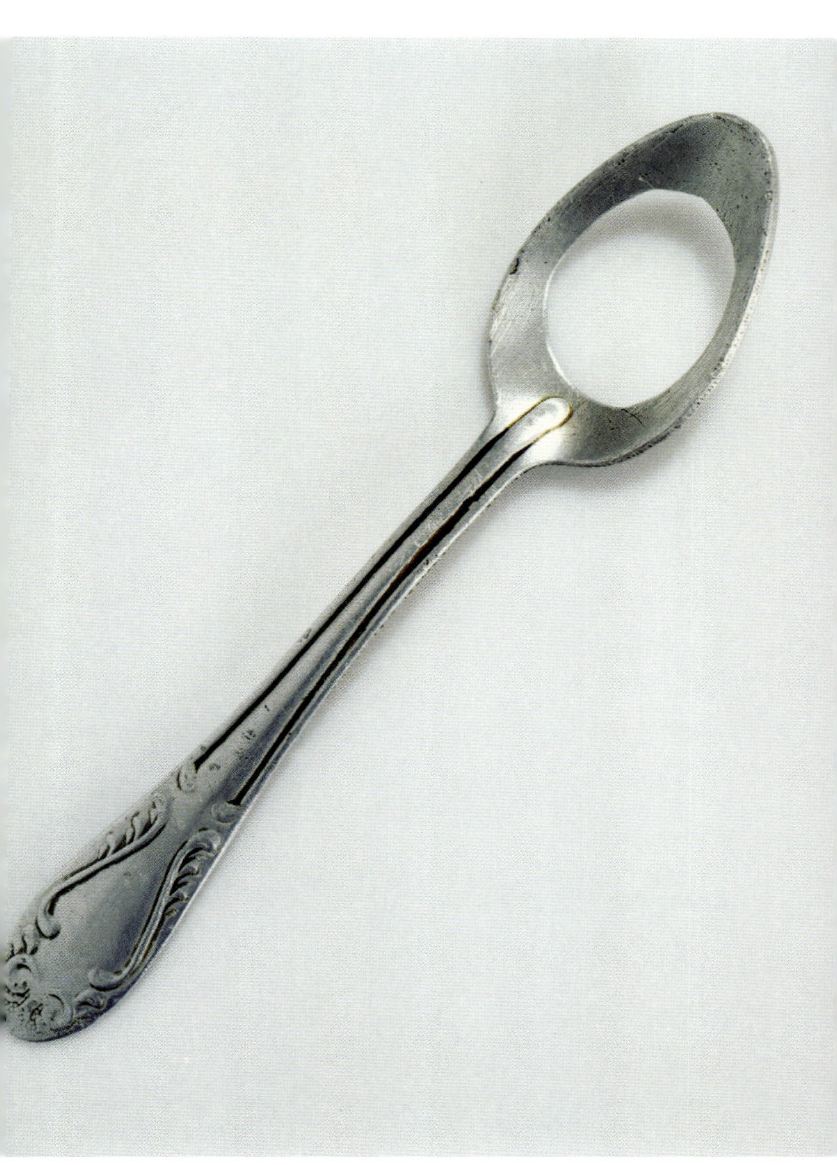

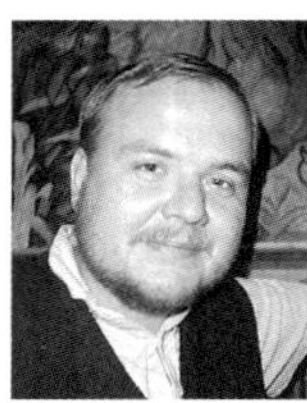

**Galina Svistakova**                                        Ryazan, c.1990

*As recounted by her son (pictured):* Well, this quilt symbolises a whole part of our family life: just like in Central Asia and in the East, carpets played the role of books, of literature, as did ornaments which depicted family traditions and legends. Stories of wars were told through ornaments, so this, in keeping with modern culture taking the place of some traditions, consists of cut-up pieces. This is my gran's coat, my brother's sweater, my father's jacket and bits of other material which also have stories behind them – there is an aura about them, or there is for me at least.

My mum gave this to me as a present. I'd asked her to make it for me like this. It's like you look at one piece and think about one thing, look at another and think about something else. It looks very organic. I think that things possess the aura of their owners, of a person who may very well no longer be with us, that things all carry information and inform us, and harmonise with other people's things. I believe they live their own independent lives and that we need to harmonise with them organically and be sensitive to them, in order for them to work in our favour.

Coat, jacket, sweater and other materials, thread

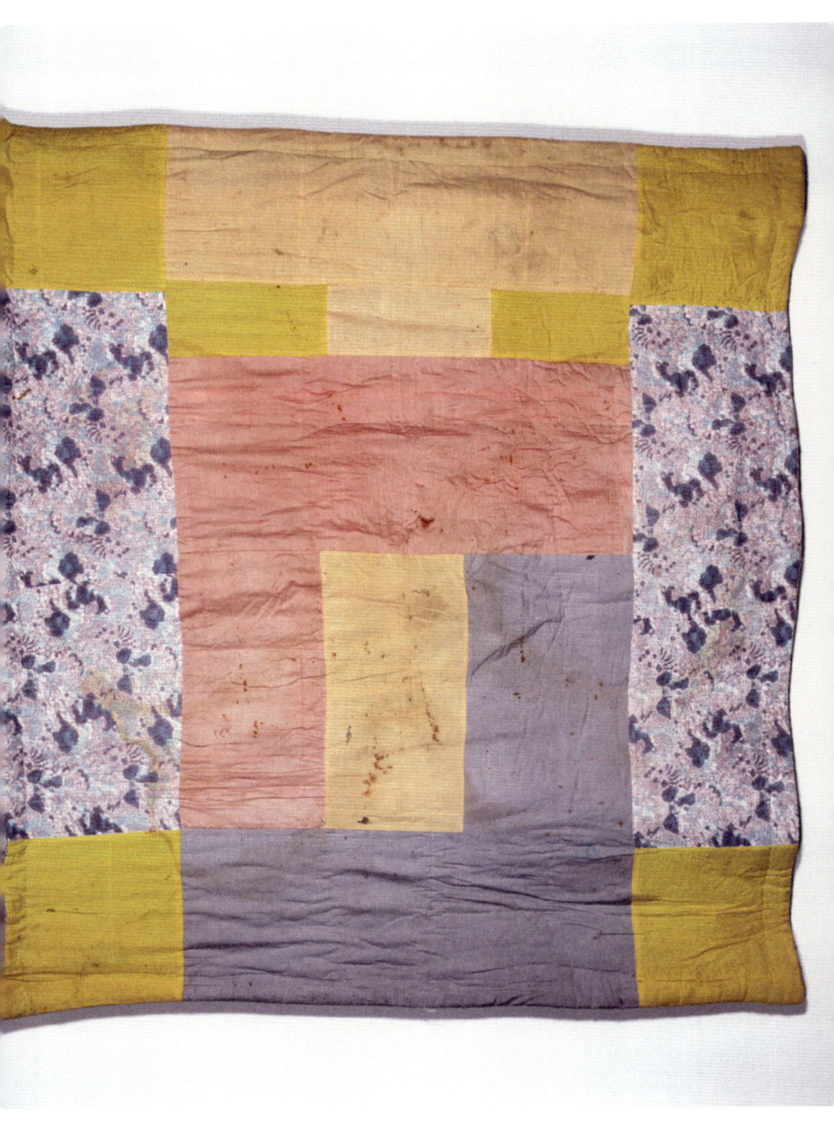

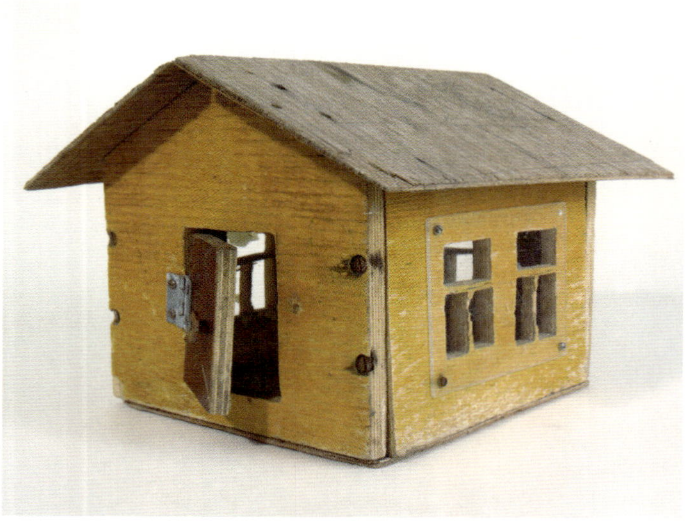

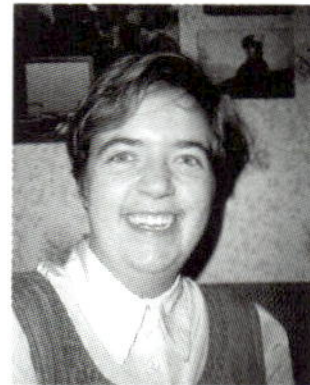

**Nikolai Ruchkin**                                     Ryazan, 1987

*As recounted by his granddaughter Katya (pictured):* This house was made by our grandad when my brother Grigorii was very ill. He couldn't go to nursery school and so he had to be taken to granny's and then my parents picked him up at weekends. Well, of course, he was very stressed out about it all because he didn't really like it there, and so grandad made him this house. But, you know, I think he just wanted to make it. It was kind of done purely for himself. Later he made me one as well, a bit bigger. This house has four walls and is made out of plywood. The windows are made of plexiglass so you can see what's going on inside. It also has a door which is very easy to open.

Plywood, plexiglass, nails, screws, metal hinge

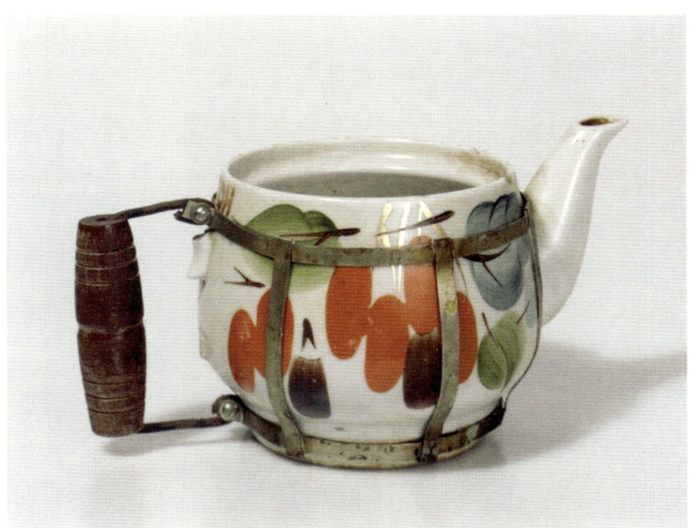

**Anonymous**                                                   Orel, late 1980s

*As recounted by his son:* My father was a journalist and he had to make tea and have lunch at work as he didn't always have time to get home. Well, how do you make tea? You need to brew it in something and you need to have some cups and spoons. But he didn't want to buy them specially because he was a thrifty man. And his conscience wouldn't let him take anything from home, and so, if anything wasn't working properly at home, he tried not to throw it out but to put it to use for the tea-making stuff that they needed at work.

Well, once, one of their teapots at home (they had two) fell and the handle came off. So using it in the traditional way became impossible, but he couldn't bring himself to throw it away because at work they only had a very small teapot. So he decided to make a new handle. He took a wooden handle from an little old milk churn, then soldered some wires together, like those that hold barrels together, and attached the wooden churn handle to the teapot. Maybe it didn't turn out quite so nice looking, but it was reliable and useable. Then, with a clean conscience, he took the teapot to work and they used it there until someone gave him a teapot for his birthday, whole and new, and better than the old one. He gave the old teapot to one of his close friends who appreciated original things, and so the teapot found itself a good home.

Teapot, copper strips, screws, milk-churn handle

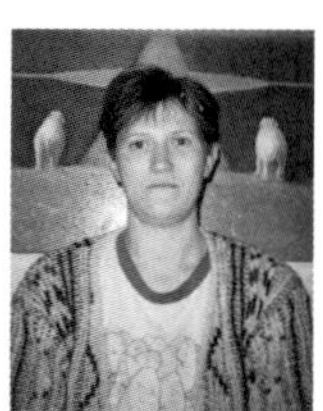

**Nastya Voronova**                    Moscow, 1997

After we had our daughter, Asya, she slept in a room but the ceiling light
was very bright, so we had to make it dimmer somehow. We had this hat
made of lace that was left over from some show – a prop. There was a dress
too, left over from some costume and I took it and sewed it onto the hat. It
did the job – little Asya doesn't screw her eyes up any more.

Hat, dress, thread

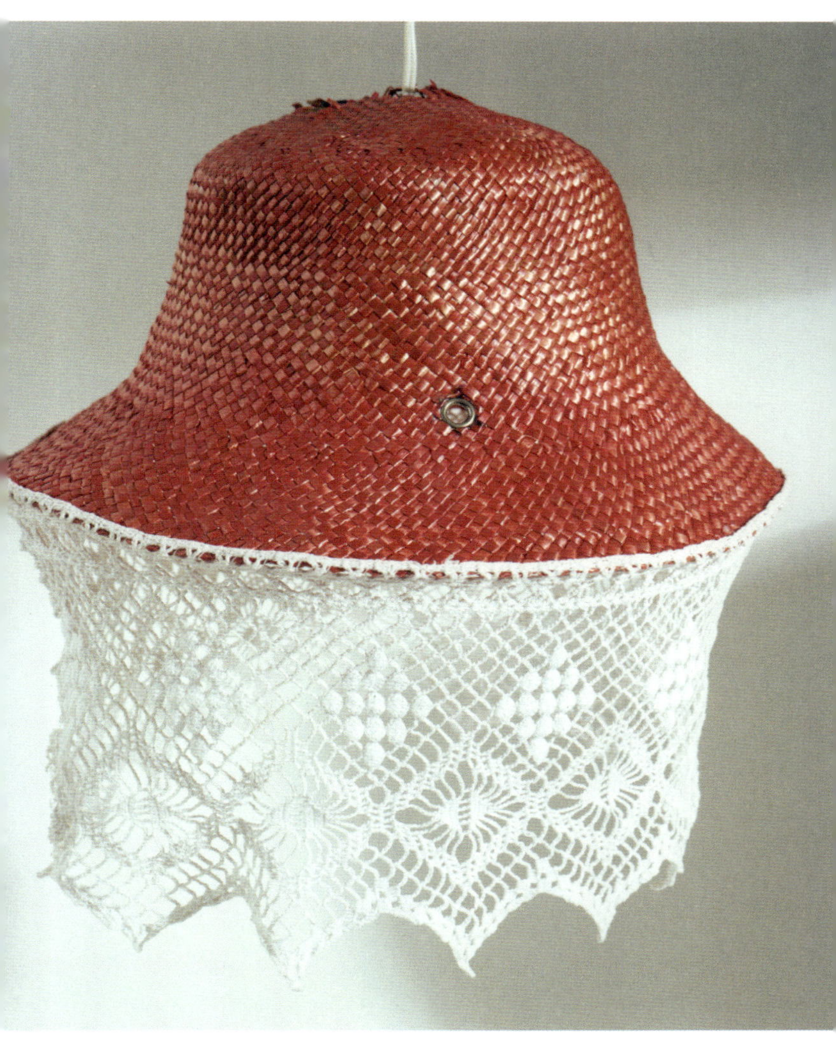

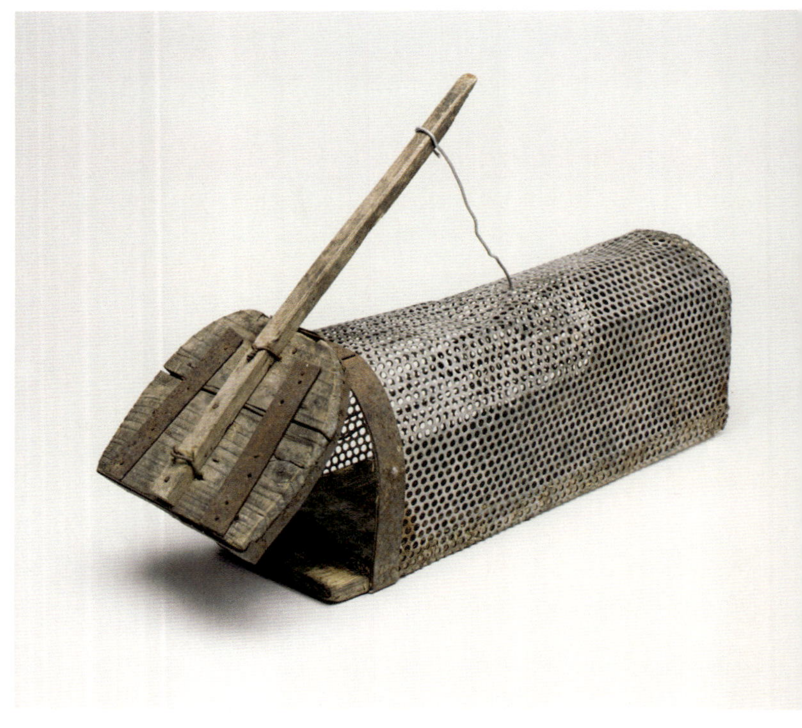

**Vasilii Shishkov**  Nikola-Lenivets, Kaluga region, c.1977

*As recounted by his wife Yekaterina:* We catch rats with this. We caught a ferret once – that was when father was still alive. We trap them in here and they start to squirm about so you turn this here and, boom, that's your lot. This was made after the war, after the occupation. My husband did everything himself. How else? There was no cash about. Did it all himself – everything for the house, he did himself.

Wood, mesh, nails, spring

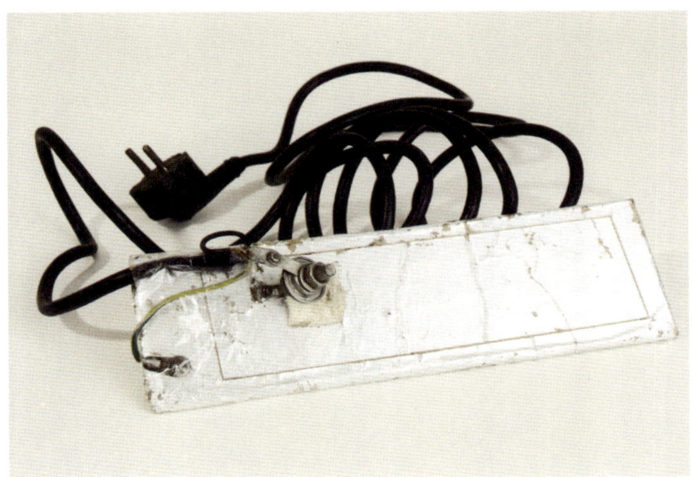

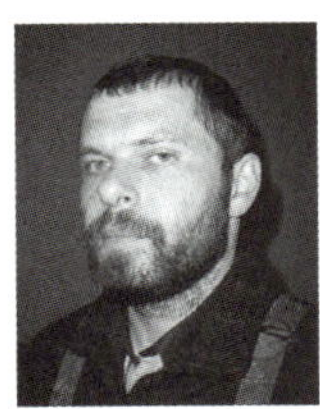

**Mikhail Akhmatov**                    Moscow region, 1992

Once we had an invasion of ants, an infestation. I thought, 'I have to make something that will kill them.' And so, here you have it, a cockroach trap. It's electric and runs on 220 volts. It's a very simple thing. You get a piece of a lamp and on both sides you fix foil from a tea packet. The foil isn't whole but in strips, so that there is a gap of 1-2mm, like the length of an ant. These strips are joined together with the ends of the wires and the lead itself is plugged into a socket with 220 volts. Then you leave it somewhere where there are a load of insects. The idea is simple. When an ant crawls across from one strip to another it should get a shock from the electrical current. But they turned out to be more cunning than me, even though their brains are a lot smaller. It crawled onto the strip, so far so good, everything was powered up, but it didn't crawl across to the next strip. It stayed there. It felt the potential voltage, felt that 220 volts were waiting for it on the other side. And that was it, it turned round... A few years later we had cockroaches. I tried to use this in a new way against them. I killed two – it turns out they're not so clever.

Plywood, foil, diode, electric cable, plug

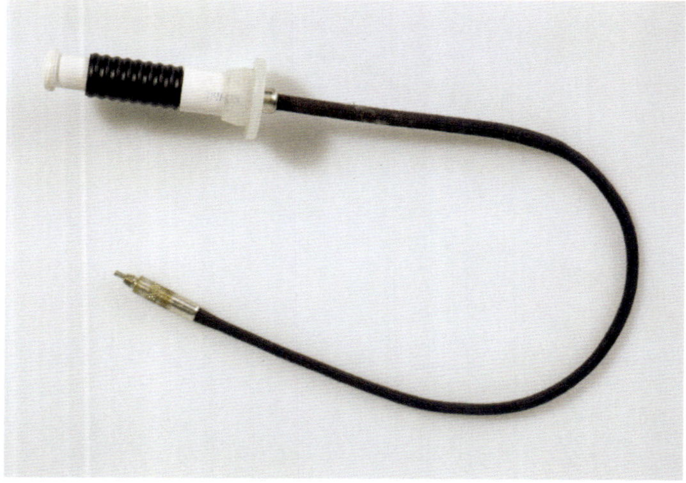

**Mikhail Akhmatov**                                        Moscow, 1999

This is a common camera, purchased for about six thousand in old money. The camera shutters have many different kinds of functions – from short exposures to medium. There are different shutters and different exposures, timed exposures and permanent exposures. You operate the exposure by hand, using the shutter release button: when you press it the shutter opens and you release the button; the shutter will continue to be open for the necessary time. Then, in order to shut it you have to press the button again. So, you press it, release it and the shutter closes. In this case you need a shutter release cable. In the shop, as always, they cost a lot. So I decided to make a shutter release cable from materials that were cheap and to hand. For this I took an ordinary switch and an ordinary pen; I cut the top off it and attached the part from the top of the pen that clicks to the releasing part of the switch. So as a result I now have a shutter release cable. The switch rises when I press it, then you can release. It works a treat.

Cable, switch, ballpoint pen

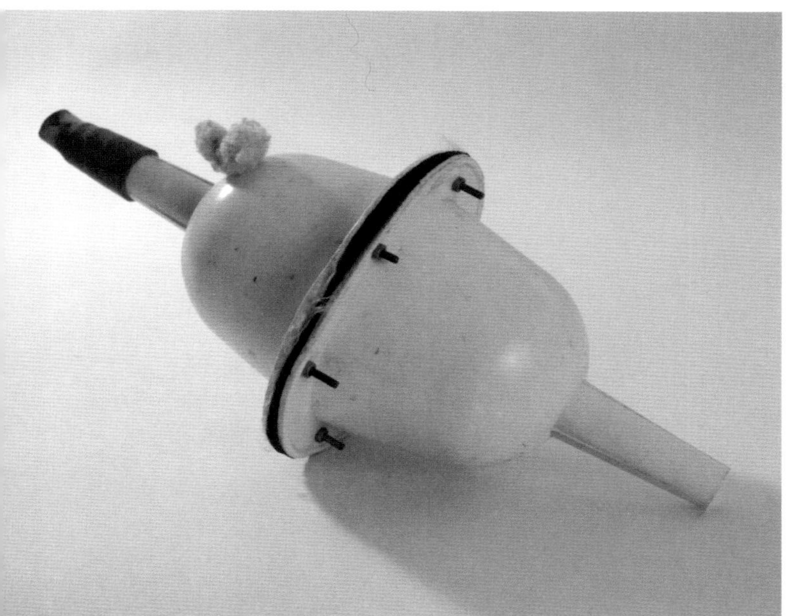

**Mikhail Akhmatov**                                         Moscow, c.1990

This is a water filter for when I used to print photographs myself. You get hold of two ordinary plastic funnels and fit the wide parts together, then between them goes the filtering element, in this case a parachute made from synthetic thread which was bought at the 42nd Kilometer (a railway station near Moscow). Then two holes are bored through between the flanges of these funnels, bored through and fastened with screws. To fix this device onto the tap I used a rubber hose end, and so that the pressure doesn't tear it away from the tap, in the upper part of the funnel holes are bored and filled up with any old shit, like newspaper or a bit of cotton wool. So, it functions like a valve. I mean, if the pressure is excessive this bit of cotton is just knocked out and it isn't torn away from the tap. It only filtered large bits but it was sufficient for me. It was possible to get cleaner results, and they needed to be cleaner, but I didn't have any time to spend on it or even feel like working on it any longer. And besides, in order to get cleaner results I would have had to nick a normal filter from some laboratory or other, without all that fancy stuff. This was before the revolution, about 1990.

Plastic funnels, rubber hose, cotton wool, synthetic thread, screws

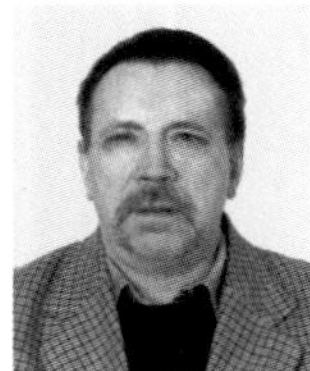

**Aleksandr Yakimovich**                                    Moscow, 1993

I came across my old punch bag which I used when I was eighteen to about thirty, to exercise. It was a uniquely Soviet punch bag, made from hard leather, like the type they use for soldiers' boots. But because I battered it for fifteen years, it turned into a very soft thing. And so I cut it up and used half of it to make myself this simple cap to have something to wear on the streets, to go to the shops, walk my dog, etc. I put a warm lining inside. It didn't need much doing to it, just a bit of taking in. These long bits of leather here are from my army boots that I used to go gathering potatoes or mushrooms in. I covered up the stiches with them, so they didn't stick out, and then added this band. Then I made the peak. I don't remember if it was made from my wife's old boots, or from some old black bag. It turned out to be such a useful thing, a very practical object, and brought me a great deal of pleasure during the making of it. Without a doubt, it's one of my masterpieces and I really love that kind of work. I love to make unusual things, to turn an object into something else, to use things in unexpected ways. I wore the cap with great pleasure – it kept me dry and protected me from the snow. Then in 1994 I went abroad and I wasn't here for a year. I wore it for another couple of years but by this time it had already turned into rags and I stopped wearing it. The lining was a warm soft lining. I changed it a lot of times but when it turned into sh... pardon my French, shit, I chucked it out.

Punch bag, boots, leather, thread

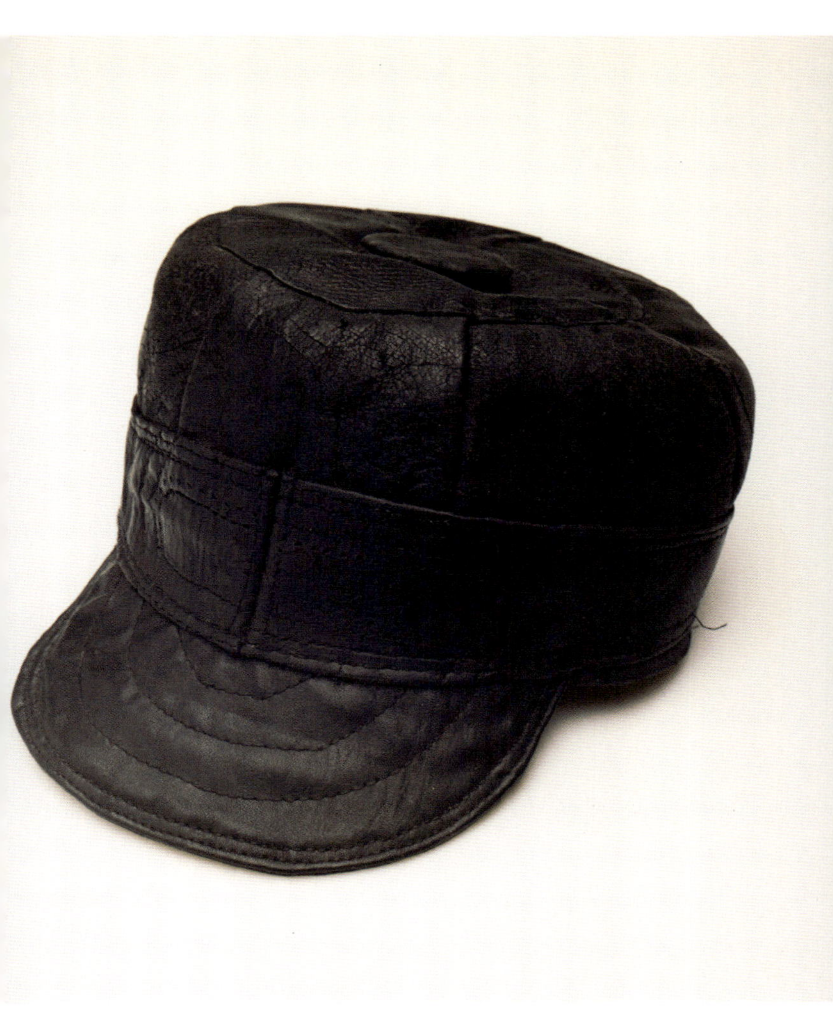

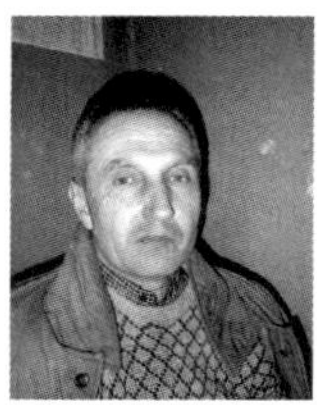

**Aristarkhov**                                                    Kolomna, 1970

It was difficult to get hold of a floor lamp thirty or forty years ago, so we made them ourselves. We got hold of some copper tubes with long ends, sharpened on a lathe, and a heavy circular base made from steel, ordinary steel, a circular ingot, thick and sharpened. We made two holes in it with a thread and beneath two 12mm openings. We got hold of the tubes, bored them, and cut them and screwed them into the base. We used black ebonite. If you take some sandpaper and rub it, then it becomes black and shines beautifully. Then at the top you put in two more beams – two at different ends and then two more long copper tubes, cut like under the socket's thread – then you screw in two more sockets, buy a nice lampshade and you've got yourself a floor lamp.

Electric motor, steel tubes, ebonite, lampshades, electric sockets, conductor

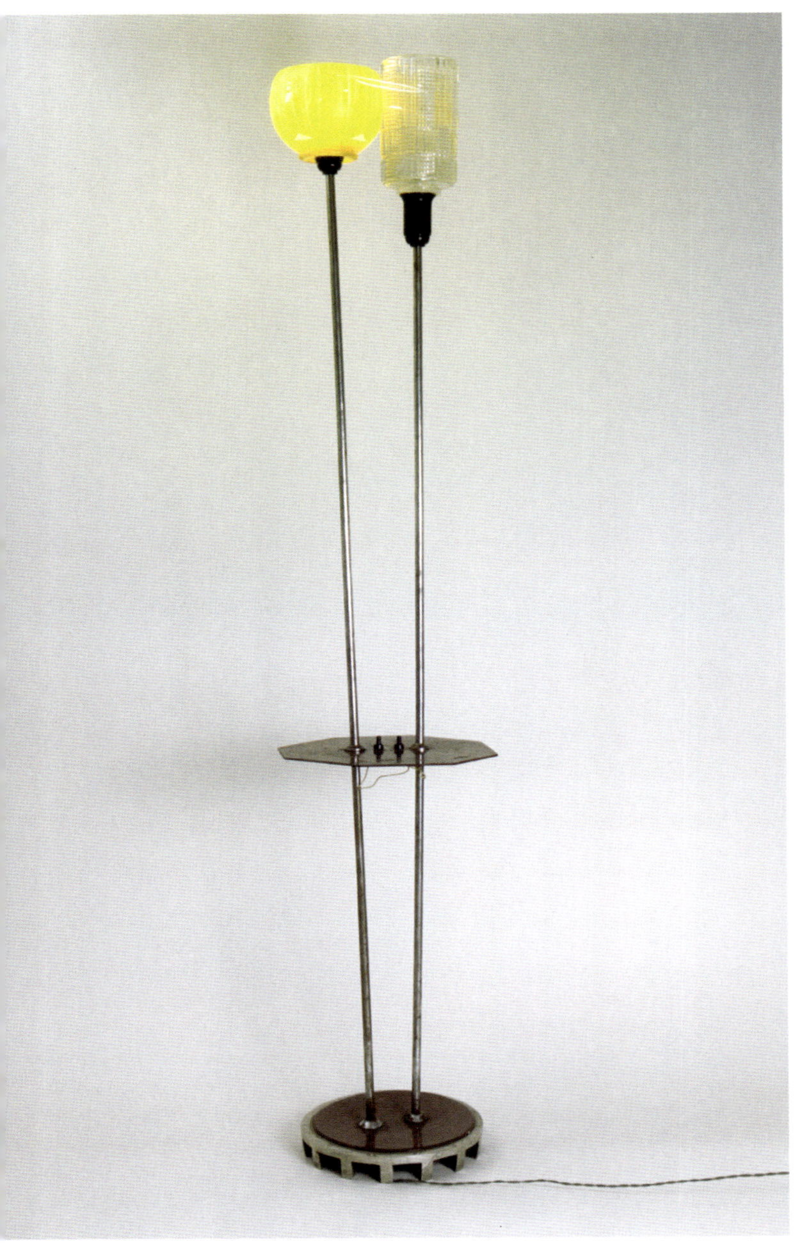

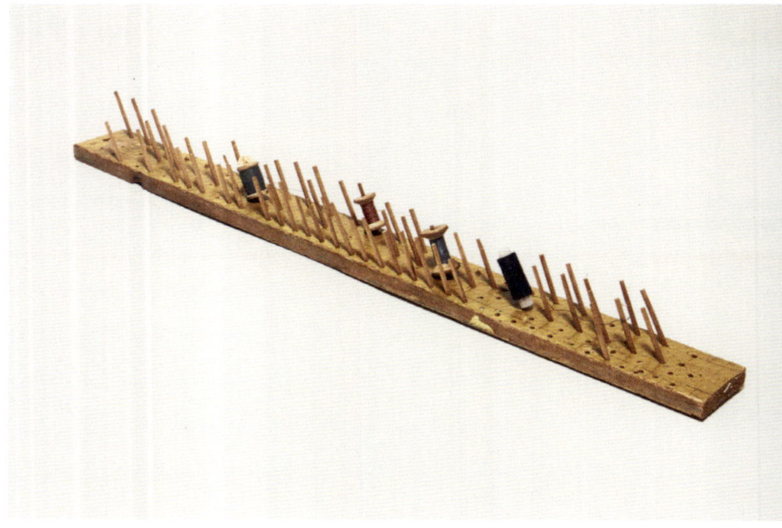

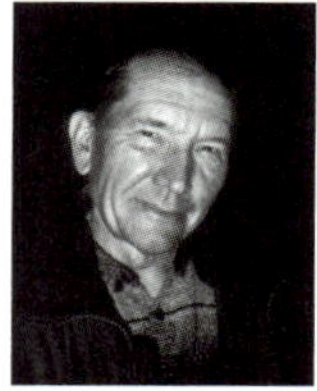

**Gennadii Nikitin**                                    Ulyanovsk, 1970s

At one point my wife decided to sew, to embroider on a machine. We bought lots of different coloured threads, and they all lay in a box and got tangled up with one another. Then we had to try to untangle them, to separate them out, even cutting them. It was a lot of hassle as they were in bunches. Well, so that this wouldn't happen I took a board, drilled a row of holes, and put in bits of beech or oak so that they stuck out. Where the coil is the distance is a little shorter, and where the spool is, it's a little greater. Well, until recently they all hung on this board. Any colour that you wanted, it was right in front of your eyes and very convenient to take off. Compact too and you didn't have to fuss around with anything. Everything was right in front of your eyes. This was back in the 1970s, but she can't be bothered with it now, she's not into sewing anymore.

Wooden board, sticks

# GRUB HOLDER

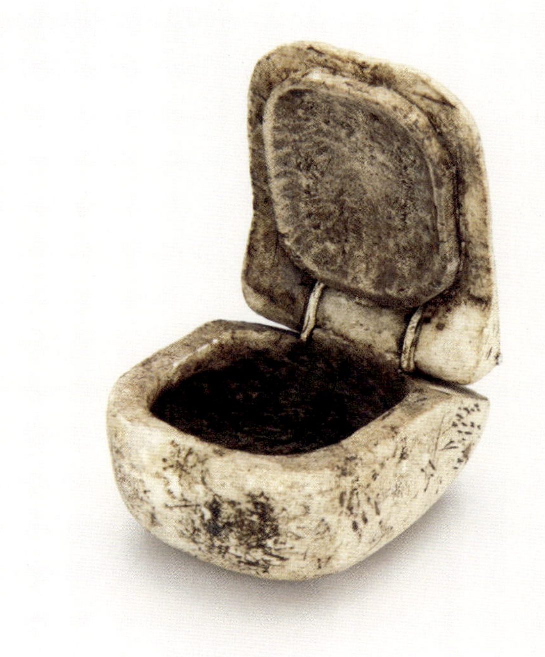

**Gennadii Nikitin**                    Ulyanovsk, c.1993

They used to sell grub holders and I'm not sure if they do now. Anyway I make them myself now. It wasn't too easy to get one out of your pocket; you'd open it up, and the grubs would have frozen. And so I thought this up myself – I had to really. I thought up how to make them more streamlined, easier to get in and out of your pocket. Also, so that the grubs don't freeze, I made the sides quite thick. But the bad thing about these grub holders is that this foam plastic lets water in, so with time, it becomes crumbly and starts to get spoilt from the grubs. So that this didn't happen, I used a hot teaspoon to bond it. The main case is very thick, like glazing, and so it stopped getting soaked, was easy to clean and the grubs didn't start to rot either. Once you've made one you can give it to someone as a present. One is enough for me. Me and my friends make our own rods, grub holders, all that kind of stuff, for bait and the like.

Foam plastic, wire

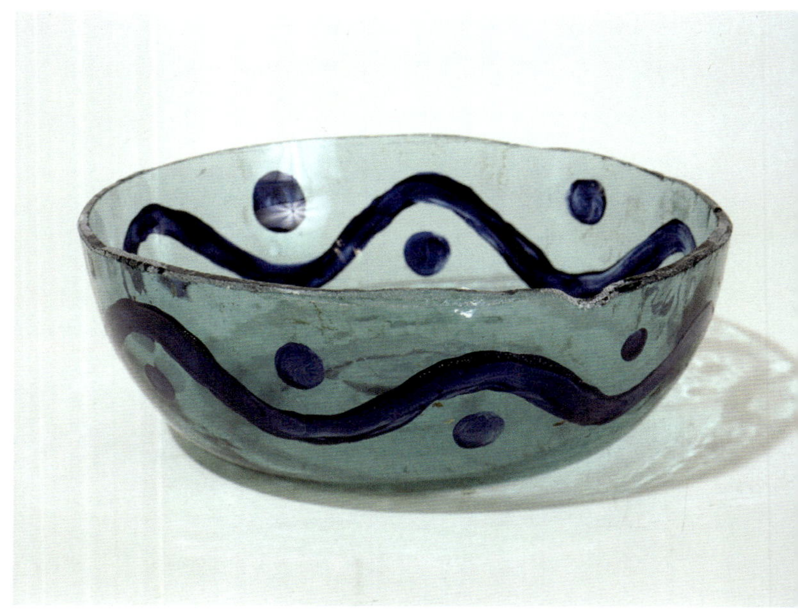

**Igor**                                                              Orel, 1995

I used to make dry wine and this was one of the bottles I used. It's very old you know – they don't make this type anymore, kind of barrelish in shape. It was a very cleverly made bottle, with a cleverly made neck. As you can see, at the bottom the glass is thicker and at the top thinner. I once knocked into these bottles and this one broke, sh-sh-sh! The wine poured out and it seemed like a pity to waste the bottle, so I cut the bottom part out with a glass cutter, worked on it a bit and got an original-looking cup. I've never seen one like this before. Because it was unevenly cut it doesn't get used in the kitchen, although I guess it would be possible. I cut it off with an ordinary glass cutter – I just traced round it a few times and cut it off. It didn't break for some reason, just cut off cleanly. Then I worked on it a bit and here it is before you, to admire.

Glass bottle, paint

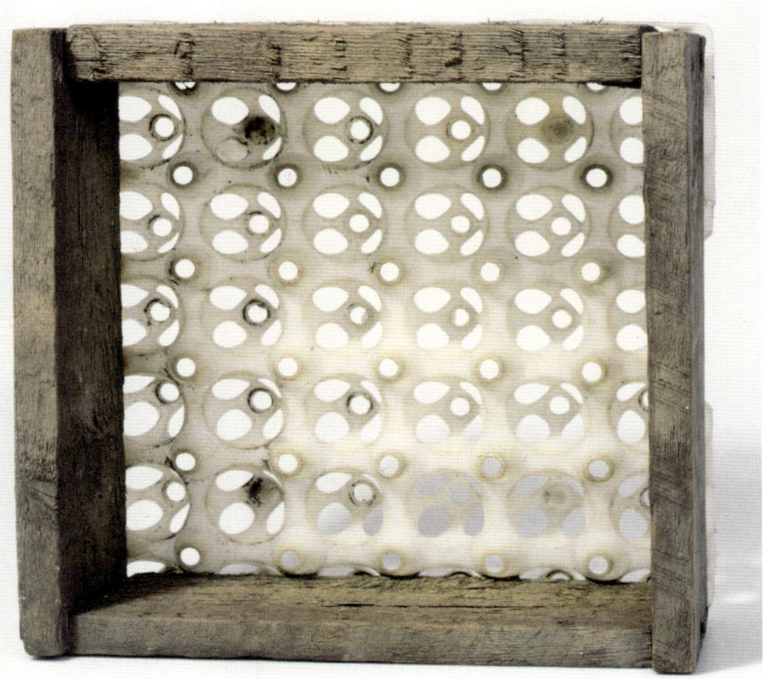

**Igor**                                                          Orel, 1995

It was autumn, the sand was damp and you know yourself that damp sand won't go through a fine mesh screen. There were also stones in the sand. I tried using a fine mesh screen but it didn't sift the sand. If you wait until it dries, you'll have to wait a week. So you need to have larger holes for the sand to fall through. I found this tray, used to store eggs, and used it for the first stage of sifting sand. There were two, actually. I tried it at first without a box, without edges, but it was very slow. Then I made this box, hooked it on and started to sift. No kidding, it worked pretty well. Almost a whole bucket of sand gets in there, then you stretch it out, and all the stones stay on the top. Taking into account that it was wet sand, damp lumps, well... they haven't forgotten about it even now.

There was a building site, and we were building a house. I'm not a builder by profession, but it was necessary, so we did it. The fine mesh screen was needed for this, so it was a specific thing made for a specific moment in time.

Wood, nails, egg holder

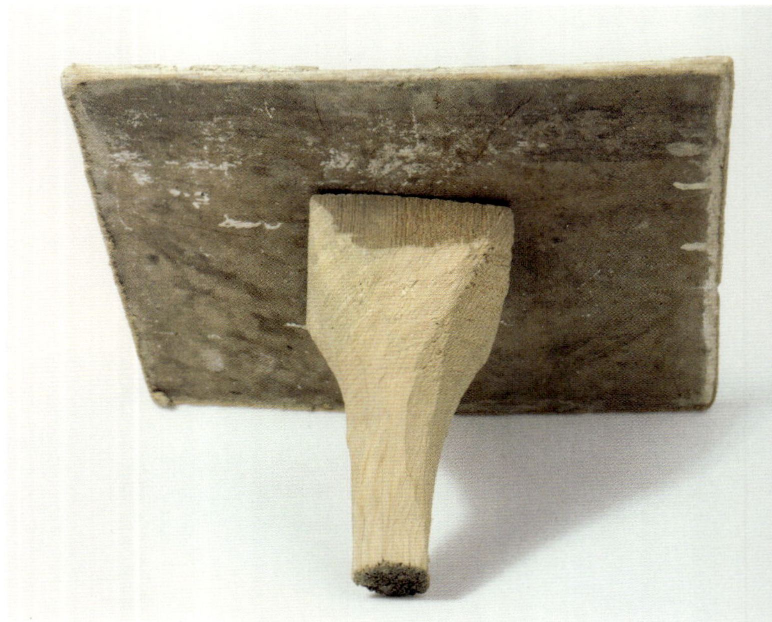

**Igor**                                                          Orel, 1996

This is an ordinary thing for holding mortar – it's for when it's difficult to hold it in place by hand. It's simpler to hold it from beneath, but it's not so comfortable, so I had to make the wide part bigger so that it would hold a large amount. This is the most primitive solution; of course you can make it more complicated, make a joint from two pieces of wood, make it the same level, one across the other, but that's tough to do. I'd spend a day on that, but on this, on this I spent twenty minutes. No, not twenty, just five. But this is only to be used once: it's made and chucked away. The less time you spend making it, the easier it is to chuck it out. This is because it's disposable, disposable, disposable. The mortar is put on top, you carry it to the wall and start plastering. The wood is just an ordinary bit of wood – not even timber, a bit cut out of the wall, what's it called... it's completely gone out of my head. Well, yeah, timber, fifteen by fifteen. It's solid, strong timber, and here at the top there are a couple of nails.

Wood, nails, plywood

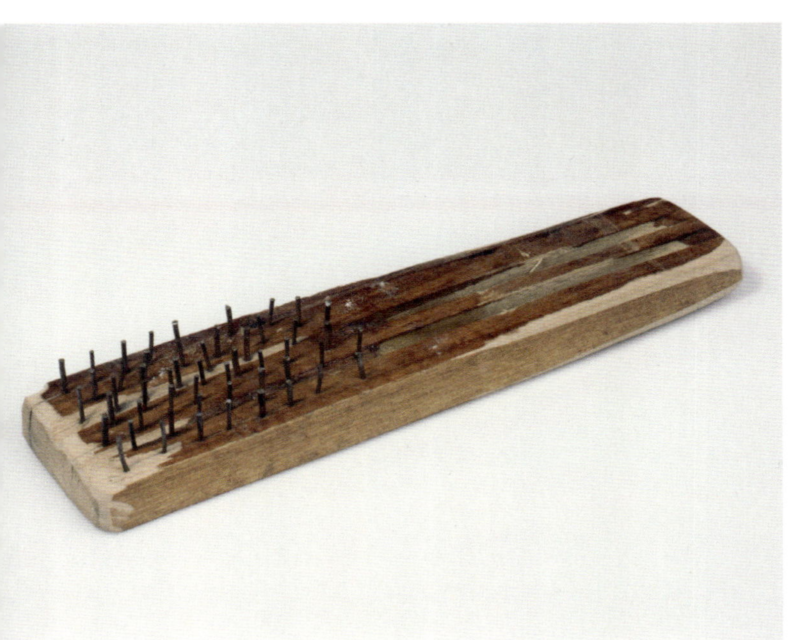

**Igor**                                                    Orel, 1996

So, this was made when we were building our house, doing the second floor and, for some reason, I felt like making the second floor from logs. We had the idea but we weren't professionals in that field and we didn't have any professional tools, and when they brought the oakum to me it was all twisted and so mushed-up that it was impossible to pull it apart by hand – you couldn't get your fingers in there. It just wasn't possible by hand. Then I remembered granny's method of pulling fur apart with her fingers and brushes. They make similar things for the flaxing of fur. I got hold of an ordinary piece of wood and these nails which have had the heads cut off them. They were nailed in with the heads and then these were cut off during the production. The nail was driven in with the head pointing upwards, then the head was cut off and a stump was left. We used a lot of nails but, well, we didn't care about that.

Wood, nails

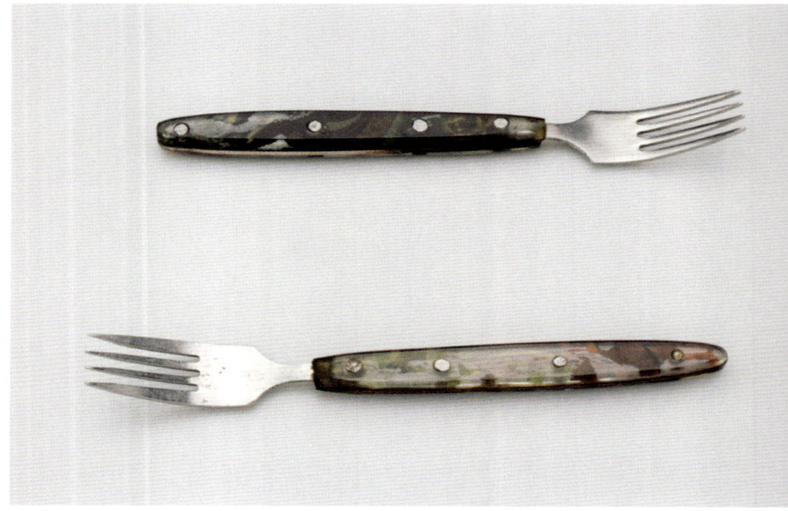

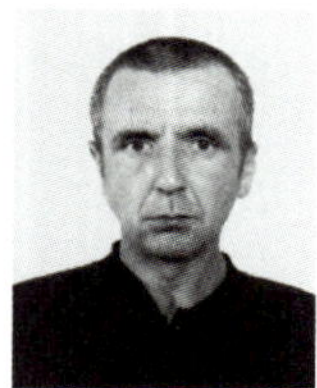

**Aleksandr Podguzov**   Vladimir region, 1997

It was when I was doing time that I made them. Five years is a long stretch, and when you're inside the time weighs heavily on your hands. It feels like you're going to be in there for ever, so if you don't start to do something you can go crazy. Basically everybody works, because of course you get some money later when they let you out, and the time passes quicker when you're busy all day long. You can choose any kind of work: metalwork, joinery or sewing. In five years I tried everything – it was interesting, learning to sew and plane wood and work metal. You wouldn't believe what class of professionals there are inside, doing time! Real high-class – they can do anything! They shouldn't be inside, they didn't do anything wrong! Do you know how many people are doing time for things they didn't do? They're not guilty, they were just stitched up and put away. Where's the justice, Vladimir? But these were waste material, from when I was working with metal – see, everything's made out of pieces. We weren't allowed to have forks, only spoons. But to feel like a human being, you need to eat properly, with a fork. We're not trash.

Metal, plastic

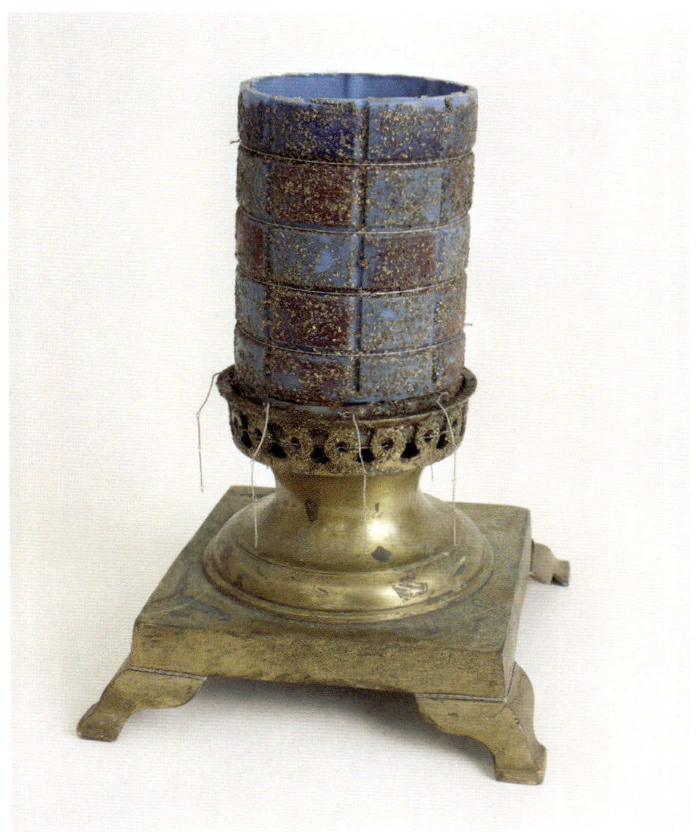

**Aleksandr Podguzov**                    Vladimir region, 1997

I made this vase as a present for my mother. I thought, when I get out I'll go back and give it to her, but the way things turned out my mother wasn't there any more… This bottom part here came from a samovar; the top part, the blue bit, was probably from a thermos flask. They let us have thermos flasks. It's all covered with copper filings and lacquer. Yes, and there's twisted wire here too.

Samovar base, thermos flask, copper filings, wire, lacquer

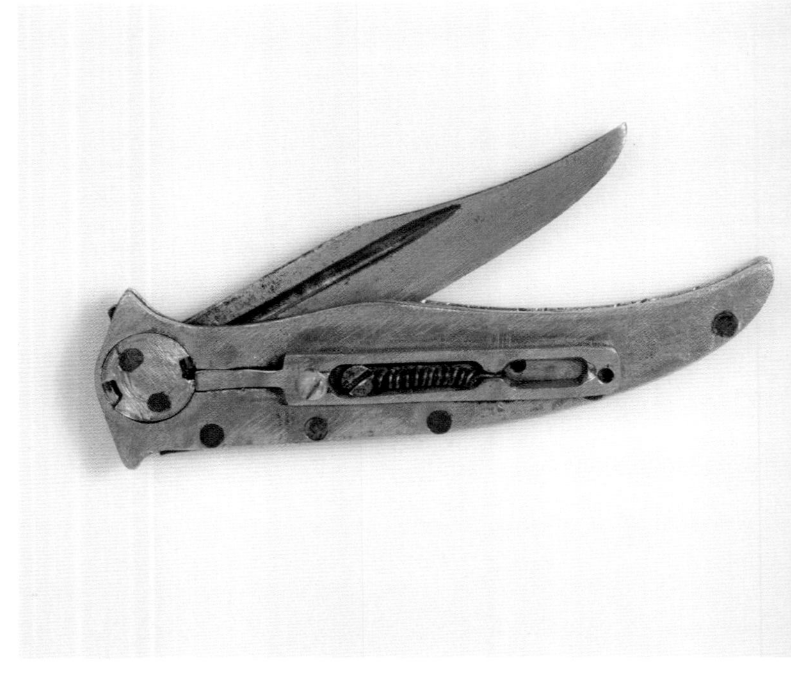

**Aleksandr Popdguzov**                    Vladimir region, 1998

I began working with metal when I was in prison. Some of the guys were top-of-the-line specialists, they could forge a flea. I wanted to learn a bit from them. There's this test – if you can make a flick knife, then you'll be a metalsmith. I made one on the quiet. You have to find a spring, a screw and a blade. Of course, it's not allowed but I wanted to. If they'd caught me, they could have put me in the punishment cell or something. They've got plenty of ways to punish you in there.

Steel, spring, screws, blade

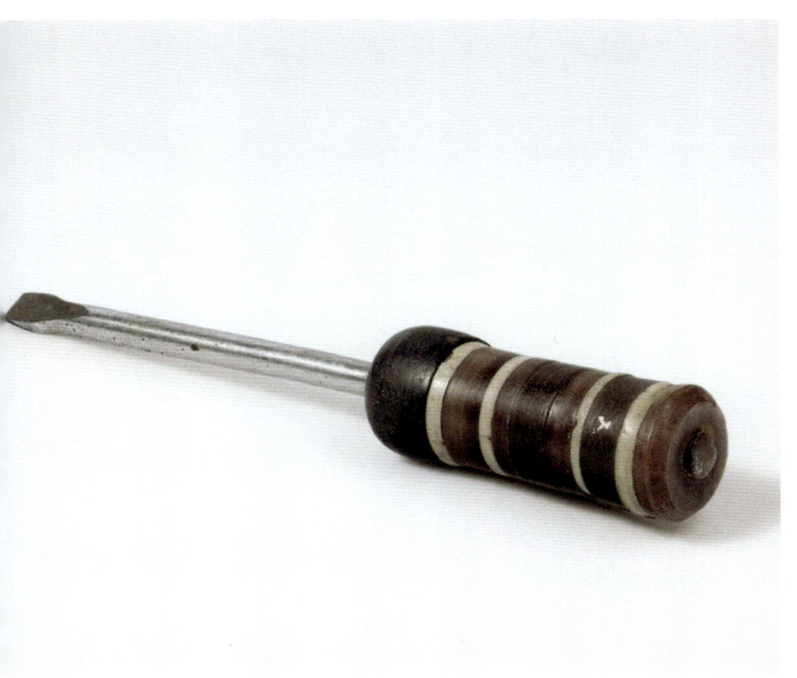

**Aleksandr Popdguzov**                    Vladimir region, 1996

I made the screwdriver when I was inside as well. I learned how to do a lot of
things there – like mending clocks, for instance. You weren't supposed to
carry any tools with you, only in the workshops. But there weren't any clocks
in there. I collected various bits and pieces of plastic and perspex to make
this. You drill holes in them, put them together, turn them and polish them
up. The screwdriver itself was some kind of shaft from a lathe; I tempered
and sharpened it.

Steel, plastic, perspex

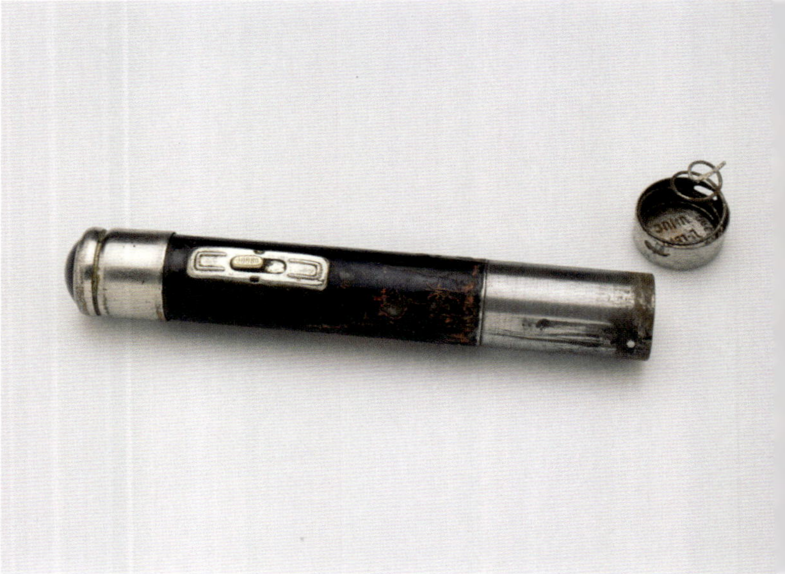

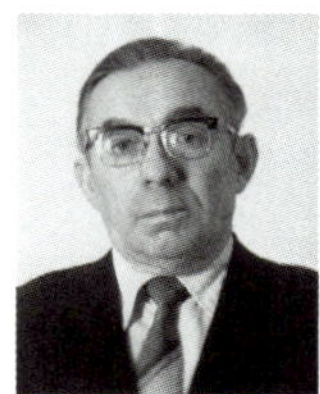

**Grigory Krichevsky**                    Moscow, c.1950

*As recounted by his son Vladimir:* Lengthening a metal object! That's the kind of thing that only my father could have thought of. He's no longer with us. Because this torch shone weakly, my father made the whole thing longer, for a third battery. By the way, it's an old Soviet torch, if not from the 1930s then the 1940s. But the beam was too weak for my father – so he lengthened the torch. Lengthening a metal item, that's a hell of a job! As you can see, he wasn't a lazy man and he found time to do such damn work. In here went three Soviet batteries, Leningrad ones by the way. It's not so effective really, but when you put it into words it's touching. Lengthening a metal object, I ask you!

Torch, rivets, steel pipe

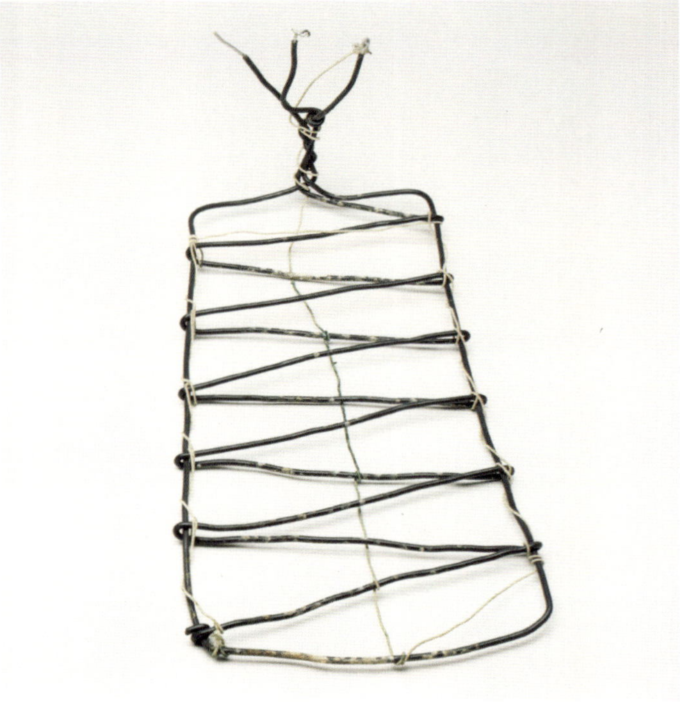

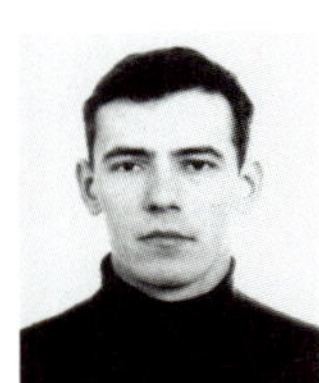

**Sergei Mikhailov**                    Moscow, 1997

This is an amateur radio aerial. My friend and I use the radio to talk to each other, but the signal isn't always good. I tried to make the aerial a bit bigger, so we could communicate better. We're at college together and we bought the radio equipment between us. We live close to each other – inside a good reception area. We've got a phone, but our parents won't let us go on talking for ever. Now we can talk to each other as much as we like when it's late – no one bothers us. A mobile phone is too expensive for a student; communicating by radio is a lot cheaper and there's no rental charge to pay.

Wire

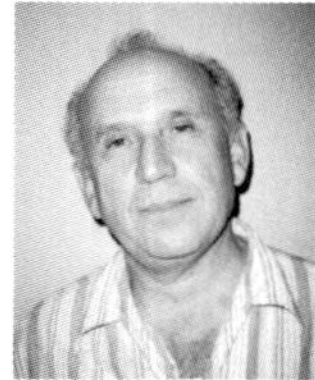

**Yakov Kladnitsky**                                        Kolomna, c.1993

Life goes on, the years pass by and I'm getting older. I felt I needed a trolley, a little trolley that I could use to transport vegetables and fruit in and bring them home from the shed. Four kilometres is the distance, no more, no less. Well, of course we use the tram then but first we have to get to the tram. And when you put a bucket of potatoes, a couple of jars of cucumbers and tomatoes in your basket, and something else, it's hard to carry it. I felt I needed to make a trolley. Of course you can buy a trolley in a shop, but the ones I found were small, and if it's small, it's awkward, it's not strong enough, the dimensions don't suit, so I decided to make a trolley myself and looked around for spare parts that I could use. The idea of the trolley and its design came to me a long time ago. I kept walking around, always looking. Suddenly on the rubbish tip I saw the handle from a child's pram, so I took it. Then I was visiting my sister and she offered me some rubber pieces from dough-mixing machines. 'Take them', she said, 'then you can make yourself some little wheels'. I shaped them, put in some little brass axles, and made some brass sockets for the axles, like a bracket. Then there was a problem with the piping, as I couldn't make it out of steel rods or it would be too heavy. Well then I saw this man had steel piping so I ordered it. I drew a little diagram, but I couldn't make it from the drawing myself, so they bent it and welded the body of my trolley for me. Afterwards I fastened on the handle from the child's pram, which I had to bend a bit for myself and fix on firmly. The method for fixing it consists of putting a ring on it, cut out of aluminium, out of aluminium plastic. You cut it into a ring like a link in a chain and slip it on and fix it, and the result is a trolley that's comfortable, light and nice and neat.

Aluminium, steel, rubber, brass

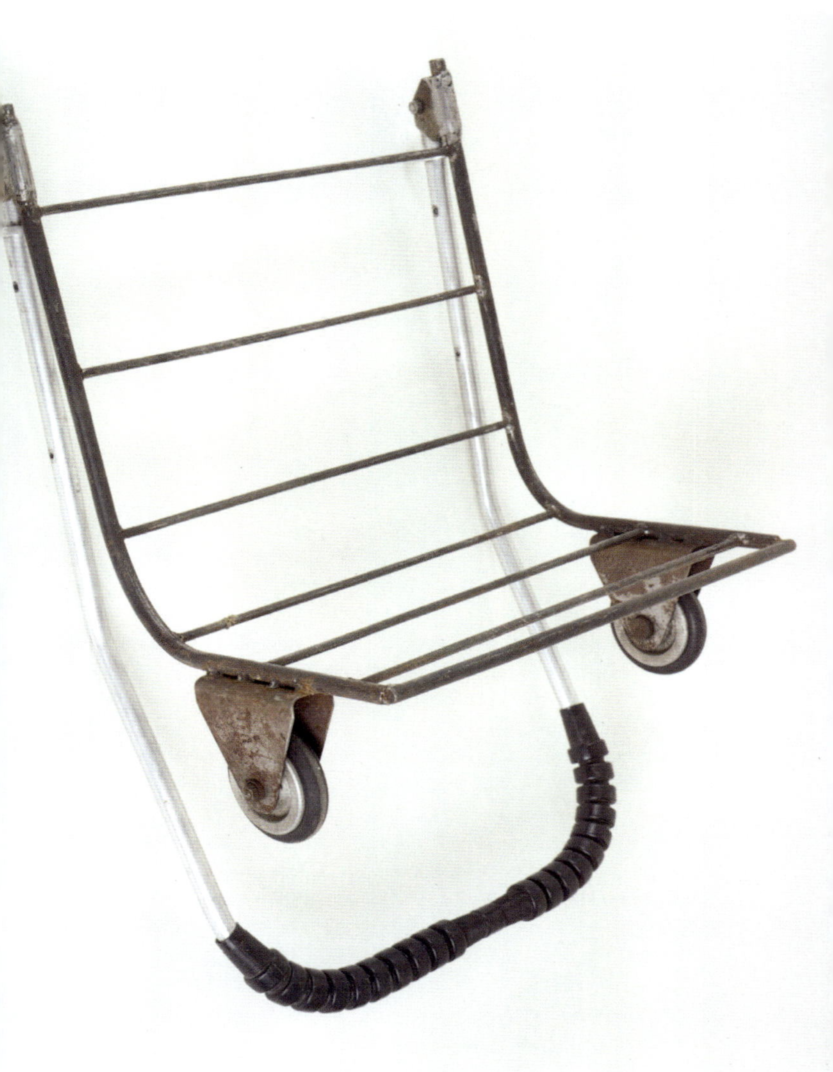

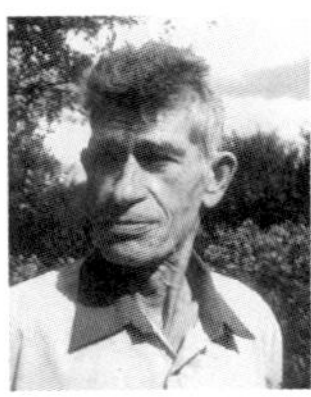

**Viktor Yegorov**                                    Moscow region, c.1992

*As recounted by his granddaughter Nastya:* My grandmother worked as an accountant her whole life, and did her calculations on an abacus. Then it got used a lot in our housekeeping affairs as we weren't so well off and every kopeck got counted. Gran sometimes used it to work out the family budget, so it wasn't just lying idly. But until recently it had been in the attic somewhere, lying with a load of old junk that we didn't need. We tried to dig it out a few times as it seemed like a shame for it to go to waste as granny had become so attached to it, having worked with it for so long. We thought it'd be good to dig it out, and maybe we could find some use for it. Then, finally, its time came. To begin with, grandad read an article in the magazine *Health*, about the benefits of massage. Both he and granny suffer from their joints seizing up and stuff like that. But we don't have enough money for things made by some company. Then grandad had a brainwave. He crawled into the attic, got out that abacus, and started to think of how he could make a massager from it. He went to the shops, had a look around, checked everything out, came back and got down to work. And so he made this thing: it looks like a real massager and, strictly speaking, it isn't really any different from one you could buy in a shop. So both of them started to massage their backs and their spines started to straighten out. You could say that this thing was reborn and our abacus is still put to some use.

Wooden abacus

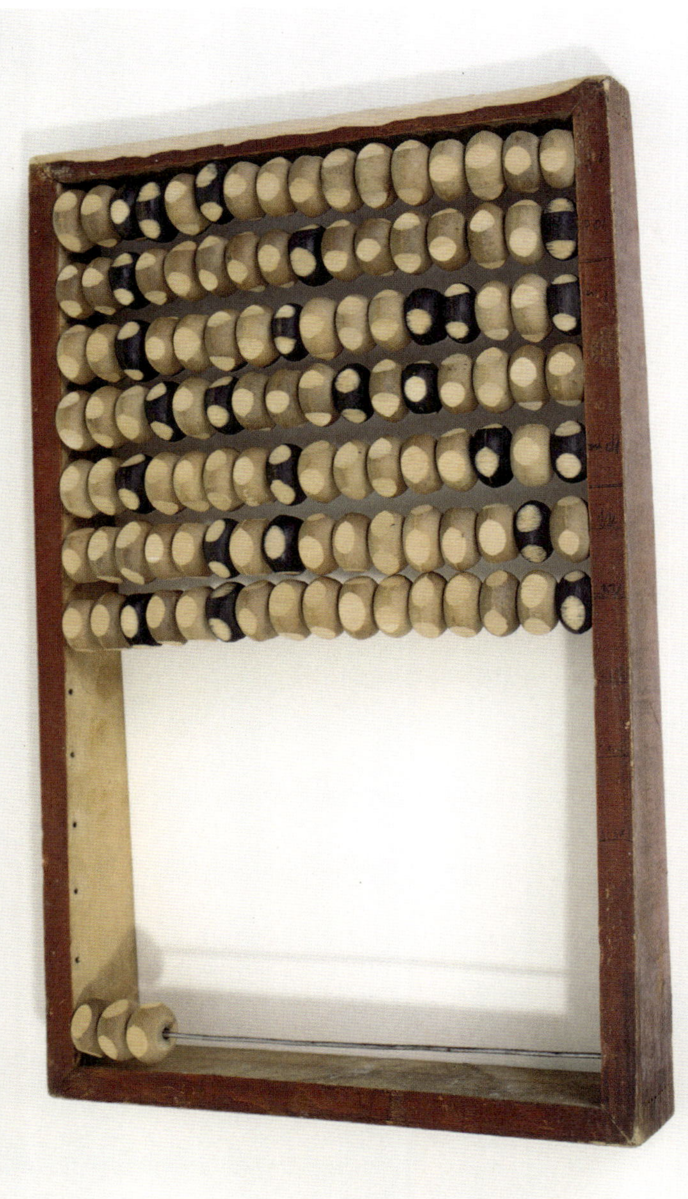

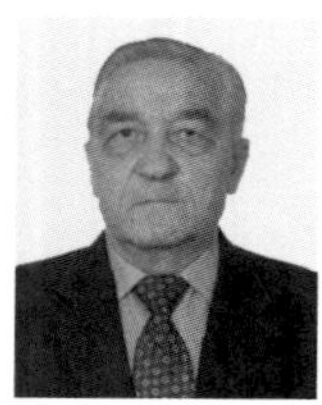

**Grigory Samorin**                                               Kolomna, 1983

When I bought a motor scooter there was damn all on it. What good is it without a windscreen? No good at all. You'd think it'd be dead easy to put on a windscreen, but there was nowhere to buy one, they weren't on sale then. So I went to my neighbour – he worked in a factory and in those days they could make anything you wanted there. Stainless-steel petrol cans, stainless-steel tubs for salting cabbage, anything you like – you just had to come to an agreement. I used to pay him with medical alcohol – I was working in a hospital at the time. It was easily done: they just cut it out of a sheet of stainless steel and bent it a bit. I attached the plastic to it myself afterwards, just bent it over the fire. My son stuck these stickers of girls on it when he returned from the army. He served in Germany – that's where he brought the stickers back from. It was fashionable then, they didn't make things like that here. But now every kiosk's full of porn.

Stainless steel, plastic

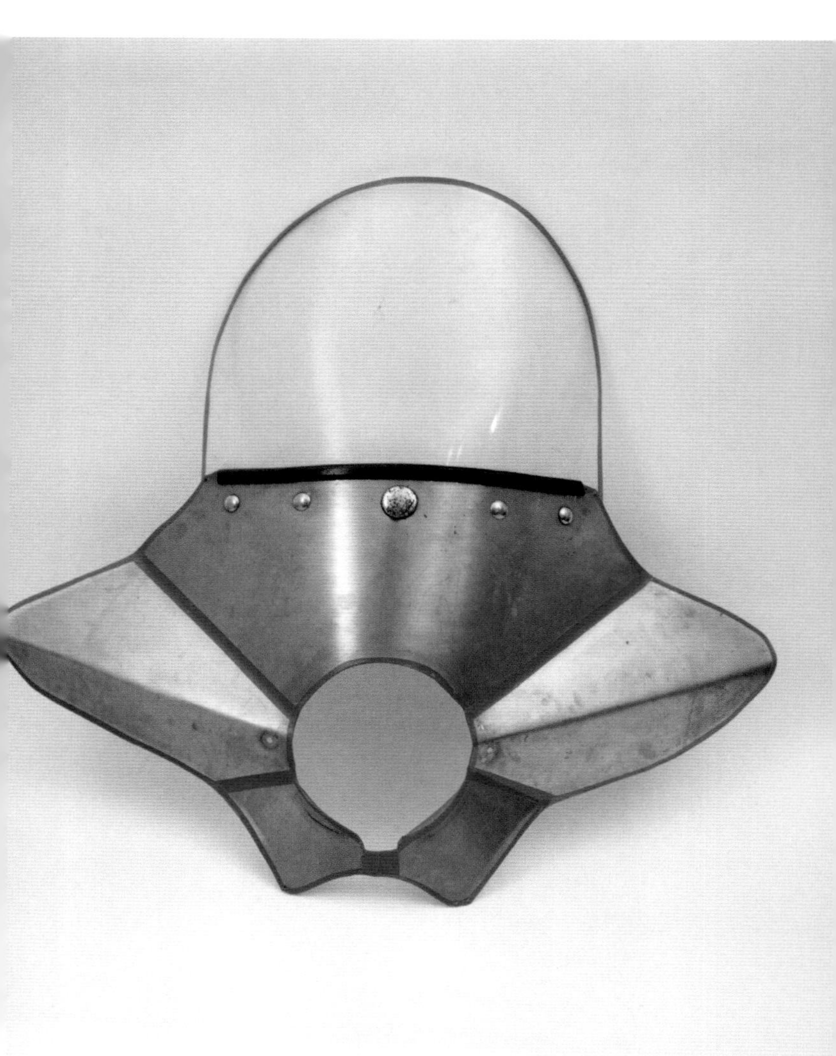

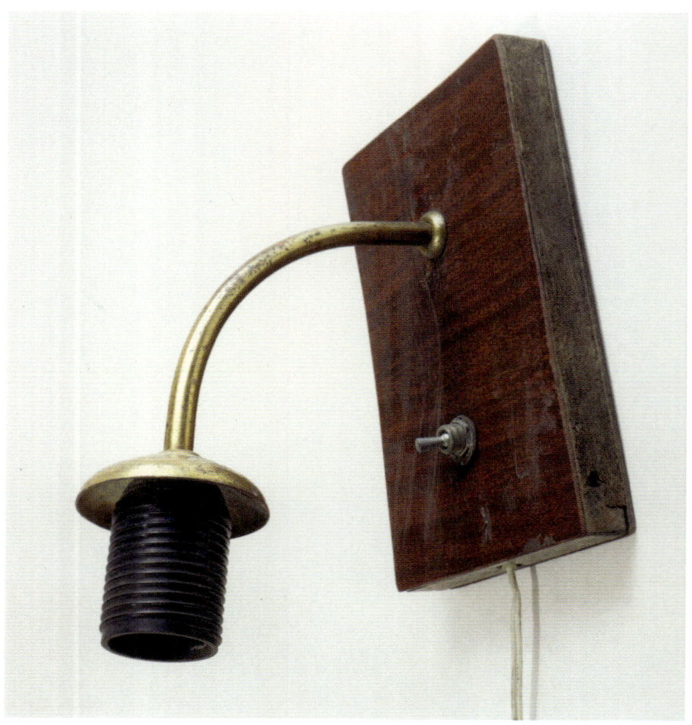

**Grigory Samorin**                                    Kolomna, 1985

When we built another bedroom onto our house, my wife said that it ought to have a wall-bracket lamp, to give some kind of soft light. But it was at the very time when there wasn't anything to be found anywhere. The prices in the street kiosks were crazy. My brother brought me a piece of polished chipboard from the furniture factory, I took the pipe from an old ceiling lamp and I found a lamp socket somewhere. There used to be a dome light on the ceiling as well, but it got broken somehow. The whole business only took half an hour. If you know how, then do it yourself – no problem!

Chipboard, lamp parts

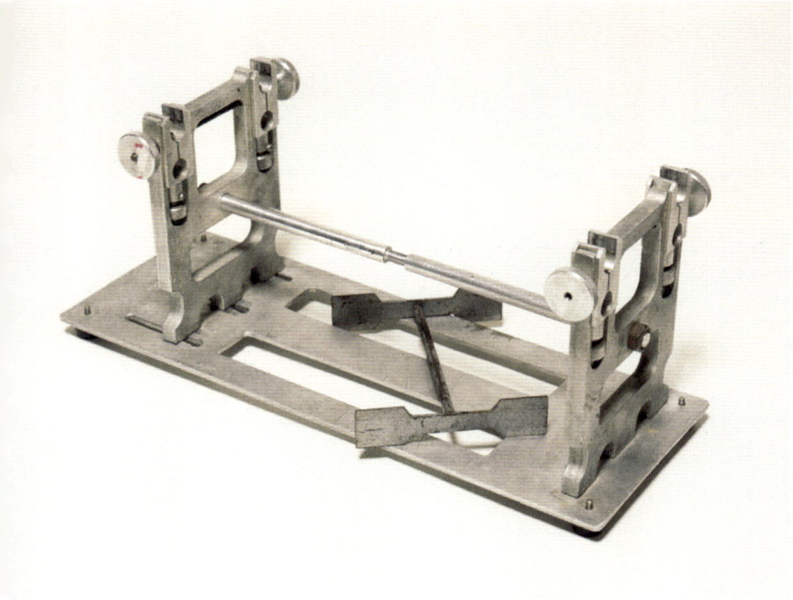

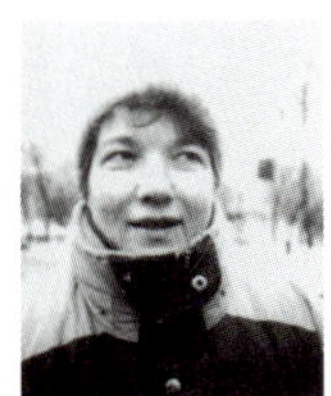

**Nikolai**                                    Krasnoyarsk, c.1990

*As recounted by his daughter Nadya (pictured):* The skate lies upside down in the frame, so the blades are up and the boots hang down. You have to move it around, to balance the blades, so that they are exactly parallel to one another. Otherwise they swing about. There's a special piece for ordinary skates – it rocks them, so that they don't knock, then you take it away and start to sharpen them. First with a rough blade, then with 'ilich', which is like a smooth sandpaper. Then you smear the 'ilich' with oil, sharpen again, then take off the burr with another bit of 'ilich'. Then you're ready to go. I made it when was I was fourteen – it took five years.

Duralumin, steel, screws

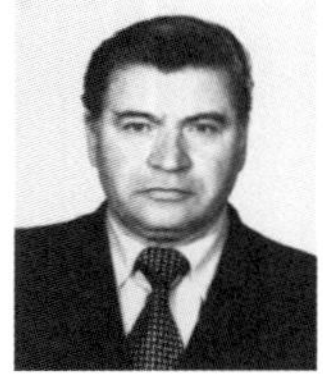

**Vasilii Arkhipov**                                                              Kolomna, 1965

It was only later, in the 1970s, that printed circuit boards started to appear –
before then we had to make everything ourselves. I went and asked a lathe
operator to cut out the framework. I got hold of a metallic fibreglass laminate.
Then the design, from a magazine, was made by hand on a circuit board. I
used some paint and some ferrous chloride, and I made a small, thin glass
tube like those for medical use. Then we bored holes and put in the necessary
parts: outline, capacitors, resistors. We worked on this for about three months.
Then it was necessary to make the frame of the transistor which I decided
to make from plexiglass as we had some big scrap pieces. We painted it black
on the inside so the outer side turned out black and shiny. We put the frame
together with screws and aluminium brackets which I bent and cut off myself,
and also the front panel where the loudspeaker was. I asked a guy who worked
in the factory to do some fine cutting for me. The figures were done by hand,
burnt in using something with a very fine end which heats up very quickly,
and from the reverse side the figures were burnt out. Then we painted it
and the extra paint was cleaned off and in the lines these figures remained.
So, we have white numbers against a black background. But the most extensive
work was carried out on the tuning. This was because we didn't have
piezofilters at that time, and we had to make inductance filters. It's very
difficult to tune them because you need special devices – an oscillograph
and a frequency generator. It could pick everything up. But it was most
interesting to hear what the *Voice of America* had to say. We quietly discussed
stuff in our smoking hangouts and then tuned into the *Voice of America*.

Textolite, radio components, plexiglass, handle, wire, screws, paint

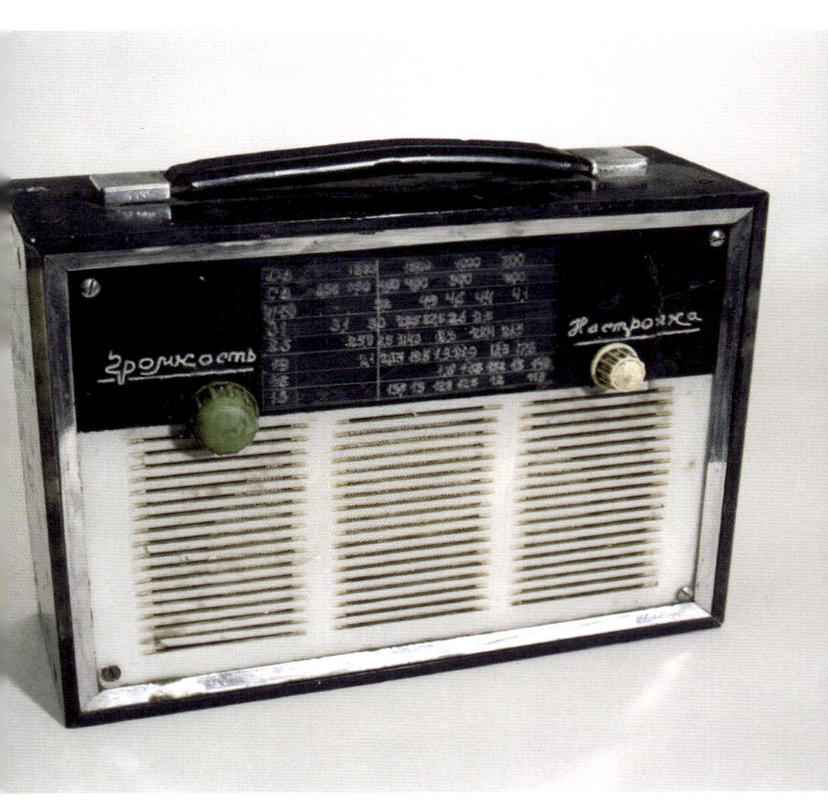
Громкость
Настройка

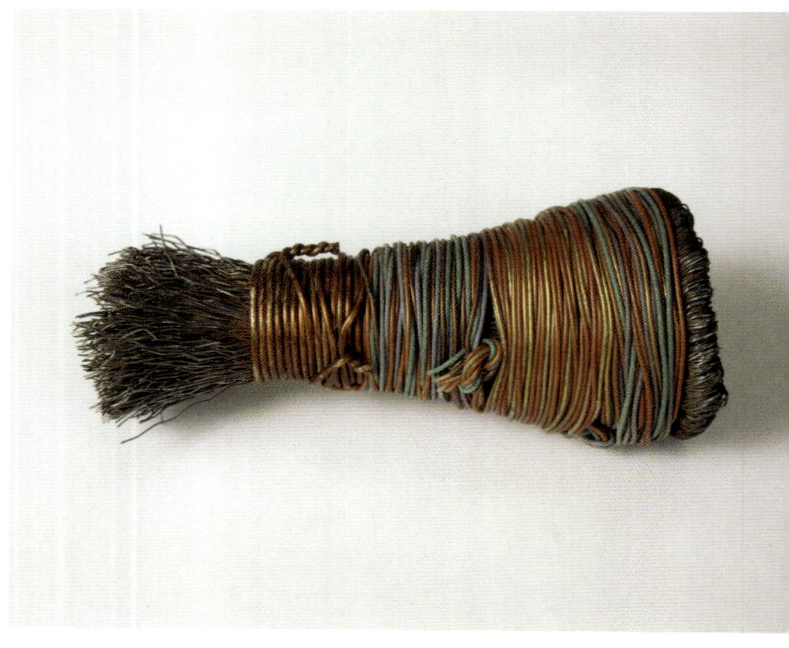

**Vasilii Arkhipov**                    Kolomna, 1992

I had to clean the back of a vehicle which was starting to rust. I had to clean it with a metal brush, but you can't get everywhere with the type of brush I had. It wasn't convenient, it really wasn't – and I had to get in everywhere. So I had to make a kind of shaving brush. I took a brush from the guys at the foundry, which was going to waste. I got some binding so I could tie up the bristles like a shaving brush. It turned out to be an excellent metal brush. It's narrow and it's very convenient to use it to get in there where the rust has appeared... and in other places where a big brush can't fit and you need a small metal brush. With this brush you can get in there, once, twice, give it a good scrub and that's your lot. Finally I used some 'anti-corrosion' and then I was able to paint it.

Metal brush, wire

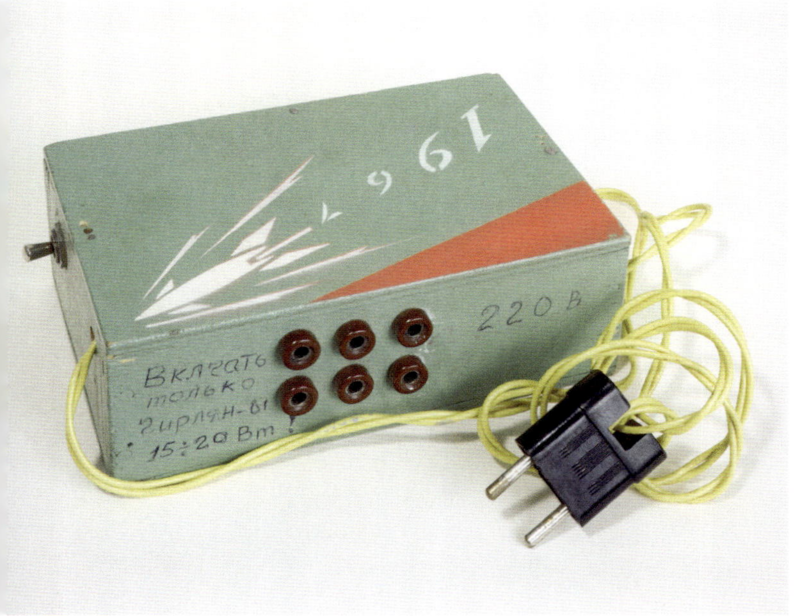


## Vasilii Arkhipov

Kolomna, 1967

The New Year was approaching and we made wooden boxes – we put the apparatus for the lights for the Christmas garlands in them. We wanted to decorate the tree so we made two or three for the garlands, which turned on and off. It's written here: 'Turn on garland – 15-20 watts.' The small lights can't take any more power. We made the garlands ourselves. We coloured the lights with varnish – red, green, yellow. We developed the apparatus for the twinkling lights. One garland had a certain timing, and another a different timing. Each garland is made with its own scheme; its connections were made differently. But you need to put them somewhere. We made the wooden boxes by glueing veneered wood together and then decorated them. It had to be safe – there were 220 watts. It was necessary to close it, to protect it. But we didn't use so much power because wood burns at high voltage. We wanted lights that blinked on and off – every light blinked in its own colour. It was beautiful like that. We also made a stencil for writing stuff. At work there were lots of bosses, second in commands, those type of people. We made garlands for all of them. We made them at work. And I made this commutation block for a Christmas tree garland for myself. There was a relay on every garland.

Plywood, glue, oil paint, radio components, cable, plug

**Vasilii Arkhipov**                                              Kolomna, 1987

It became necessary to make automobile parts – rubber items – because I couldn't buy them anywhere. Because the car was imported, an Opel Record 1970 issue, I travelled to Moscow a few times to a service centre for imported cars, but they didn't have much to say and charged crazy amounts of money. So I decided to do everything myself. I was able to do this because of my education – I mean, I knew how everything had to be done. I had the raw rubber already – all I needed was the stove. But how to make it? I decided to take a piece of piping, about 100mm in diameter. On one side I welded it securely and on the other I drilled some holes for the die. To produce the die, I took the old parts to a lathe operator, who made a mould of them for me. I made my own stove, which I put on a gas cooker and heated to the required temperature. The temperature control was carried out by a special instrument I have. The raw rubber was put in the mould and then lowered into the chamber, which was sealed by a disc. A screw was screwed into this disc in order to press down onto the raw rubber and fill the entire mould. The disc was nailed on. Well, the second and third times it produced OK rubber. I use these parts in my car now. This was the first mould and then, after that, there was another for casing and for work cylinders. But the most interesting one I had to make was a membrane for a fuel pump. Everyone was using a varnished insulating cloth then, but it wasn't reliable and was a lot of fuss. This stove solved the problem very simply. I put gauze into rubber in this stove and got an excellent membrane for a fuel pump with no trouble at all.

Steel pipes, metal disc, nails, screws

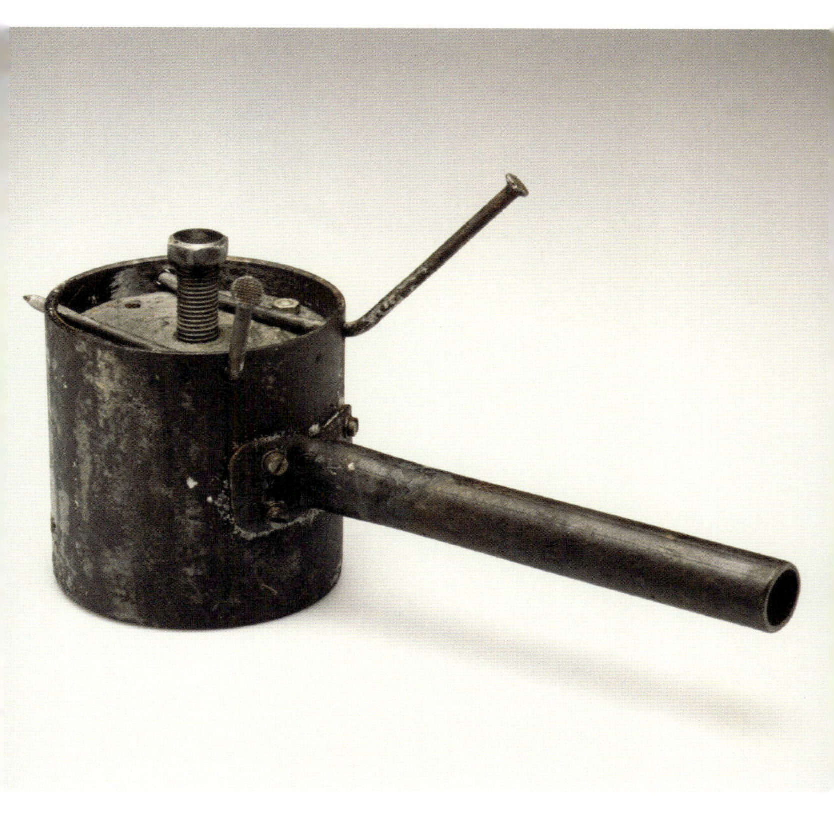

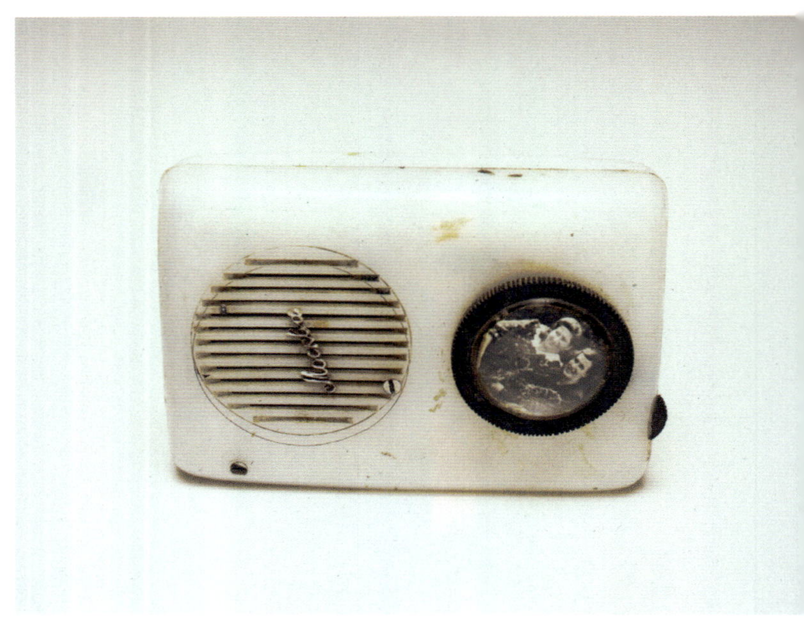

**Vasilii Arkhipov**                                                    Kolomna, 1960s

The 'soap dishes' – they were all long wave. Long and medium wave – there wasn't anything else. They were made after the war, in the 1950s and 1960s. They were small – that's why they were called 'soap dishes'. Everyone was trying to make stuff as small as possible. The home-made loud speakers were made from foam plastic. I made a diffuser, which was flat. I added it to the magnetic system, and got a speaker, thinner than usual, a 015 speaker. The VEF was, at that time, the only transistor radio that specialists, amateur radio hams, tried to put together themselves. It was well made and good quality. The design was very good. The only real problem was with the batteries. There weren't any small button batteries available, although to be more precise, there were FBS ones, but they quickly packed in.

Plastic, radio components

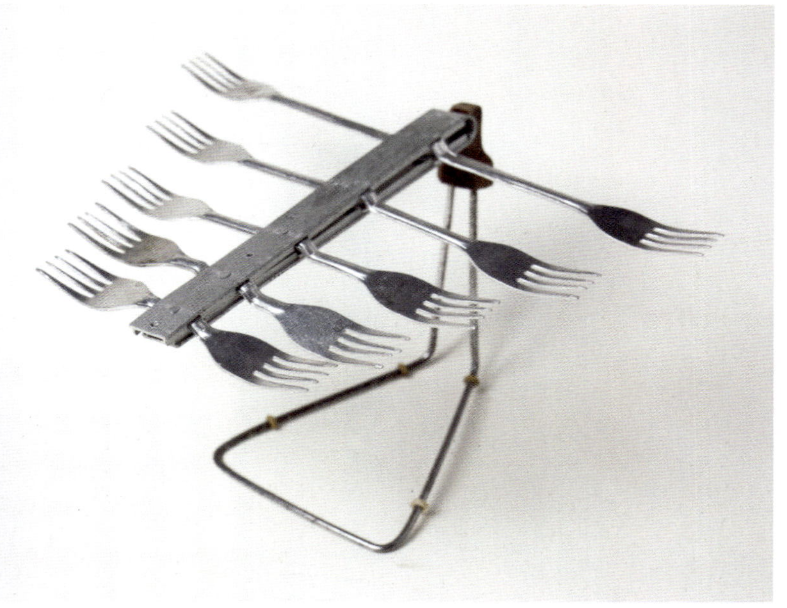

**Vasilii Arkhipov**                                        Kolomna, 1993

We prepared this aerial according to the dimensions published in *Radio* magazine. But, you know, resonators are everything. They were made from forks so that the reception would be better. In my opinion it all worked out very well. The effect was noticeable from the very start. Everyone particularly wanted to watch the programmes from Saint Petersburg. My mother had the forks in her cupboard. She bought them when everything was collapsing around us. There wasn't anything else but forks to buy in the shops then. They weren't even very good forks, in a practical sense. But they went well with that aerial.

Aluminium forks, rivets, aluminium pole, ventilator base, screw connection

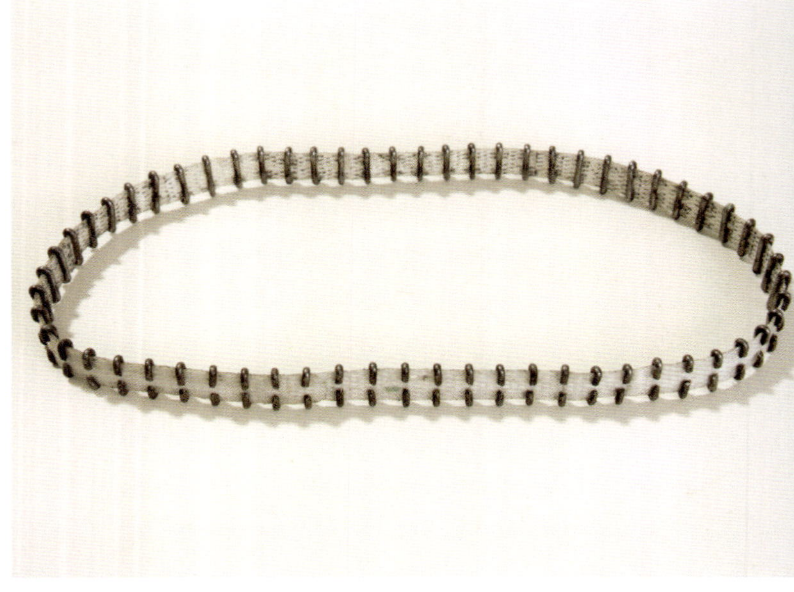

**Vasilii Arkhipov**                                                    Kolomna, 1989

The 'Tula' sewing machine has a drive belt, but it was stretched out of shape and we didn't have a replacement. Someone suggested I should boil it in soda so that it would shrink and fit properly, but that didn't work. There's this ribbon, for packaging, that they throw out on the rubbish tip, so I picked some up and decided to use it to make a drive belt. I measured out the span I needed in metal wire, got a pair of pliers – the wire was dead easy to bend – and squeezed it all together. But that didn't work, as the wire turned out to be harder than I thought and the span didn't match up. With a soft belt you get one span, and with a hard belt you get a different one, even though the staples are the same distance apart. The old belt was made out of some kind of threads glued together – I couldn't find any like that and I had no idea what to replace them with. First I tried using leather ribbons, then nylon, but none of it was suitable. This didn't work either. It's a pity: it's a good sewing machine, but there's nowhere to buy a ribbon for it. Maybe there's somewhere in Moscow, but I'm not going all that way for a drive belt!

Packaging strip, wire staples, glue

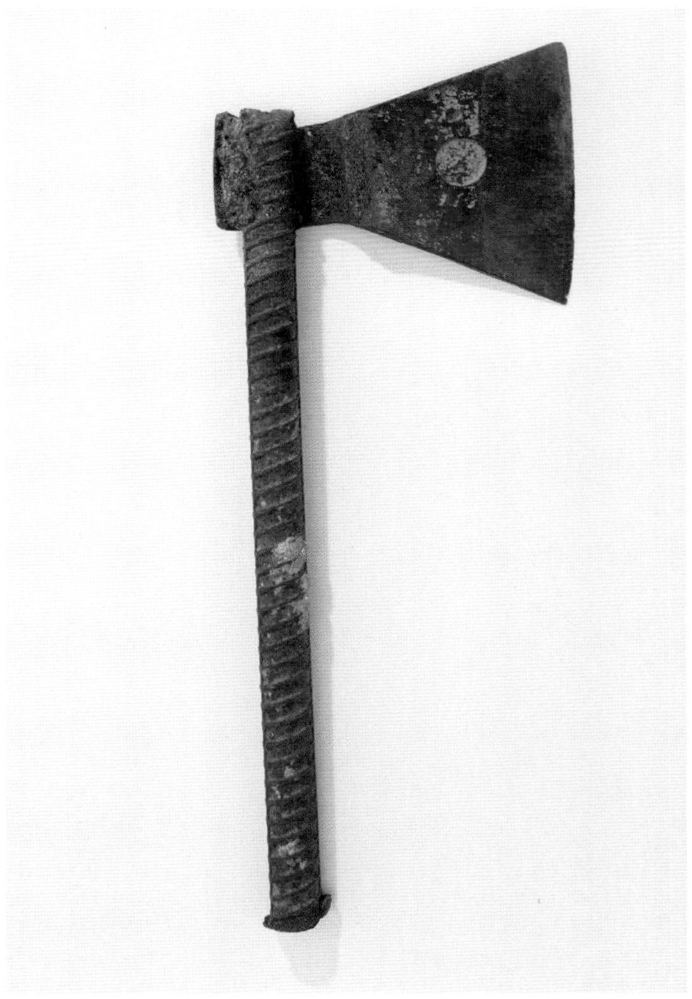

**Vasilii Arkhipov**                                        Kolomna, 1992

I was trying to chop something, to split it, so I hit my axe with a lump hammer and it cracked and split. But it was a pity to throw it out. So I welded the head to a piece of steel bar. That's all. What else can I say?

Steel

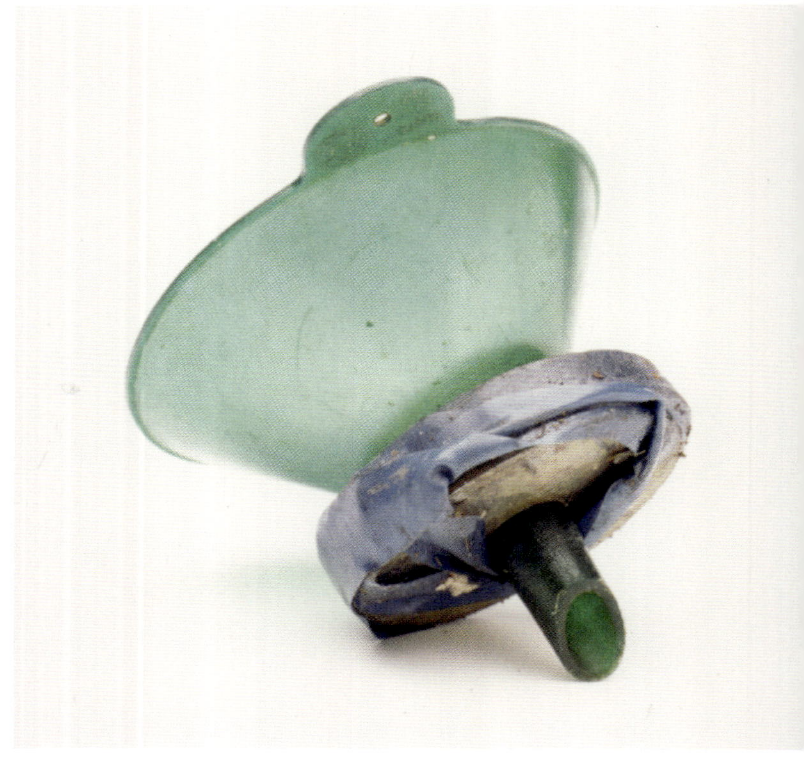

**Vasilii Arkhipov**                                      Kolomna, 1996

What can I tell you? It's not that interesting... I read in a magazine that magnetised water is good for you. That's all. So I decided to try to make magnetised water. I had a magnet from a radio speaker and I had a funnel, so I just had to put the two things together. I put the magnet around the funnel, took some insulating tape and fixed it on. That's all. I put the funnel in a bottle and poured in the water – it was supposed to be magnetised and acquire healthy properties. But there was something wrong. I used the device for a year with no results at all. Either I didn't do something right, or maybe what they said in the magazine was wrong.

Plastic funnel, magnet, insulating tape

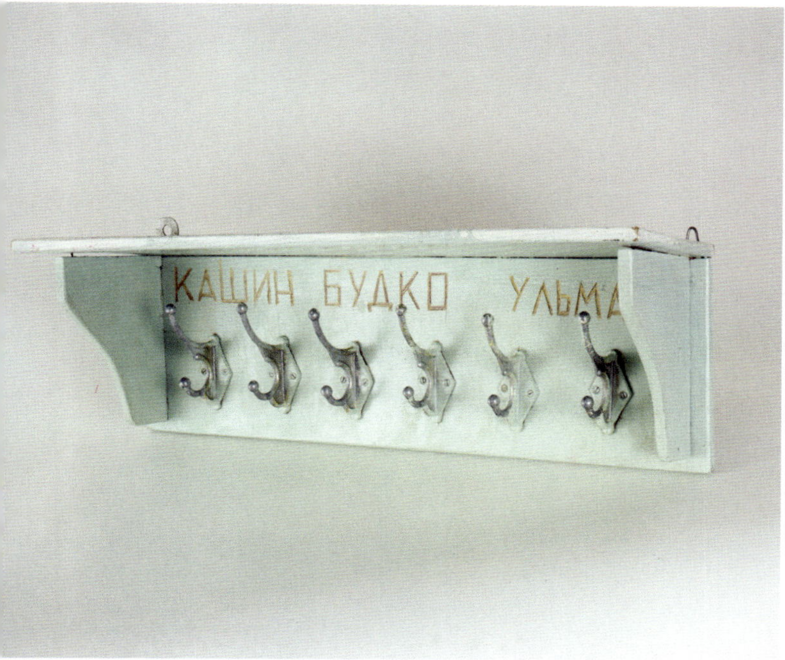

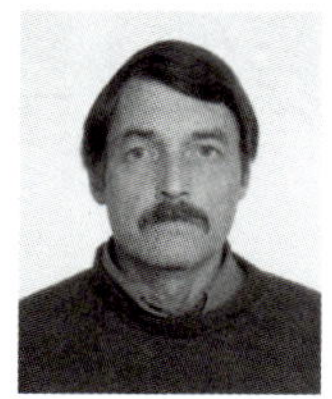

**Viktor Kashin**                                              Moscow, c.1987

There's not much space, but lots of people. We have to economise on space: the entire corridor's cluttered with all sorts of old rubbish anyway. Well, I made the coat rack a bit more compact. I wrote their names on hooks so everyone would put their coats on them. But since then everything's changed – it was a long time ago. Yes, life has changed. Ulman works in a bank – he's bought a flat – and Budko's got his own car wash now and he's built a dacha. We're the only ones left of the old tenants; our neighbours are all new.

Wood, hooks, paint

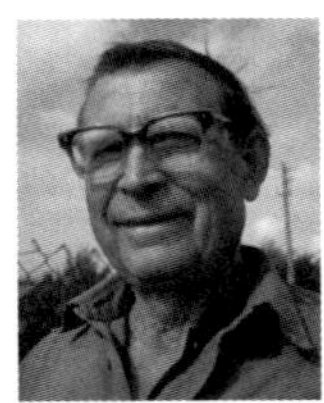

**Viktor Tabankov**  Kolomna, 1971

This is a device for producing captions for my amateur 2x8 films, when I was shooting with a 'Kvarts-2'. The films had no sound, not like today's video. I had to write the captions on the film, then glue them on, to make a kind of montage. They're like silent films. You put the captions in, for example, 'Holidays–76'. I'll turn it on – these captions are already done. Then another bit of writing, we put it in, turn on our camera and the text is already on the film. Then you develop the film. I remember I bought these two brackets in the shop 'DIY' on Gorky Street in Moscow. Then from Textolite and stuff that was hanging around I made the frame, and this little window was the result. You stick the text in there. I made the captions myself as well. There was a film shop on Leninskii Prospect, but they never had anything like this – though I'd read about them. My camera's got a fixed focus, so I worked out how to set up the captions and they all came out very clearly.

Duralumin bracket, Textolite, rivets, screws

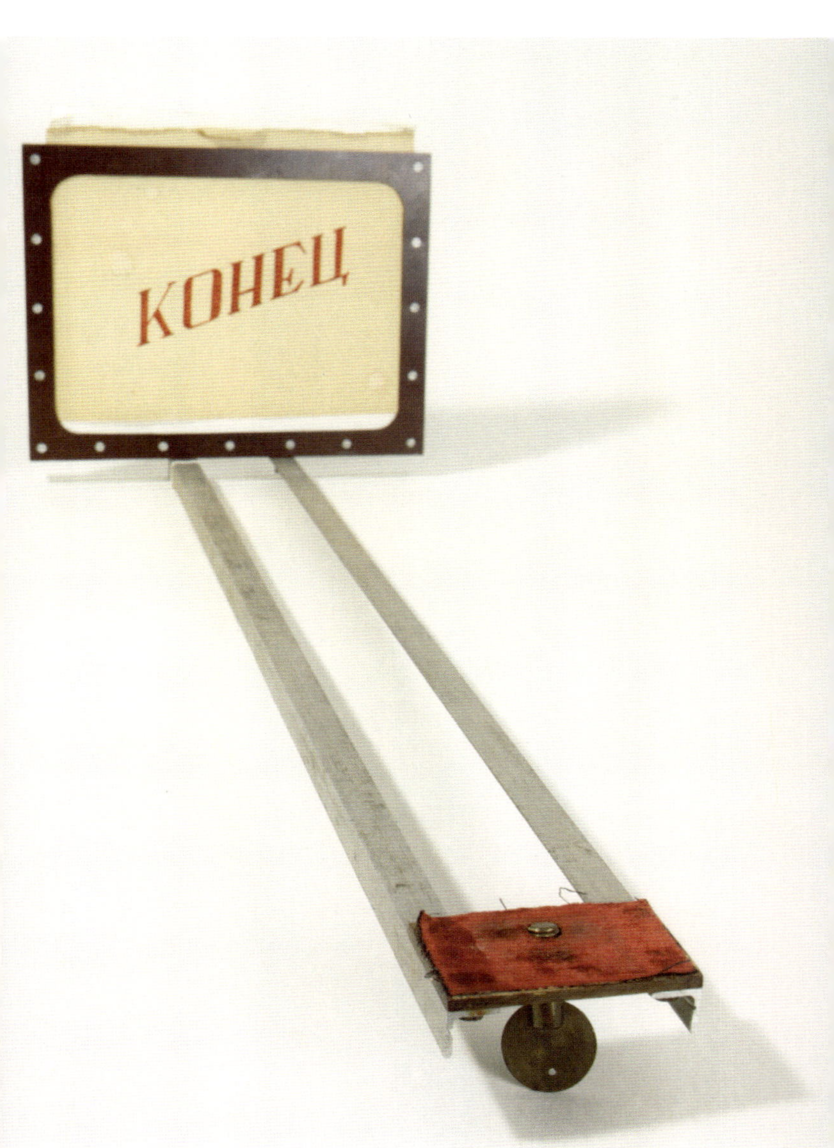
КОНЕЦ

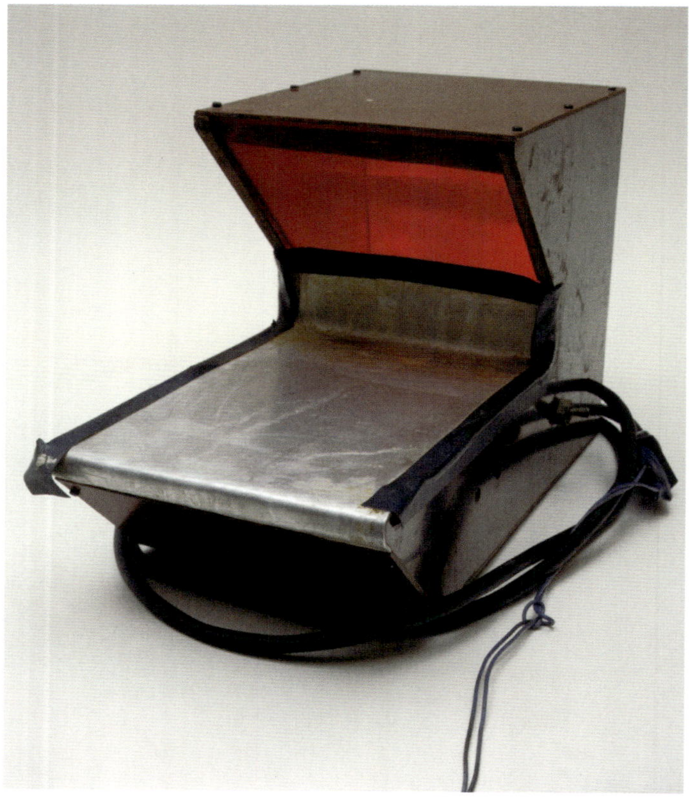

**Viktor Tabankov**                    Pechenga, Arkhangelsk region, 1968

This is a lamp with preheating, not from a spiral but from an ordinary lamp
which fulfils two functions. The first is this preheating here on which a tray
with a developer is placed, and the second is to illuminate all the photos
that we get here. I made it myself from Textolite that was going to waste. It
was a long time ago – about twenty-five years. I've never seen lamps like this
in the shops and it came to me that I could make one lamp that would do
two jobs. I made it when I was in the army, serving in Pechenga, the northern
fleet where we used these lamps. I brought this lamp with me, and then
used it to print photos. It's made from materials I had at hand – there's
nothing special here – and I did the tracing and the plans myself, which my
mates also made lamps from. They were very happy with it.

Textolite, duralumin sheet, red glass, wire, rivets, screws

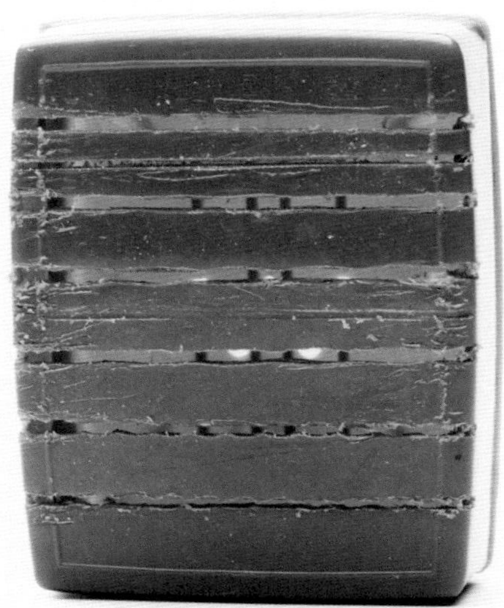

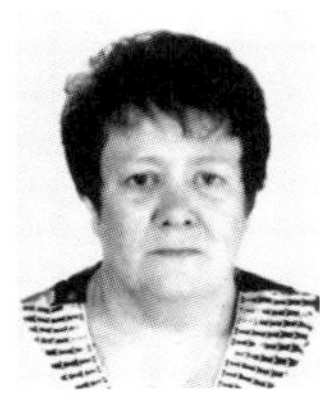

**Nina Potapova**                    Ryazan, 1992

This strange little box used to be a soap dish. Yes, and before that I finally bought myself a good coat. All my life I'd dreamed of having a good wool coat. My dream finally came true. I bought it. A black one. But the slightest dust showed on it. What could I do? I was absolutely desperate. I tried everything you could think of. Maybe it was the type of cloth, or maybe it was something else, but everything stuck to it. It was impossible to clean with a brush. But Valka, my neighbour, told me she'd seen this special brush that cleaned because it sucked in the dust. And it looked like a little box, not like a brush. I found a box – it was a soap dish – and my husband made some slits, cut through it with a hacksaw. When you rub it over the coat the plastic gets charged and the dust all gets sucked into the soap dish. So you could say it turned out to be a real invention. It's only for light dust, of course – you couldn't clean any other kind of dirt with it.

Soap dish

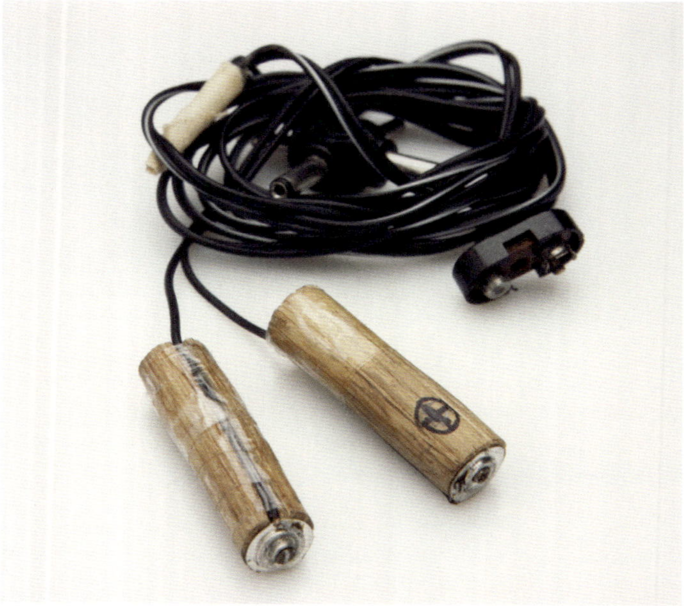

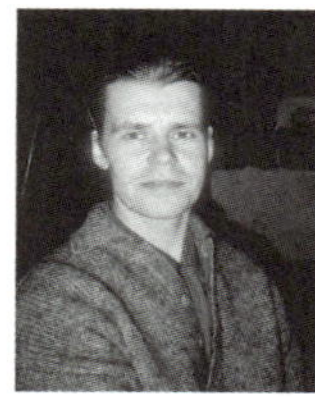

**Vadim**                                                   Yaroslavl, 1998

When I bought my Walkman I needed to listen to it not only using batteries but also mains. But there wasn't any jack socket that I could use to plug it in. What there was wasn't suitable for the electrical system. So it was necessary to make something instead of putting in these small batteries every time. Instead of the small batteries, this was pushed into the battery section and was connected directly to a transformer. In principle jack sockets for this exist, and naturally, you need to look for plus/minus. This was probably made about two years ago, in 1998. I don't really feel like wasting money on buying a special adaptor with this kind of jack socket.

Wood, wire, jack sockets

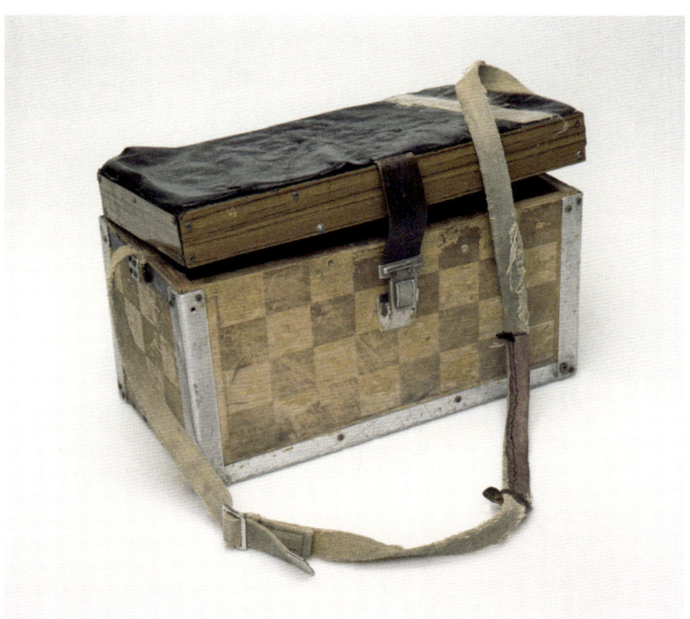

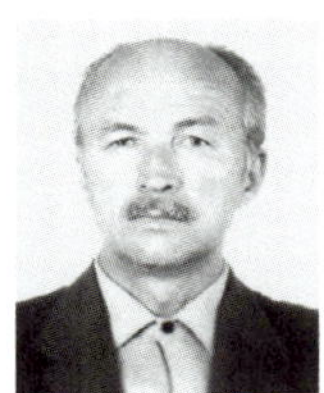

**Viktor Lukin**     Moscow, c.1988

This board was just a normal chessboard. You just need to be able to make a good case out of it. There are brackets everywhere, at the bottom and on the sides – everything done with screws. The chessboard was already there, so as far as size goes, its height and width were determined. I didn't need to do anything else with it except knock together a good case out of it. The buckle is cut off a run-of-the-mill briefcase and held together with straps. The straps are on the top so that the fishing rods stay in place; you can make them from any pair of trousers. You're dressed in fleece-lined trousers, so you've got some warmth there, and you're sitting practically on wood so that water or snow or early rains don't get on the case.

Chessboard, duralumin bracket, briefcase lock, strap, metal hinges, screws

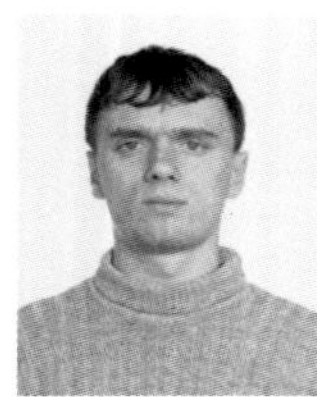

**Albert and Ivan Khmelyov**  Kaluga region, 1999

We had a television but there wasn't any aerial so my uncle and I began making one. We wound copper wire round two spare bicycle wheels – around here everybody used to have aerials like this. To get a good reception we sank this sort of cylinder into the ground and nailed a stick to it, so that we could turn the aerial to where it got the best signal. We hung it on the stick and attached the TV cable. Look, it gets two stations just fine – channel one and channel two. I used to have a bike, but it broke, so the wheels were just lying around. And our pensions aren't very big – we've nothing to buy one with. Some Moscow people's house here caught fire and something must have happened to the electricity – it just went 'fizz' and cut out.

Bicycle wheels, wood

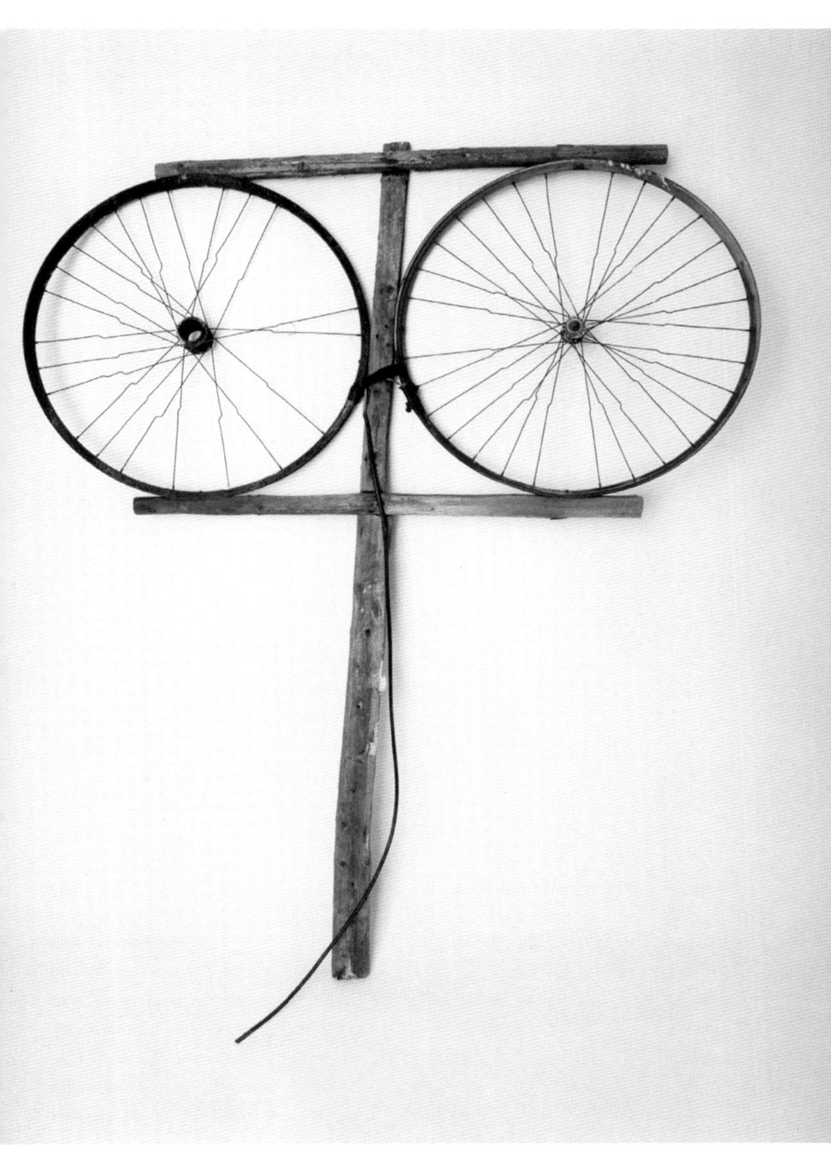

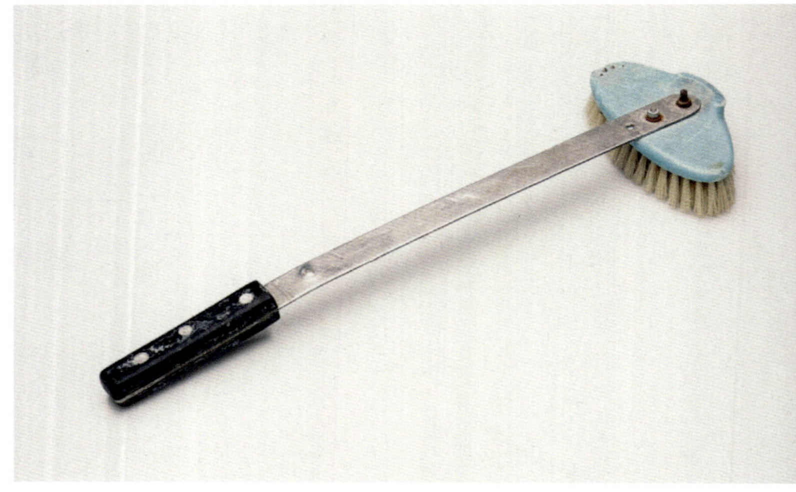

**Evgenii Liberman**                                    Mariupol, c.1980

*As recounted by his granddaughter Vera Khlebnikova:* My grandfather, when he was very old, had forgotten some things but was still able to do some stuff – he still had a passion for DIY. But he didn't have much strength, so this is one of his typical household improvement jobs. These are the remains of brushes of a very high quality, German, good plastic and good bristles. It looks as if at some point its handle gave out, or maybe he deliberately sawed it off, and so that old people didn't have to bend over quite so much when cleaning the bath he added this handle, made it longer and turned the brush around. The brush's previous handle he then attached onto another brush made from iron and ebonite. It looks like the iron strip has been taken from something else because there are extra holes here – they haven't been drilled especially for this. The rivets are ordinary ones, rusted from water, as it was in water for a long time – the rust also had a part to play in the cleaning of the bath. So, the head of this brush has been screwed onto this handle, which ends with thoroughly worked-on ebonite. And riveted on with these rivets. This ebonite handle looks like a hamburger because in the middle this iron bit comes out of the brush and lies between these metal strips and then on the two sides there's this ebonite, which played a part in a lot of grandad's DIY projects.

These aren't the kind of things you can find readily available in the shops or that are so cheap to make yourself. It was simply that it was necessary for him to make a lot of stuff himself.

Brush, non-corrosive metal, ebonite, rivets

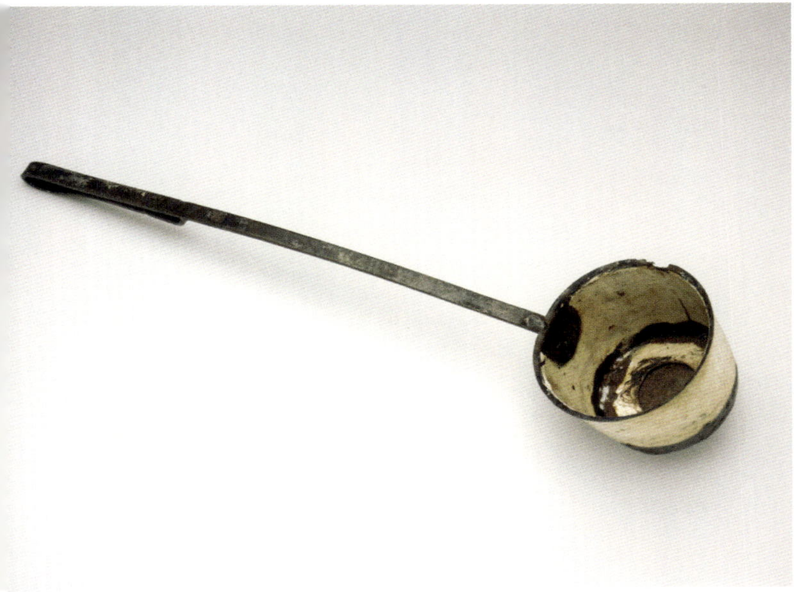

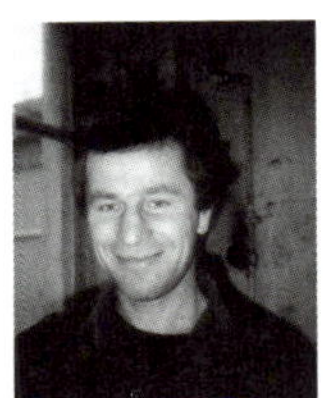

**Nikolai Fedorov**                    Kaluga region, 1994

*As recounted by his son (pictured):* They've got two or three greenhouses each. When it's hot I open them up; when it's cold I close them. I'm here the whole time but they just come at the weekends. He was born in 1926 – he's seventy-three years old. He hasn't worked for a year, but before that he worked the whole time, didn't let anything by – he was a good welder. Well, all these shovels, all this different stuff, 'Look after them', he said, 'I can't work any more, so who else is going to make them for you?' Metal's expensive now. Last year he brought it over once it had been made. The ladle is back there somewhere in the greenhouse – you can use it to water the plants, the tomatoes and cucumbers.

Lampshade, metal bar

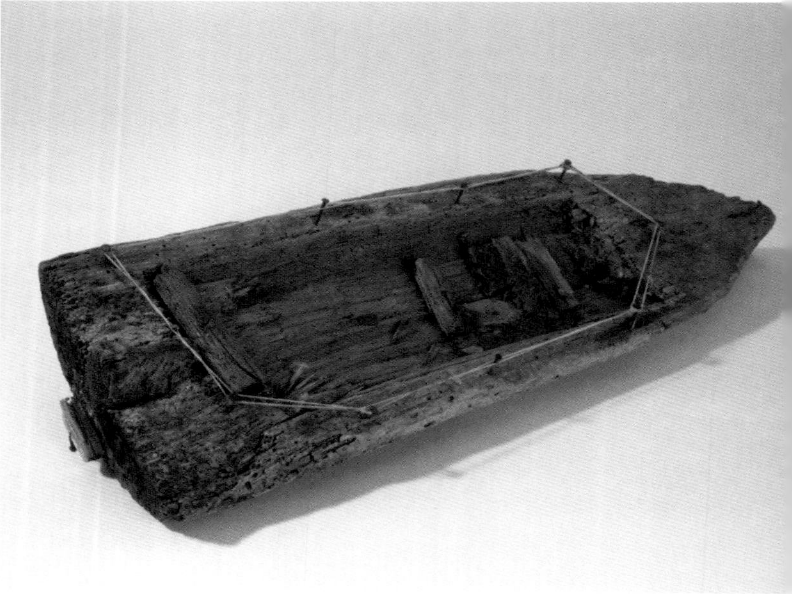

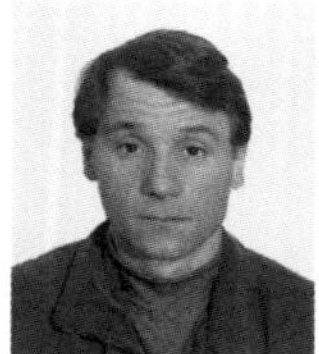

**Gennadii Konychev**                    Ryazan region, 1992

I made it during a summer in the country, maybe five years ago now. He must have been about four then and started pestering me: 'Make me a boat, make me one.' Well, I found this old block of wood, so I just sawed a bit off and chopped out the rest. I hammered nails into it round the edge and twisted rope round them. There used to be a mast here, but it broke, and afterwards, that same year, he nailed on a rudder. And what else? I don't know. I stuck on some putty, and that's all.

Wood, nails, rope, putty

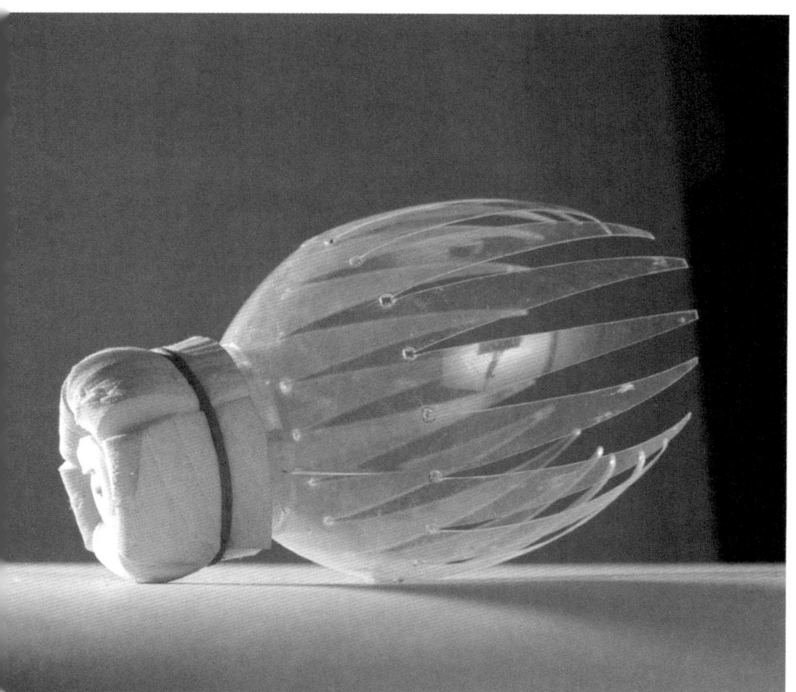

**Gennadii Konychev**                                    Ryazan region, 2000

There was this time when we went for a holiday on the Oka river – we took a badminton set, but we forgot the shuttlecocks, or else we didn't buy any. Anyway, we found we didn't have any shuttlecocks. We tried playing with a sock and a cellophane bag, but it's just not the same. And my wife blamed me for forgetting. In other words, I had to do something about it. So I took a plastic bottle and cut out something looking more or less like a shuttlecock. These stabilisers are supposed to be the feathers. And to soften the impact I covered the end with soft pieces of material and an elastic band.

Plastic bottle, cloth, elastic band

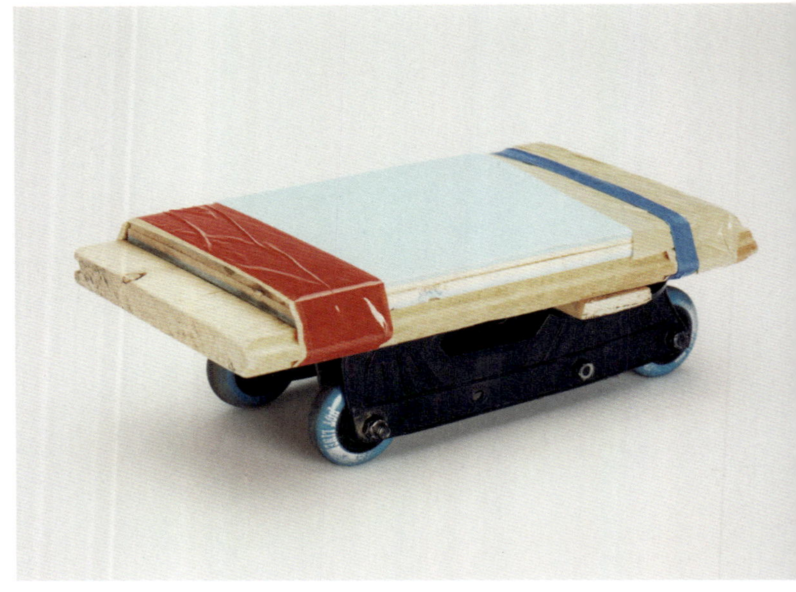

**Gennadii Konychev**                                        Ryazan, 2001

We bought our son some roller skates, ordinary cheap ones, and they fell apart the following year. I told him: 'Don't jump, they're not built for you to do all that aggressive jumping on, they're just ordinary skates, for skating.' The wheels were plastic and couldn't take it. We didn't have any money to buy him new ones, but it seemed a shame to throw them away. I had to make use of them somehow. My wife was nagging me to buy an exercise machine. All right, I thought, you'll have your exercise machine. I took some plywood and screwed on what was left of the roller skates, then I taped some foam to the top to make it softer on the backside. I bought a big rubber bandage that you slip round the radiator. Then you sit down on this contraption, press your feet against the radiator and ride backwards and forwards, pumping your legs and abdominal muscles. Great! It makes a fantastic exercise machine.

Roller skates, plywood, foam, tape

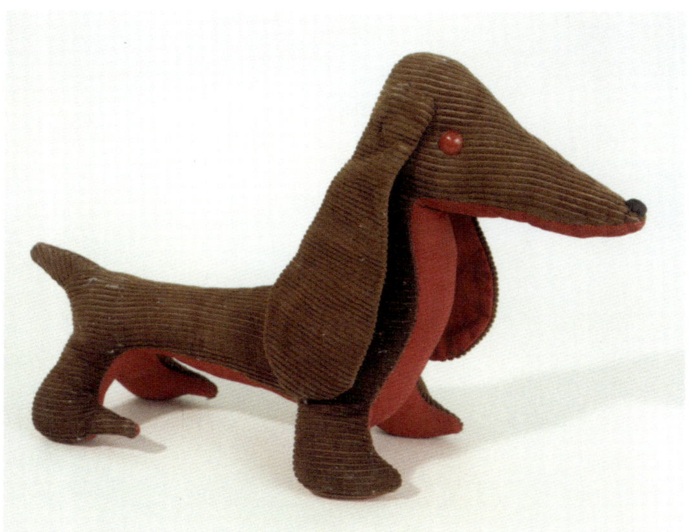

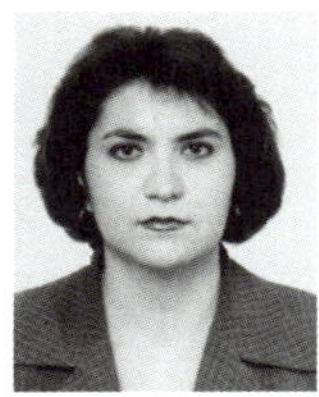

**Masha Chekalina**                    Moscow region, 1984

I made this dog in the summer of 1984, at the young pioneer camp. On the second day these men and women, bold promoters of mass culture, announced to us, 'Children, we have such-and-such clubs where you can make such-and-such a thing for your dear mummy and daddy.' I was no good at handicrafts – but of course I joined the 'Soft Toy' club. When I got there I saw all sorts of mice, dogs and cats. Of course, like any other child, I wanted a big dog. So I thought, I'm going to make a dog so that it looks like it's alive. Well, as it couldn't be big, I decided to make a dachshund. For a dachshund I needed some kind of smooth material, so I chose corduroy. The parts are carefully cut out, then sewn together, turned inside out, and stuffed with small pieces of material and cotton wool to fill everything out and give it body. I brought this dachshund home from the camp like a 'war trophy'. I was terribly proud of it. It was my favourite toy for a long time – it slept in my bed and took regular baths. Now the seams on its back have split.

Corduroy, cotton wool, buttons, thread

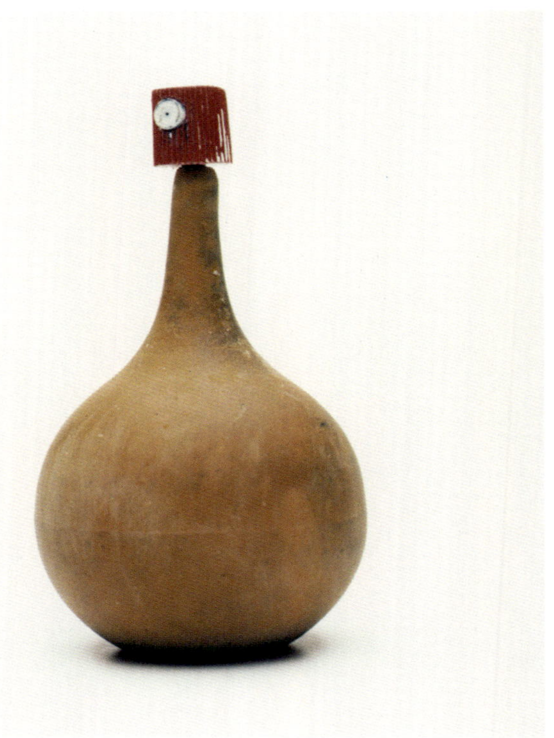

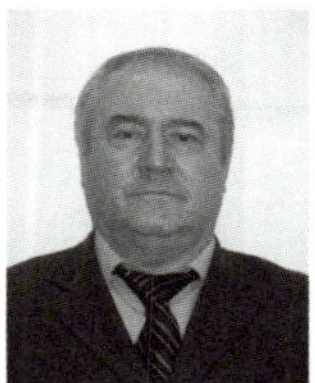

**Valentin Plitkin**                                    Ryazan, 1990

I couldn't make it work, though. I thought it would work, but obviously there was a mistake somewhere... you can't atomise water using this spray and an aerosol head. It doesn't atomise. I don't know why. I made it a long time ago, when the shelves in the shops were empty. It would have been some time around 1990. I don't remember what I needed it for, something – otherwise I wouldn't have made it.

Aerosol nozzle, spray canister

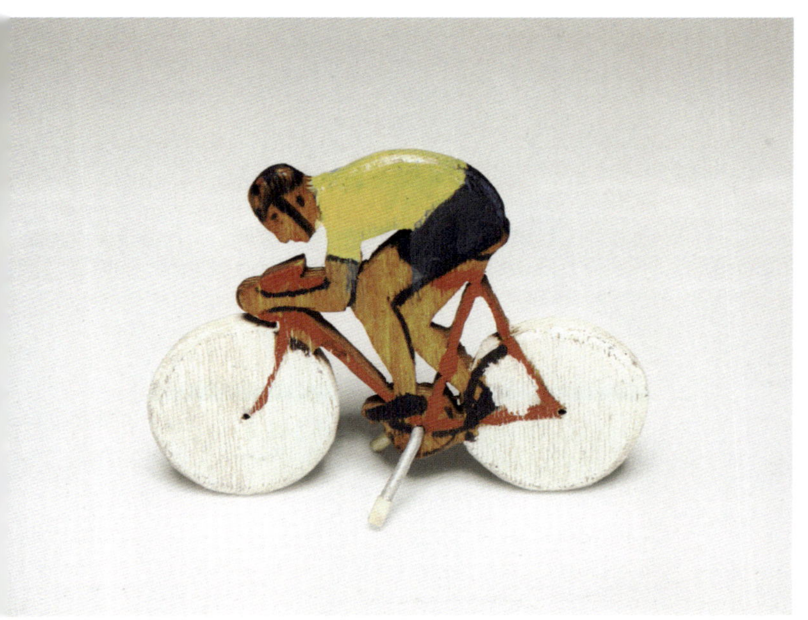

## Vladimir Piskun

Kiev, c.1980

*As recounted by his wife Nadya:* Well, this is a wooden cyclist cut out using a fretsaw. We had eight of them, these cyclists. My husband is a distinguished sportsman and trainer to the Ukrainian national team. He used them as a teaching aid in racing tactics, to show his pupils how team racing is organised, how to turn, what to do on the highway. He also made a polystyrene track which he used to demonstrate sprint tactics and to show who should take which position, who should begin at which moment. This was a way of supplementing pure muscle power with theoretical knowledge. This is a model, a cyclist – you can arrange them on a table, say, and even mark out a road with chalk, and demonstrate all this to your pupils. Of course, there was no such thing as video then. These cyclists must have been made at least thirty years ago and well, this wasn't something you could buy in a shop. So now, thanks to the models, you could gather a group to sit and listen without any special preparations of any kind. He drew the shape and made the templates himself. He also painted various parts. The model of the cyclist is made of wood. My husband is a creative person – always wanting something, searching for something.

Wood, paint, metal

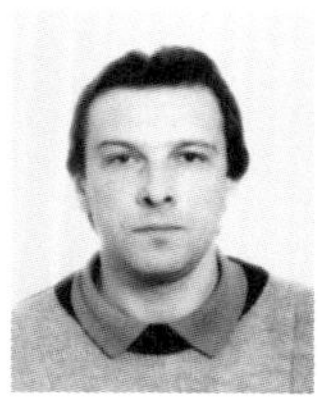

**Vladimir Antipov**                                          Moscow, 1997

I'm a street cleaner and this is my dustpan. I don't know what else to call it.
I made it from a plastic container – it must have been in 1997 or 1998. It's
very handy for sweeping up all sorts of dirt in the street, and it's light and
easy to work with. What else? I found the container on the rubbish tip – I
think it was from a 5-litre mineral-water canister. They make us clean up
the streets, but what tools do we have? A spade and a small twig broom if
you make it for yourself, and nothing else – just imagine trying to sweep up
with that. But I took this container, cut it with a knife and fastened it to an
old mop. The mop's stick has a very useful sort of clip on it. The design
turned out light and it holds a lot – very handy. I invented it myself!

Plastic container, mop handle

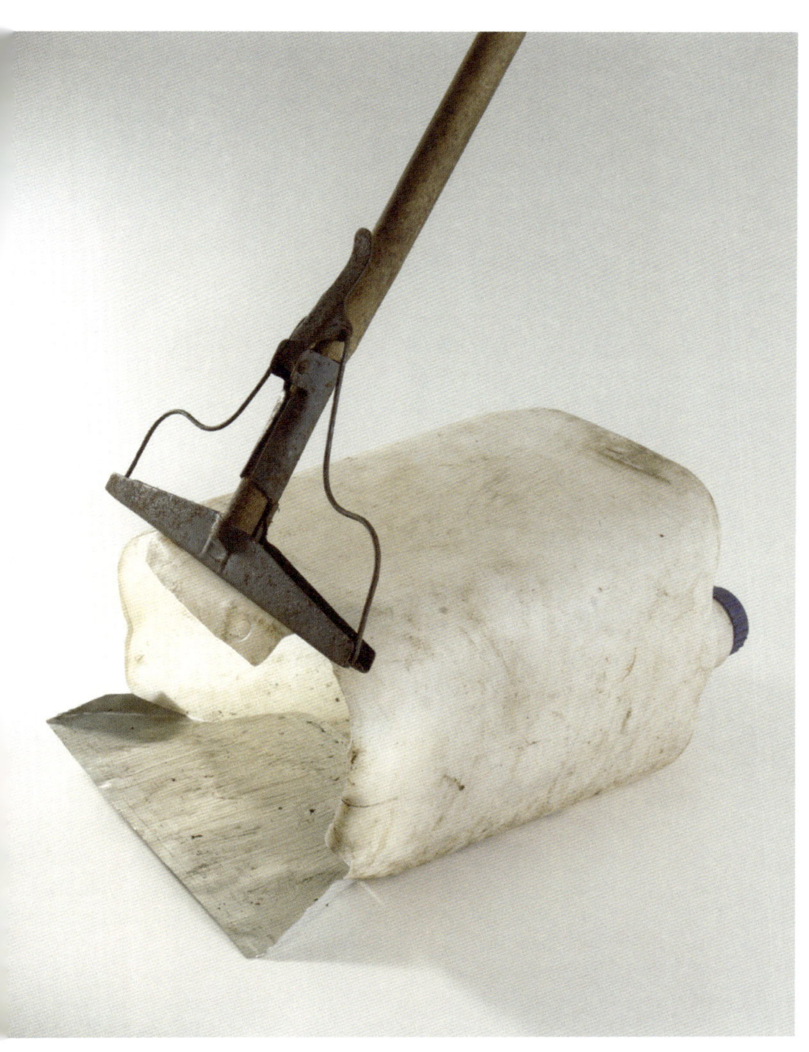

**Vladimir Antipov**                                    Moscow, 1998

In 1998 I was working as a street cleaner, on Kutuzovsky Prospect. In June that year we had the famous Moscow hurricane. I can't remember ever seeing so many trees blown down and roofs blown off. Right there in the section that I used to clean, practically all the trees were down. It was terrible when they made us street cleaners clear away all that fallen timber. We worked nine or ten hours at a time – the number of truckloads of branches, logs and roofing metal that we took away was something incredible, absolutely incredible. When we were loading those trucks, we sawed up the trees, cleared the obstructions – honestly, they didn't pay us a thing for it. We slaved away like that for two months and they paid us a bonus of 100 roubles – but then that's another story. That's the way things happen here. They brought in some soldiers to help us. They stood in the backs of the trucks while we handed them up branches, leaves and all sorts of filthy rubbish. The number of heaps we took apart! Well, there I am throwing all sorts of trash into the truck and I came across this sign. I was all set to swing it, but then I felt it in my hand – it was really light. Hey, I thought, that would make a fine spade for clearing the snow in winter. They used to give us bloody useless spades, so I decided I'd make a decent one myself. I sawed off two corners or broke them off and bent the third up. I drilled a hole, riveted one corner back on itself to make it stronger, and bunged on a handle. There, I had a spade – that's the way a real worker works. It might look like it's good for nothing, but when I started clearing snow I really appreciated it. It turned out to be really useful. We were in a very heavy district, Kutuzovsky Prospect, everyone zooming past in their big Mercs. They couldn't give a damn that you're working, scraping up the snow. Just step on the gas down the Prospect – the bastards don't even give you time to dodge. I got fed up with it and started holding up the face of the spade to them, vertical, so they could see the sign. Well, some of them braked a bit, but the ones in the biggest hurry rushed along the same as ever. Twice it was a miracle I got out from under their wheels. Bastards! You're clearing away the snow for them, and they... I used this spade to clear away the snow in 1998 and the beginning of 1999.

Road sign, wooden handle, rivets

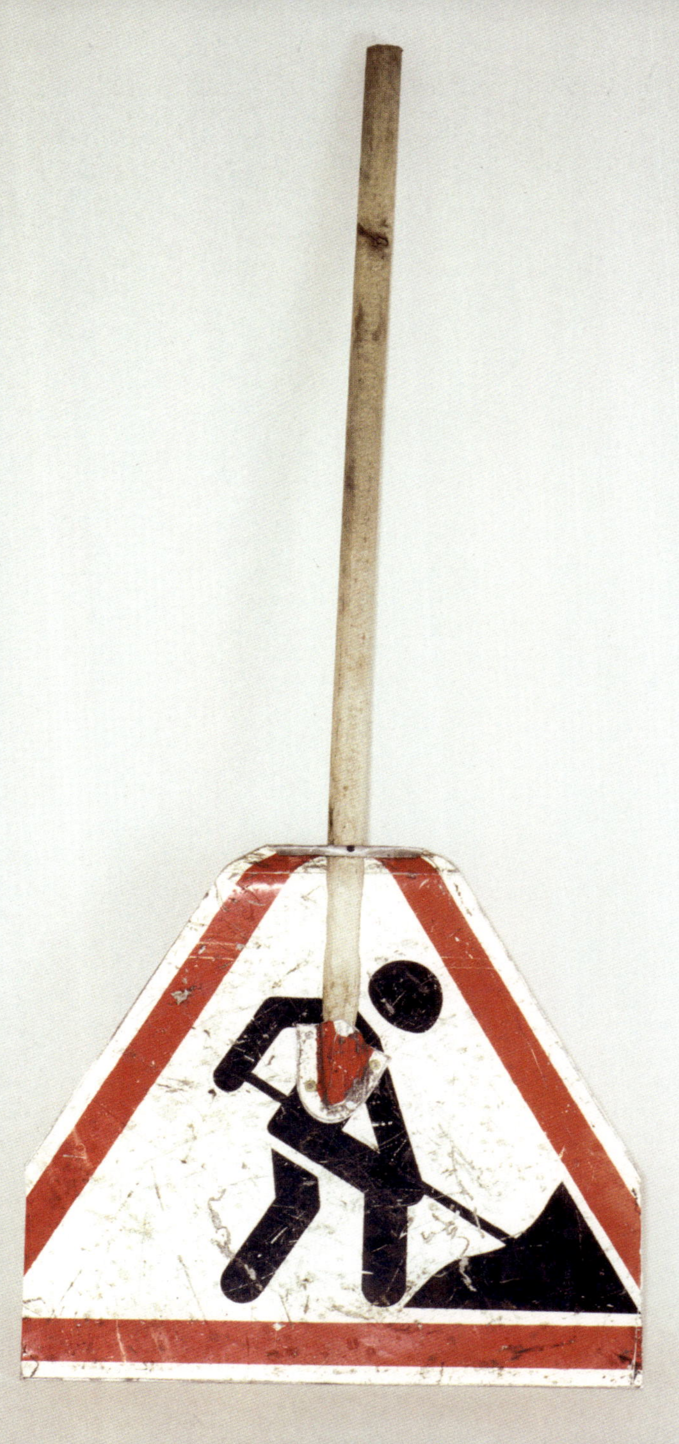

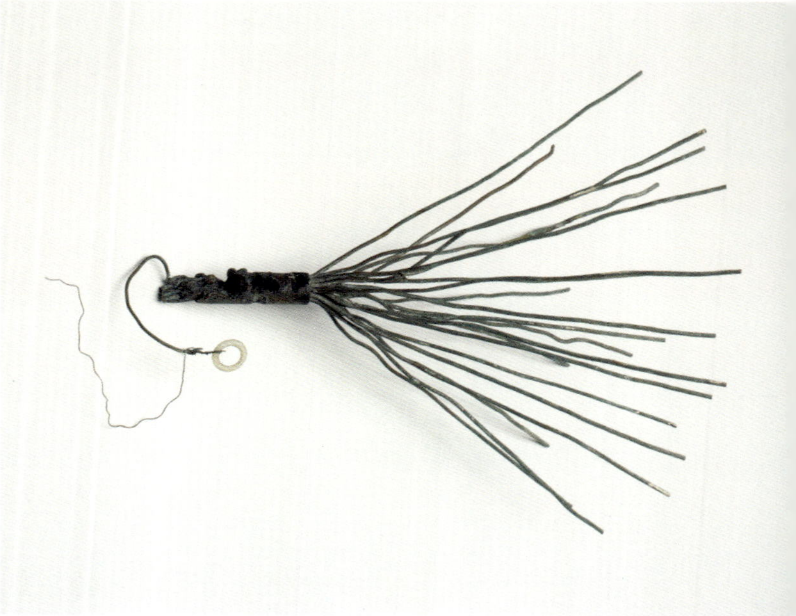

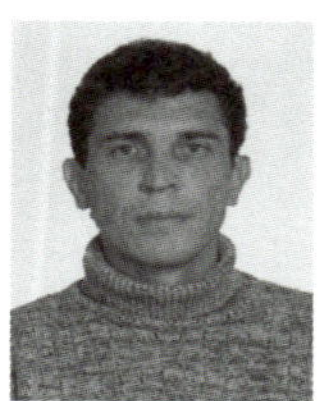

**Anton Kalashnikov**     Tver region, 1995

We bought a television but there was no aerial. We couldn't go all the way into town for one. We used to have a television and an aerial in Bishkek. We had everything set up there, lived a decent life, like everyone else. But when they broke up the Soviet Union life got hard for Russians everywhere. So we had to move away from trouble too. We sold everything down there, the flat and everything we owned, for silly money. Anything to get away. And here we had to build from scratch, 80 kilometres from town. You can't go driving into town for every little thing and you can make an aerial for yourself – if you really want one and you have something handy you can use. I happened to have some copper wire – that's what I made it from. It shows the first and second channels OK.

Copper wire

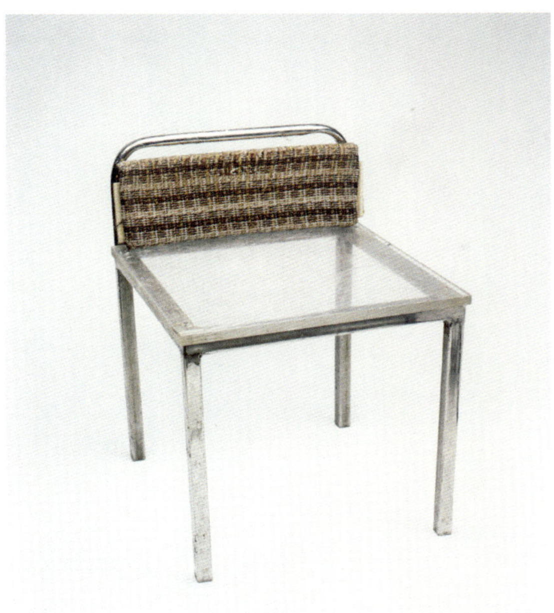

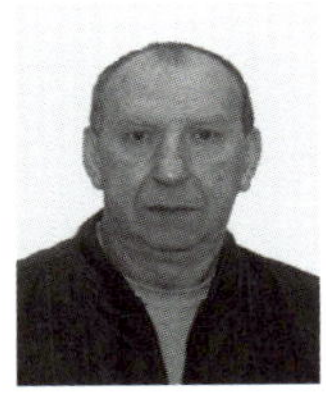

**Anatoly Uvarov**                                        Moscow, 1993

The chair was very easy to make. There's a big rubbish tip right beside us
here. They bring garbage there from all over the district and next to it there's
a school, a hospital, a fire station, a pumping station, blocks of flats, garages.
When I walk to the garage I always walk past it, and if there's anything that's
any good I take it and make good use of it. So anyway, when I look I see this
shiny frame lying there, from a chair, or maybe a locker. I welded a back onto
it, a soft back that I picked up on the same rubbish tip, and I cut the acrylic to
size – I still had some left from when I used to work in the factory – and then
I had a chair that'll last forever, like as not. It won't burn, it won't rot, it won't
fall apart – and that's just the kind I need for the garage – solid and reliable.

Metal, acrylic, fabric

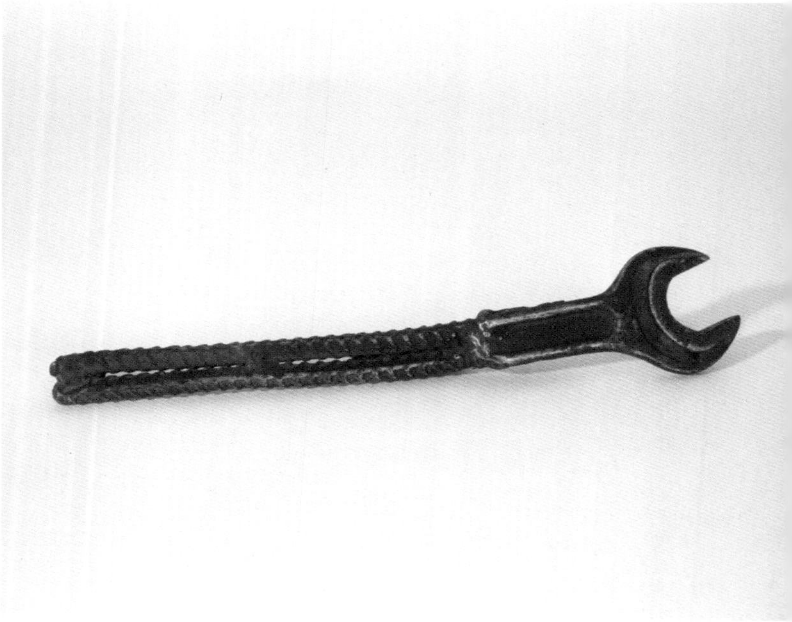

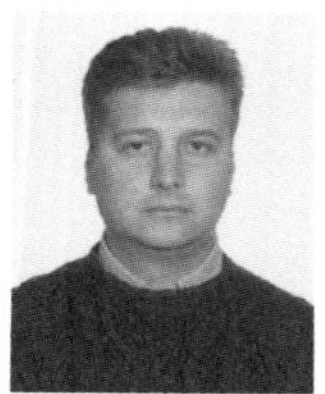

**Vasilii Nazarov**                                    Ivanov region, 1996

There's not much to say, it's a crying shame. They don't pay you anything, there aren't any spares, so you get round things the best way you can. I was unfastening something and the nut wouldn't move. I hit the spanner with a hammer and it broke. Made of pretty weak metal apparently. You'll never get a new spanner out of our boss, and so I welded it.

Spanner, steel

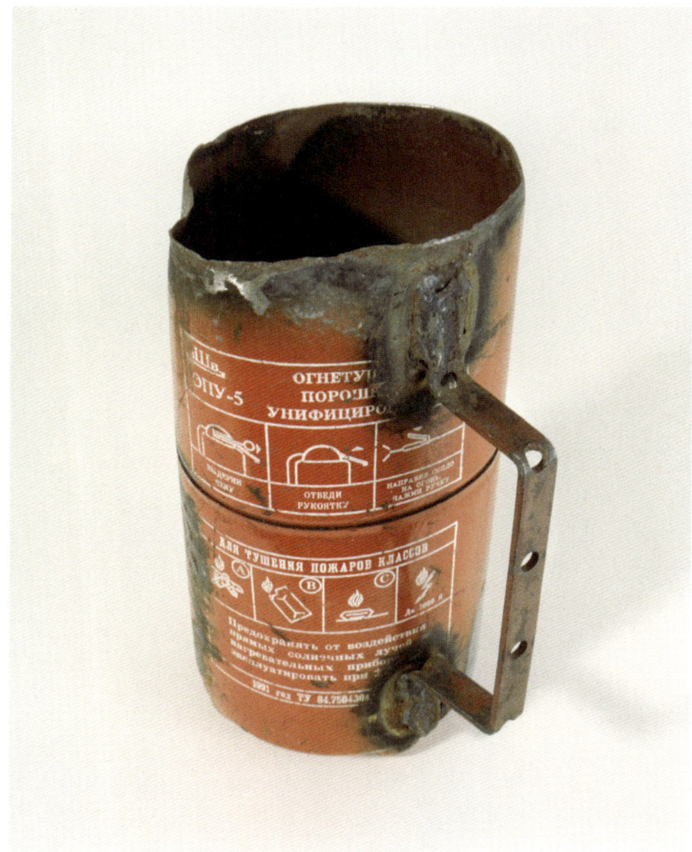

**Vasilii Nazarov**                    Ivanov region, 1995

That year they gave me a 'Kirovets' tractor. It's a good tractor, but it guzzles no end of oil, and getting under it to put the oil in is awkward. It's OK at the filling station – just stick the hose in and there's no problem – but when I'm out in the field or somewhere else it's really awkward. I tried doing it this way and that way but I always kept missing. There was an old used fire extinguisher lying around in our workshops, so I cut off its nozzle and welded on the metal bar for a handle. It holds just the right amount – not too much, not too little – just right, so I don't have to go climbing underneath with a fuel can and a funnel.

Fire extinguisher, metal bar

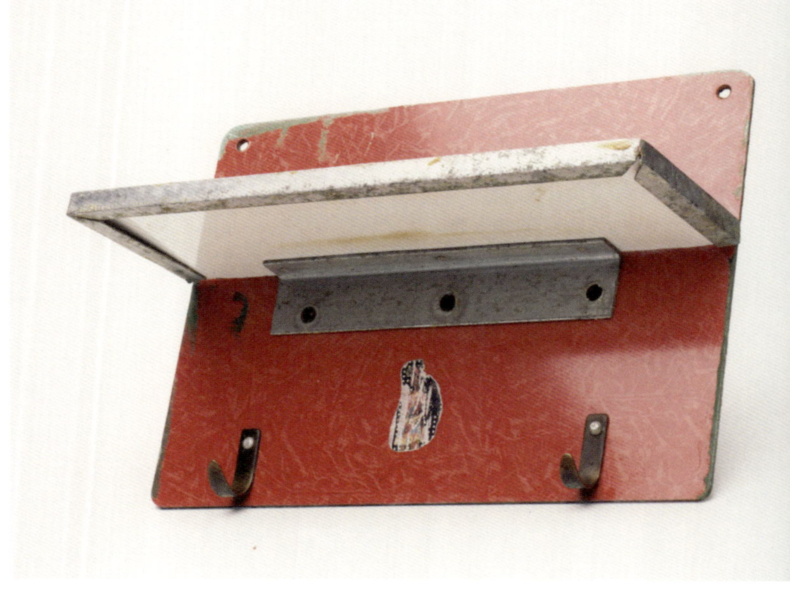

**Vasilii Nazarov**                                    Ivanov region, 1996

There has to be a shelf in the bathroom, doesn't there? There does. So I made one. Nothing to make really. I bent some hooks and riveted them on. We brought the plastic from town for the workshops, so the lads could learn how to work with it in their craftwork classes. We have bits and pieces of metal left over. I chose pieces that wouldn't rust and didn't have to be painted. The shelf turned out perfect. There's nothing in the shops here except vodka, sprats and rubber boots. When the district trade office used to run it, they had goods to sell, but no one cares about us now, I suppose.

Galvanised metal, perspex, hooks, rivets

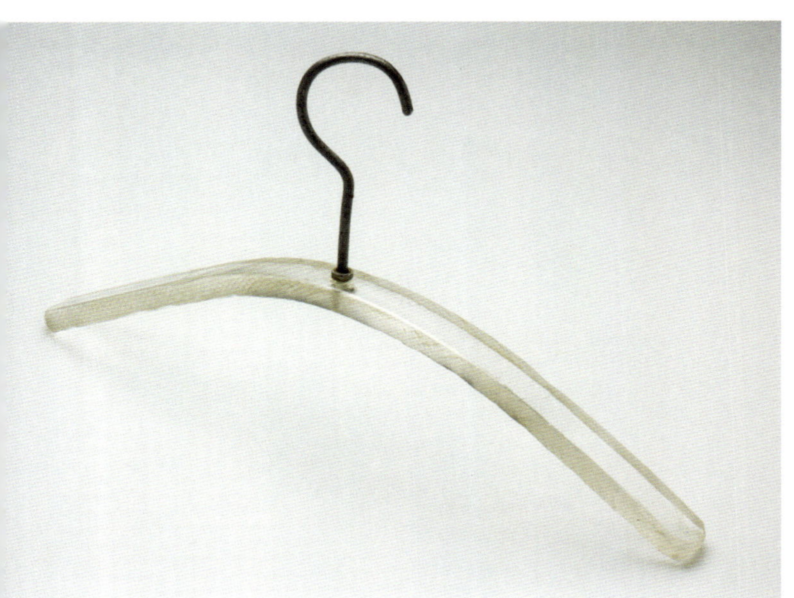

**Anonymous**                                     Moscow, pre-1998

*As recounted by Georgy Nikich:* If you haven't got a coat-hanger like this then take it for your collection. Of course I didn't make it, I found it here in the workshop. Somebody left it behind. It's hard to say who it belongs to, or even who you might ask.

Perspex, steel

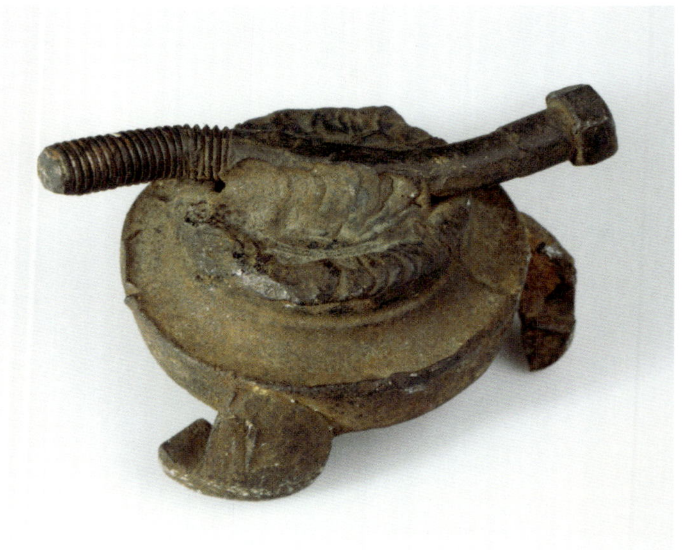

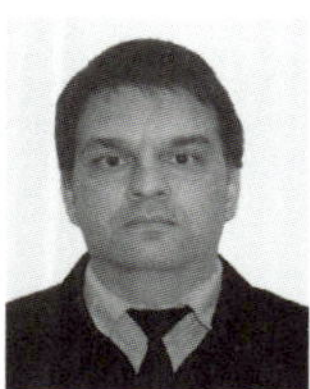

**Oleg Surkov**                                        Vladimir, 1994

As part of my job I have to check the condition of the fire hydrants and the mains, to make sure everything works in case there's a fire. I go round opening and closing the covers, tightening up the nuts and the valves. This hydrant is in a spot that's wet – well, not wet, but damp – for some reason there's always water on the floor there. As far as a fire's concerned that's good, nothing's going to catch fire, but the pipes there were always rusty. When we check them we unscrew the cover, attach the hoses, open the fire hydrant and the water flows. Then the same thing in the opposite direction, and we screw the cover back on. But this one was rusted on. I hit it with a hammer, and the handle fell off. But I had to unscrew it, so I welded on a bolt with an electric welder. As soon as the bolt was solid, I gave it a careful tap with the hammer and the cover turned. We attached the hoses, pumped the water through, took them off again, and screwed the cover back on.

Steel bolt

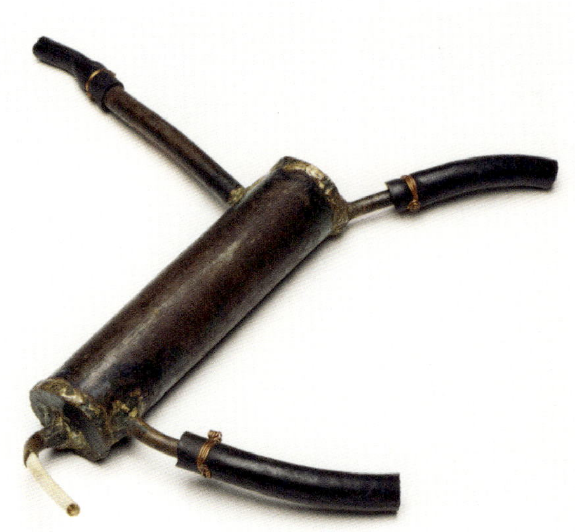

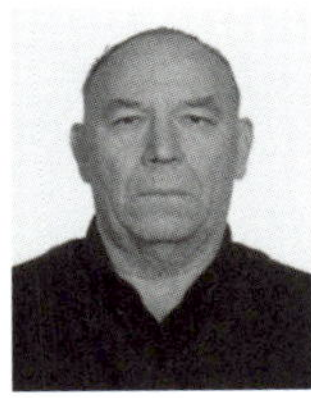

**Nikolai Smolensky**          Nizhny Novgorod, 1985

It's just an ordinary coil. Haven't you ever seen one before? Ah, it's a shame I'm not distilling right now, or I'd show you what connects to what and how the vodka's made. As it happens, this is the most important part of a home-brew still – the very heart of it, you might say. It's a large diameter piece of copper pipe and inside that you put a narrow copper pipe, twisted into a spiral so that it holds more liquid. The ends of the big pipe – not really a pipe, more like a cylinder – are soldered shut. But two holes are made in it for welding on a piece of pipe – for feeding in cold water. What happens is that the hot steam with the vodka in it goes through the coil, and the coil is cooled by the cold water in this cylinder, so that the steam condenses and you get your home-brew. I made it when Gorbachev was trying to ban vodka. It must have been 1985. That's some idea – banning vodka in Russia! Our folk know what they're about: they'll distil it from sawdust if they have to!

Copper pipe

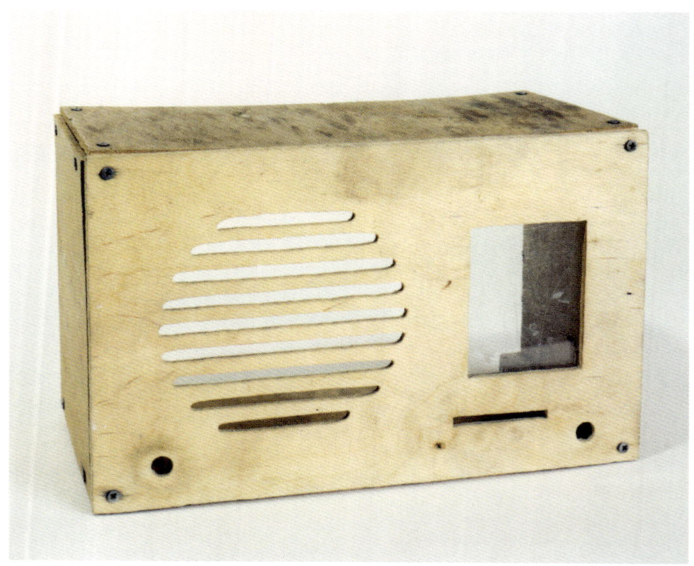

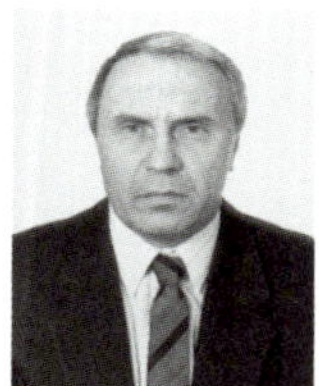

**Andrei Petrov**                                              Kaluga, c.1975

This was when I was planning to teach my son about radios. He was at school then, about twelve or fourteen years old, and he didn't seem to be interested in anything much. So I wanted at least to get him interested in radios. In those days they still didn't teach anything about radios in school, and I started telling him a bit about transmitters and waves and receivers and so on – how it all works. I used to bring home from work valves, diodes and resistors and explain all their functions. We started building a frame for a receiver – we had to assemble all the parts in something. We made the frame out of plywood... and then my patience gave out. He wasn't interested in the whole business, and I suppose it isn't possible to force someone to be interested in anything. Anyway, I couldn't do it. But thank God, he managed to finish college and developed an interest in life. And so this box has just been lying around – I've been wanting to make something out of it, but never got around to it.

Plywood, screws

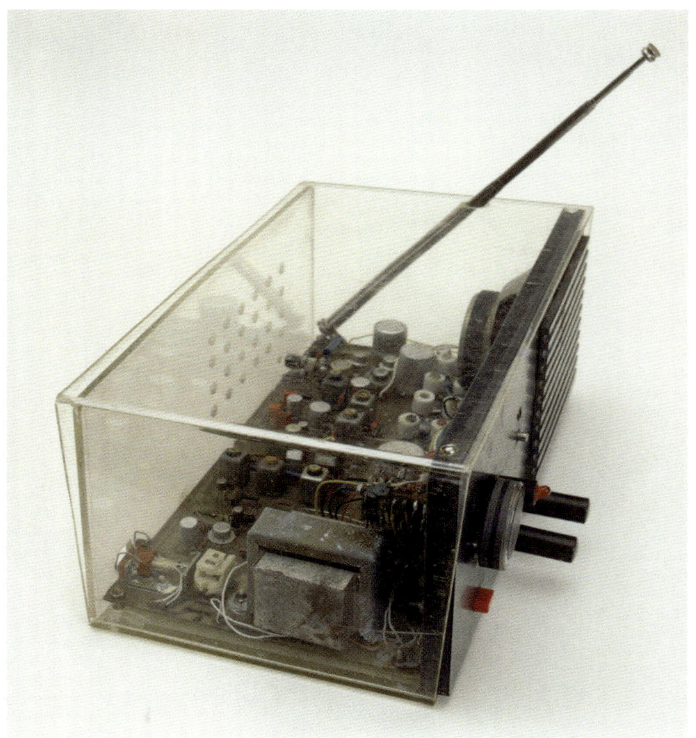

**Andrei Petrov**Kaluga, c.1974

I suppose you could say this is a remnant of my enthusiasm for design. I saw a clock with a transparent case somewhere, and I decided to make a transparent box for a short wave radio receiver. There weren't any then, and with a radio like that you could listen to the *Voice of America*, and to jazz and other music – we were young then and everything was interesting. Fortunately acrylic plastic had already appeared in our secret factory. We had all the other components in our design office, or at least it was possible to find them. Compared with a long wave receiver, this short wave one was a lot harder to tune and of course its circuits were a lot more complex. It was my pride and joy, and we kept it on display. It worked until just recently, for thirty years. I've had to replace a few bits, to repair it. This all seems incredible and ridiculous now, after you've seen the Chinese radios in the shops. There's so much of everything now, it's hard to understand the way we lived then. And how we should live now.

Acrylic, radio components

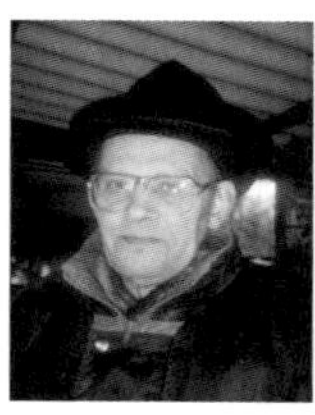

**Konstantin Kiselyov**                                        Nizhny Novgorod, 1979

At forty-eight I had my first heart attack, then three years later I had my second and then several years later, my third. Well, three heart attacks and all three due to work. I worked as the boss of a laboratory where I had to deal with stressful situations every day. I was officially recognised as an invalid eight years ago. I'm fifty-nine now. We don't get any financial assistance from anyone, apart from a small pension. So because of this, it becomes necessary to earn money to live on. I'm an old radio ham – I've got a load of old stuff here, left over from those days. Most of its going onto the dump – none of my relatives would be interested in inheriting it. What's left is all in parts. I've had this box all my life. The small parts go straight in here and other parts in there – everything gets chucked into its own section. The transistors, the resistors, capacitors, diodes – that kind of small stuff. Because, firstly, if this system goes wrong then it doesn't take a long time to replace it. You stick in a new one and it costs nothing. When it wears out you make a new one. You get some ordinary office glue and glue it on – most importantly, it's cheap.

Matchboxes, glue

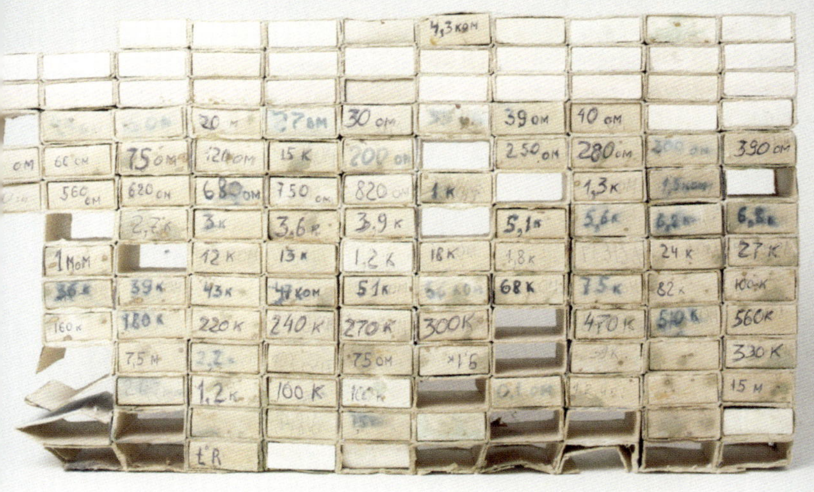

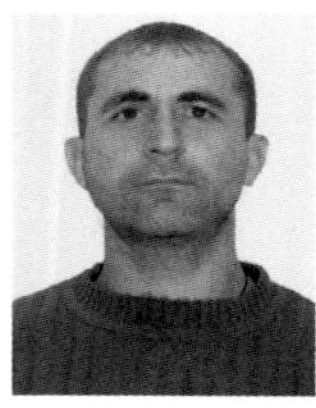

**Said Magidov**                                    Moscow, 1996

This is my little trolley. I don't know what I would do without it. It's the only thing that keeps me fed. I can't carry much by myself, so I need a trolley. I picked up the wheels from different prams on the rubbish tip, and a friend helped me weld the metal. God grant him good health! I can tie on the load with rope and carry as much as I like.

There's no work at home and I have to feed my children. All the work's in Moscow now, which is why we're here. We help people to bring in and send away whatever they need. All the stations in Moscow are divided up: some have Azeris, some have Armenians, some have Tatars. I've been here five years already – at the Kiev Station.

Steel, pram wheels

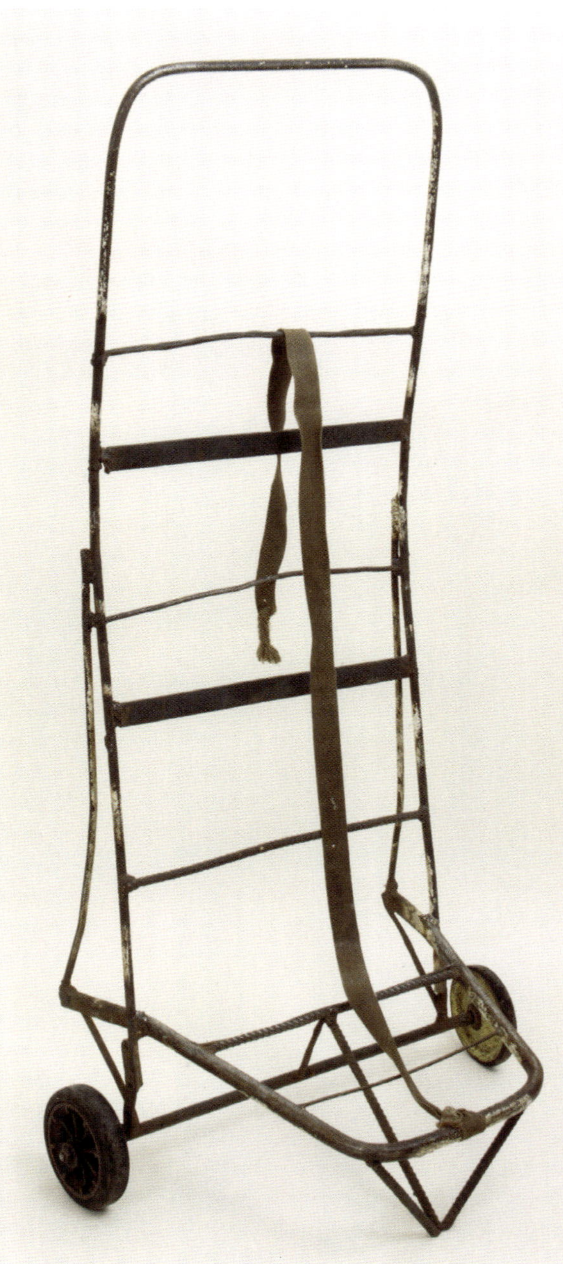

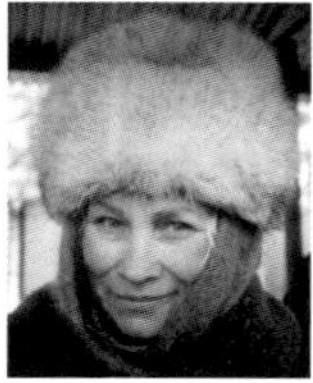

**Nina Kotova**                                           Moscow region, 1998

I'm a woman on my own. I don't ask for a man's help more than I need to, because I don't like to feel obligated. Of course, it's tough in the village without a man – getting the firewood in, fixing the fence, digging the vegetable patch – it's really hard without him. I buried my husband five years back, and I haven't found another one yet. Where would you find one here? They're all dead now, every last one of them. So I get on with things myself. I hammer nails in myself and kill chickens myself too, but when it comes to chopping wood, I hire men for that, any who happen to be around.

It's very snowy in winter, and I have to go out into the yard. At the very least I have to clear a path to the chickens and the firewood. I had an old shovel, but it broke, and a new one has to be paid for. Where would I get the money? You have to count every last kopeck. So I thought: what can I make a shovel out of? I had this old bread board, and this pipe left over from an old vacuum cleaner. I fastened on the board – and there was the shovel. You can't really call it a shovel exactly, but I can clear up the snow in the yard, scrape it off the roof and clean up a bit beside the house – that's all I need. I don't go anywhere, just to the neighbour's house and back. No one clears the snow away in winter here, not like they do in the town. They just clear a bit for themselves, and for the postman, so the snow won't cause him too much trouble. Oh, the poor man has a hard time of it in winter.

Plywood bread board, vacuum-cleaner pipe, nails, screws, wood, insulating tape

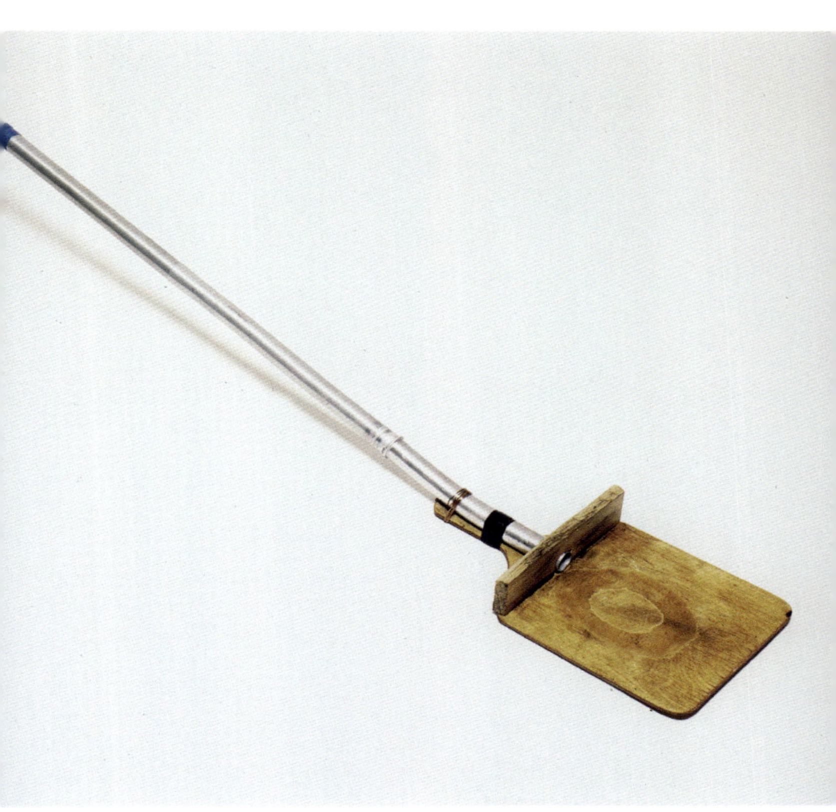

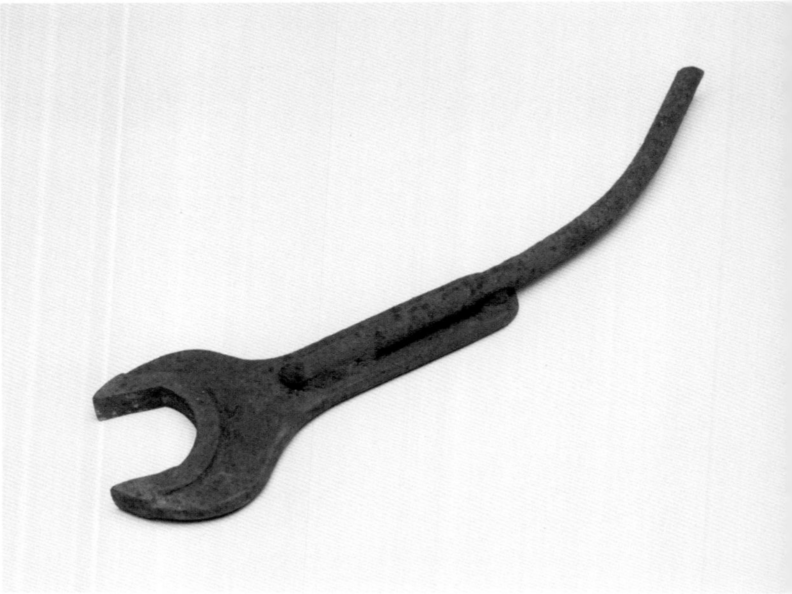

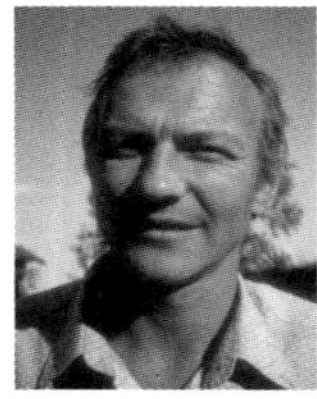

**Sergei Volkov**　　　　　　　　　　　　　　Tula region, 1988

It's an ordinary spanner for a tractor. They gave me the tractor at the collective farm, and a tractor ought to come with a set of tools for servicing it – different spanners, a hammer, a sledge hammer and all the rest of it. But what's normal round here? You see 'prick' written on a fence, but it's still a fence after all. The same thing here. Never mind what ought to be there, never mind what it says... there were two spanners there, size 16 and size 24, I think it was. How was I supposed to get a wheel off when the nuts are a different size? This piece of metal welded on to it is to give it more leverage. Just you try unscrewing those nuts the way they usually are – they're stuck tight. You can't turn them with a short spanner, and you have to screw them back on tight. That's why I made the handle longer. But even then, I'm never strong enough – I have to hammer it – look, it's bent there.

Spanner, steel

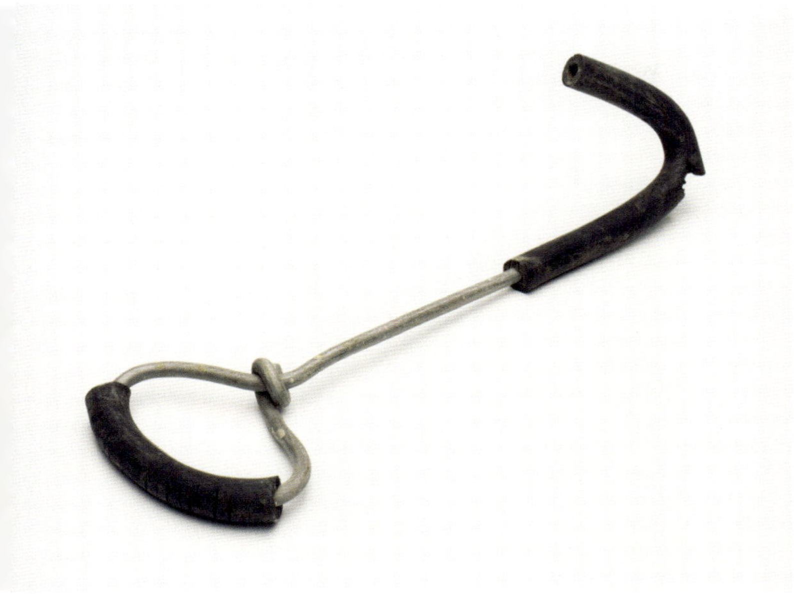

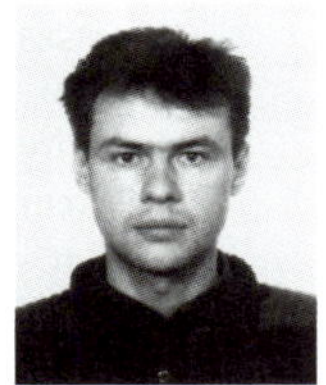

**Andrei Petrov**                                      Moscow, 1997

A hook. I made it for carrying around glass. When you cut glass, you can't always pick it up with your hands that easily. You can move it a bit, but if you have to take it somewhere it's easier with the hook. You stand the glass on the hook, hold it with one hand and use your shoulder, hold the hook in your other hand and carry it.

Metal wire, rubber pipe

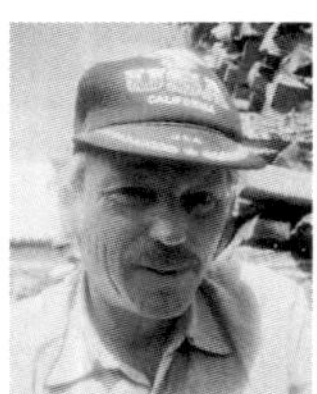

**Nikolai Karpov**                              Onega, Arkhangelsk region, 1997

It's just a chimney. A chimney for a smoking shed. I'm building a smoking shed just now, to smoke fish and meat for the winter. And that's the chimney – all I have to do now is set it in place and secure it. Why a bucket? Well, what else would do the job? So I used a bucket. It's an old bucket which had a hole in it, so I riveted it on. And the pipe, I found that at the state farm, from a combine harvester probably.

Metal pipe, bucket, rivets

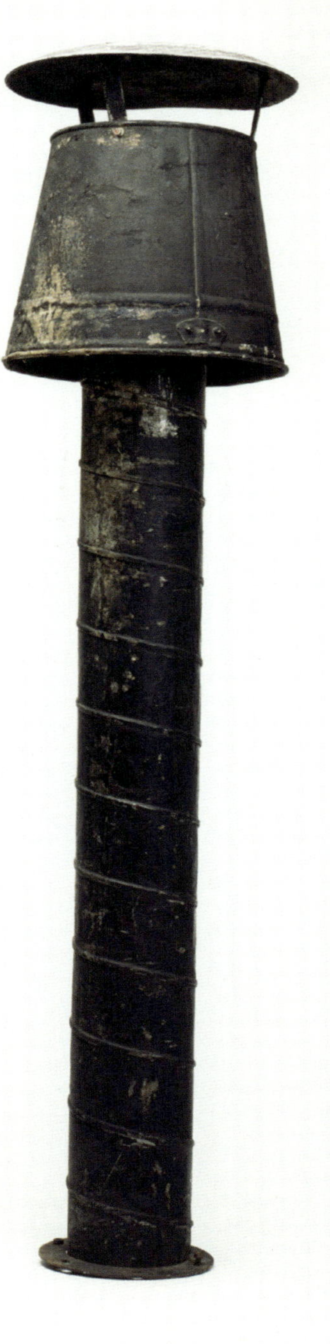

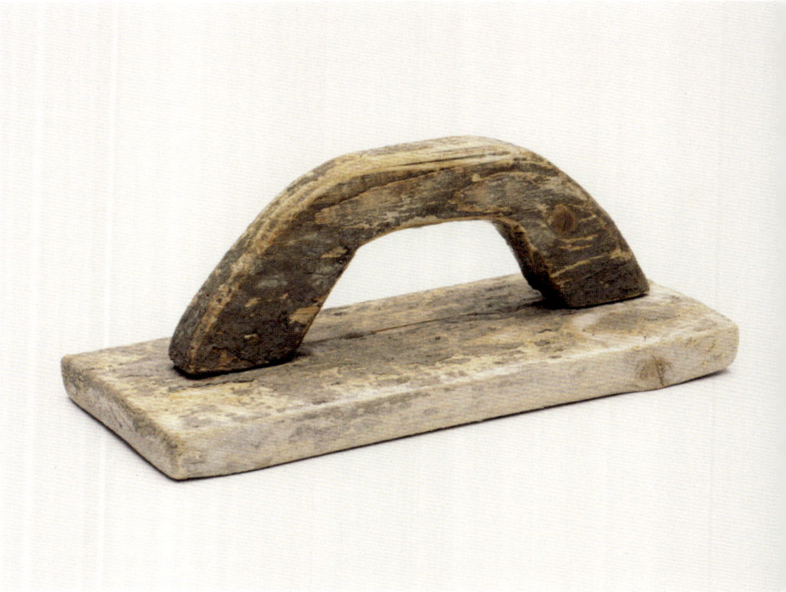

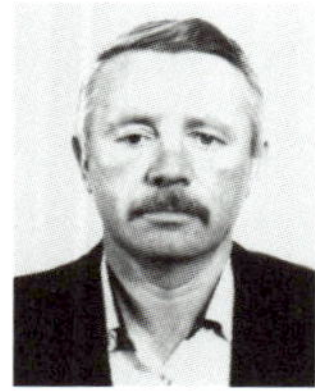

**Nikolai Serov**                                         Tver, 1996

We'd moved into this new flat and I had to do something about the walls. I've never seen such crooked walls in my life. Whoever built it should have had their hands cut off! Moldovans or some such. I took a plank, sawed a bit off, cut out a handle and nailed it on, and then I had a float – not a big one, but I didn't need it any bigger. I'm not a plasterer, but I remembered from my army days when I was doing my service, we built a dacha for a colonel and that's where I learned how to do it. I don't use it now, but it might come in handy some day so I keep it.

Wood, nails

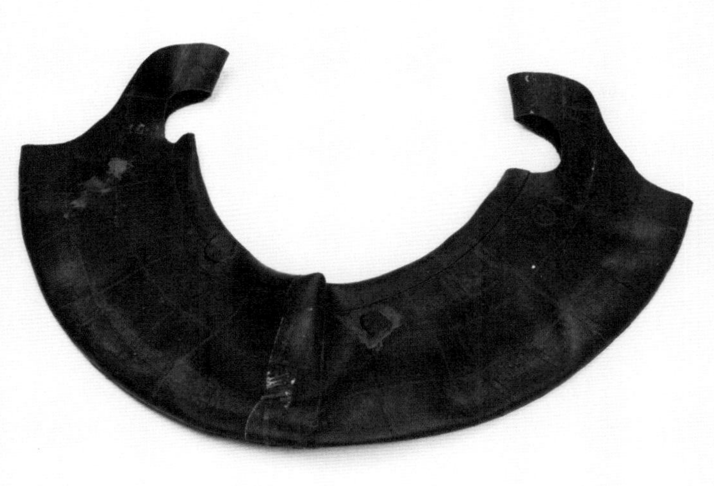

**Nikolai Serov**                                                          Tver, 1998

It's a really handy item and really easy to make. You take an old inner tube
from any wheel and cut off the part with the hole in it. Then you cut out
handles and you have your bucket! It's light, doesn't take up any space —
throw it in the boot and away you go! The only thing that's awkward about it
is you can't stand it on the ground, but it's OK for scooping up water and
washing the car, and all sorts of other things. All the cars round here have
them. Why buy it when you can make it yourself?

Rubber inner tube

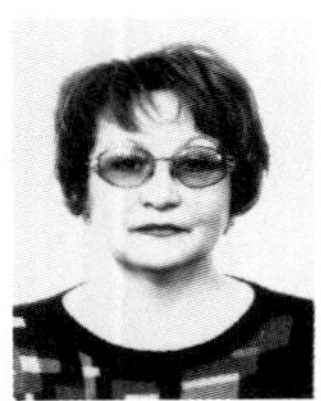

**Nina Gorshkova**
Moscow region, 1997

We have a holiday camp that has a big canteen with over a hundred people eating together at the same time. The tables each take four people and there are sixty tables altogether. Each holidaymaker has a table reserved for them with a unique number. So that people can get their bearings quickly and spot their tables from a distance, we have number signs from one to sixty standing on the tables. We had these numbers specially made at a factory, but somehow number '38' disappeared. They are my responsibility, so I had to do something to put things right. The numbers are made of stainless steel so '38' had to be made of stainless steel too. I found part of a broken masher for making mashed potatoes, and asked a welder to make the number, the same kind as the ones we have standing on our tables. I gave him my part and he welded a disc to the top. We painted the numbers on ourselves.

Potato masher, steel, paint

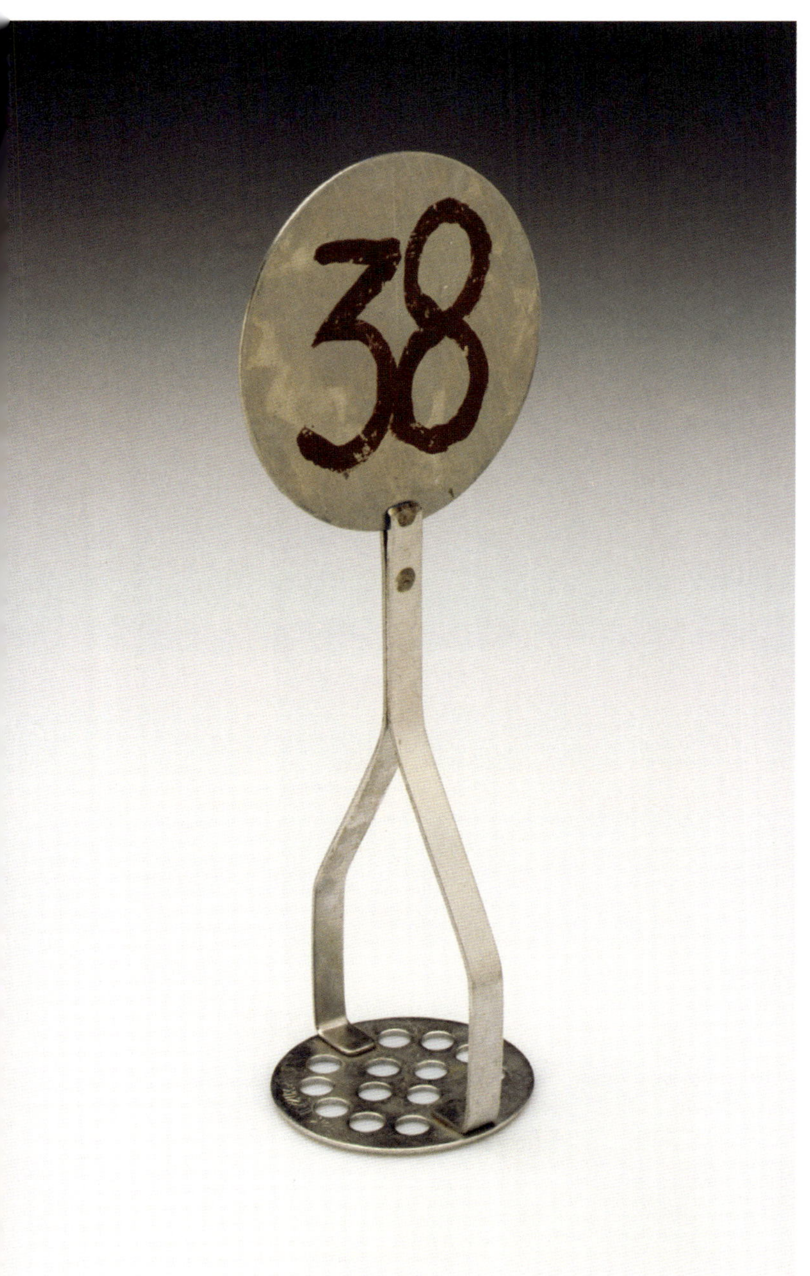


38

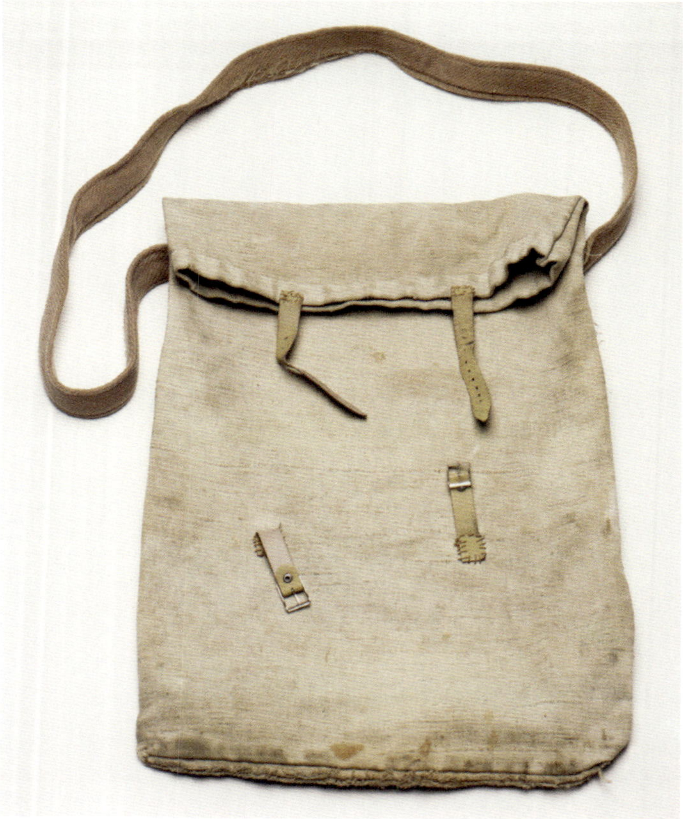

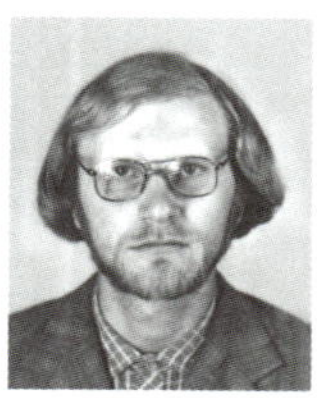

**Pyotr Yevgenievich**                    Moscow, c.1990

Well, it's like the sack was already sewn. I just added these handles. The straps are from watches that I had worn until they broke. The shoulder strap is just a belt from an old coat. At work I had to drag junk from floor to floor or a load of bottles – you could stuff a load of bottles in this bag.

Canvas sack, thread, watch straps, coat belt

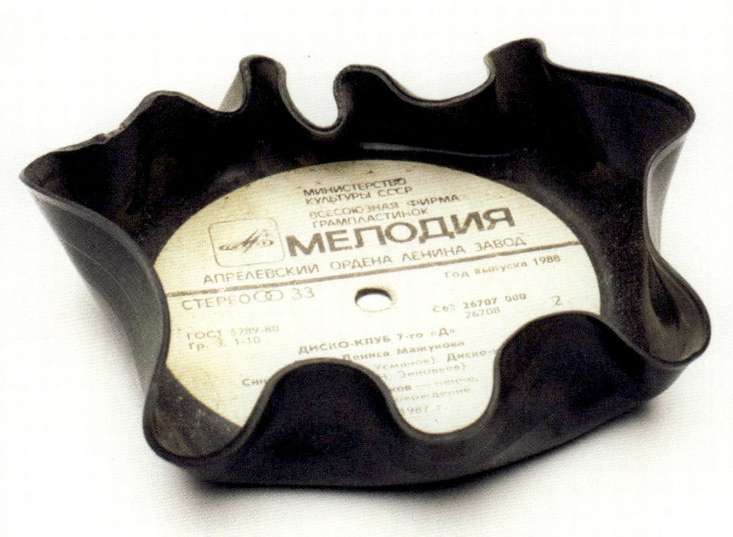

## Svetlana

Moscow, 1997

*As recounted by her husband Pyotr Yevgenievich (pictured left):* Flowers
stand in it, you know, that kind of thing. Well, it's moisture proofed. This
hole is like those you find on the bottom of a flowerpot, so that the surplus
water flows out into the saucer or into the surrounding space. You can plant
stuff there. My wife made it. She got hold of an old record which no one
wanted, and which was worn out. This was made not so long ago.

Vinyl record

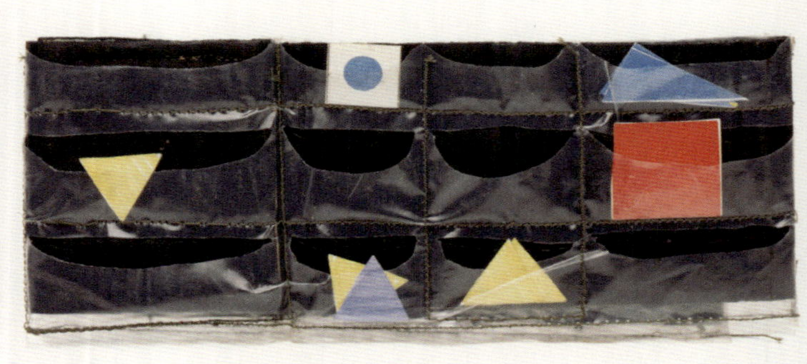

## Svetlana

Moscow, 1994

*As recounted by her husband Pyotr Yevgenievich:* This is what you could call a numbers sheet, for teaching a child to count. My wife made it when our little girl started the first class at school. The numbers are represented by different colours and shapes, so that she could find the number she wanted easily. I cut the numbers out of coloured paper.

Cloth, plastic, thread, coloured paper

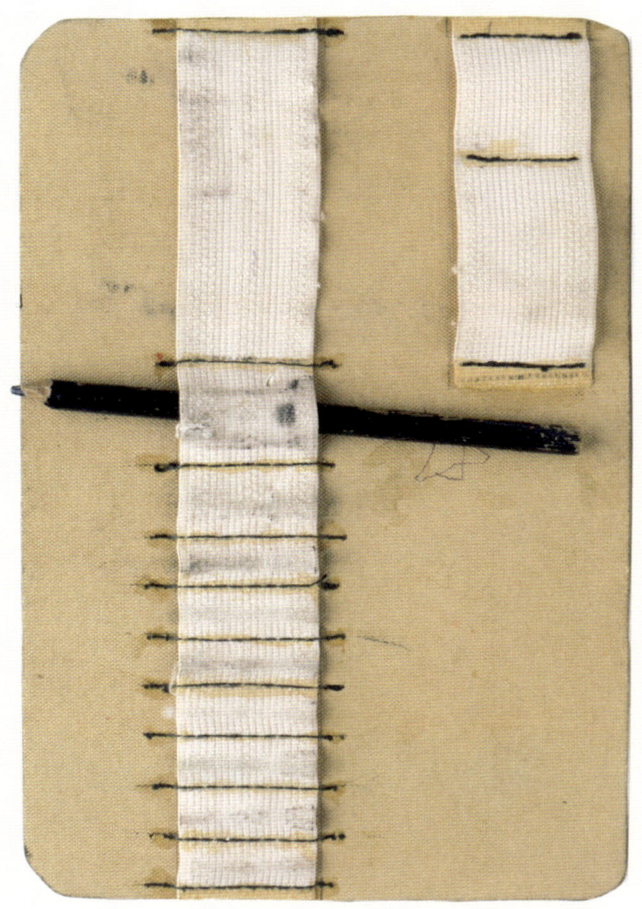

## Svetlana

Moscow, 1994

*As recounted by her husband Pyotr Yevgenievich:* This is just a child's school pencil case. The pencils go in here, pens in here and in here go, say, cards with figures and letters. My wife made it on an ordinary sewing machine, but the material is very fine. It's very simple – she picked up her thimble and sewed it.

Cardboard, elastic band, thread

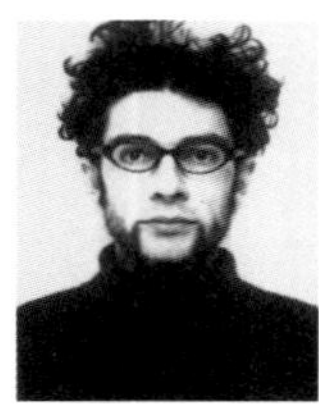

**Jan Kalnberzin**  Moscow region, 1991

This was my first guitar. My school classmate Shurochka Finogenova lent it to me and I promised to give it back. It got taken to the dacha, where my dad sat on it. I put it on the bed and he sat on it by accident, breaking the sound box. All that was left of that lousy fucking Leningrad guitar was the fingerboard and the bridge. Nothing else. I realised I couldn't give it back in that condition, and I wanted to play it. So I put this guitar together out of whatever I could lay my hands on – rough bits of wood I found at the dacha. I couldn't take proper pieces of board from my father, things that were meant for shelves, for instance. Just look how elegantly the fingerboard is attached! Of course, if I tried putting in a nail and it wouldn't go, I just hammered another one in right next to it. I wasn't concerned with aesthetics back then – that's probably why it turned out looking so brutal. It was an ordinary acoustic guitar once, about ten years ago. I realised I'd never manage to play it the normal way, so I made it for playing like a crazy bastard. The sound it makes is wild – you can never tell what it'll do next. But it turns me on and I like it.

Wood, nails, string, guitar parts

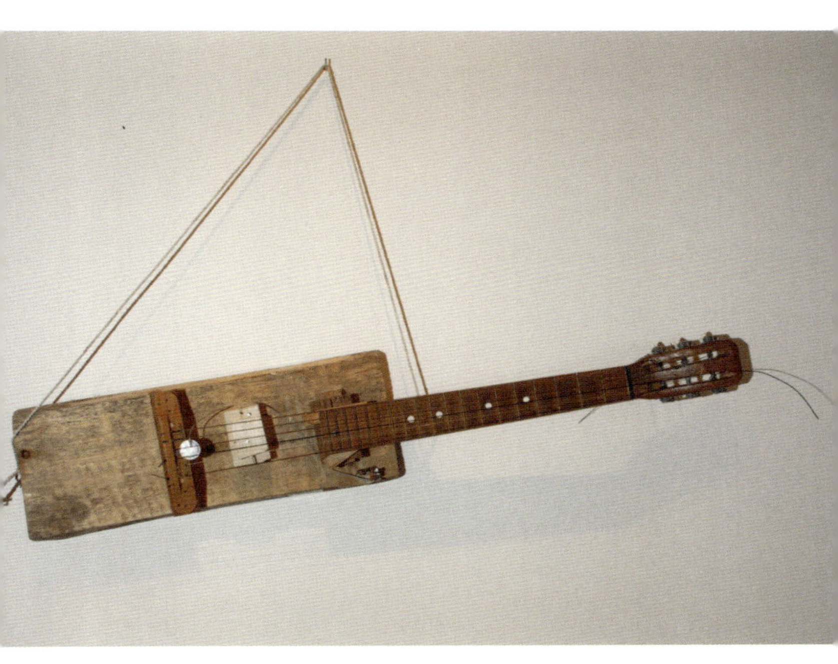

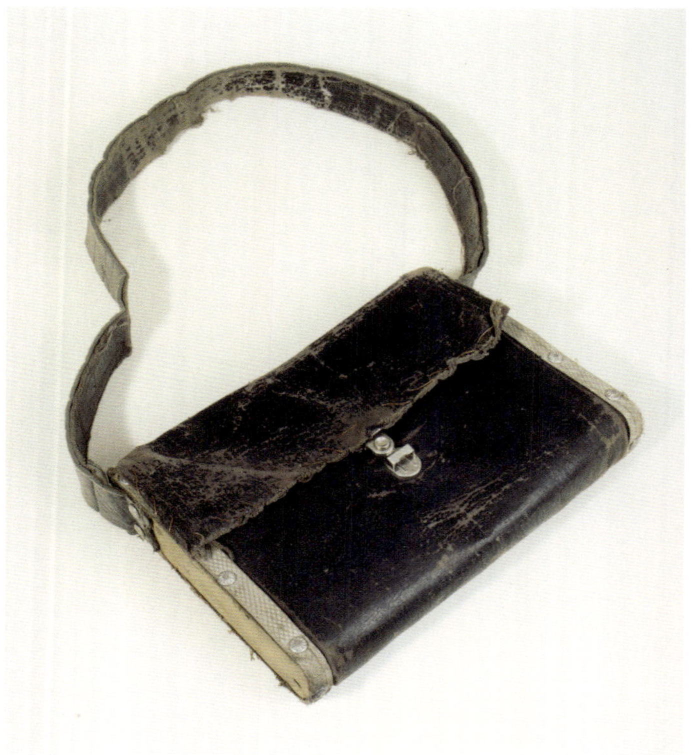

**Pyotr Gritsenya**                                        Rostov region, 1993

I made this when I used to go down the pit, in the Rostov region. There's no work there now. We used to do a normal job and get paid for it, but it's all stopped now, everybody's gone and I made for Moscow. I used to work as an electrician down the mine – putting in lights, connecting up all sorts of electrical gear, there was plenty to do. You're usually using a screwdriver, pliers, insulating tape and wire. They used to give us these big bags which were too awkward to drag around with you everywhere. What you needed was a little bag, something handy and light, so you could get through everywhere with it. So I made this one. It keeps its shape – the side panels are made of wood and this is imitation leather. It tears easily of course, but I can rip it off and tack on a new piece using ordinary furniture tacks I hammer into the wood.

Imitation leather, clasp, wood, tacks

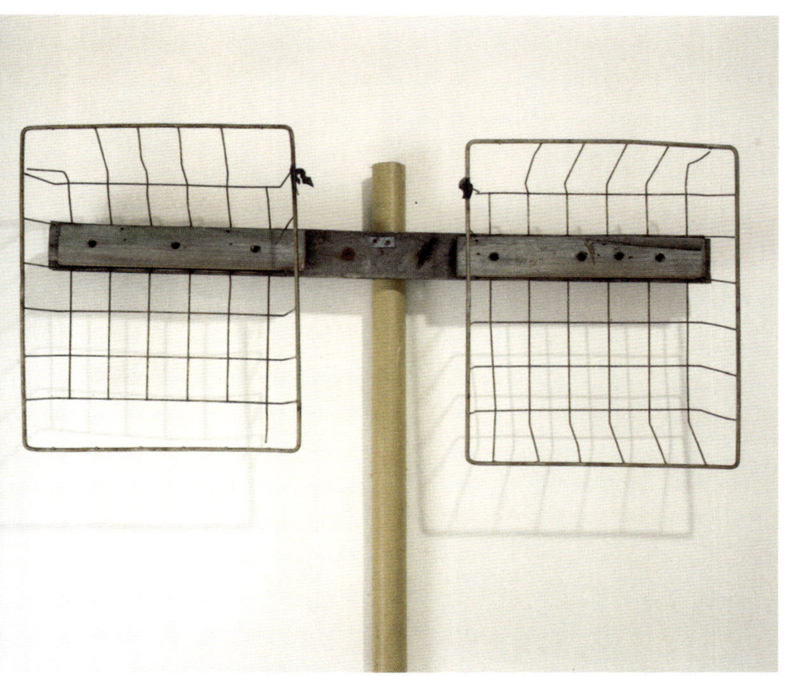

**Pyotr Gritsenya**                                        Moscow, 1996

This was the first aerial I made, but it didn't work properly. I found these baskets on the rubbish tip. The shops used them to sell vegetables. They look like they're made of steel, which doesn't pick up a signal like aluminium does. So when I found an aluminium disk and made a new aerial, I threw the old one out. Well, I didn't throw it out, but I switched the cable to that one with the iron *(overleaf)*.

Steel baskets, wood, screws

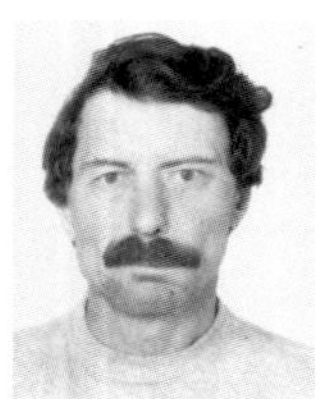

**Pyotr Gritsenya**                                    Moscow, 1996

Round here we live where we can and work until it gets dark. But sometimes you have a free moment and you want to amuse yourself with something, maybe even just watch TV. I found a TV here on the dump, only a black and white one. All I had to do was change a resistor and make some kind of aerial. I found this old iron and aluminium disc in the same place. Aluminium gives a good reception, so I connected them and that was it. The guys got the cable from somewhere or other, then we had an aerial. We watch it in the evening, or in the afternoon if someone's ill or injured. But as we don't have any medical insurance here and they won't take us in the hospital, it's best not to get ill.

Iron, aluminium, bracket, cable

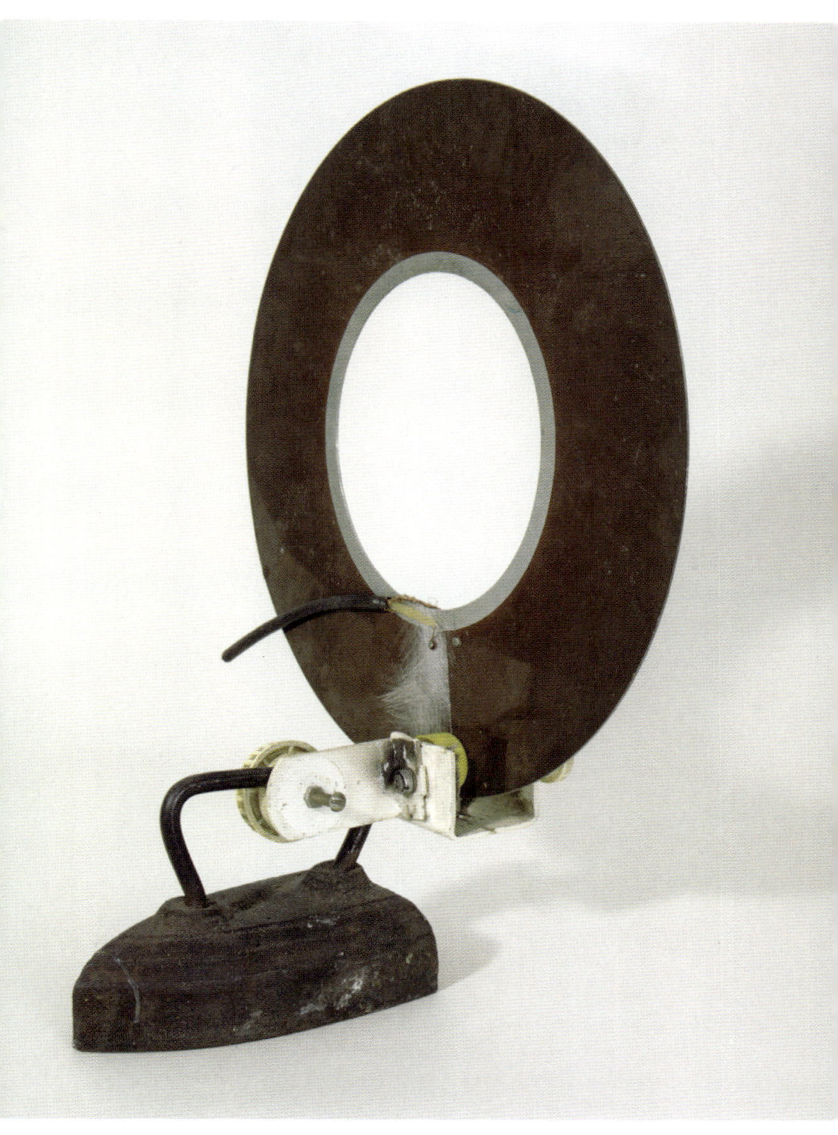

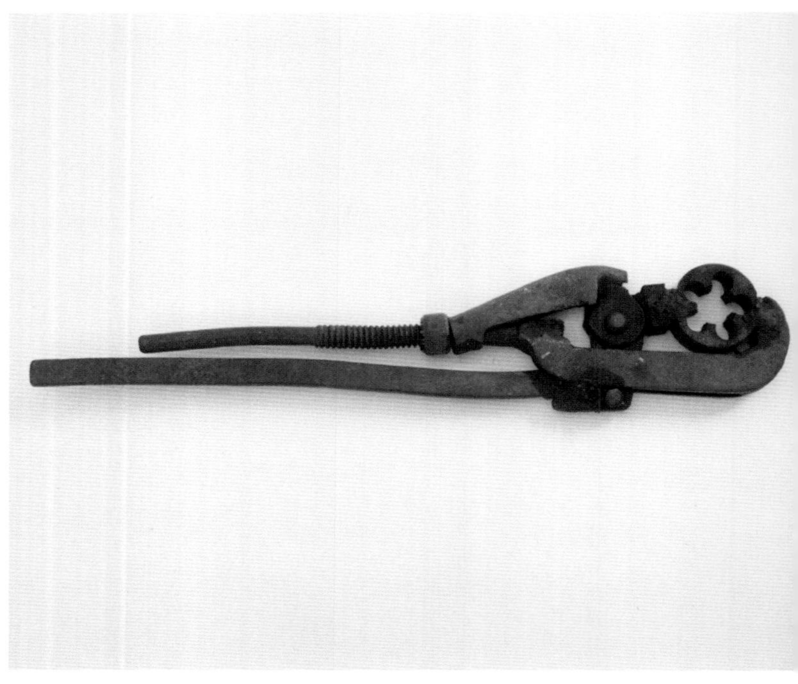

**Pyotr Gritsenya**                                        Moscow, 1996

We've been in Moscow for about a year now. They pay me, thank God. I'm listed as an electrician, but in reality you do what they tell you, otherwise they can sack you or not pay you. I don't lay bricks – I mostly work on secondary jobs, making moulds and connecting up the services, water mains or sewerage. I'm a carpenter, a plumber and an electrician – all my tools are my own. I've got screwdrivers, pliers and a knife. Once I needed to cut a thread and I'd nothing to do it with but my bare hands. Nobody cared that I didn't have a die – so I had to find something and make it myself.

Steel

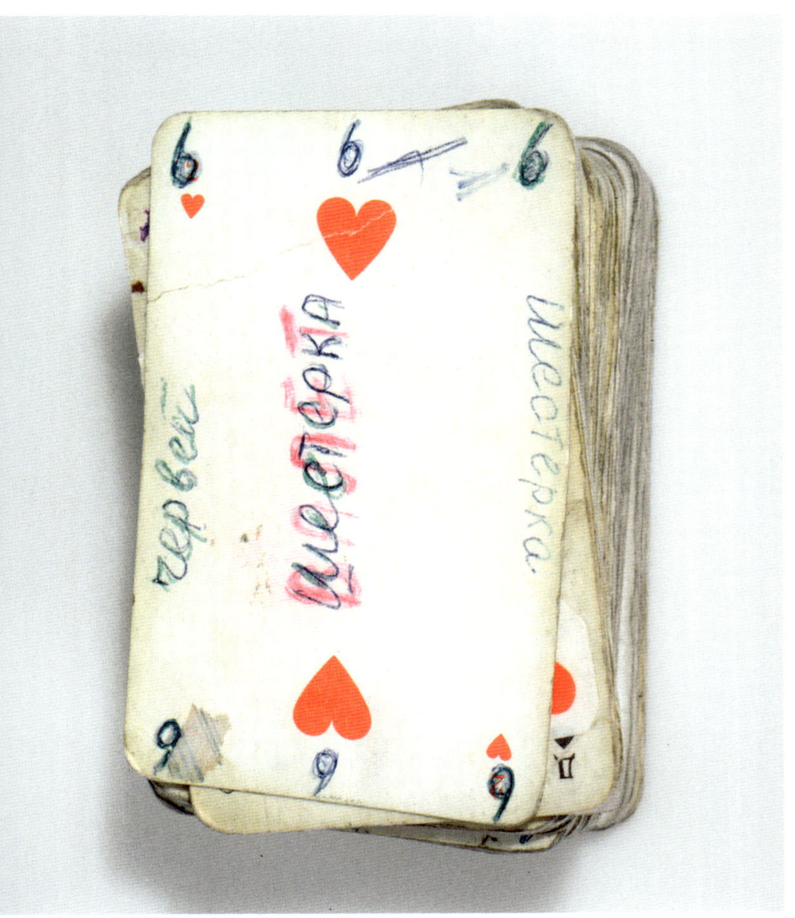


**Pyotr Gritsenya**                                    Moscow, 1997

Sometimes you have to idle away your free time, to take your mind off things. These are playing cards. We often have a game, just for fun, not money. I don't know whose cards they are – everybody plays with them. Now and then one of them gets lost, so I just draw the one that's missing.

Playing cards, pen

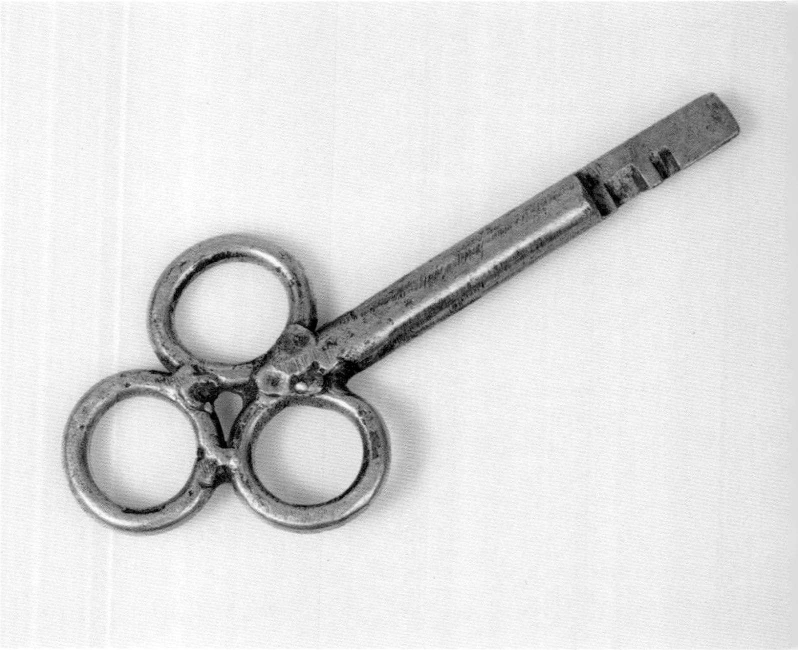

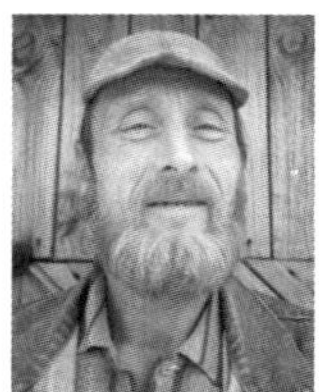

**Mikhail Eryomkin**                                        Ryazan region, 1994

This is the key to the garage. Why should I buy one when I can make it myself?
I need it to be as strong as possible as it's a big heavy lock. The parts are
heavy, and it takes a lot of effort to move them. Basically, this lock is like an
ordinary one, only bigger, and it's harder to open – even the diameter of the
key is different. The rings are there to give me more leverage, so I can open it
even when there's a frost.

Steel

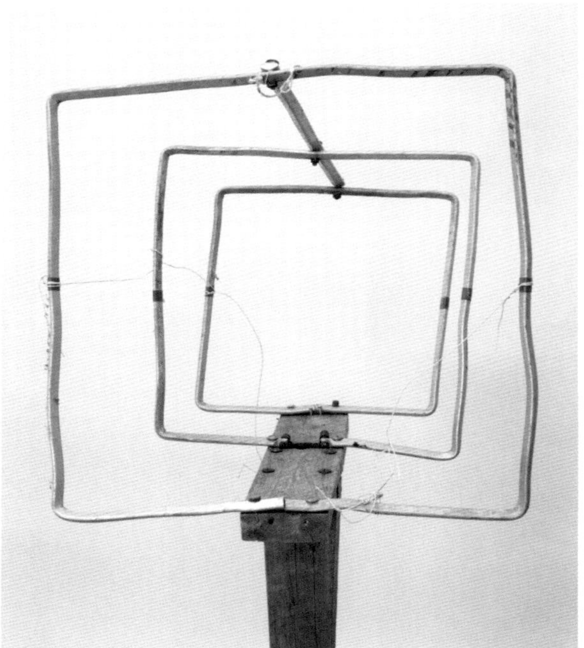

**Mikhail Eryomkin**                                    Ryazan region, 1993

Ryazan television started showing interesting programmes on a decimetric channel, but all the aerials we had were metric. There used to be nothing but metric channels – one and two. Nobody in the village had made any aerials like this before and you couldn't buy them either – there weren't any for sale. At that time I subscribed to the magazine *Radio* and they showed some drawings for decimetric aerials. I tried making one of their versions. I found a piece of power cable – it was somewhere on our pig farm. I pulled it apart: there are four aluminium strands inside it and I made the aerial out of them – more or less like in the magazine. But my wire had a larger cross-section and I made the whole thing a bit bigger, in proportion. I found an oak plank for the frame and cut strips off it – I have a lathe that I made myself too. I screwed it all together and raised it 5 metres to try it out, but it didn't work very well, so I decided to raise the aerial higher. This time I took a pinewood pole, about 15 metres long, dug out a hole and we set it up. My neighbours helped of course, as I couldn't have set it up alone. But even then the picture was bad. Either I did something wrong or the signal wasn't reaching this far.

Aluminium, wood, screws

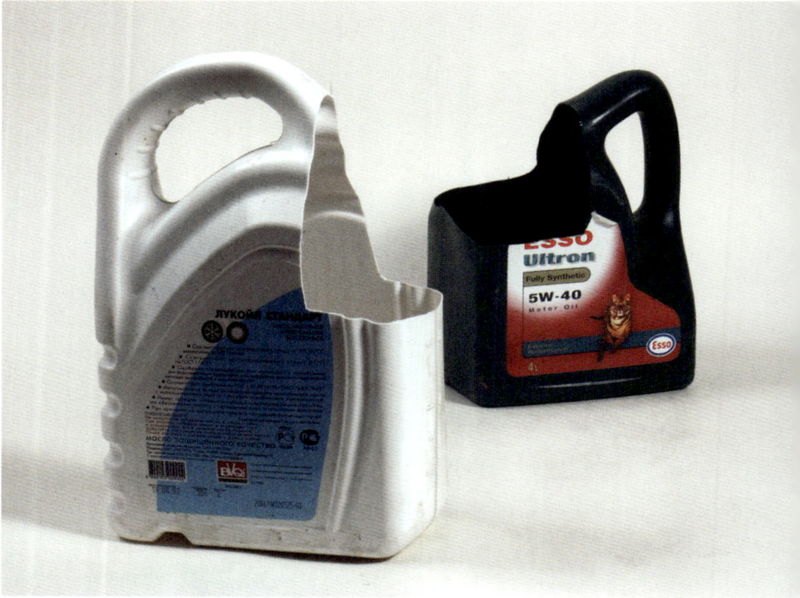

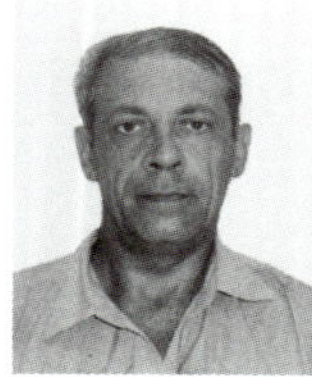

**Aleksandr Prokhorov**                    Ivanovo, 2003

There are all different sorts – these were full of engine oil. What makes them handy is that they don't clatter about if I have to stick something in the boot. I cut them in different ways and use them for different things. Very handy. The thin ones and the boxy ones – you can put rags in them, or taps, nuts, bolts, whatever. There's all sorts of clutter in the garage. I repair everything myself. I cut my first container like that when I bought my first car, in about 1985. As soon as my first oil container was empty, I had to think what to do with it. It seemed a shame to throw it out and I didn't want to pollute the environment, so I cut it down, without even giving it a second thought. Of course, I wasn't the first to think of it. I probably saw one of my neighbours at the garage doing it. I cut these ones this year.

Plastic oil container

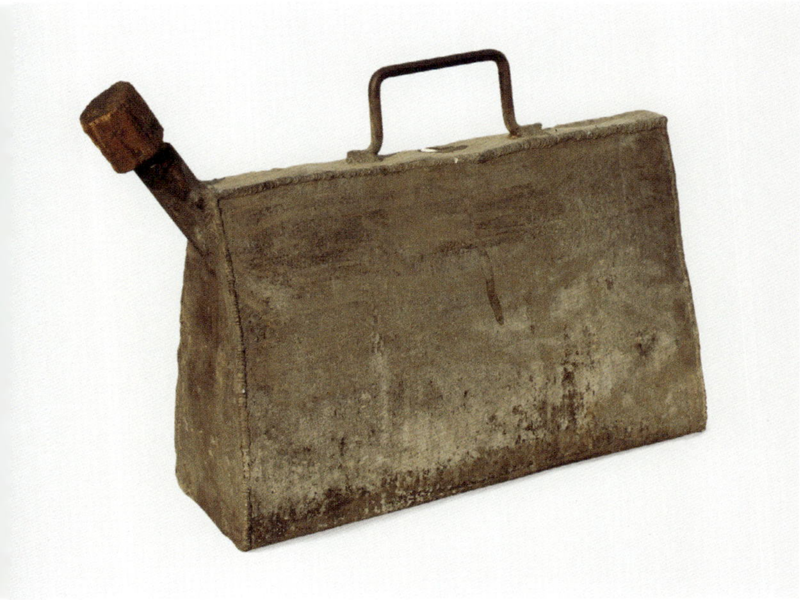

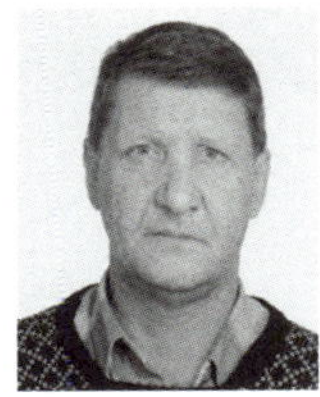

**Vyacheslav Suranov**                                    Kolomna, c.1970

*As recounted by his brother Sergei:* There weren't any petrol cans back then, but we still had to drive around the place. The same goes for petrol stations, not like now – one on every corner. You had to have a can for petrol and there weren't any, so we made them for ourselves. My brother made his own too – he had a few. Fill up two or three and you could drive anywhere. They held 15 to 20 litres. There were all kinds and one turned out shaped like a briefcase. He used to drive the boss – maybe that's why it turned out like this.

Steel, wood

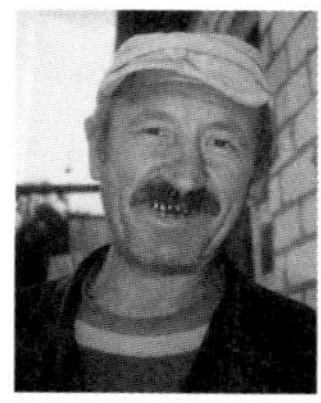

**Konstantin**                                        Michurinsk, c.1985

Well, you know, there weren't any pens. I mean, of course there were pens, but none for sale. All they had was the little refills and as my children were going to school, they needed something to write with. I'm handy at putting things together. My wife works in a hospital and she brought back these little tubes – droppers, I think they are. I made them into pens – nothing tricky about it.

Ballpoint pen refills, plastic tubes

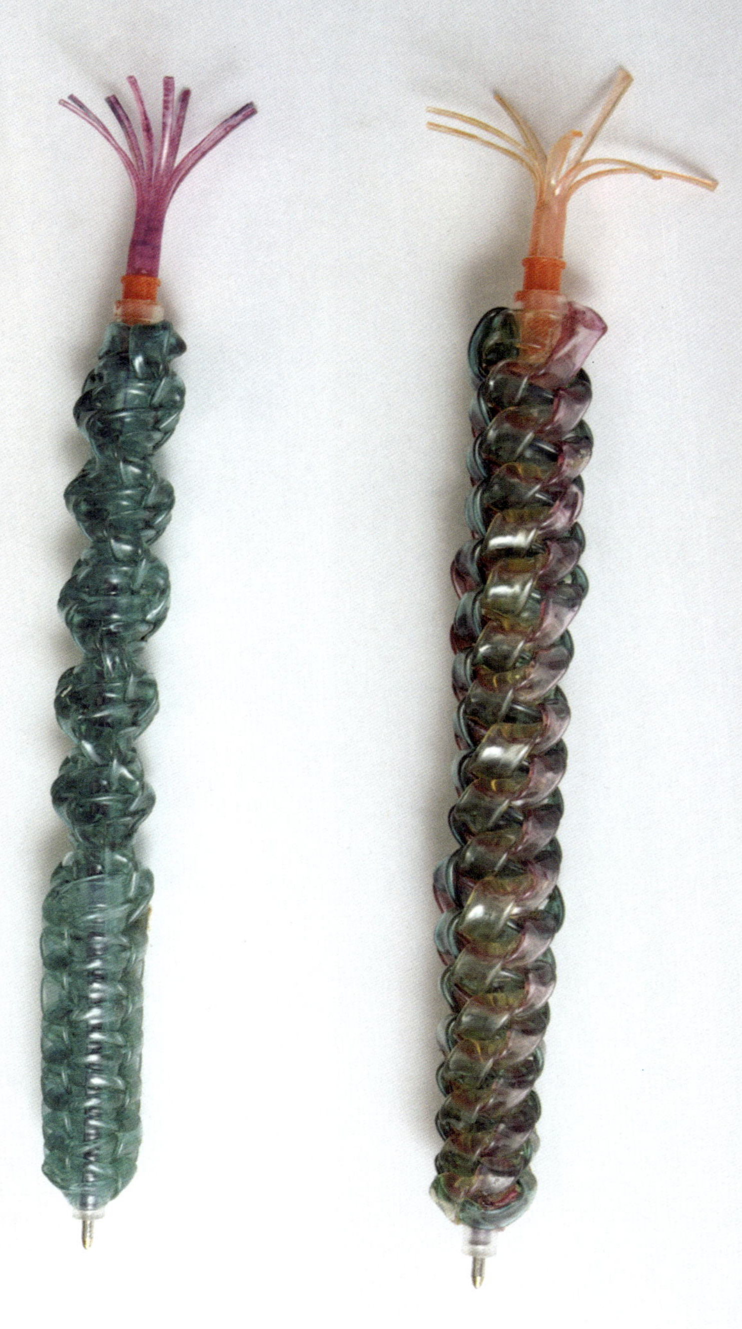

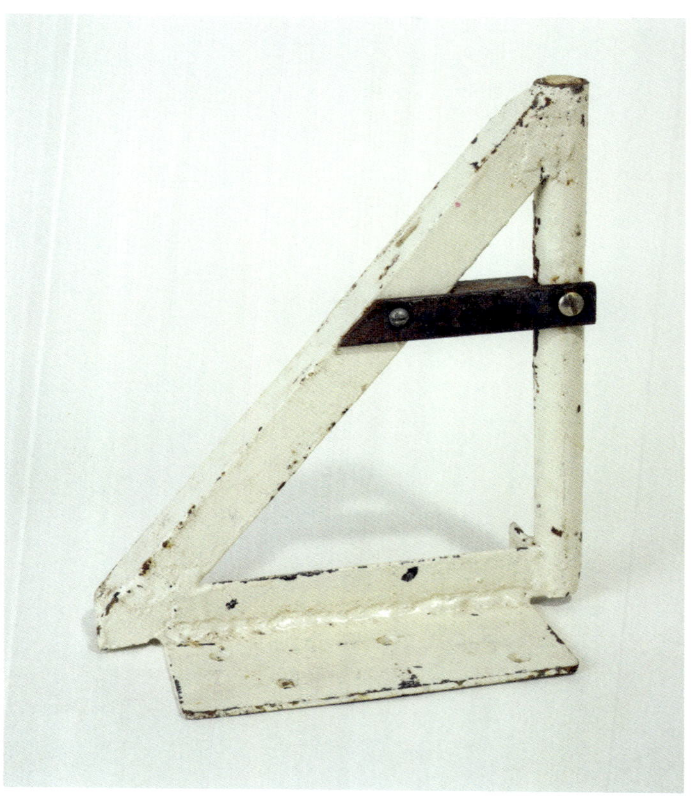

**Konstantin**                                        Michurinsk, c.1996

My garage is small, you see – there's not enough room to swing a cat. Where can I put everything? It all has to fit in there, I can't take it home. I have to charge my car battery. My welders are there, the rakes, the spades, the trolley, and the workbench. So I made these brackets, strong ones. They'll hold anything. The shelves are really secure. I welded them myself – who else would weld them for me? I made the welder myself as well. Wound the coils, found the little wheels...

Steel, screws

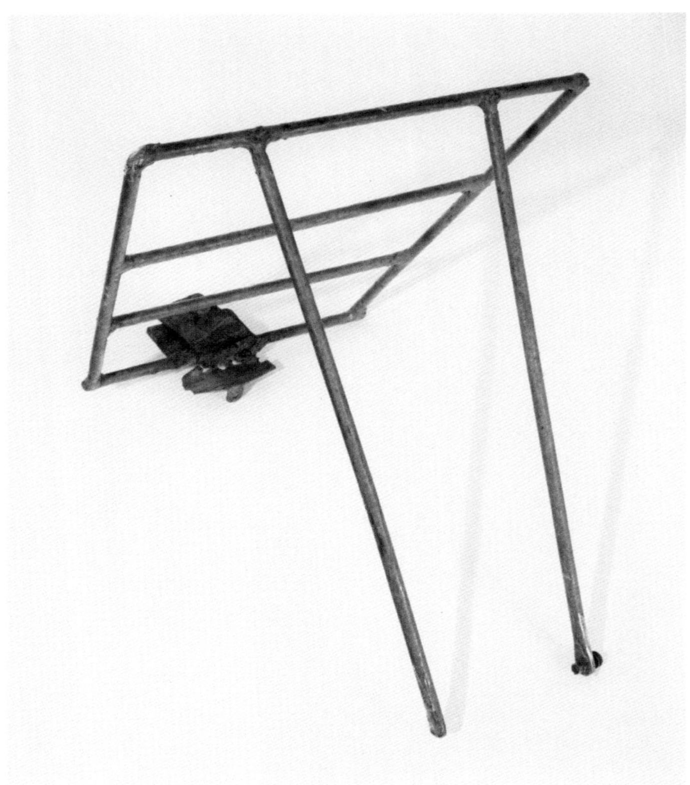

**Konstantin** Michurinsk, 1993

I made this at least ten years ago. I improved it, because I welded it myself. I fastened it on and now it carries stuff just fine. What good is a little rack? You can't put anything on it, you can't carry anything on it – and where can you buy a decent one? So you just improve things yourself. I put good ball-bearings, real big ones, in the back hub as the little bearings it was made with fall apart straight away. If you're buying, buy something decent as you can pick up the other stuff lying round the back of the building. Make use of whatever you can get. Of course, it could be a bit more civilised, using stainless steel, but I haven't got around to that yet.

Steel, bolts

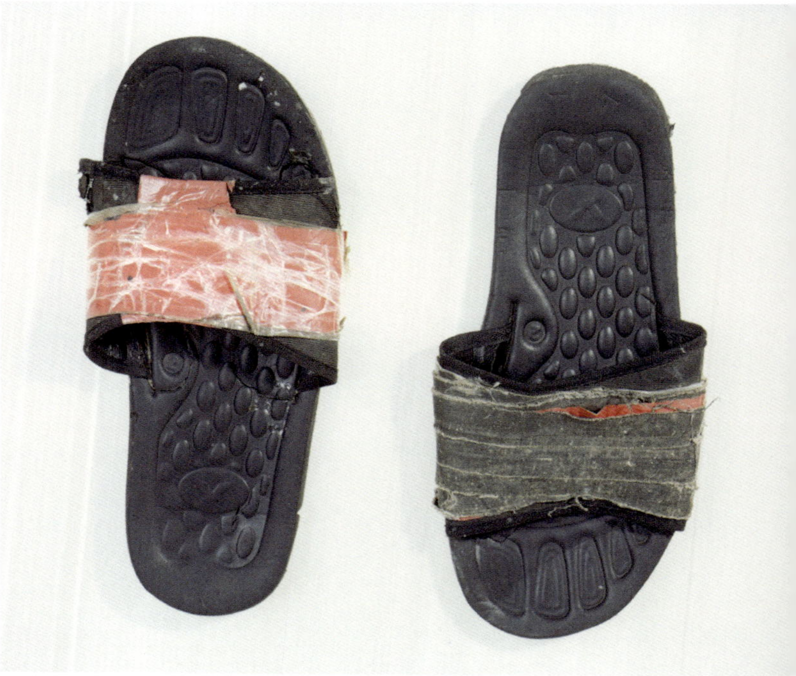

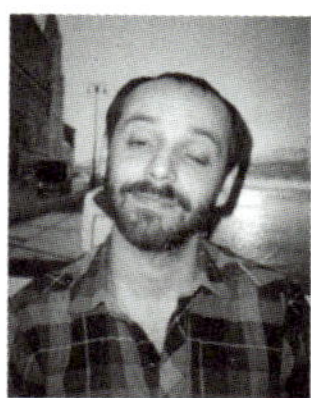

**Semyon Voronov**                                            Novgorod, 1994

Right, this is what happened. I'm only telling you so you'll leave me alone. I went to the market and bought these slippers for me and Naska. The slippers were cheap and comfortable, but the lousy things fell to pieces. Well, after all, they were my little slippers – I mean they were comfortable, it seemed a shame to throw them out. So I took some sticky tape and some insulating tape too, and I wrapped it round the lot. It's holding so far. We've got what you'd probably call modified slippers – a new design.

Sellotape, insulating tape, slippers

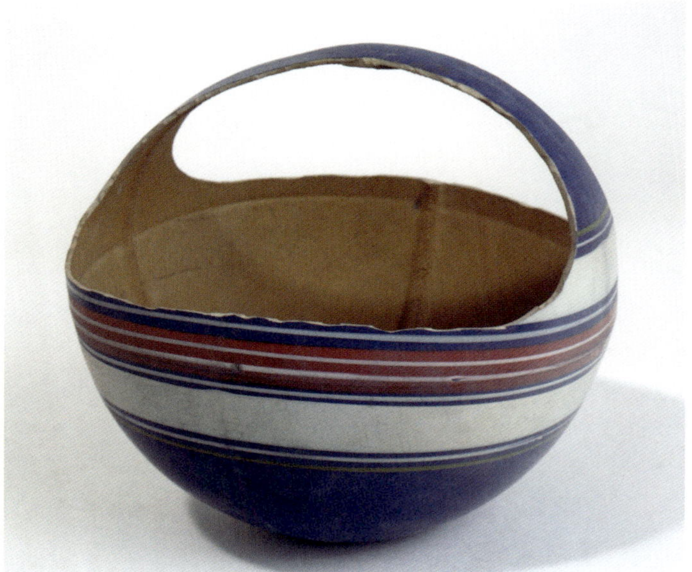

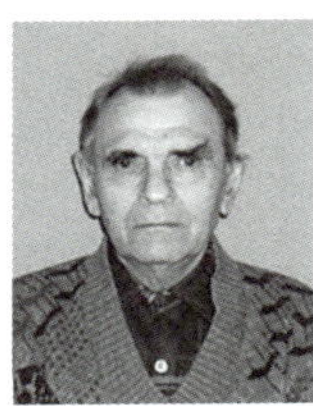

**Yurii Fesun**                                                    Novgorod, 1994

*As recounted by his grandson:* My grandfather calls it a basket, although no
one's ever gone gathering anything with it. I had this punctured ball and we
were going to throw it out. But my grandfather cut out a sort of handle and
said, 'There you are. Now you can go gathering mushrooms and berries in the
forest.' I've never gone gathering mushrooms in my life and I don't ever intend
to either. But it would be awkward to throw grandad's present out – he'd take
offence. He's always picking up all sorts of trash in the street and bringing it
home – I'm sick to death of it. Take a look in his room – he's got planks in
there, bits of plywood, pieces of lino, plastic foam, some pipes or other – you
name it. The bed's the only place he hasn't piled up with stuff. I feel sorry for
him – I don't think he's ever had any decent things in his life. He told me he
used to wear his older brothers' hand-me-down clothes and shoes.

Plastic ball

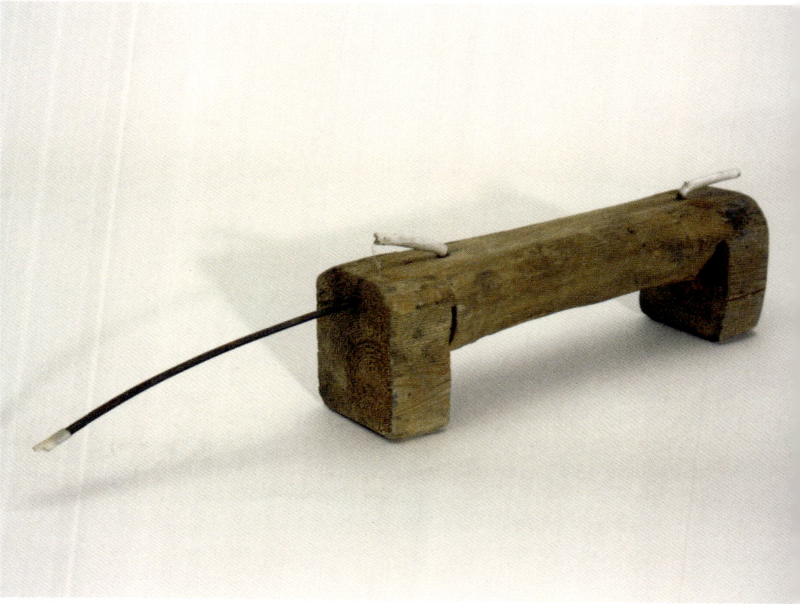

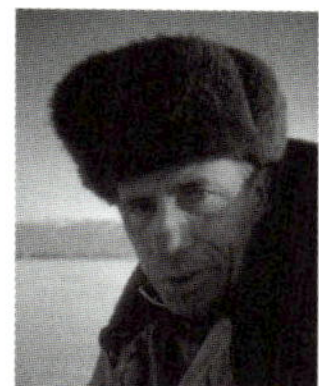

**Pavel Anisimov**　　　　　　　Serpukhov, Moscow region, 1996

I don't use a good rod from the shop because of the strong frosts. When the line winds onto the drum and there's still some water on it, in a strong frost it freezes, and with a shop rod the drum won't turn. But like this I can just take it, pick it up easily, unwind it, then wind it up and unwind it again. I find it very handy, so sometimes I use a home-made rod. In the frost it's actually better in this respect. This wooden rod is called a 'bridge'. That's because you can freeze it onto the ice and it will stay there: you dip it into a hole and press it against the ice for a minute. Then you can go and check your other holes.

Wood, wire, fishing line

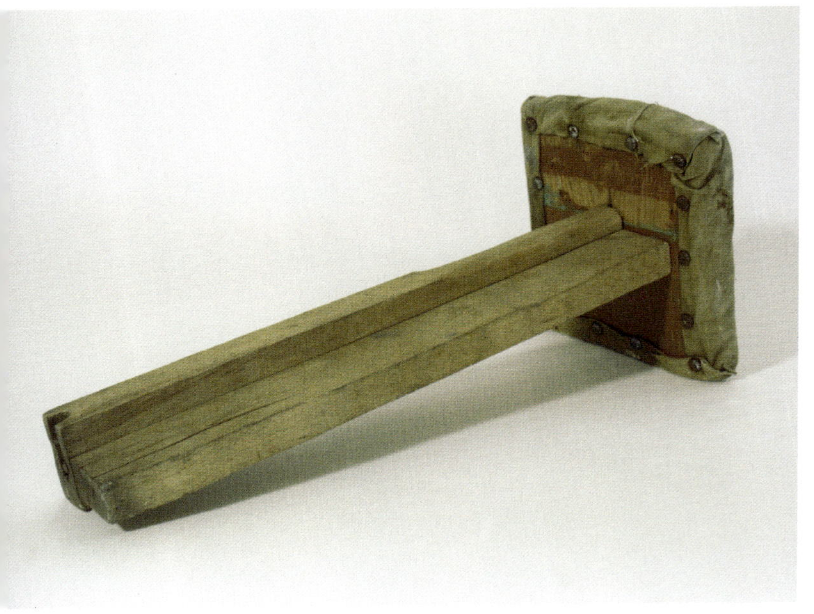

**Pavel Anisimov**                    Serpukhov, Moscow region, 1995

Before you find a fish you can drill any number of holes. Throw a line in here, drop a weighted one in there, freeze a rod on somewhere else. You have to walk round and check them all. Sit here a bit, sit there a bit – your legs are killing you. You can't carry a box around with you everywhere – it's not made for dragging around all the time like that. But tie a 'goat's leg' to your belt and go wherever you like – you'll always have a chair under your backside. This version of mine is a bit different from the usual design. This 'goat's leg' I made you don't stick into the ice, like a lance, you freeze it on like one of those wooden rods. It's a bit on the heavy side, but then I don't live far away.

Wood, cloth, nails

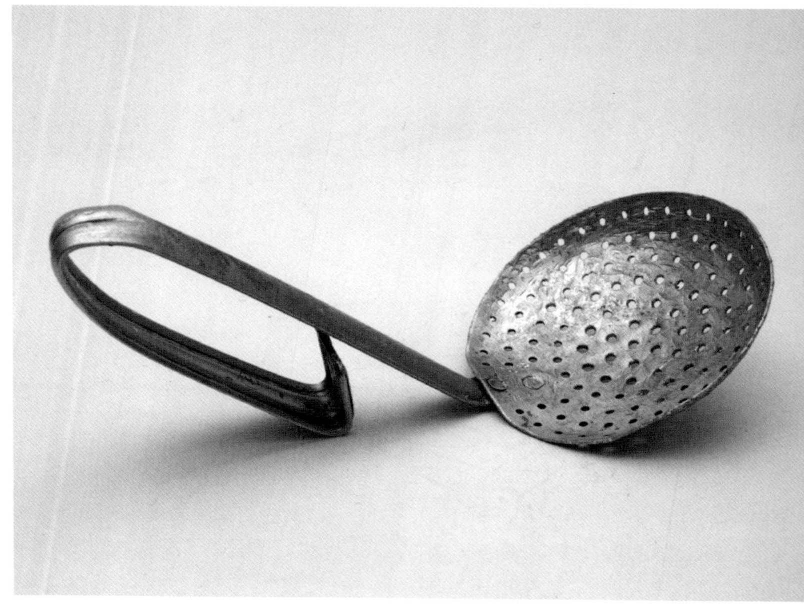

**Pavel Anisimov**                    Serpukhov, Moscow region, 1997

It's just a scoop, for scraping snow out of the drain. I dropped mine down it just recently – not deliberately of course. It happens – it falls in there and you can't get it back out. Sometimes you can lose a pickaxe, never mind a scoop. I had a good one, stainless steel, very strong. It's important for it to be strong, because when the ice freezes onto it, it gets heavy and sometimes it won't fit down the drain. So then you smack it against the ice – and it breaks. But if it's stainless steel it won't break. I'm using this one for the time being. I took my wife's ladle and bent it so it would fit into the hole, then hammered in the edges a bit.

Stainless-steel ladle

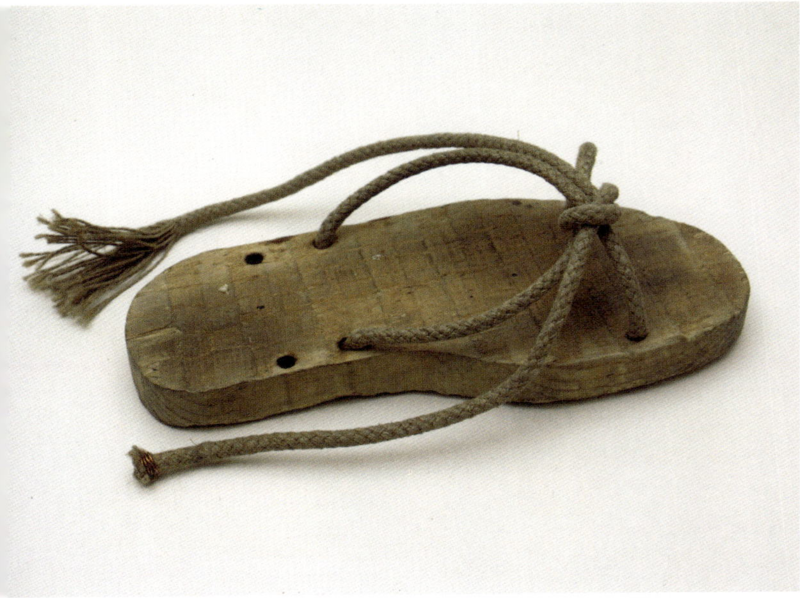

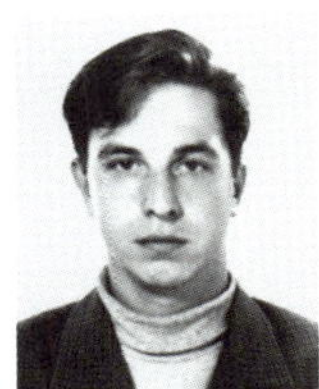

**Aleksandr Gromov**                                   Moscow, 1998

I made these sandals when I was studying at college. We had guys from Vietnam studying with us and in the summer they all walked around in sandals like these. It was a gas. I wanted to show my solidarity with them somehow: they were from a poor country that the Americans had pounded. Basically, I wanted to give them a bit of moral support and give myself a bit of a buzz. I tried them on, walked around in them, worked out what size I needed and sawed some out of an ordinary plank of wood. It was dead simple! I drilled the holes, put the strings in. I wore them around the college a lot.

Wood, rope

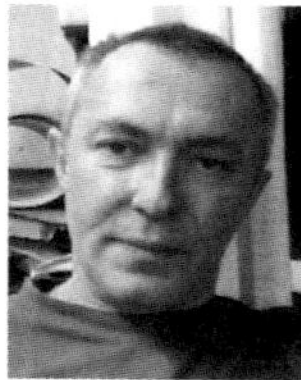

**Sergei Bazilev**                                    Moscow, 1985

I was rummaging about in a dump full of aeroplane parts, not far from here, on the site of the old Zhukovsky Academy. This thing's some kind of light guide, it's silvered inside and out – so I made it into a lamp. The soldier who was guarding the dump said 'light guide' to me, and that started the whole business. What could you make out of a light guide if not a lamp? When I look at it now I don't think I would have made it into anything else. You can use it as a wall lamp and at the same time you can move it around from place to place, because it's pretty mobile. You can stand it on the table as well. I needed to use this object, not just let it lie around idle, because society requires you to justify your 'squirrelling'. You've found an item in the street and brought it home, it's lying there in front of you, and as long as it's just lying there, your family regards it as clutter, a thing that can potentially be thrown out. But if it's transformed into something useful, then it's harder to throw out. I've simply socialised it – made the members of the household respect it like I do. That was all I wanted to do, nothing else. It was probably made in 1985, a long time before perestroika. I definitely bought the socket for the bulb, because I was amazed at how cheap it was. I sharpened it, so it could be stuck in. The shiny piece is a reflector that I picked up near here – at the Moscow street lighting depot. There are all sorts of reflectors there, and I've made lots of useful things out of them – my car's radiator grille, for instance. When I learned how much it cost, I decided to make one myself – it turned out like a piece of chased metalwork.

Aeroplane parts, lamp socket, bulb

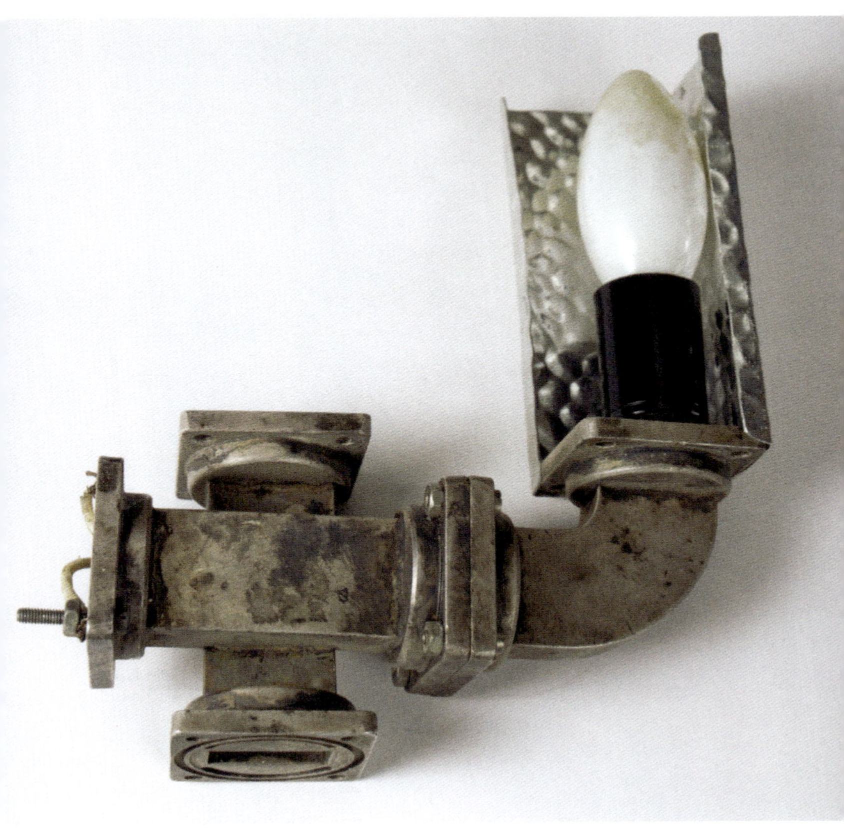

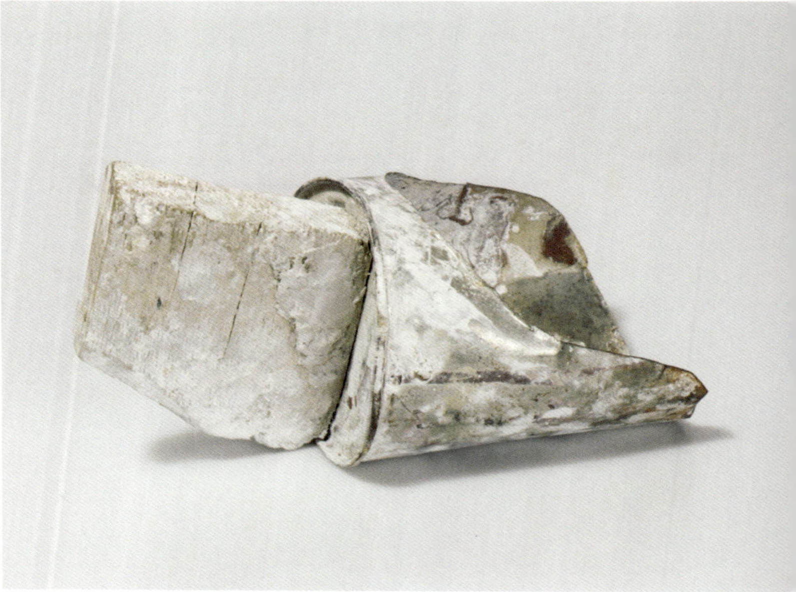

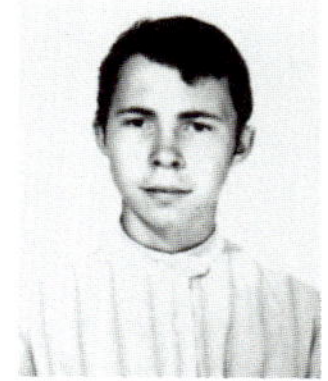

**Denis**                                                    Moscow, 1999

I made the scoop when I went to sculpture classes in college. First we worked with plasticine and clay, and then we moved on to moulding things in plaster. The plaster comes in sacks. You need to have some kind of scoop – you can't go using your hands. First we used to buy them, but they always disappeared. So you'd turn up to do some work and there'd be no scoop. You had to improvise one out of whatever you could find. We made them out of plastic bottles, tin cans, linoleum, plywood. This one is from a tin can and a piece of wood – put together in a hurry.

Tin can, wood

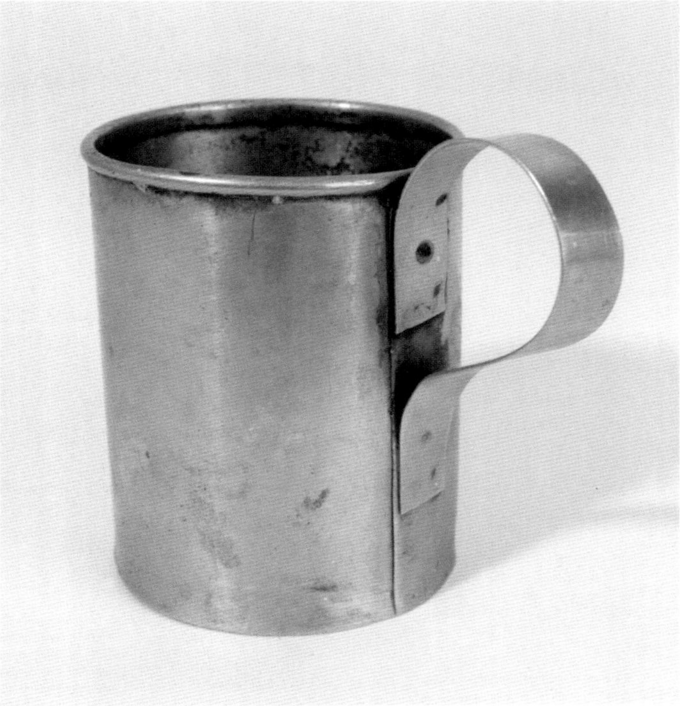

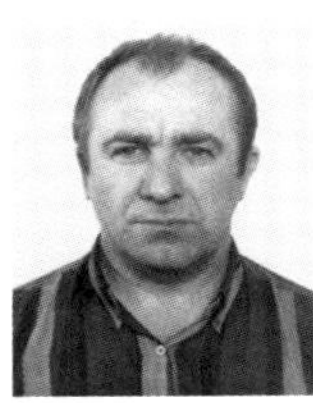

**Aleksandr Babushkin** Samara, c.1988

Since there weren't any of these goods in the shops, people made them for themselves, to suit their own needs. They weren't used in the domestic setting – only when you went fishing or on holiday. When things had to be light and convenient and you had to boil water in them, then clean them with sand. For material we used whatever was available. In this case it's stainless steel. The kettle's basically made with the same technology and the same material, for one purpose – going fishing.

Stainless steel, rivets

## Mikhail Kozin

Moscow, c.1985

So I happened to end up in a secret factory, where you could do fine turning work. That was where we made some of the components that went into this tape deck. And I had another stroke of luck because by chance I managed to get my hands on a fourteen-channel recording head – that was just too much! And when I took some tape from a computer and held it against this head and discovered that it covered ten channels, I realised I'd soon have a ten-channel tape deck in my hands. I was working in a factory, I knew plenty of lads who were lathe operators, and if you had any questions you showed them, gave them a bottle of vodka, and your problem was solved. And at that time we already had a tape deck on sale. It used to be called the 'I-302' I think. The guys made the parts for me. Since it was only a playback head, but it covered all the channels, the erasing head had to be lifted and lowered across the channels, and there's a little set of steps in here that made that all possible. There are exactly ten channels here, so when I had to erase some channel or record on some channel, I moved it one step. Basically it was very simple – you could see the number of the level. This little thing went under the erasing head, and about here say, where my fingernail is, channel one is recorded, then at level two it's channel two, at level ten channel ten. They made the little piece for me and I made a support for it, a bracket with two screws. At the factory we had a microscope that was accurate to within two microns, so that was the precision with which I defined the necessary levels for playback and recording with this tape, the computer tape. I checked the tape and it really was good enough for playing back and recording. Of course, it was meant for 01 binary recording, so its transitional moments were a bit tricky, but in principle it was suitable for recording all these ten channels with noise masking. I thought through all these points because, after all, one half... one hemisphere of my brain's not really technological. I suppose, I don't know, it's impetuous and creative, and the other's implacably logical, technical, focused on maths and physics and so on. As soon as I could, I made a tape-head system that you could record with. Sticking in the rest of the electronics was very simple, and I was already pretty good at working on radios. I just took my soldering iron and set about it. I got the transistors from a secret factory as well, by the way, a place that made very serious sorts of things, I won't say what. When I got together an entire circuit that worked, I had a tape recorder with ten independent channels that could be fed into a single mixing console so that you could do some pretty serious sound recording. So everything here in this tape recorder is made on the ten-channel principle, because we couldn't buy a ten-channel switch, they only sold five-channel.

Tape deck parts

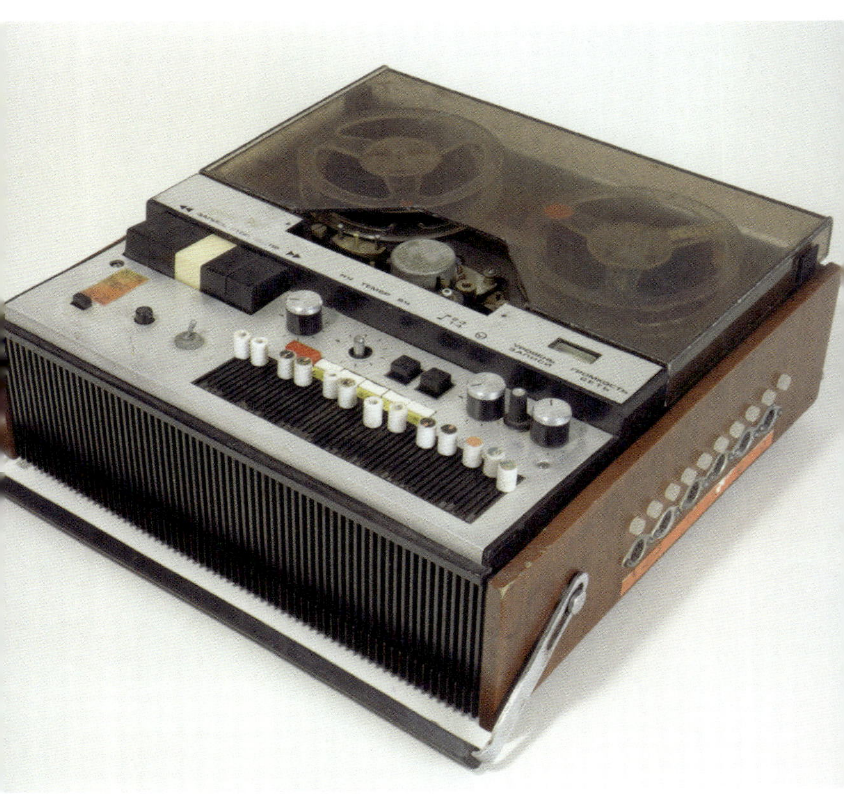

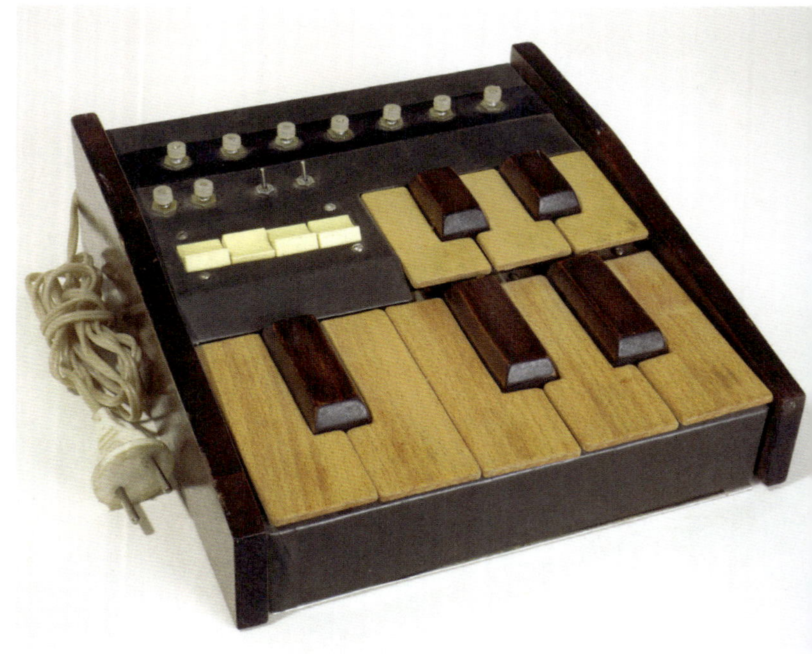

**Mikhail Kozin**                                        Moscow, c.1986

This is my percussion group. I made all sorts of drums and other percussion instruments after I'd made my tape recorder. There used to be a mixing deck, various microphones and vibraphones as well, including one made out of some sheet metal that got blown off our roof. After two or three years had gone by, I was able to record complex pieces of music that I composed myself. Of course, I was only interested in all these devices because I needed them. Perhaps they were interesting discoveries, but if I'd had a computer then, it's unlikely I would have made anything of the kind.

Wood, electrial components

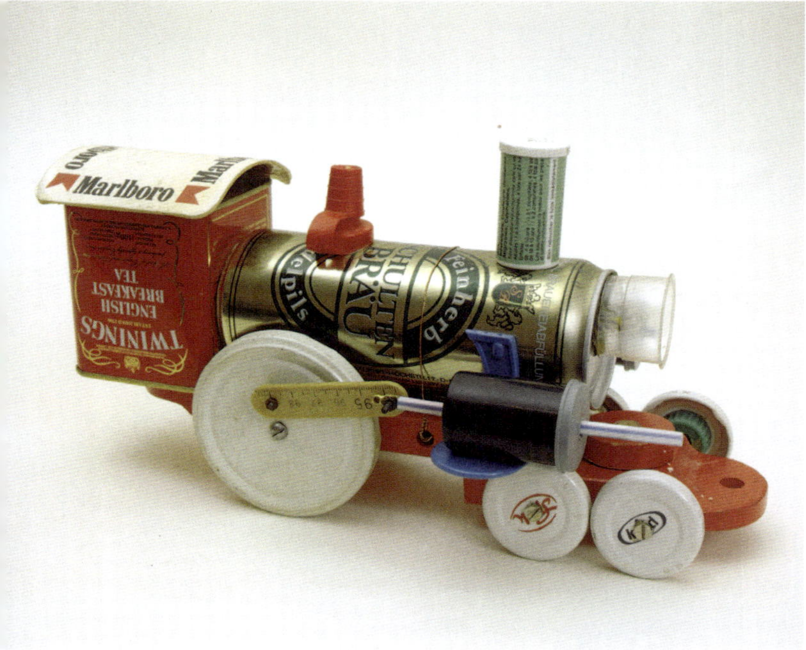

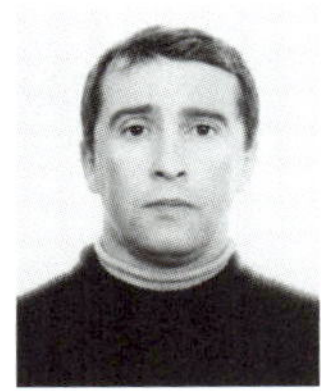

**Aleksandr Chebotaryov**  Zhukovsky, Moscow region, c.1996

I made the locomotive when Mitka was little, six or seven years old. He had pneumonia at the time. He was playing up and I wanted to distract him with something, to amuse him. I sat at home and drew various kinds of cars and ships with him. Then I remembered I'd seen a little locomotive in some German magazine, made out of different sorts of tins and lids. I was in the army in Germany. We had lots of that stuff lying around at home. I raked it all into a big heap in front of Mitka and started making the locomotive out of it. I deliberately did it all slowly, and we had it finished off in about a week.

Beer can, tea tin, coaster, film canisters, bottle tops, wood, ruler, drinking straws

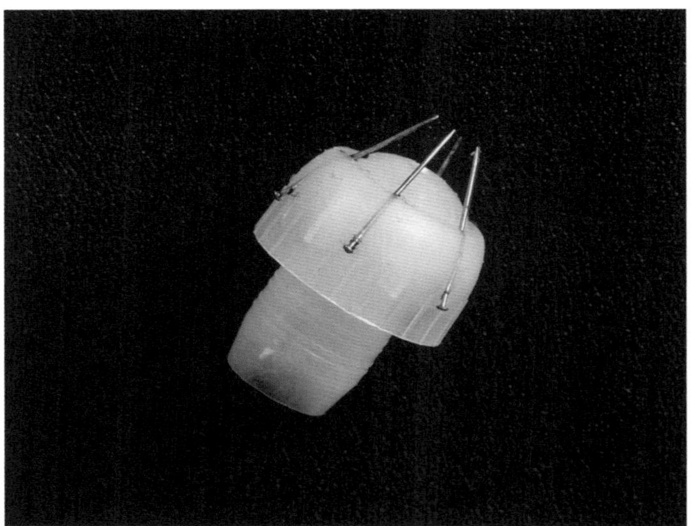

**Nikita Kuzmichyov**                              Moscow, 1987

This is a piercing cork for making jam. When you make jam you have to pierce every berry so that the juice comes out, so that it's good and tasty. My grandmother loved making jam. At first she used a hairpin for piercing the berries, but a hairpin isn't sharp enough and she had to poke every berry several times – the more holes, the better. My grandfather found an old champagne cork, left over from some party, and stuck pins into it – the kind of pins that you use on men's shirts. He put the pins in it and it was very easy to hold in your hand. It was convenient for my granny and for me too. I was very small then, about five or six years old. I loved holding it and piercing the berries with it. My gran used to call me when she was going to make jam. I remember how we made gooseberry jam. We brought a whole bucketful from our dacha. I pierced every single gooseberry and then I put them in a separate bowl. I really loved doing it. It was fun. The jam turned out so tasty, perhaps not just because of this piercing cork, but maybe it had a part to play too. Then granny lost it. We only found it again a long time later – it had fallen behind the cooker. We had to replace a few of the pins, but once we replaced them it began to serve us like before. Well, it's such an interesting little thing.

Champagne cork, pins

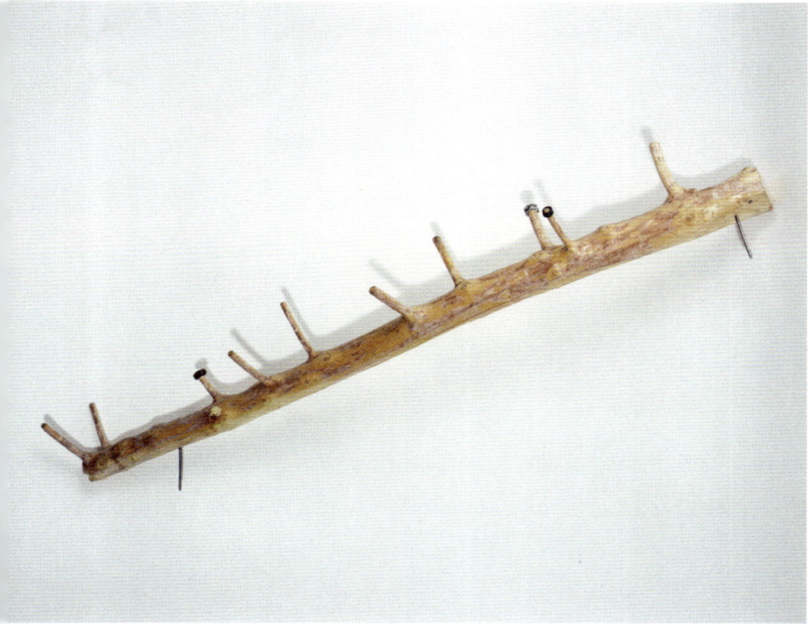

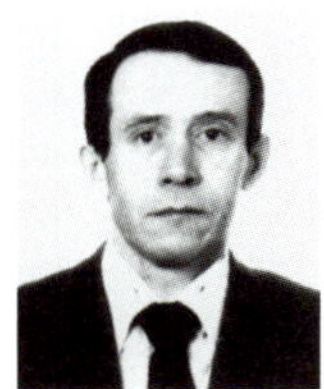

**Vitaliy**                                                    Moscow, 1998

The children are growing up – they're proper members of the family. They
have the same things that we do, only smaller. We come in from outside,
take our coats off – they reach up to the coat rack to hang their things up,
but it's too high. I decided to give them equal rights and I made this 'family
coat hook' out of a New Year's tree. It was supposed to be thrown out after
the New Year but I cut it shorter, cleaned it off and hung it up – not horizontally,
but at an angle, so everyone could reach the right part for their height.

Tree branch

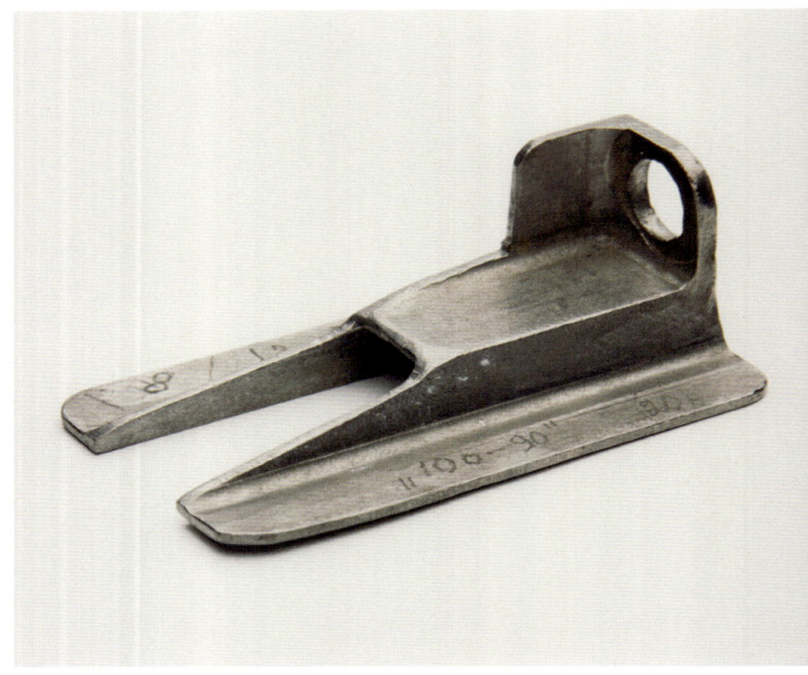

**Vitaliy**Moscow, 1988

This is a peg for mountain climbing made out of titanium. I worked in a factory where we had all different kinds of stainless steel and titanium. I started climbing when I was still in college, but there was no equipment, and we often used to ask our friends to make us an ice axe or a crampon. We used to make drawings and they made them for us from those. When I went to work at the factory, I got the chance to make them myself, to experiment. You need different pegs for different situations, depending on what the cracks are like. It's a temporary point of support – it isn't hammered into the rock like a piton, but inserted into a crack. This isn't my first peg – I made others before it.

Titanium

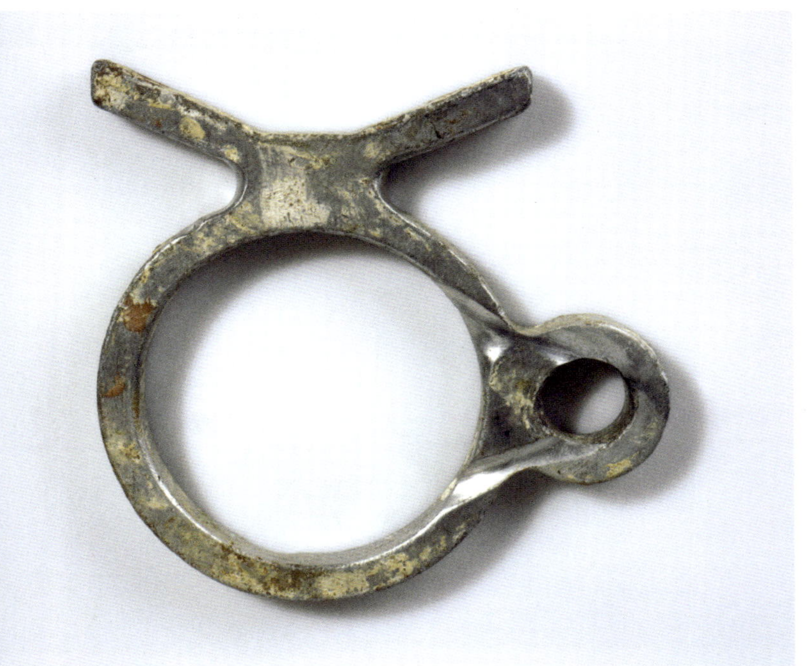

**Vitaliy**                                           Moscow, 1987

This is a device that mountain climbers use for abseiling down a rope. We call it a 'releaser', or a 'figure of eight'. I made it myself as well, when I was setting up the programmable lathes. It didn't make any difference what I made out of the metal – I had to adjust the lathes, set the programme going, and run them in. So I was practising. And this is what I made as a result. I took this thing up into the mountains about five times, until I bought a professional one.

Metal

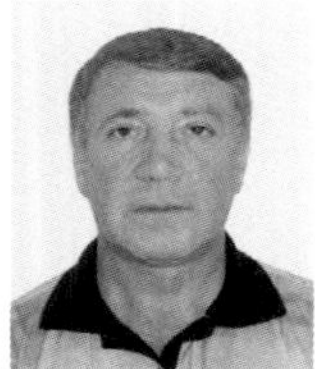

**Sergei Voroshilov** Moscow, c.1960

*As recounted by his son Andrei (pictured):* This letter box was made by my father when we moved here. That was probably around 1960. I was still little then, so naturally I don't remember too much, but I do remember him making it – because that was the first time I saw it was possible to make something useful around the house from pieces of ordinary plywood. I didn't know how to hold a hammer or a saw back then and the deft way my father handled them made a lasting impression on me. Of course, I learned too. I used to make myself swords and machine guns. My father only helped with the most difficult parts. We were poor back then – it was as if the war had only just ended. Life still wasn't organised yet – everyone made their own letter box. I think the only place they had them already built in was the new Stalin construction projects. But we moved from one communal apartment to another. They called it an improvement in living conditions. If they gave you 5 square metres more or an extra room, that was really good. It wasn't usual for people to take their letter boxes with them – in a communal apartment every family had a letter box hanging in the corridor. It was almost impossible to manage without one, because someone who received lots of letters and newspapers was regarded as important. But I was the one who painted it. It was a responsibility that I had, to paint the letter box every three or four years – there are eight layers of paint on it.

Plywood, nails, metal hinges, brackets, paint

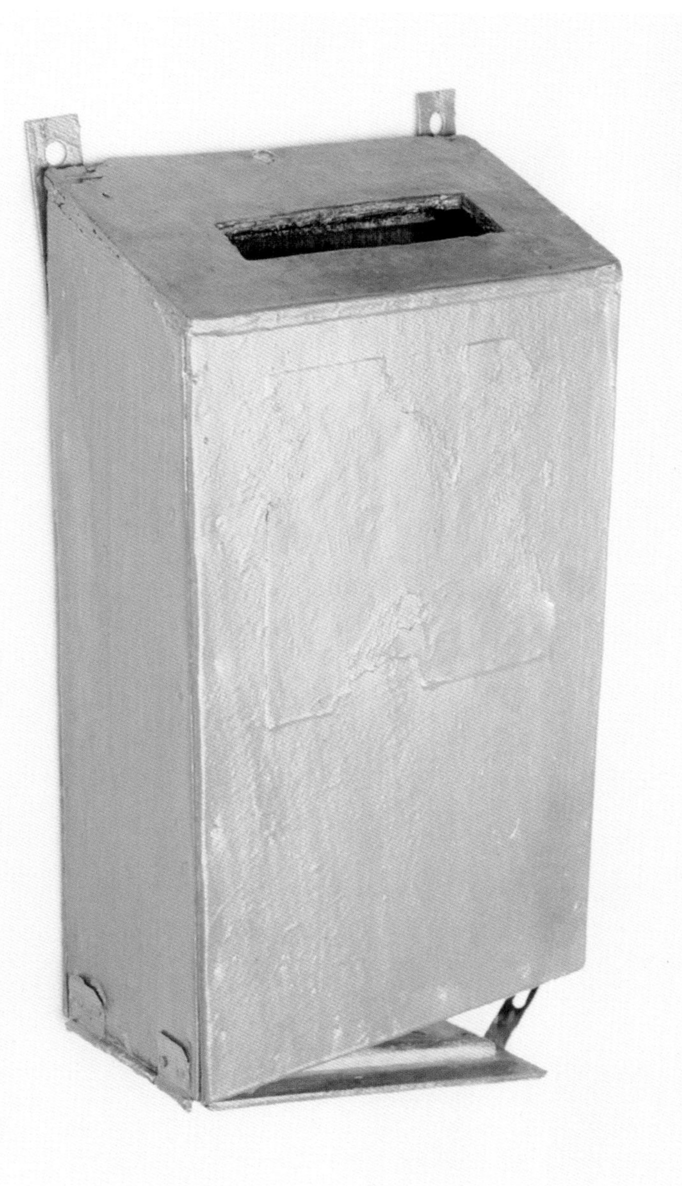

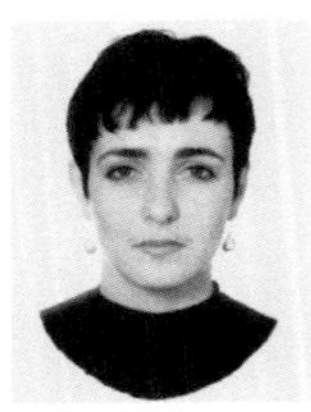

**Nikolai Kudelin**                                    Moscow, c.1994

*As recounted by his daughter Nastya Kudelina (pictured):* My father catches songbirds. At home we have big cages, but for carrying them around he uses little ones. He made all the gadgets for catching the birds as well as the cages himself. There's lots of different shapes and sizes. Some are made of wood, some metal. There's even a triangular one that hangs in the corner. He gives people a lot of birds – some as presents and others he sells. He always needs cages. He made this one around 1994.

Wood, wire, plastic

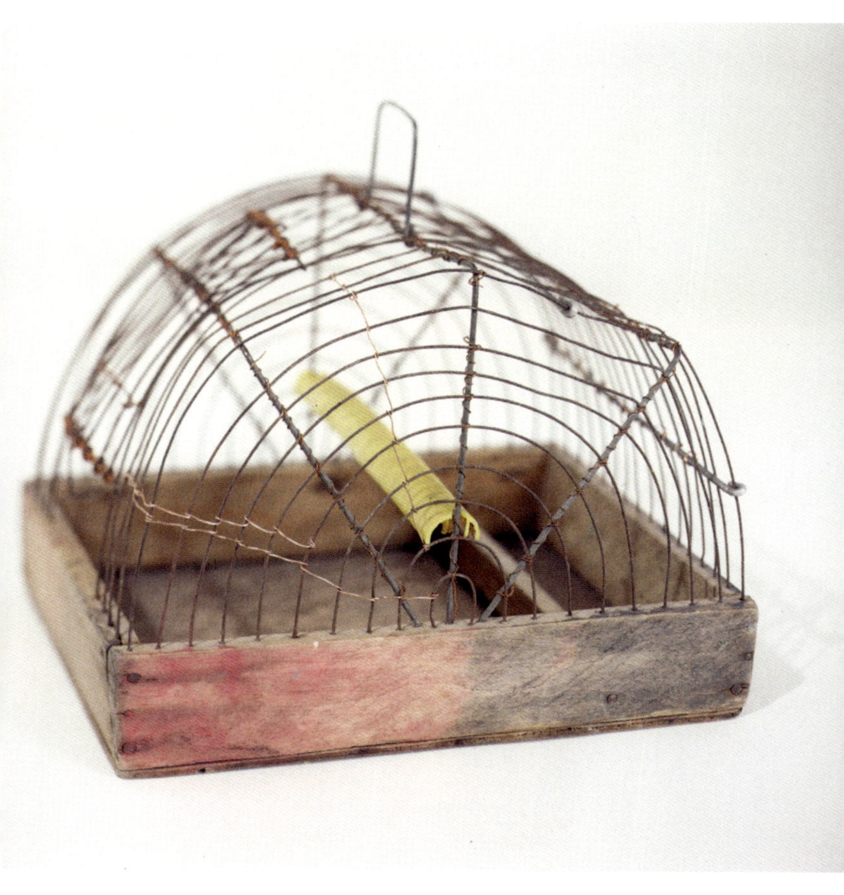

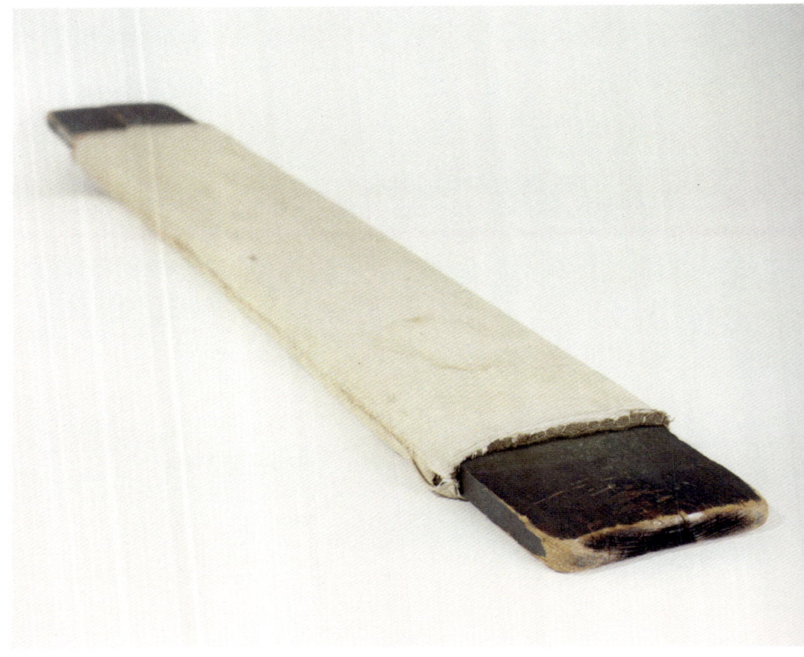

**Darya Kudelina**                                     Moscow, c.1980

*As recounted by her granddaughter Nastya Kudelina:* This is my grandma's
ironing board – for ironing the laundry. It's been here for as long as I can
remember. There's no sure way of finding out who made it, now that she
and my grandad are both gone. It's just a plank, a piece of wood, wrapped
round with layers of old blankets and coats. It's all been carefully sewn by
hand – that looks like granny's overstitch. She used to set one end of the
board on the windowsill and the other on the table and iron like that. We
wanted to throw it out ages ago, because we'd bought a new imported one,
but she wouldn't let us. And so the ironing board has outlived grandma.

Plank, blankets, thread

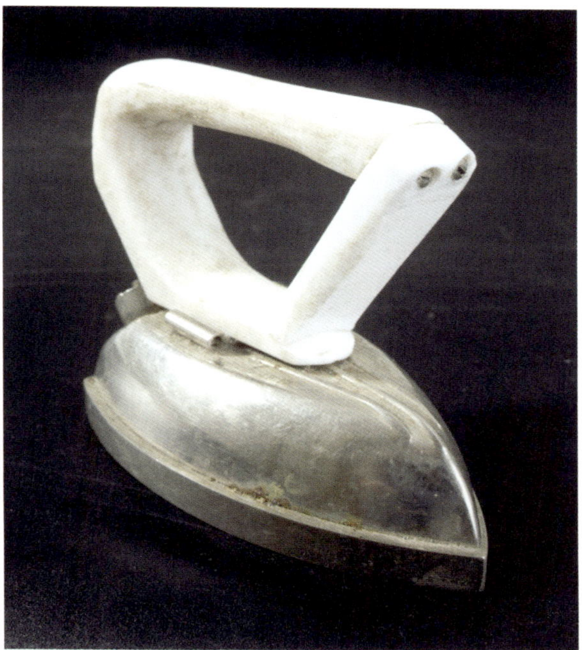

**Alla**                                                              Kolomna, c.1960

*As recounted by the author's daughter:* I remember this iron from my childhood. It belonged to my father, who was an important boss at the military factory. He always used to take this iron with him on business trips because everyday life at that time left a lot to be desired. His business trips were, for the most part, in places where, not only was it impossible to iron, but sometimes even to wash, or have something to eat. Because of this my father used to take it with him in order always to look smart and well turned out, like a boss should be. The handle was a completely different one then – this one's been attached. It's made of material that doesn't heat up. There was lots of material lying about in my father's workshop and so it wasn't difficult for him to get it together and make the iron from it. He couldn't make it satisfactorily with his own hands, but after a long time, basically the iron began to look different, with a Teflon covering. And so, you could say, the iron's already fulfilled its function. But it would be a shame to throw it away because it reminds me of my father and my childhood. Because of this I've decided that the iron's life should continue in some way.

Iron, teflon, screws

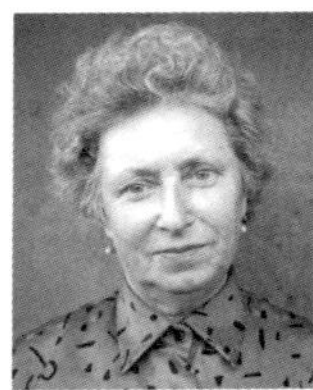

**Valentina Bobryashova**                                    Ryazan region, 1990

Well, about ten years ago, I suppose, we had shortages. All manufactured items started to disappear, and factories couldn't provide people with even the most basic things. At that time I was working in a slaughter house on a factory farm, as a production engineer, and I had to wash my hands quite often, because I was handling food a lot. But they didn't supply us with proper soap there. So I had to use my head, and I remembered the time when I used to work in the Orsk meat factory, where we used to make soap for industrial purposes. And so I thought I could give it a go myself. I got together the things I needed, sorted out the correct quantities, and the soap turned out to be OK. It washes off dirt and grime pretty well. I made that soap in fairly primitive conditions, on an electric cooker, in an enamel container. I made quite a lot – there are twenty people in the slaughter house and it was enough for a week. The factory managers found out about it, and started ordering soap, made under the same conditions, for the whole factory. I also tried to sort soap out for the poultry women and I started to cut it up into pieces.

The ingredients needed to make that soap are very simple. You use some animal fat, any kind will do – pig, beef fat, stuff that we used to use at the factory anyway as bird food. We didn't need to go looking for it. And sodium hydrate that we used to use for disinfecting the shops. I can't remember the exact proportions. We boiled up that soap on the cooker at the factory in our workshop.

Fat, sodium hydrate

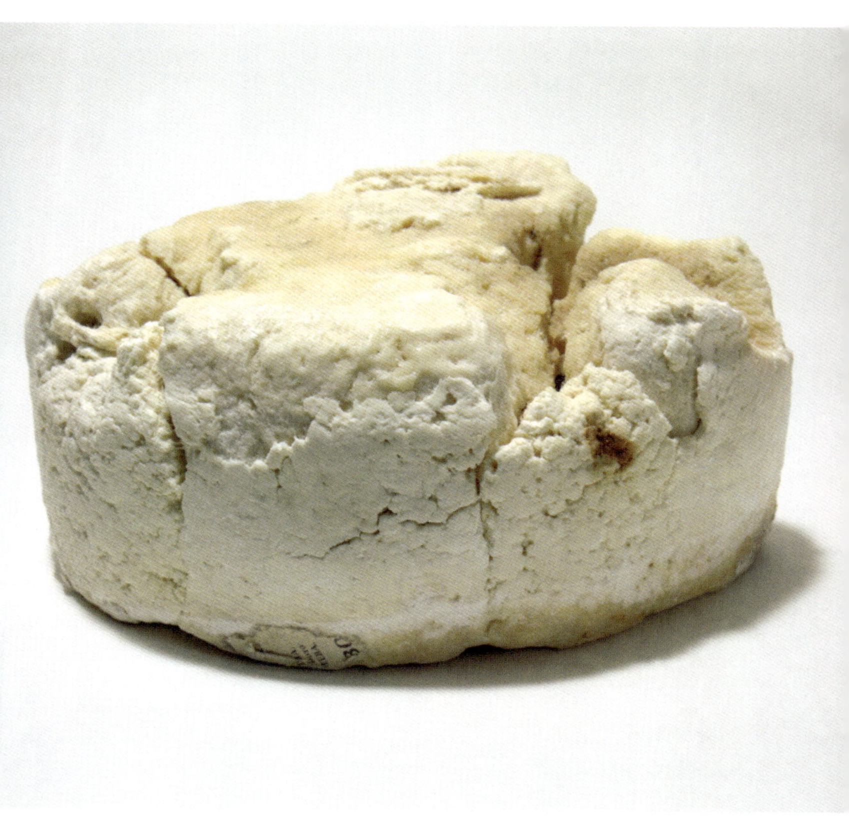

**Mikhail Bobryashchov**                    Orsk, Orenburg region, c.1959

*As recounted by his wife Valentina:* There was one year, probably 1959, when I'd just got married and we lived in the Urals, in Orsk, and we were young and happy and everything was still ahead of us. I worked with my first husband at the Orsk Meat Combine. There was a big refrigerator, a sausage workshop and a canning shop too. There were plenty of young people and newlyweds like us, and at the weekends and holidays we used to get together in big groups. But where could we get together? In those days almost everyone lived in hostels and there wasn't a single square metre of space to spare. We were all members of the Komsomol and through the Komsomol committee we used to hire a truck from the combine for cultural events, as they used to be called then. Usually we had about ten or fifteen people. We took balls, fishing rods, drinks, snacks and went off to the river to relax. It's the southern Urals, surrounded by the Steppes. It's especially lovely in the spring – when the poppies bloom the Steppe turns a beautiful red.

Those were hard times, after the war – everything was in short supply, especially out there in the provinces. You couldn't buy a bucket anywhere and even an ordinary basin or saucepan was a rarity. We didn't have much. But we had to boil water to cook something to eat, and there's no firewood on the Steppe. Then our Komsomol organiser said, 'We need to make a special campfire saucepan, so it comes to the boil quickly.' My husband was a metalworker – he could turn his hand to anything. If ever anything broke, they called for him. So he made two saucepans – one bigger and one a bit smaller. See how big the bottom of it is – so it boils quickly on a campfire. He found special material for it somewhere too: it's what we used to call food-quality aluminium.

Aluminium, steel, rivets

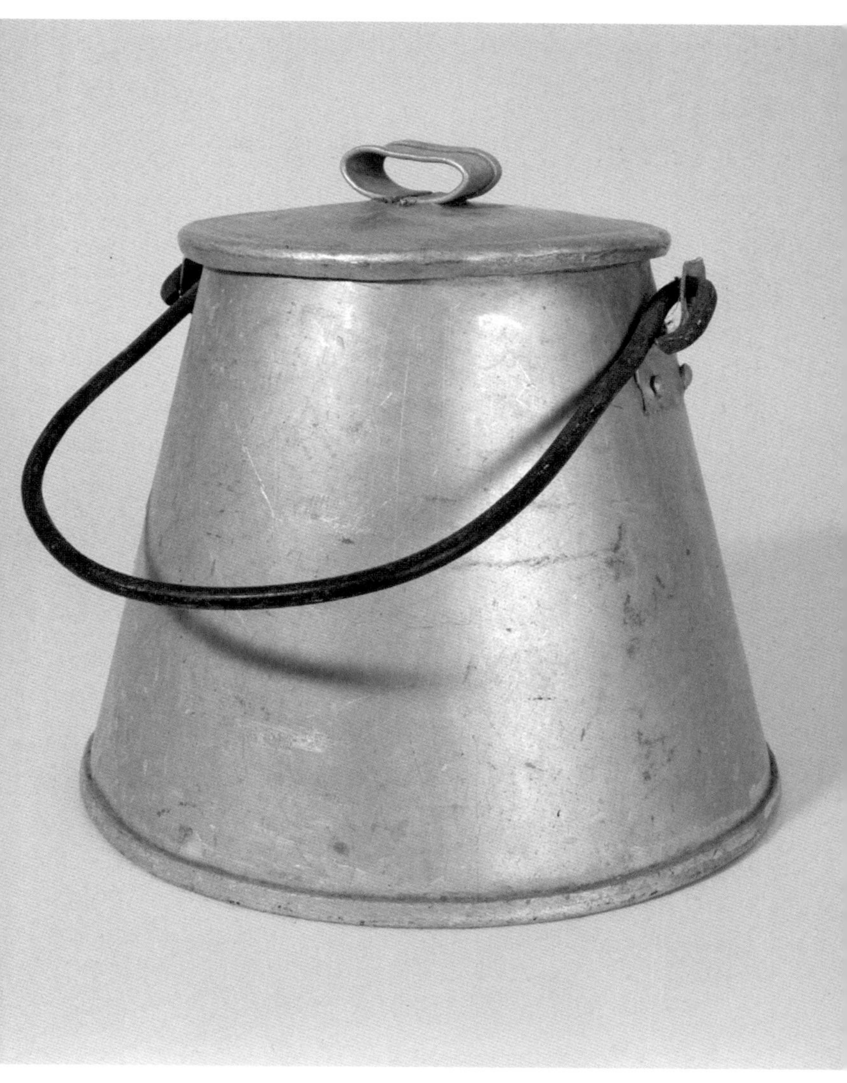

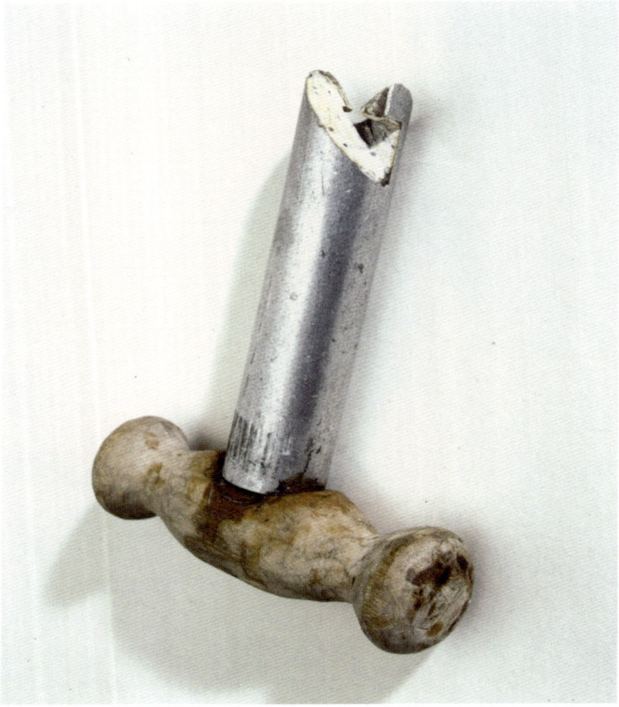

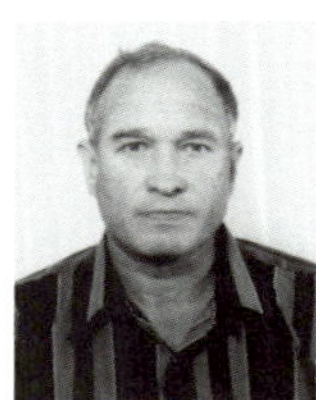

**Viktor Laptev**                    Klin, Moscow region, 1999

This is another of my contraptions. We make wire netting. It's all fairly simple: we cut the wire, twist and stretch it together, then we weave it into netting and roll it up. Sometimes, to make absolutely sure the wire doesn't come unwoven, we have to twist it tight with something. So I invented this spanner for twisting two wires beside each other together. It can be used for twisting over the top edges of the netting when it's being put up as well. But this is just a model, I've still got to test it. What an invention! Life forces us to think and adapt. If we had good equipment, maybe we wouldn't have to invent anything.

Wood, aluminium

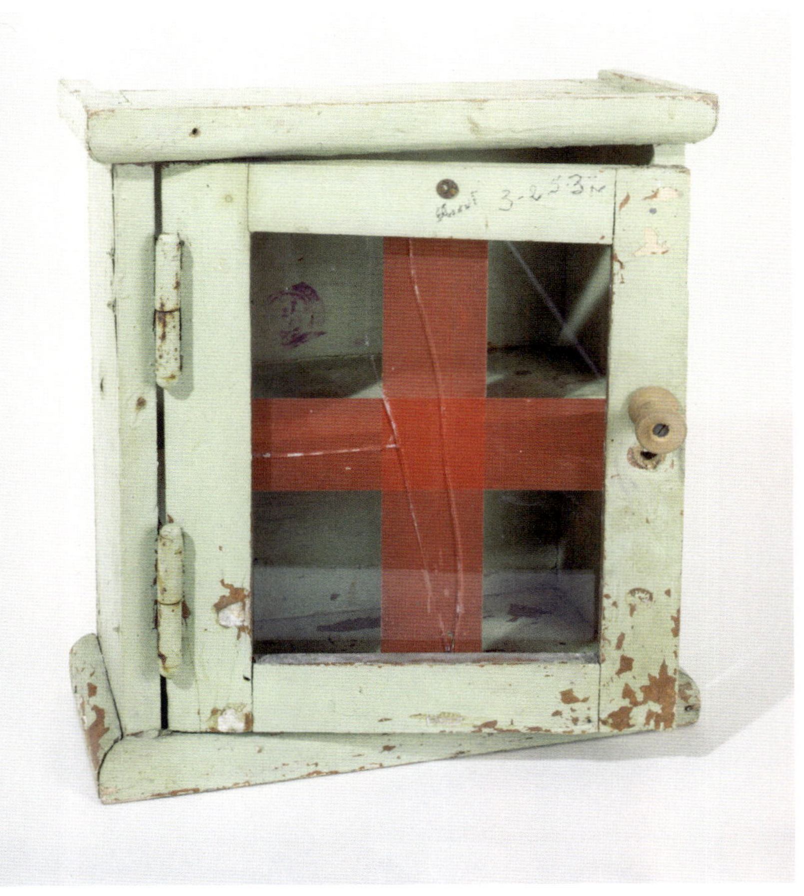

**Viktor Laptev**                    Klin, Moscow region, 1996

Anywhere that people work, relax or play sport there has to be a first aid kit, just in case. It's supposed to be there. We were supposed to have a first aid kit too, so at least there'd be a bandage and some iodine and everyone would know where to find it. There has to be a special place for it. So I made this box with a glass door, so you could see what was in it. I stuck a red cross on the glass, the way it's supposed to be. Someone broke the glass and it would have shattered if it wasn't for that cross. As it is, the box may be wounded, but it still does its job. I just can't get around to changing the glass.

Wood, glass, hinges, screws, tape

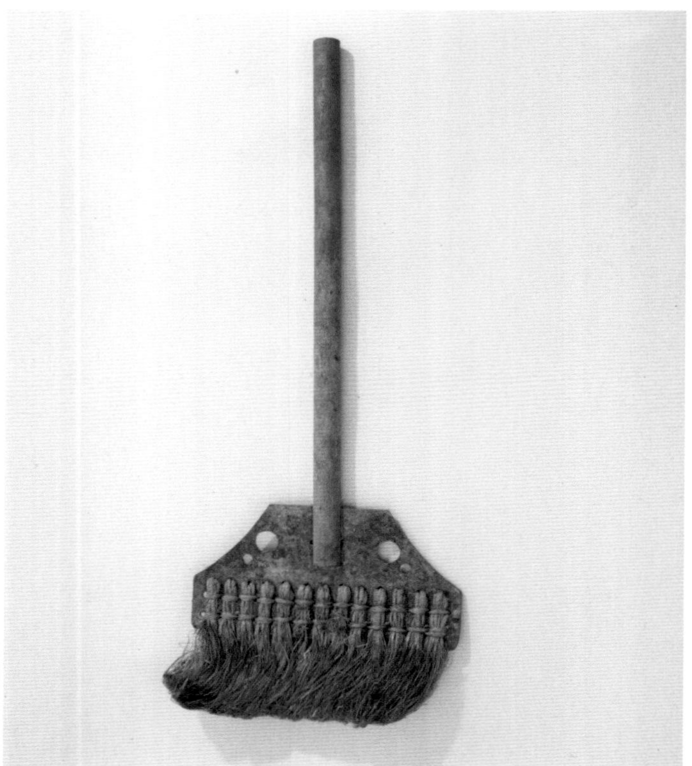

**Viktor Laptev**                                    Klin, Moscow region, 1997

You need a little broom in a workshop. But why go to a shop for it, when you've got a pair of hands? I can make one better than one you can buy in a shop, the kind I need – not just what they happen to have. It's made of nylon string and plastic, with a wooden handle just the right length. I found it all – it didn't cost me a kopeck. And if you look after the kopecks, then the roubles...

Nylon string, wood, plastic

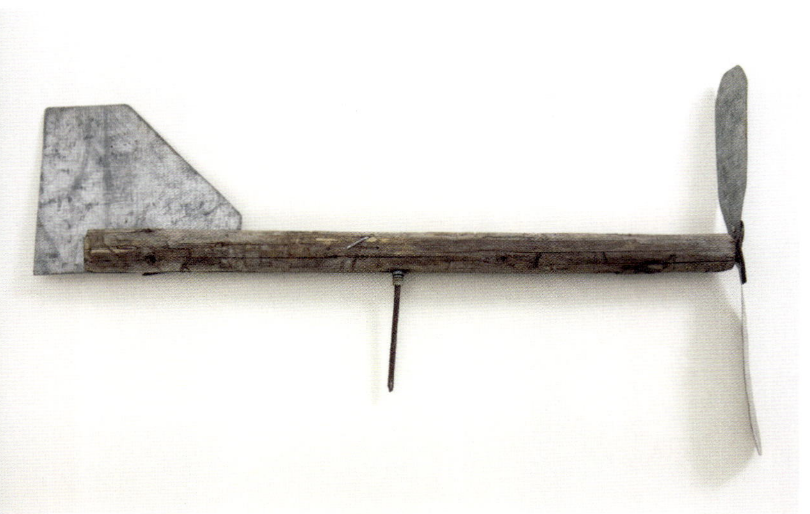

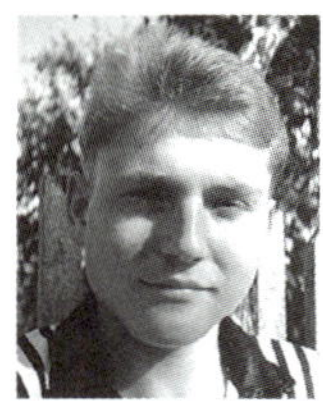

**Sergei Yeryomkin**                    Stolptsi, Ryazan region, 1994

Basically this was made to determine the direction of the wind. It's made with iron and wood. The wind indicator has had leather fixed onto it to stop it getting scuffed up. A tail was made to catch the wind and show its direction. You need to fix it somewhere high up, somewhere where there's nothing to get in its way. It's had nails hammered into the axle and wire fastened on so that it revolves without friction.

I made it with a friend in 1994. Our neighbour had one and we'd been inspired to make our own. It took us a long time, but we kept at it, and eventually we finished it and put it up. It had been there a year when some bad people took it down and dumped it somewhere. But in the end we found it, did some repair work on it and here it is now in, you could say, good condition and finally finished.

Wooden plank, tin, nails, aluminium wire

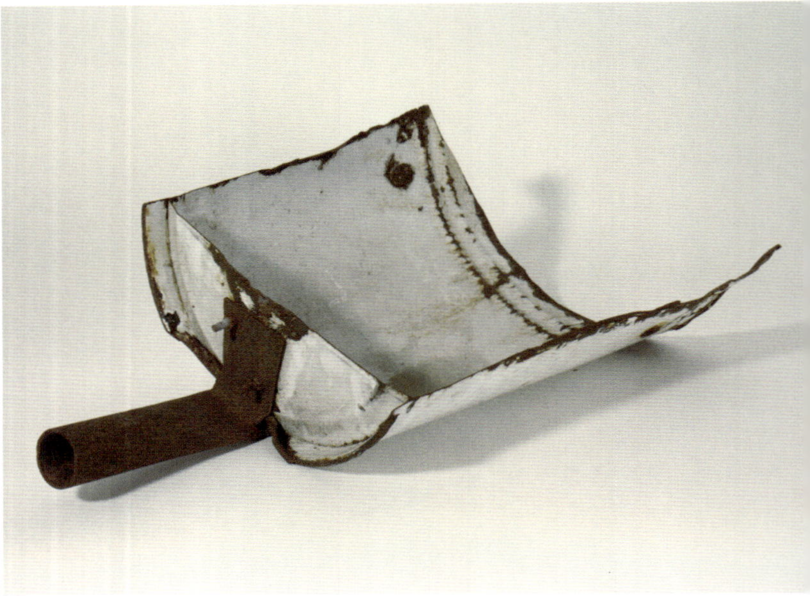

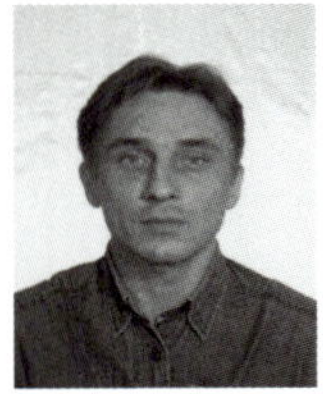

**Yurii Syomin**                                    Moscow region, 1998

It couldn't be any simpler – if you need it, you make it, that's all. I made this three years ago. I have to clean up the cow's shit after them. There was this old enamel bucket, full of holes, lying around in the yard. I couldn't just throw it out – it might come in useful for something. So I got hold of it and cut it in half, fastened on a bit of pipe to put a handle in, stuck the handle in and there I had my shovel – just right for shovelling shit. You can't scoop it up properly with an ordinary spade, but this is perfect for scooping.

Enamel bucket, metal pipe, nuts and bolts

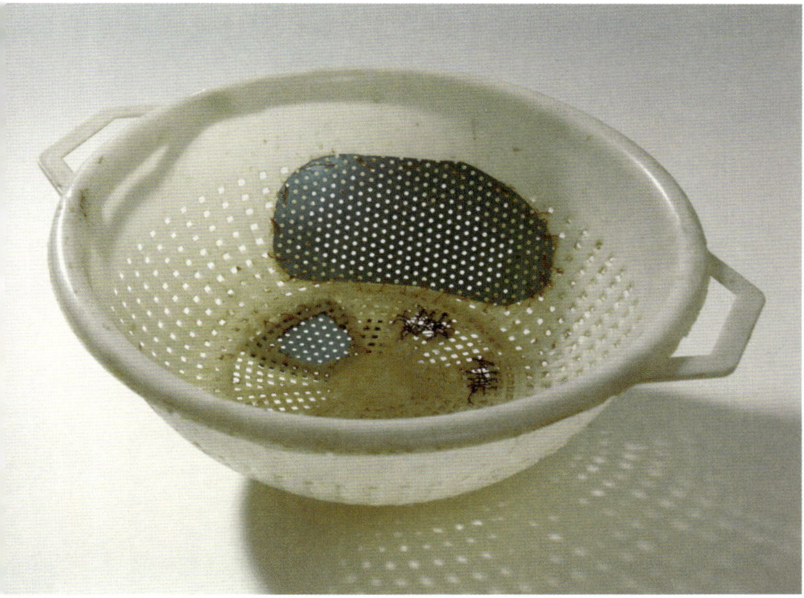

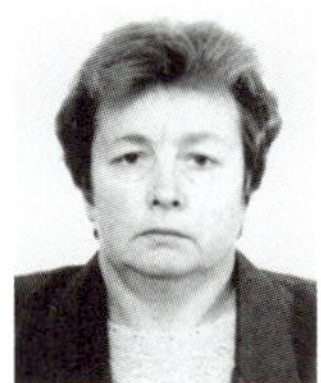

**Olga Mysina**                                    Moscow, 1995

It sort of just happened. First a little hole appeared, then it got bigger and
bigger. Why should I go traipsing round the shops looking for a new colander,
when I can still use this one? The things that were going on in those shops
– the bakery selling socks, the cinema selling cars! In the shop where I
bought this colander they sell televisions now. Life's moving so fast, you
can't keep up. What shop should I go to? I took some wire and darned a
hole, then another one. When more of them appeared, I asked my husband.
He fixed the other pieces over the holes.

Plastic colander, wire, perforated plastic

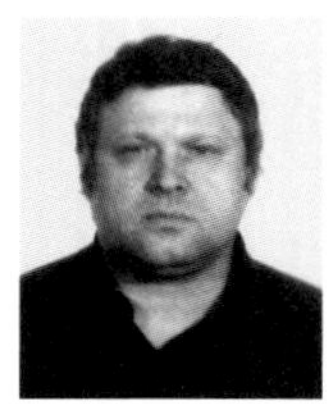

**Vasilii Kozhedub**                    Nizhny Novgorod, 1997

When I was a kid I used to have a submachine gun like this. Well, not exactly the same – it was wooden, home-made by my father. He fought as an infantryman in World War II. There weren't many toys then, in the 1950s, and my parents didn't have any money for them. Anyway they were badly made, and unconvincing. Us kids, we wanted to play at war, so my father made me this submachine gun. He called it a PPS. He carried a PPS all the way through the war, and he made me one just like it out of a piece of wood – it really looked like it. All the other kids envied me. Now I see my five-year-old son Sanka has started running around with a stick too. I decided to make him something like my father's submachine gun. Only mine turned out simpler. I don't know what it looks like, but my kid enjoys playing war with it anyway. Not long ago he broke the magazine off it somewhere and I had to make a temporary one out of an old lamp.

Wood, aluminium, nail

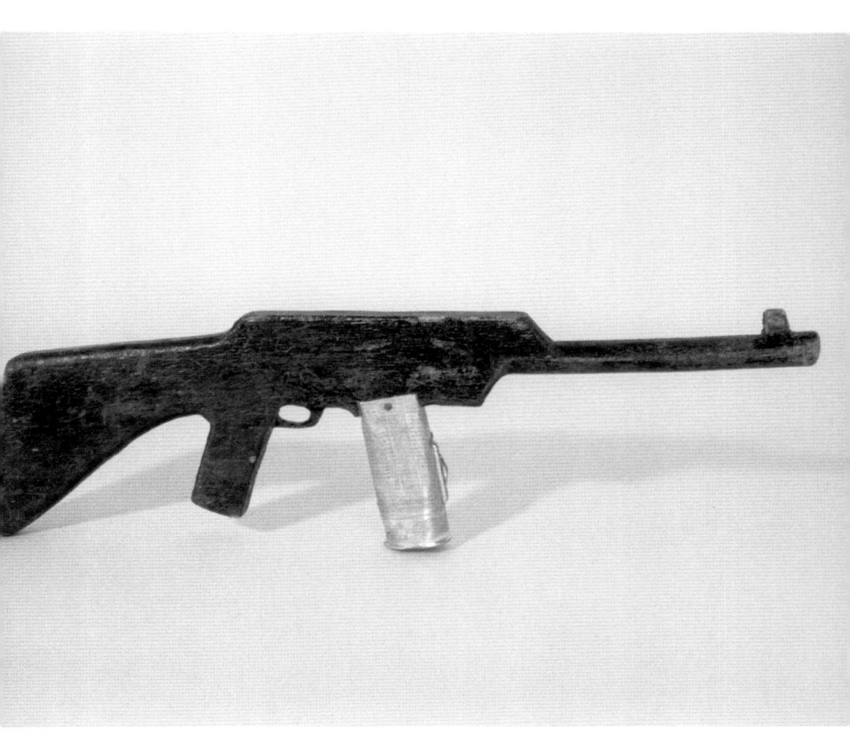

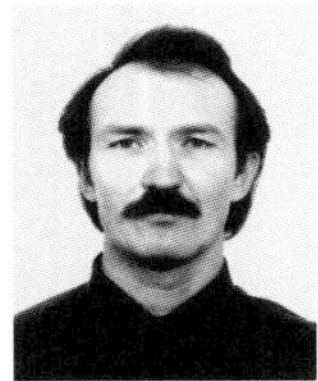

**Sergei Petrik**                                                    Ryazan, 1990

I remember at the dawn of perestroika there were these YCCs – Youth Construction Cooperatives. The Party allowed Komsomol members to participate in improving their own living conditions. What a scramble! As soon as I heard that I could go and work on a building site in order to get a flat, I put in an application. They promised me a flat in two years. Some of us ended up at the Dacha Construction Cooperative, some on the building site. That was what the building was called – YCC House. It looked beautiful on paper: twelve storeys, with arches, built of brick – not concrete slabs – with triple glazing to stop the noise from the nearby airport. I was officially transferred from our enterprise to the construction department, as a bricklayer. Do I look like a bricklayer? But never mind, I learned. It was a bit of a blast really, you know. You fling this cement and these bricks around all day long, and the wall only goes up by half a metre. In a week we'd only put up one storey. At first I was handing up the cement, and setting out the bricks. Then I got fed up with that – you're not in charge of anything. I began learning how to lay the bricks myself. They gave me a trowel and a little pick, and bricklayers have this thing to make sure the walls are vertical – a 'plumb line' it's called. It's this sort of heavy metal cylinder on a string. Every bricklayer has his own, usually kept in his pocket. But I wasn't a real bricklayer, only a temporary one. I cut off some pieces of steel reinforcement, welded them together, made a loop for the string and welded the end. But if you're naturally cack-handed, you won't be able to get a right angle anyway, even with a professional plumb line.

Steel

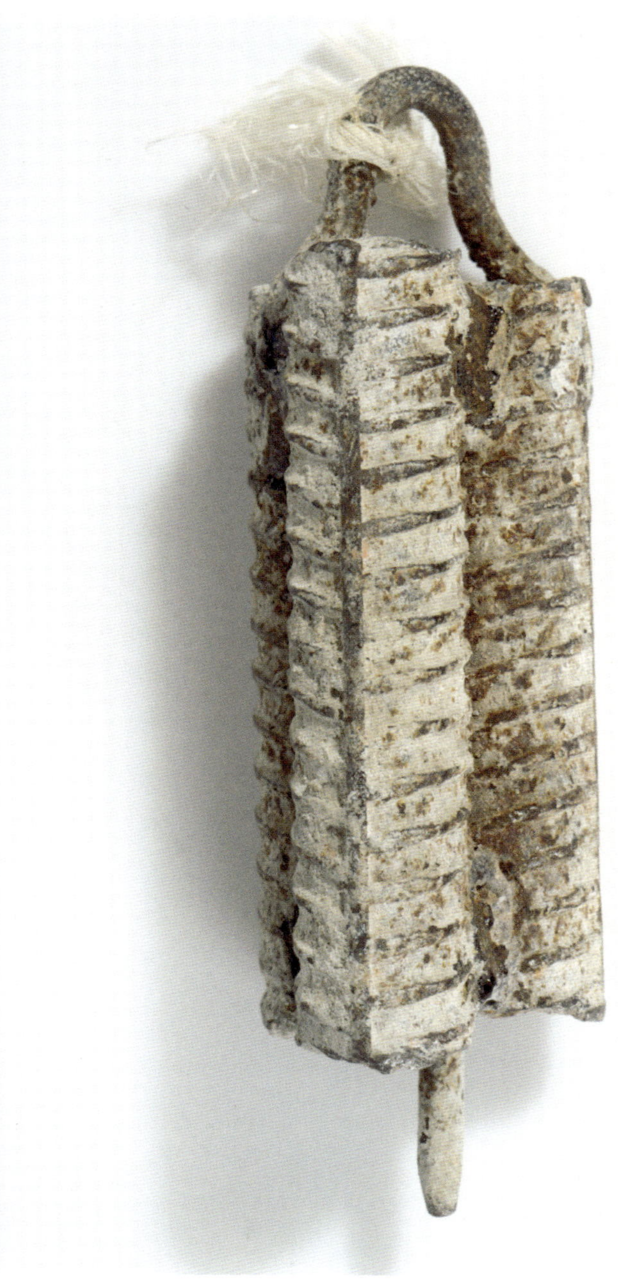

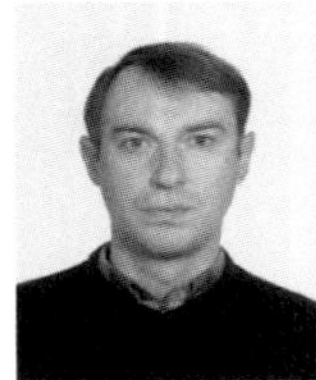

**Nikolai Vasiliev**                                         Tula region, 1975

This is a mudflap. I made it when I was still a kid. I was twelve or fourteen at the time. I was still going to school at the collective farm. That was when the communists were still in. They'd only just started producing mopeds. Nowadays you can get anything you want, but then everything was in short supply. I bought a moped. Only it wasn't that simple: I didn't just go and buy it, but in 1973 or maybe 1975, we set a record collecting the harvest and so we got sent goods that were in short supply, probably from Moscow. My aunt – in the country everyone's related – was working in the shop that received all the manufactured goods. They were allowed to choose which goods they wanted in their shops for the record-setting collective farm workers. I asked her to get a moped for me and my mother ordered a washing machine as well. So then she brought me my moped. I paid for it with all my own money; I didn't take a kopeck from my parents. I earned good money working on the harvest – they gave me a bonus and a certificate too. The kids my age were envious – I'd started straight away as an adjuster on a combine harvester, setting the rollers. Only fourteen-year-olds were allowed to do this and I was about twelve then. But my father was a brigade leader and he trusted me. I tried not to let him down, and worked honestly. So the money, the bonus, the certificate and the moped – they were all well earned.

But the mudflap, that's nothing special. A mudflap is a mudflap, what else can you say about it? Well, there weren't any on the moped. You know yourself what the roads used to be like in the countryside, and they're still shit. By the time you get home from a dance, you're all covered in mud. To stop the mud flying up quite so much, I made mudflaps out of an old conveyor belt – they used a lot of it somewhere on the collective farm. But nothing ever got dumped in the pit, even if the equipment was written off – everybody took what they needed home to use. We had some in the shed too. My father helped me cut the shape out with a knife, and I unscrewed the reflector off an old truck that had been written off in the graveyard – that's what we called the piece of waste ground where all the old obsolete equipment stood.

Conveyor belt, reflector, screw

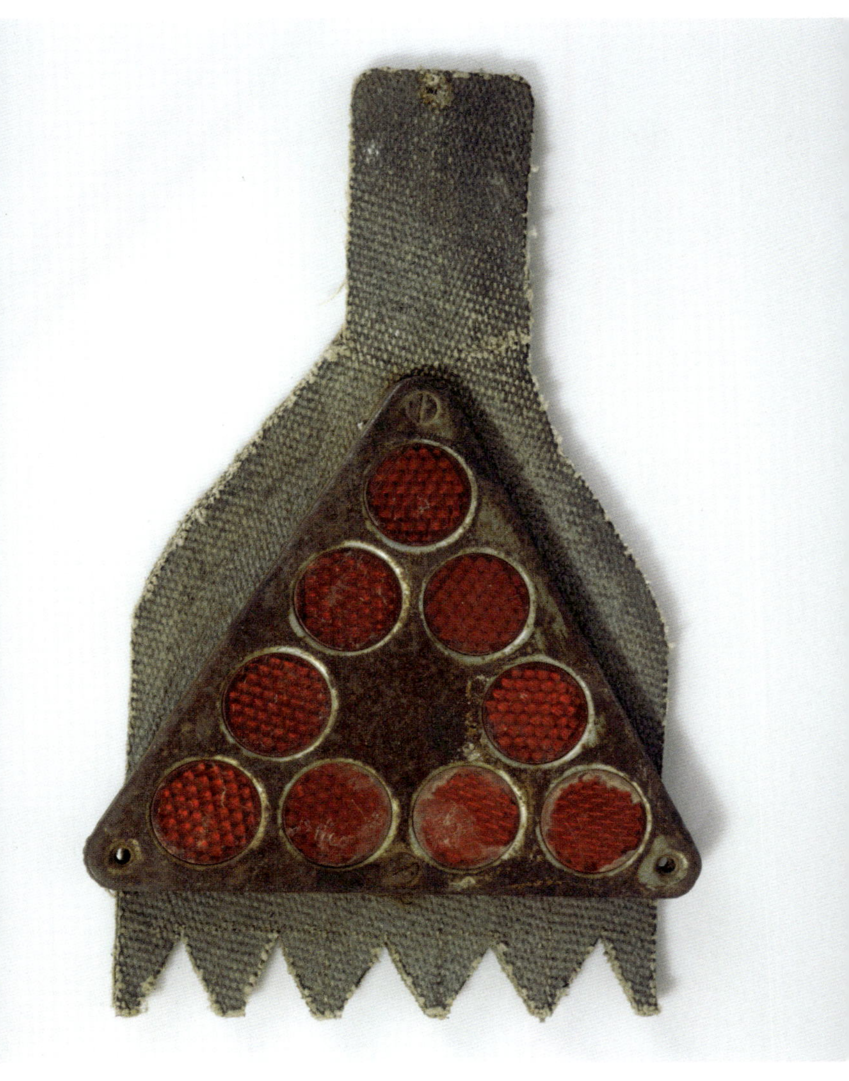

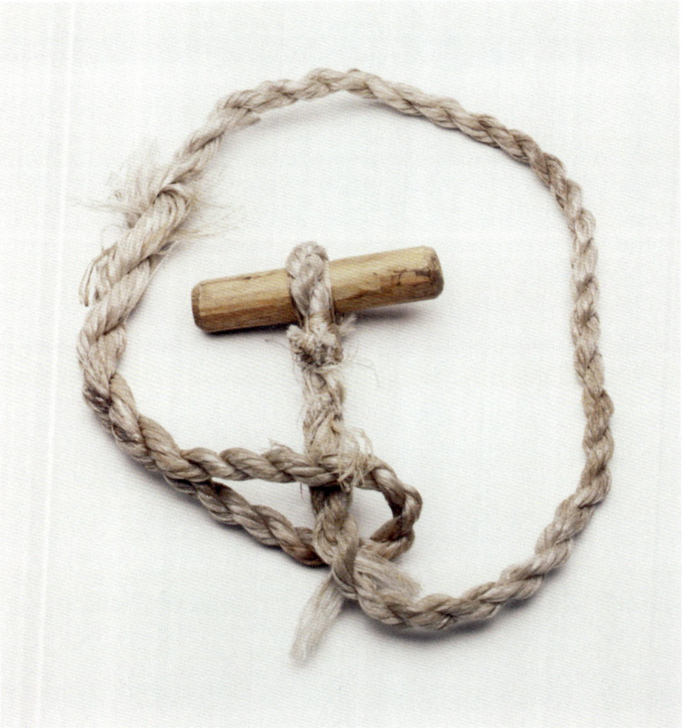

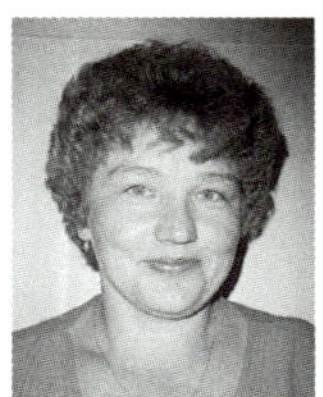

**Natalia Volkova** Tver region, 1995

Well, you get hold of an old rope, which is used to tie up straw bales, and you bunch it up into a kind of lasso. The end of the loop is called a 'gagger', which is made into the noose. You can tie up horses with it so that they stay in one place without wandering off too far.

Nylon rope, wood

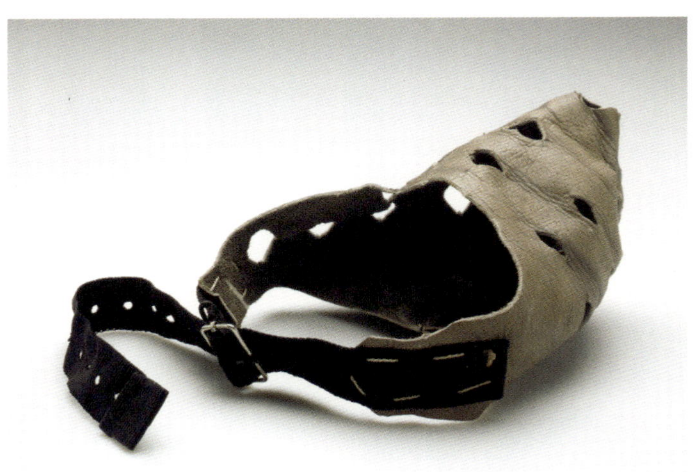

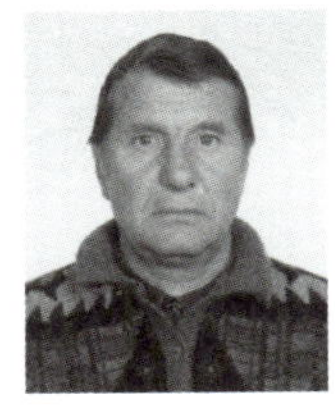

**Alexei Titov**                                        Smolensk, 1997

*As recounted by his son Andrei:* We had a collie called Gerda. She was a gentle dog, never attacked anyone, and I don't think there was ever any need for a muzzle. But four or five years ago my father made her a muzzle anyway. Only he didn't make it because the dog needed it, but because he couldn't bring himself to throw out my mother's old boots when they split – she'd worn them for ten years. My father held them in his hands and said, 'That's great leather!' The leather tops were really lovely and soft. So he cut them off and threw out the soles of the boots. Then he made a muzzle for Gerda out of one of the pieces. It's very simple: he stitched it with nylon thread, found a black nylon ribbon somewhere, made a buckle out of bent wire and stitched it all together to make a good strong muzzle. Of course my father couldn't just throw such fine leather out, because his father was a cobbler and he'd always cut off the parts of the old worn-out shoes that could still be used, to make slippers from them. Everybody in our family had slippers made by grandad.

Leather, nylon thread, ribbon, wire

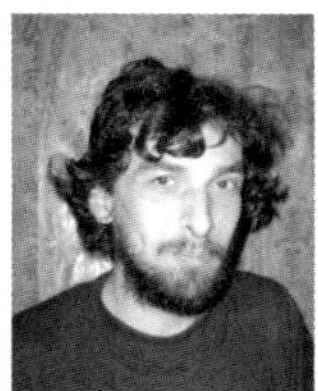

**Georgii Mnatsakanov**                                    Moscow, 1980

This is connected with that romantic poetical period in a young man's life when the muse only takes it upon herself to visit him at night, at the time when he should already be asleep. So, this pen has a plastic tube added on to it into which a battery, a bulb, a pivot and as a switch, two bottle tops are jammed. It's a very convenient thing. You can hold it under your pillow and use it for all your youthful musings. If you are meeting your muse in difficult circumstances – if someone is snoring away in the next bed – it's recommended to keep a pen, pencil and some paper under your pillow so, when the muse comes to you in the depths of the night, you can get this out and, without bothering anyone, record the results of her visit.

Plastic tube, light bulb, battery, wire, ballpoint cartridge, bottle tops

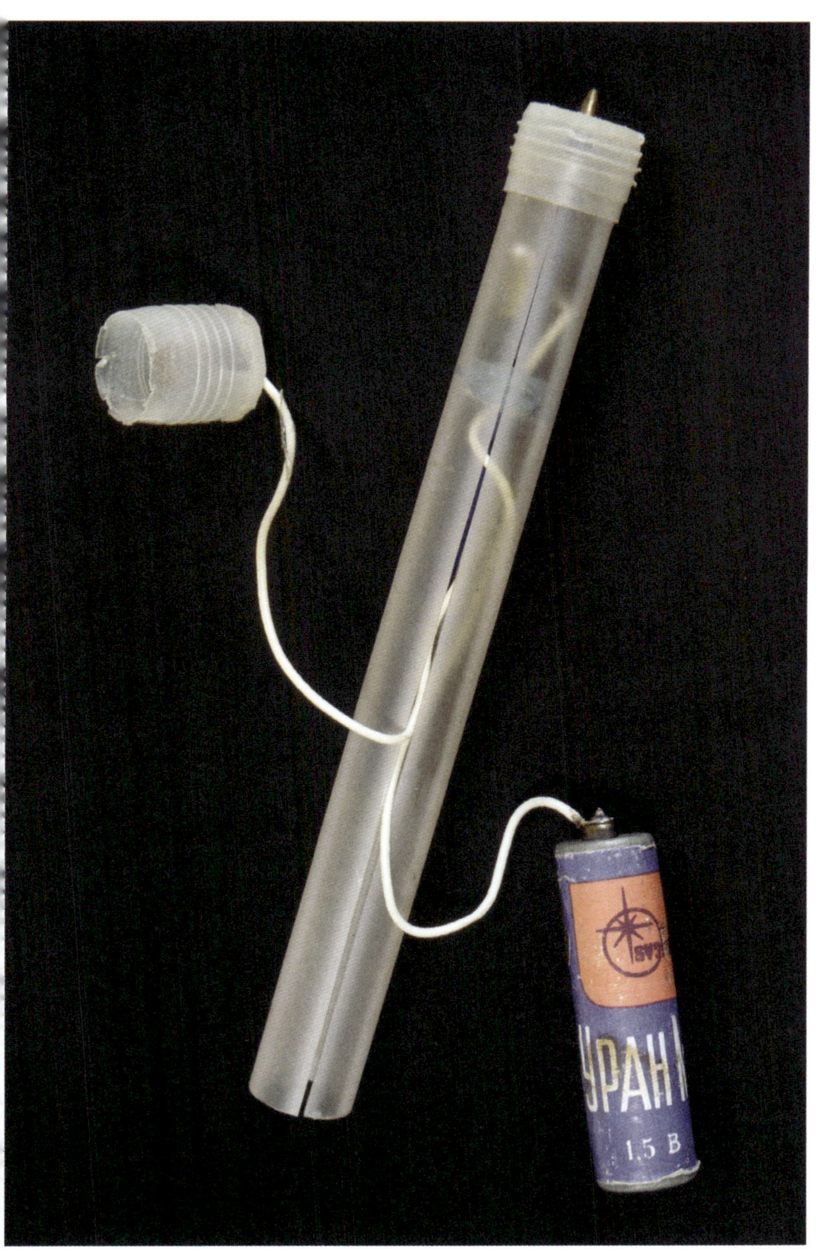
УРАН
1,5 В

**Georgii Mnatsakanov**                                        Moscow, c.1993

This episode took place in about 1993, when I was living with my friend Volodya in a basement on Mayakovsky Street. He was working as a janitor and he knew all the basements around there – which were lived in and which were empty. So we moved into one. There were some other spaces next to it, but we didn't know who was living there. There were problems with the lock right from the beginning, because we all shared the same metal door out onto the street. Pipes kept bursting all the time and the repairmen cut the lock off the door without bothering to find out who had the key, or even where to look for it. We had to keep buying new locks and having keys made for everyone. As we didn't have much money, any expense was significant for us. When we saw the lock had been cut off yet again, we tried something different. We simply went to the welders in the yard who worked on the pipes and asked them to weld the metal loop back on. No problem! They did it straight away, hammered down the scale around it and then asked if it opened properly. Fantastic! They didn't want any money! But then things got serious. Property prices rose – including those for basements. We were literally thrown out onto the street. When we came home all our stuff was lying in the road and they were already starting repairs on the basement.

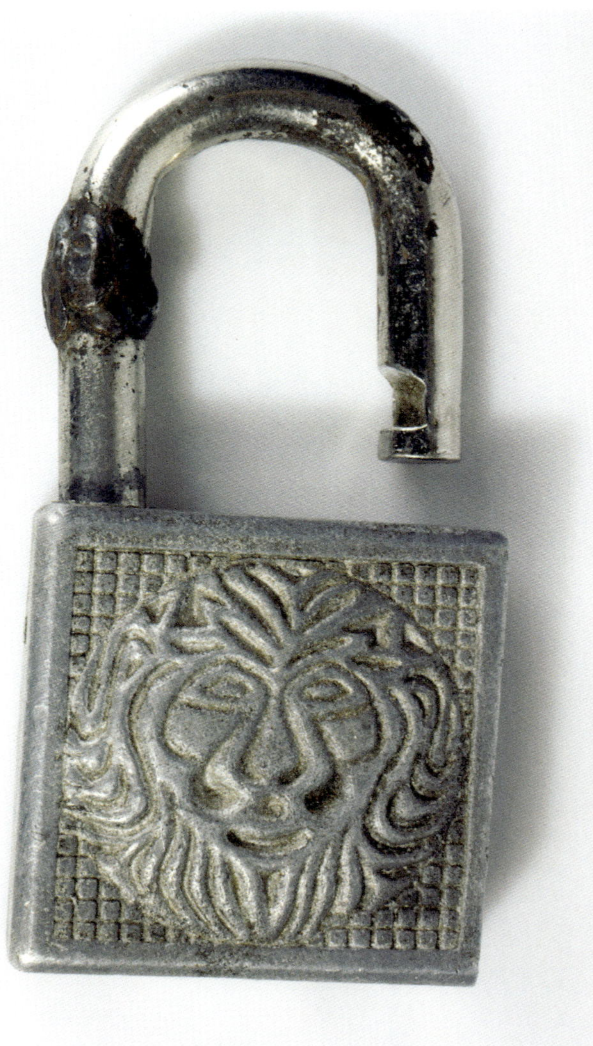

**Georgii Mnatsakanov**　　　　　　　　　　　　　　　Moscow, c.1978

This goes back to the days of my carefree youth, when we were the local street kids, getting up to all sorts of mischief. What fun we had then! We used to put nails under the wheels of the trams to make little knives, we threw snowballs at the girls, we lit bonfires everywhere we could, especially where it was forbidden. We were always digging something up, burying all sorts of little secrets, firing our catapults at the jackdaws, making guns that fired bullets of aluminium wire.

Before this catapult, I remember I had a few others made out of aluminium wire and 'Hungarian' rubber. To this day I still don't know why it was called that. But they weren't powerful enough for me, they didn't shoot far enough, so that's probably why this 'international version' got made. A stick, a rubber strap from the chemist's, and a piece of leather. Of course, it's all just messing about, sheer hooliganism, but we had to do something to keep ourselves busy.

Wood, rubber, leather

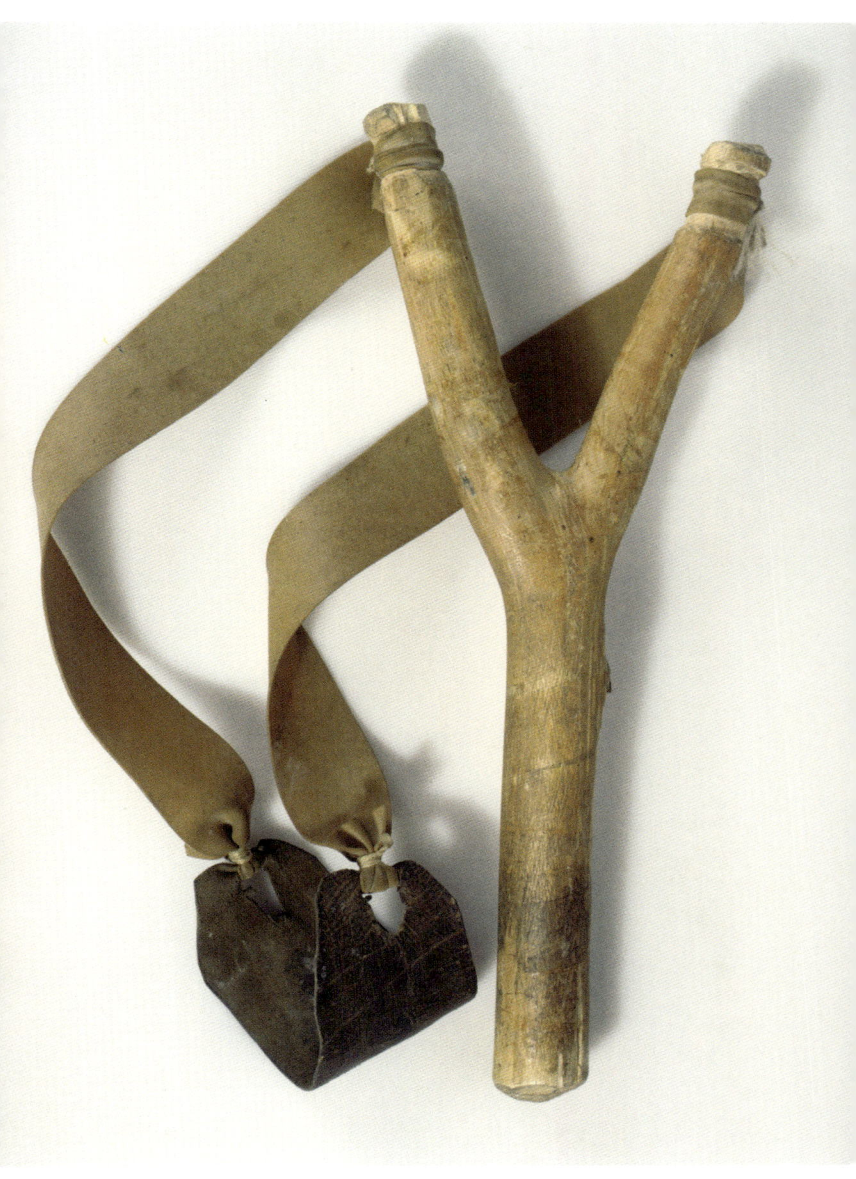

**Elena Mnatsakanova**                                                    Moscow, c.1985

*As recounted by her brother Georgii:* My sister loved to sew all kinds of dolls – she sewed baby deer, a bear, an elephant and a beautiful flower elephant. But this isn't at all like that: this was made from a load of Kinder Surprise eggs. I ate them and my sister made it. The idea most probably came from a sewn snake made from a tie. The tie was silky with a strange texture, like scales. The snake had huge jaws, was very long and was stuffed with cotton, and the caterpillar probably came from here because they all ended up in net bags. I don't know where the net bags came from – from potatoes, from carrots, from beetroot – I don't know. I haven't got a clue. It was made when my sister had already settled down, when she had become an adult, had already finished studying at university. She didn't have time to make soft toys any more, and so she made this. She has an almost pathological love of fluffy toys and so she made this simply for pleasure. But because she didn't have much time it was made very quickly. Dried peas were poured in, and the sections were knotted together. It was given to me as a gift for some reason, after I left university, in about 1985.

Kinder Surprise eggs, peas, nylon, vegetable bags, insulating tape, thread

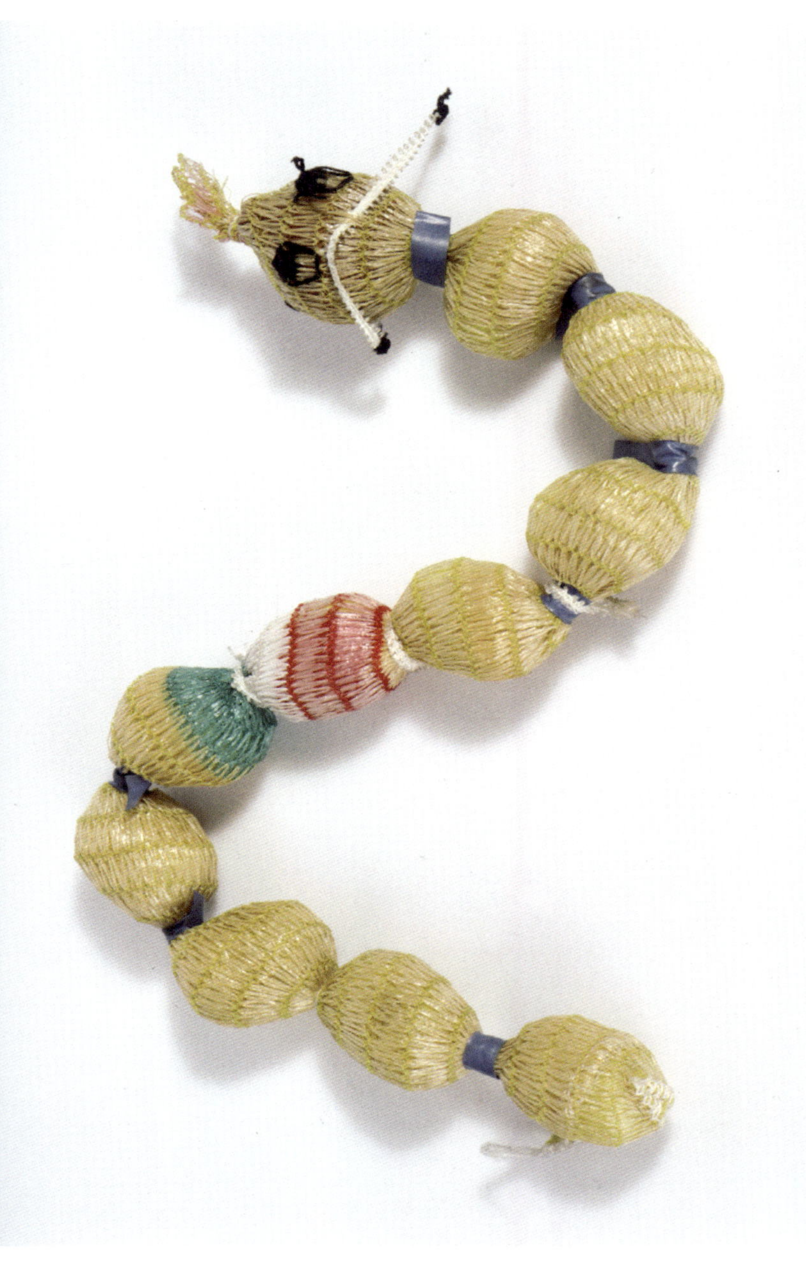

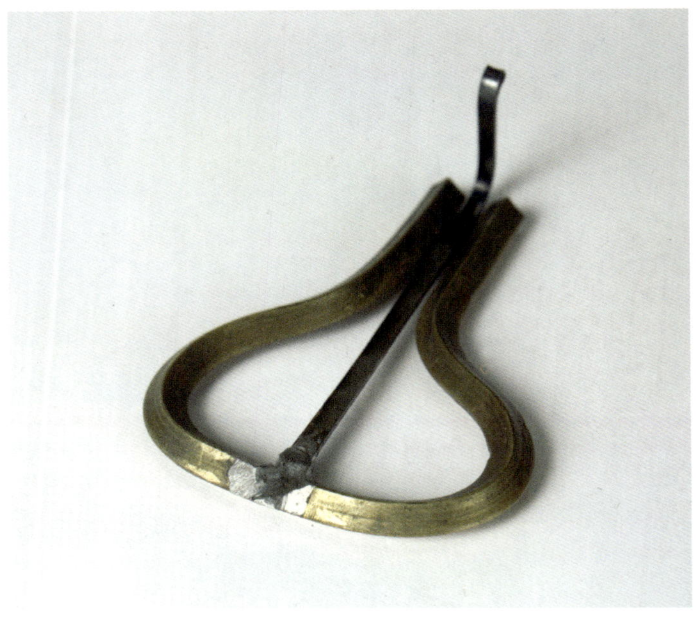

**Georgii Mnatsakanov**                                        Moscow, 1987

This is called a 'jew's harp' or a 'khamuz'. All the primitive peoples had them – the Chukchi, the Koryak, the Uymen and others. It was the favourite of the Nganasani and the Tefalari. At first they made them from bones, and then, when steel started to appear they began to forge them. Basically it had to be forged so that it would sound right. But since there was no real possibility of forging then... This thing is made from a brass strip, which is bent, then a metal strip is soldered on which gives the sound. It's made from a trimmed bit of saw, though it's possible to make it from a ruler. Before this I made one from a metal ruler. The sound depends on the length of the strip – higher or lower, and the bass sound is produced by the thicker strip.

Brass, steel

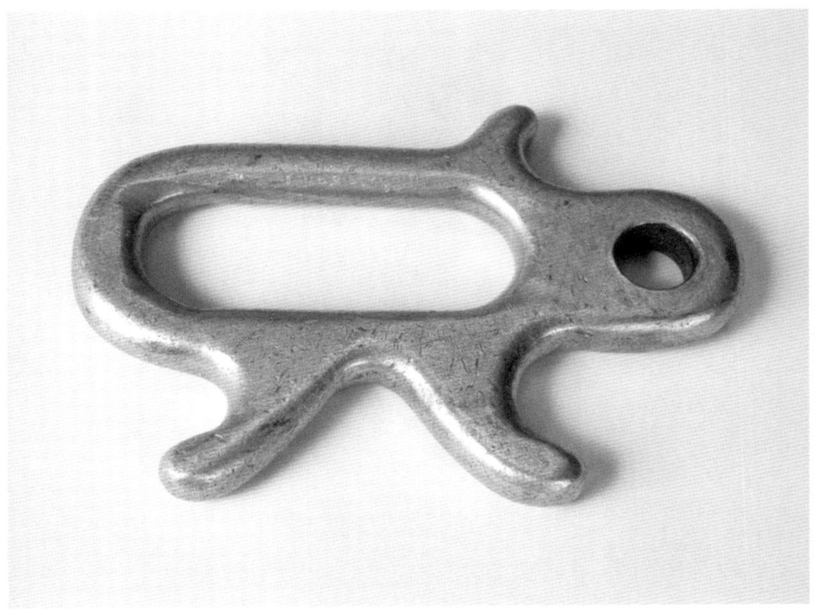

**Dmitrii Saveliev**     Zhukovsky, Moscow region, c.1980

This is an abseiling device commonly known as 'an eighter with horns' or 'horner'. Someone I know gave it to me as a present. His friend at work gave it to him. They used to use it in mountain climbing, in mountain tourism for descending from heights by rope. Into the lower 'eye' – into the small opening – the device was put; into the big 'eye' – into the upper opening – the rope was put, as well as into the device. The rope was wound around the horns, the device was fastened to the safety harness and then it became possible to wind rope from the horns and, by holding on to it, to climb down. Now such devices are produced by lots of different companies. But, in the past, you basically couldn't find them for sale anywhere. They were all home-made. This one is made from aluminum. I don't know what year it was made in. It was given to me at the end of about 1988 or 1989. But it was made ten years earlier, or thereabouts. From what they told me, it was made at a factory by my friend. He sharpened it a lot by hand – it's pretty evident where he was filing it. It's not such a successful piece actually. The things they use these days are a lot more convenient.

Aluminium

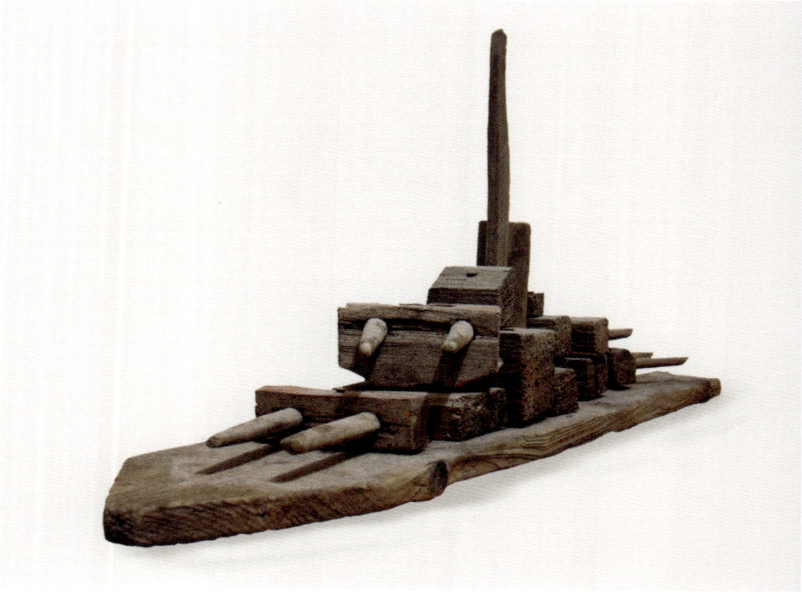

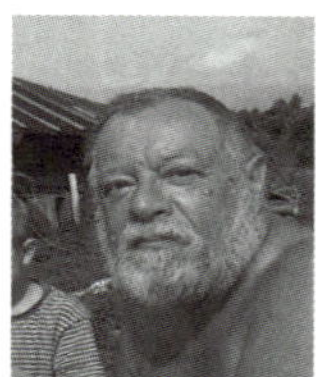

**Evgenii Skrynnikov**                    Vologda region, 2000

It's what I'd call a monitor. It's for the children really – it was built as a toy for them. But since I'm very fond of naval architecture and I know a lot about it, it looks very similar to the old flat-bottomed ships called monitors. I made it out of spare materials, some old planks, and for the funnel I just sawed a piece off an old rake handle. They used to have an entire fleet near where we live – a gunboat, battleships, a destroyer. I made the lot myself. This is all that's left now.

Wood, nails

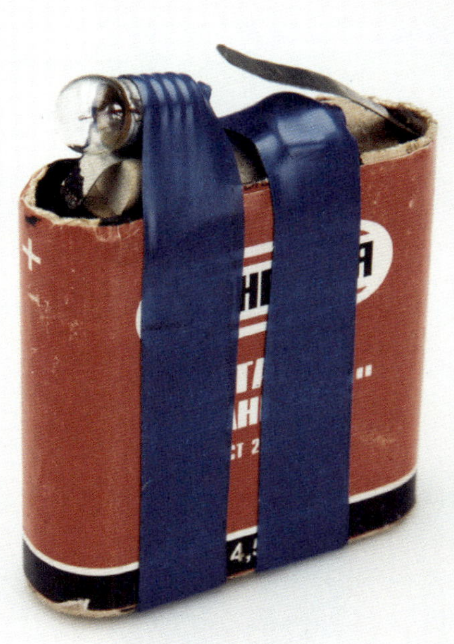

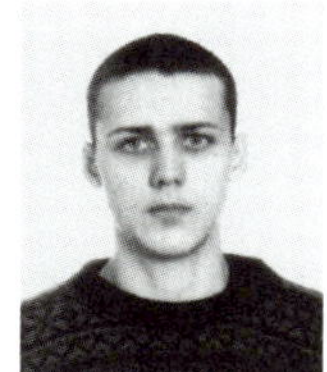

**Petya**                                              Yaroslavl, 1999

It's something I made when I was still a kid. Round here we all made them,
so we could run around at night, playing at war. You take a square battery
and tape a bulb onto one of the contacts, then you press the other contact
onto it to light it up. Your parents would never get you a torch, but you could
get them to give you the money for a battery – just tell them it had gone flat
and you needed to buy a new one.

Battery, bulb, insulation tape

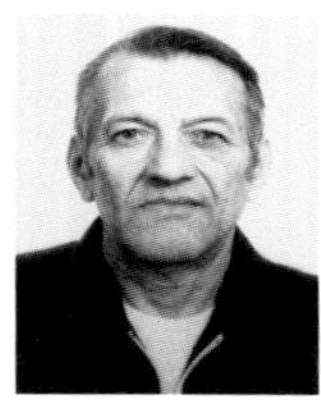

**Mikhail Sergeev**                                    Vologda, 1996

I just need to clean my hands sometimes, have a wash, or whatever. So I made a wash stand. I put it up in the corner, behind the door – there isn't any other space. The house is only 3 or 4 square metres, a dacha – what kind of dacha is that? You can shelter from the rain and stand your spades and rakes in it. But sometimes in the summer we sleep here anyway, collect the Colorado beetles, water the vegetables, heap them up. You can't keep anything valuable here – they'd steal it. Last year they even cut the aluminium wiring off the fences – things had never gone that far before. So you invent things out of whatever comes to hand. We had a basin here, and some buckets. First I bent a bucket to fit the corner. My wife said, 'We've nothing to water things with as it is, and now you've taken the bucket and made it useless too!' So I straightened out the bucket and gave it back to her, for the garden. Then I took the basin. I bent it to fit in the corner under the wash stand and put it on a stool so it's easier to carry out. Where would I find something like that in a shop?

Metal basin

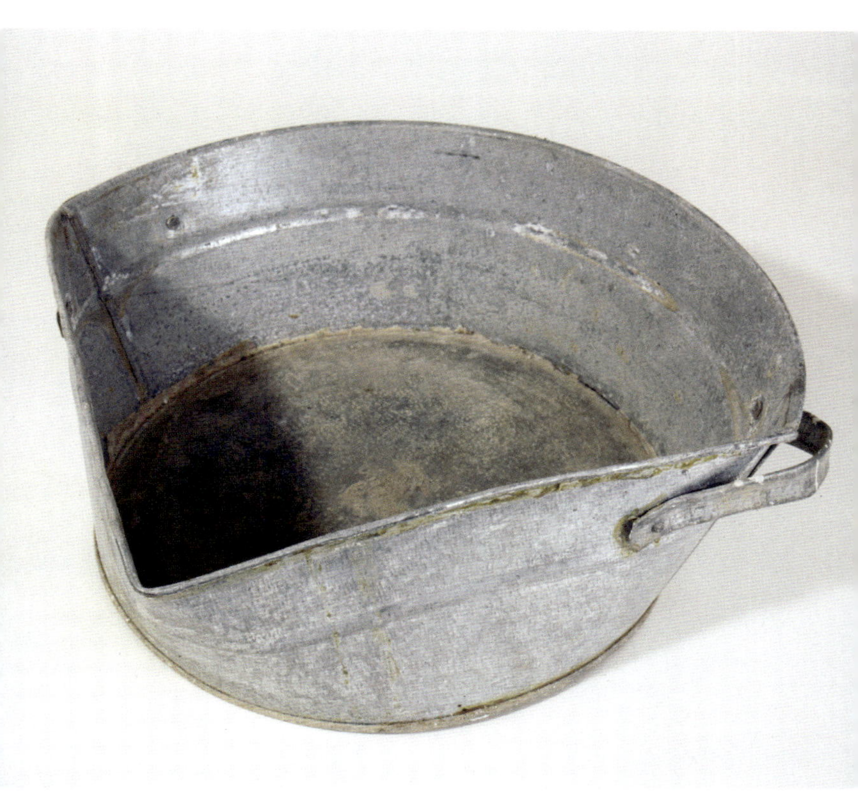

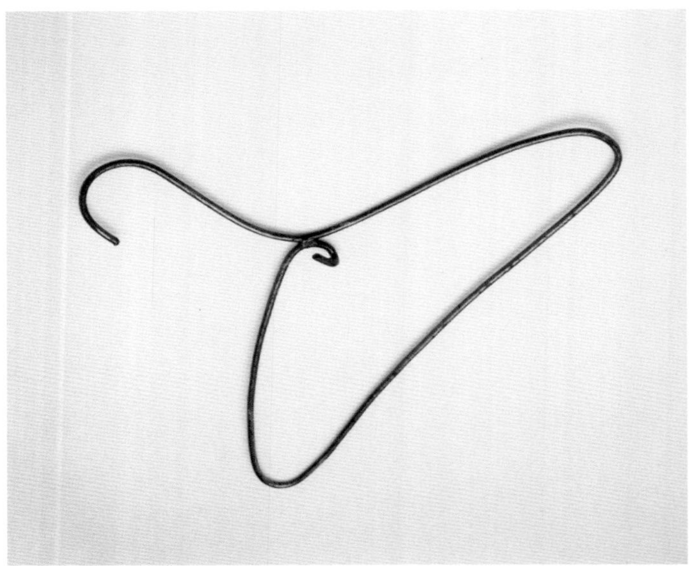

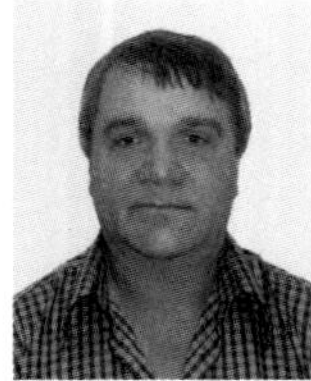

**Ivan Pogodin**                                    Ivanovo, 1999

A coat-hanger's a coat-hanger, what other shape could it be? It only took a moment – after all, I am a welder. There's all sorts of wire on a building site. I cut off as much as I needed and fixed it at one spot, that's all. If it gets lost or stolen, it doesn't matter, I'll make another one. Our work huts often get broken into, mainly to steal the heaters. In my house all the hangers are steel – I made them myself. Little ones for the children, bigger ones for me and the wife. They'll last for ever. You take a thin rod of number-five steel, bend it, and there you are. Wire's soft, easy to form. You can make them smaller or bigger – whatever size you like. When my daughter was little, I made little hangers for the kindergarten – for the whole class. And what kind of hangers do you get nowadays? My wife bought a coat, brought it home and hung it up. A really beautiful hanger, plastic it was – one week later it broke. When I make one, you can hang a bulletproof vest on it.

Steel wire

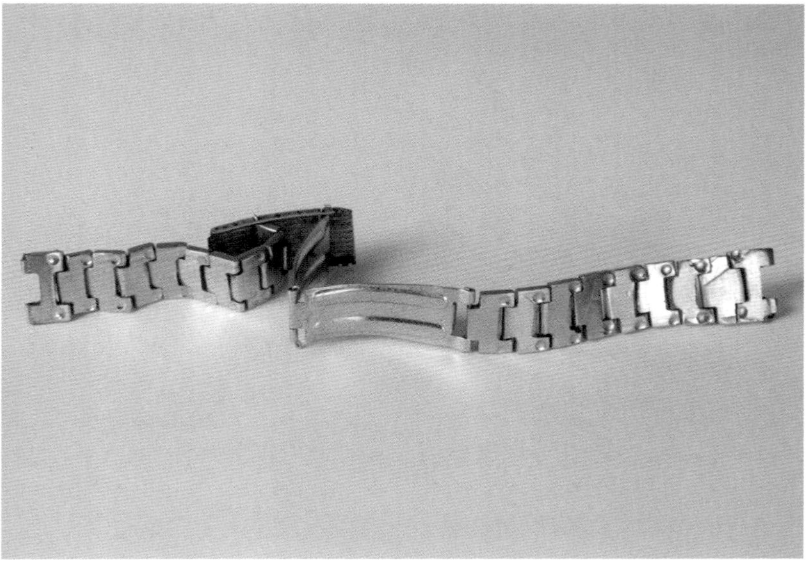

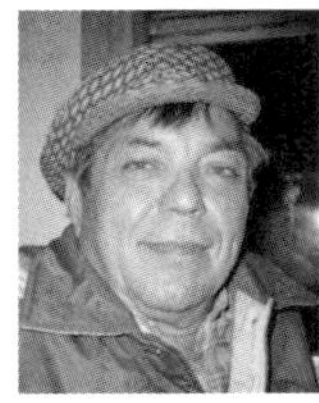

**Ivan Chernyshov**          Moscow region, 1993

Home-made – how did you guess? Because it's a bit uneven? But then it will last forever – why? Because I made it myself. Look here – you can see the clasp's a piece of the old strap, but I made all the rest from new. My old one had gone completely loose and kept coming unfastened, because it was made out of soft steel. Our factory's doing next to nothing now – we used to make rockets, but that's all I'm going to tell you. There's no money or orders now, but I still go to work. I've only got one year to go to my pension. You try just sitting there, doing nothing for eight hours. We've got some materials left around the place, some stores and equipment, and I've got a pair of hands. What else do I need? You can see how I turned this, rolled it, ground it a bit, cramped it and put new spindles in. I gave it to the lads in the thermal treatment shop and they tempered it, good and hard! Now I can wear it for ever. For as long as I've got left, that is. Maybe it'll outlast me.

Stainless steel, brass, clasp

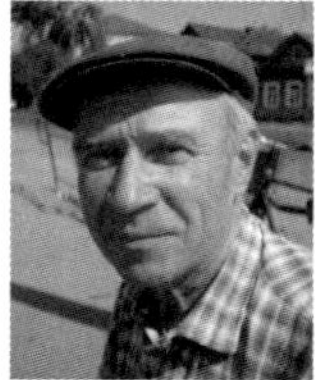

**Anatoly Yamanov**                                     Ryazan region, 1993

A chair's just something for sitting on, right? Well now, I bought a house, I moved in, and there was nothing to sit on. At first I sat on a bucket, then I said, 'Why don't I make myself a chair?' So I did a bit of planing, put this here, that there, and in a couple of shakes I'd made a stool. My wife said, 'Look, we've got no window frames. Make some frames.' I said, 'I don't know how to do that.' But then I started planing and planed away until I'd made us some frames. I haven't put them up yet, but they're standing there, all ready. I'll be putting them up soon. It's a shameful story really. I was living in Ryazan, working as a plumber, but when I got too old they sacked me and left me with my pension. How can you live on our pension? So I had to decide what to do. Nobody wants me at my age. I went to a shop as I wanted to get a job as a porter, but they wouldn't take me, said I was too old, said I should stay at home and take it easy. I went to the market as I wanted to push the trolleys about, but the street bums work there for a glass of vodka. Where else could I try? There is nowhere else in Ryazan: nothing but military factories and aerodromes, none of the offices are doing anything, nobody's taking anyone on – they're lucky if they can find work for the people they've got. The wife and me started wondering what to do. We decided that if we sold the flat in Ryazan and bought a little house in the country, we could save money. We're from the country, village people used to village work – we know all about it. We thought if we planted potatoes and cucumbers, then maybe the pension might just pay for some bread. And that's how it turned out. We bought a small house, but it's got a stove. Without a stove you can't survive the winter. That's the main thing. There was no furniture at all, so I made the most essential things: a table, a bed, some chairs, out of anything I could find lying around.

Wooden stool, chair back, wood, nails, screws

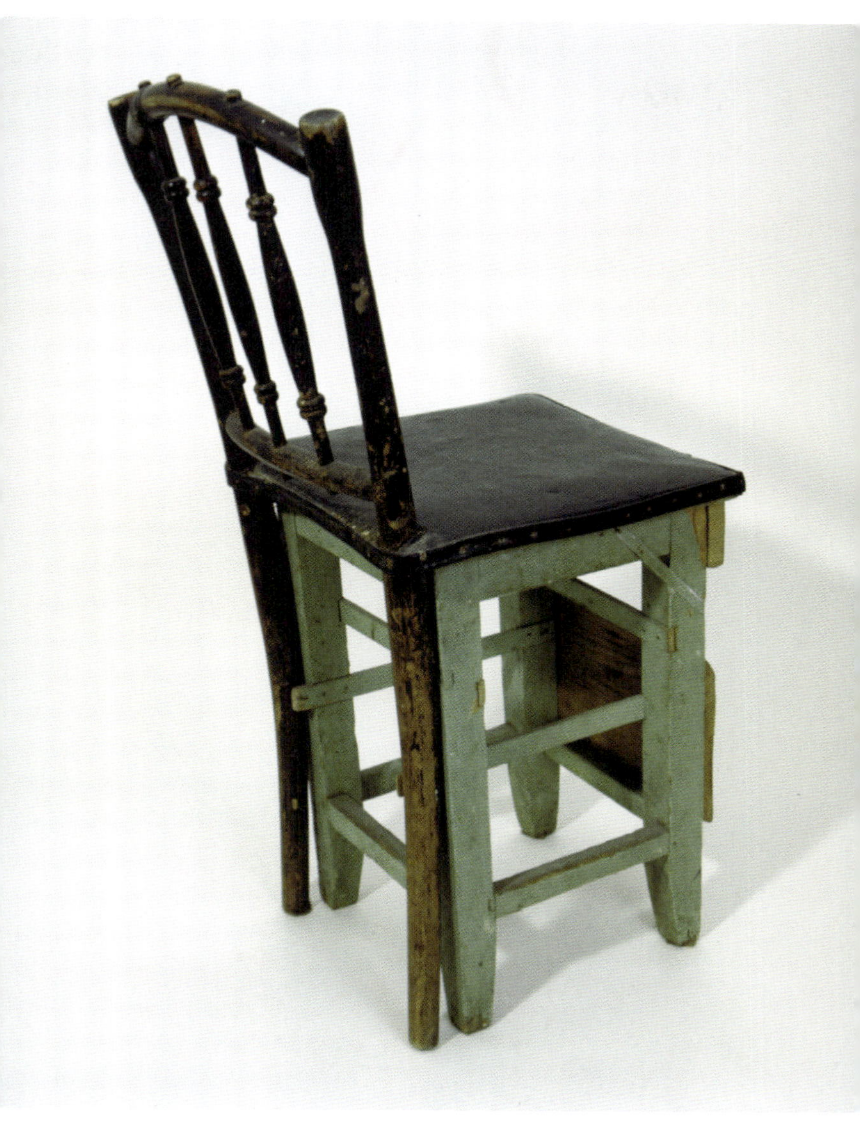

# TOILET CHAIR

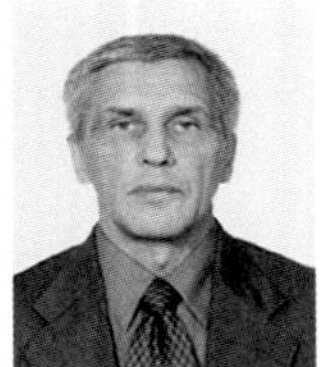

**Lyosha Tikhhonov**                    Ryazan region, 1990

*As recounted by his nephew Alexei Tikhhonov (pictured)*: Our granny had a country house in the Ryazan region and every summer lots of relatives used to come to stay. She lived on her own in the village – her husband had died from his wounds soon after the war. The lack of a pair of man's hands around the place was pretty obvious. Out in the country the toilets are usually cold – they're outside the house. This makes going to the toilet in winter a big problem – you really don't fancy the idea at all. So everyone has to think of other ways of relieving themselves.

In the late 1980s Uncle Lyosha, a distant relative from Tula, stayed with granny a couple of years in a row. He was a pensioner, already retired. One time he brought this toilet seat with him, made of plywood with lots of layers. He said he'd been doing some repairs to his flat and had decided to make granny's life a bit more comfortable. At first we didn't understand why he'd brought the seat, until a little later he produced this strange contraption. But, as we found out afterwards, it really was comfortable. He took a stool – I think it was granny's daughter who brought that, my aunt. She brought four stools with her once, because they didn't sell them in the village shop. Anyway, Uncle Lyosha asked for one of these stools and spent a long time in the shed looking for some tools and material. A few days later he showed us this new contraption. He'd attached the toilet seat to the stool using a piece of rubber because he couldn't find any hinges. The rubber's springy and absorbs the shock somehow, so the toilet seat stays vertical when you use the stool to sit on. At the same time it's very easy to lift it up, turn it round and put a bucket under it. The seat's attached to the legs of the stool with dowels. So you don't have to go outside in the winter – you can use this comfy temporary toilet. He made it around 1989 or 1990. It was still used up until granny died in 1995.

Stool, toilet seat, screws, wood, rubber, (bucket)

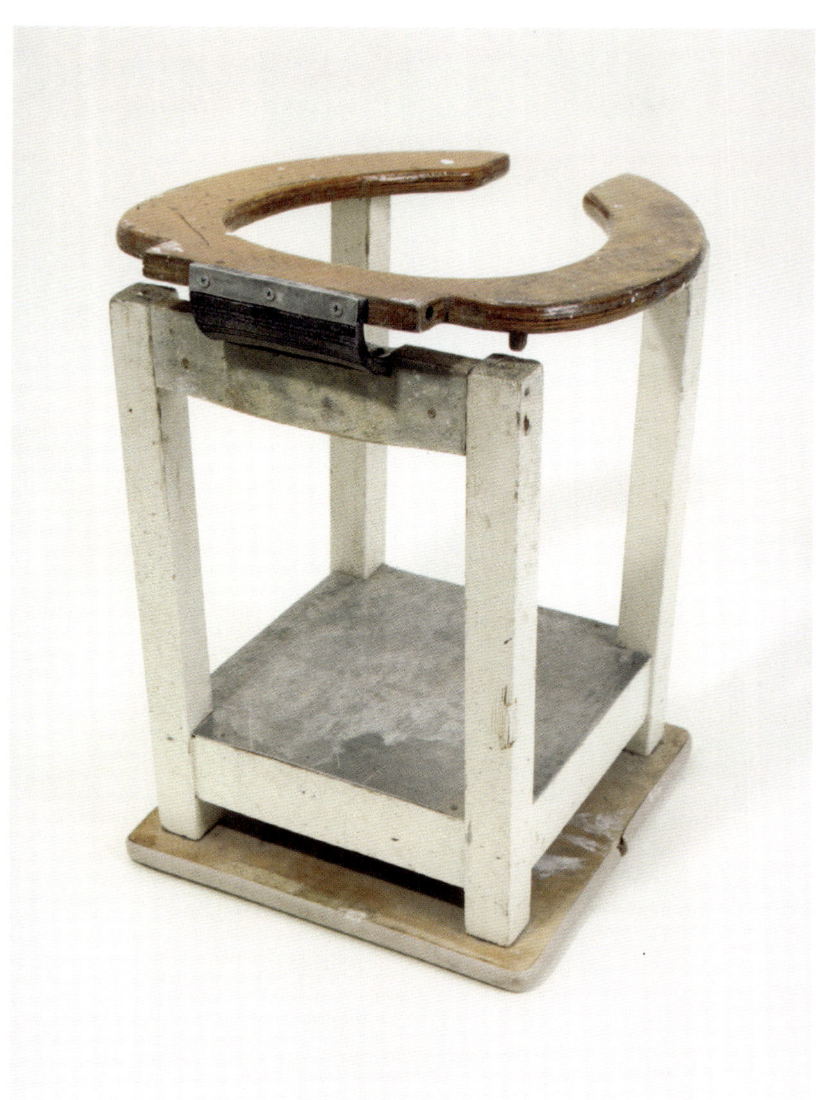

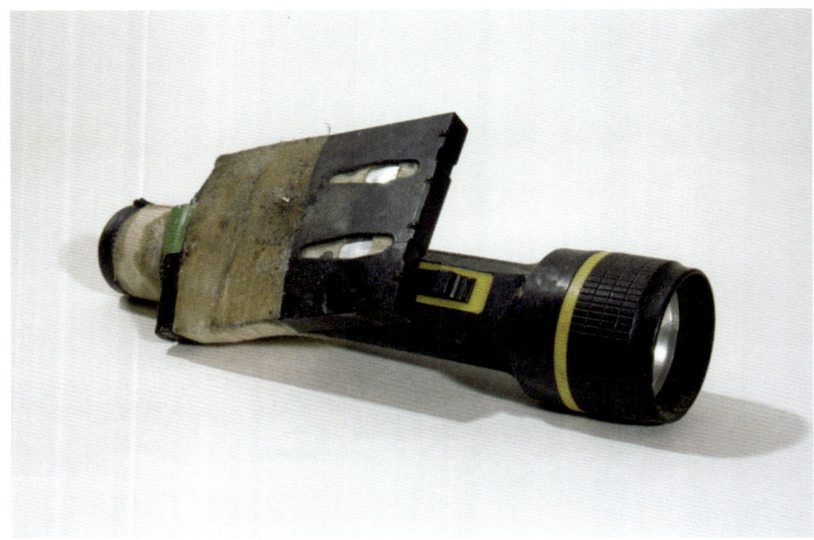

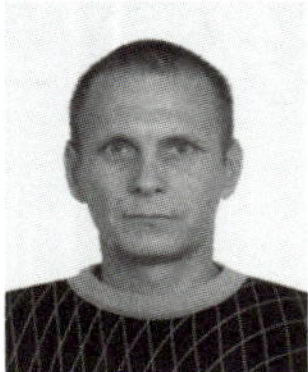

**Vladimir Titov**          Ivanovo, 1998

I found a torch, but of course there weren't any batteries in it. I didn't fancy buying any – a bottle of beer costs the same as a battery. Anyway, I found these ones from a Polaroid on the rubbish tip. I tested the charge with a voltmeter – it was still OK! I had a torch, I had voltage, all I had to do is put the two of them together. I wasn't planning to carry on using it forever – just enough for a couple of trips out to the shed – so I only fastened them on with sticking plaster. They cut off the power to our sheds when the bill wasn't paid. All the people who live here used to work at the factory, but now it's been sold off and they've sacked everybody – we're not needed any more. They say they're making it into some kind of warehouse, so it's just, 'Push off!' On top of that they go and cut the power. We got the light back on in the houses – we held a demonstration, but they still didn't put the sheds back on again. It's dangerous to go in there with matches – they're all wood and some people use them to store kerosene or oil.

Torch, adhesive plaster, Polaroid camera battery

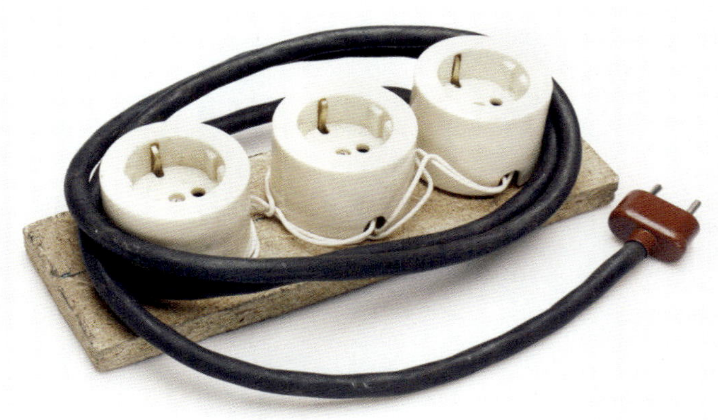

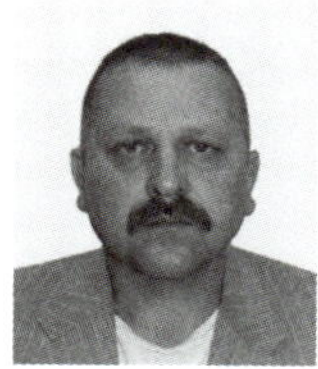

**Pyotr Anisimov**                                             Ivanovo, 1999

I have to plug all sorts of tools into the mains, but there aren't enough sockets. So I just 'nationalised' three sockets and made an adaptor out of them. You can get commercial extension leads and adaptors in the shops, of course, but they're expensive. Sockets, wire, screws – we've got all that stuff at work, it only took ten minutes. The bosses are never in a hurry to buy us any tools or improve our working conditions. We use our own tools. We work with whatever each of us has bought or been able to make. Hammers, floats, drills, trowels – anything you can find, that's what you use. Earlier, in Soviet times, they gave us all the tools, everything. We used to modify all of it then too, to suit our needs, but at least we didn't spend any money on it. Our construction trust was rich: we used to get free holidays in the south and there was a pioneer camp for the children – you could stay there all summer if you wanted – but everything has to be paid for now. How can I pay? There's no work, nobody's building anything now, there's nothing left but repairs.

Sockets, electrical wire, plug, wood, screws

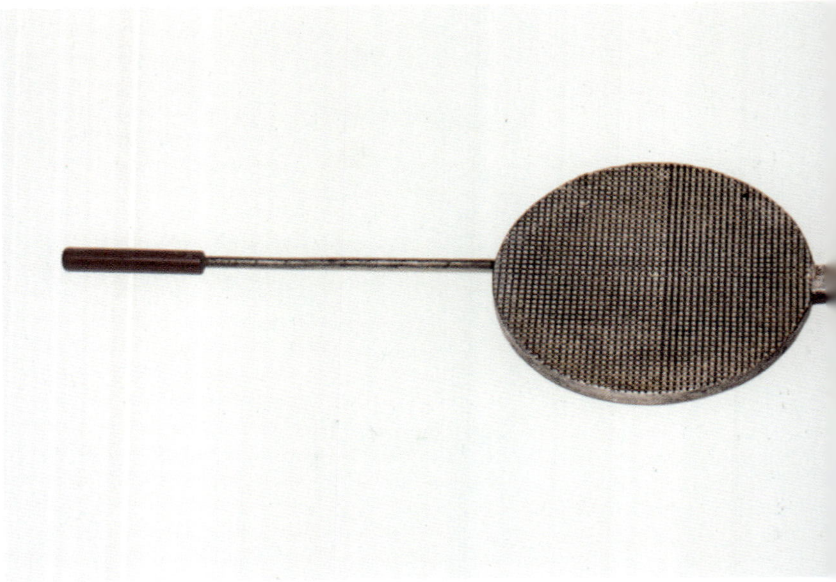

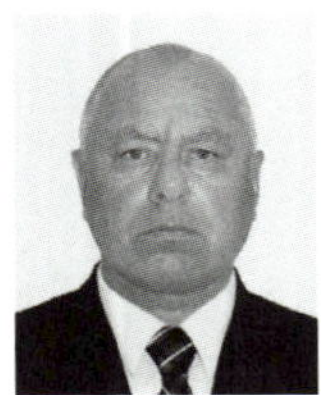

**Pyotr Sachivko**  Kiev, 1985

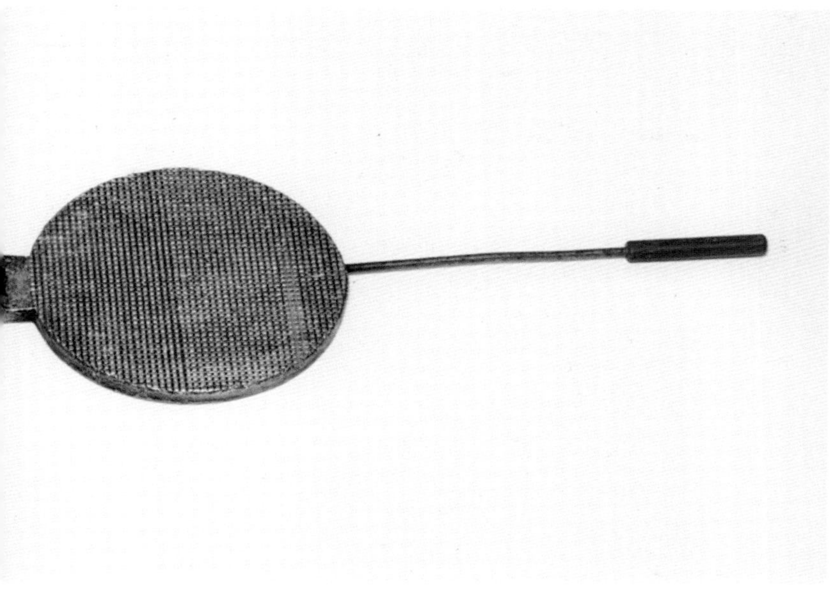

I worked in a big factory. Everything was there. We made all sorts of different things – whatever people wanted. It was only later they messed it all up and everything got filched. But before perestroika – what didn't we make? Tanks, rockets and all sorts of small stuff for the home. What a factory it was – a giant! They just screwed the whole thing up. I don't even know what's left now – some say the Germans are going to make their cars there. But back then the factory was a regular champion of industry. We had good bonuses, our own farm and a rest home in the Crimea for holidays. What's wrong with a life like that? If you needed something for the house – no problem. If you could cope with your job, you could do whatever you liked – so long as you didn't let the bosses down. You had a pair of hands, there was any metal you could possibly want, not to mention lathes and all sorts of other equipment. We could do anything with metal: cut it, turn it, sputter it, grind it. As for these waffle-irons, I don't know, it was just the latest fashion. The wife said everybody had one and we didn't – so make one! I went across to the mould operators and said, 'I need a mould for a waffle-iron'. 'Take that one', they said. I went to the foundry shop: 'Give us a few drops of duralumin, will you lads?' It was done in a moment – why shouldn't they help? If they'd have asked me, I'd have helped them out too. Well, that was it. I put handles on it and gave it to the wife on March 8th for Women's Day.

Duralumin, steel rods, glass cloth laminate

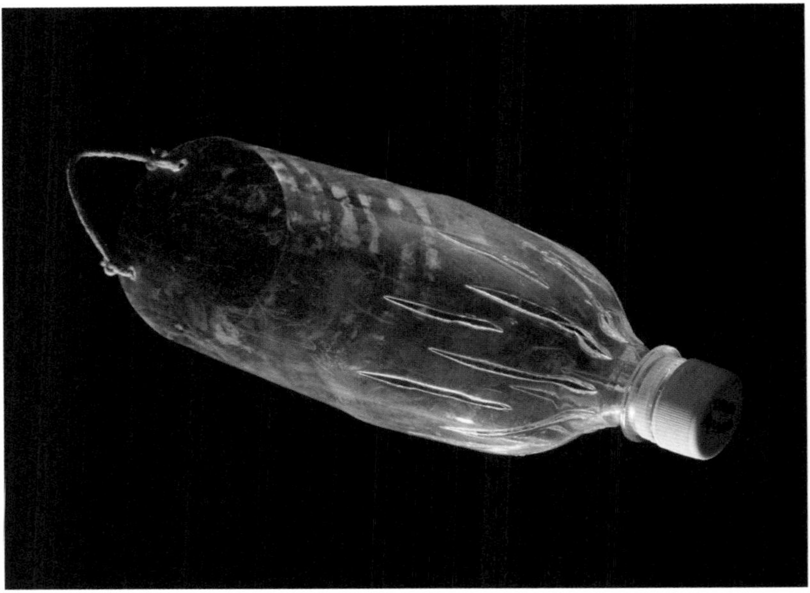

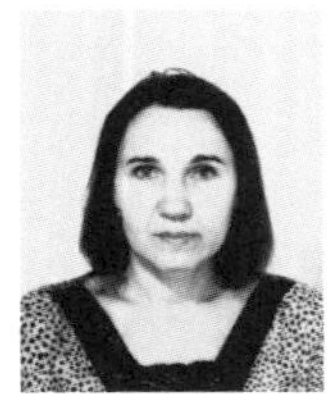

**Elena Rasputina**                                        Moscow, 1993

This is a mould for paskha, an Easter dessert made with cottage cheese. I just took an ordinary plastic fizzy-drink bottle and cut it 15 or 20 centimetres from the top, to get this kind of funnel. Then I used a hot knife to make the slits. You put the cottage cheese wrapped in muslin inside the funnel and the slits let everything drain out, just like granny's old wooden mould. The next day your cottage cheese will be ready. Thank God they still bring a big barrel of milk into the yard and pour it out for us – like they used to in Soviet times. The collective farm here hasn't collapsed yet, so I can buy a litre of milk for a third of what it costs in the shop. It works out that a packet of cottage cheese I make myself is five times cheaper. As for the taste, mine's the real thing, it's alive. The stuff from the shop is dead somehow.

Plastic bottle, wire

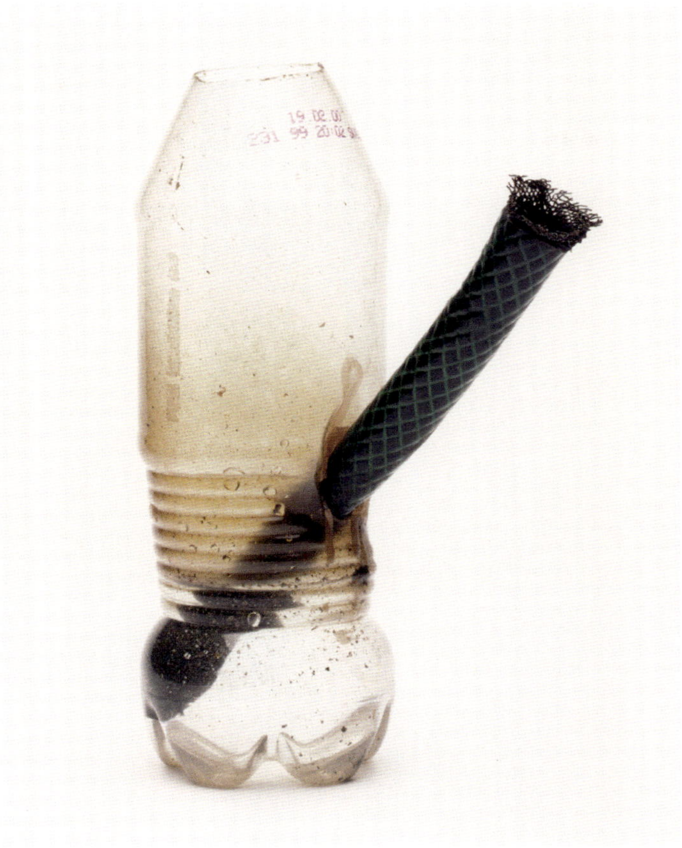

**Alexei Bonk**  Moscow, 1999

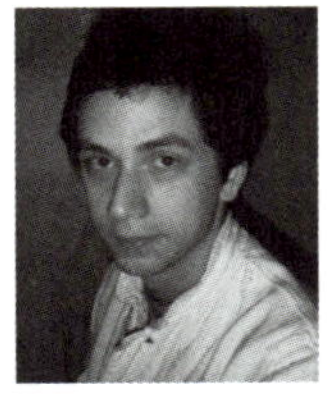

Sometimes I fancy a smoke, but I don't have a hookah. So I invent something quick and easy. I go to the market near here where you can buy bits of tubing, and those plastic bottles are lying around everywhere. After that, all you need is a good pair of hands to put them together. And Bonk's flying! Better than any hookah. It's a real high! Ooh!

Plastic bottle, hose

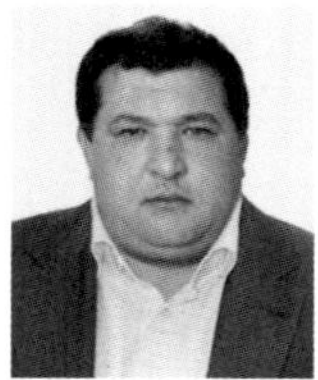

**Oleg Kudriumov**                                     Moscow region, c.1992

You know the way it is: all sorts end up in the army. Some are from the backwoods, some are only just down from the hills – this used to be a big country. It's good when someone has brains and has graduated from a technical school or college – you can talk to him like a human being. He understands you and you understand him. But they're not all like that. There are some, you tell them 'left turn' and they turn right. You tell them 'about turn' and they stand there grinning, making sheep's eyes at you. I ask them: 'Do you understand Russian?' They understand 'mess hall' all right, but 'left turn, right turn' – they don't want to understand that! How can you leave anyone like that on guard or send them on active duty? You're afraid to give him a rifle – let him peel potatoes instead. So the normal guys stand duty for them and never get enough sleep. That's the way it works out: some have an easy time sitting in the kitchen for two years, while the others are on constant guard duty. That's why we need this seal, this stamp, so that certain idiots won't get their face and foot towels mixed up. Just recently they haven't been giving us towels any more, but big sheets of towelling that you cut the hand and foot towels out of. They end up looking the same. So the soldiers won't get confused, we mark them with stamps: 'fo' for foot, 'fa' for face. The rubber came from a boot heel, and the handle's made out of a piece of wood, to make it easier to stamp. You dip it in the paint and stamp away.

Wood, glue, rubber

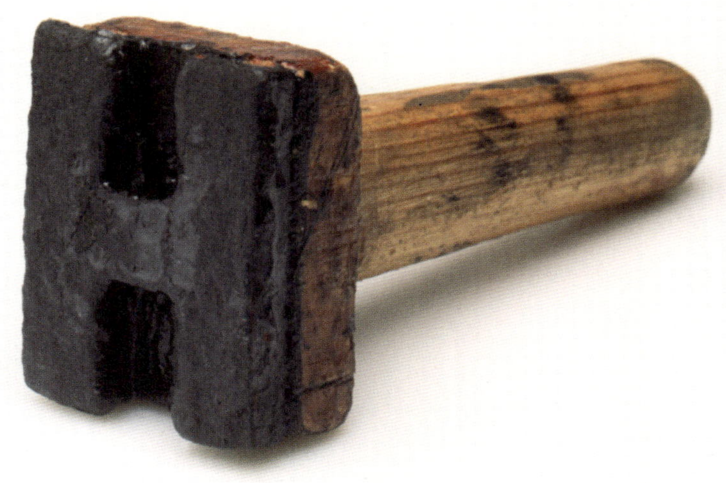

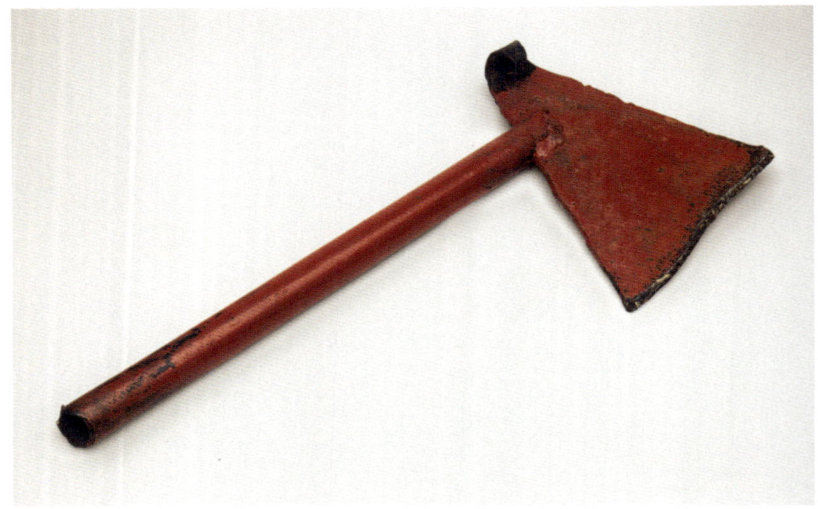

**Oleg Kudriumov**                                    Moscow region, c.1995

We made this ourselves in about 1995. The corner part was cut out of thick metal. One side we sharpened to make an axe and the other turned out like a pickaxe. We bent it so that it wouldn't give way. It's kind of a relic now: it hangs around here as a reminder of those years. It's simple metal – not hardened as if it was there wouldn't be any burrs. I sharpened it myself. The commission needed it – the fireman had a job to do. It was kind of my initiative. There was inflation in around 1994 and we didn't live so well until 1996. Financing started in about 1997, when they started to pull themselves together and so axes and shovels started to appear – I mean all the necessary stuff. But axes break you know, whether you want them to or not.

Steel, paint

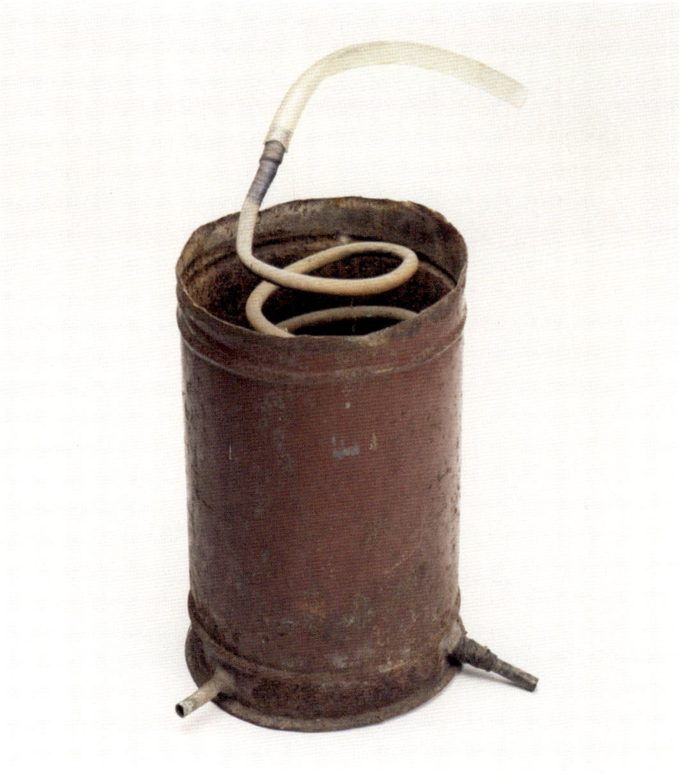

**Lidia Vasilieva**                    Ryazan region, 1981

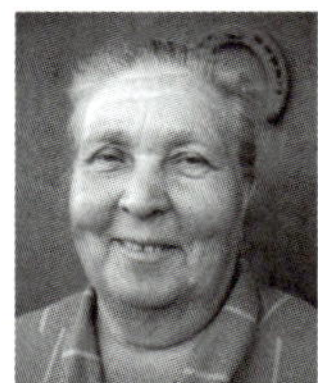

This is a home-brew still. Or rather, it's the most important part of one – you can't make any vodka without it. My late husband made it out of a big old can that we used to keep our flour in. The can developed a hole and so, to get some use out of it and not just throw it out, we used it as a still. My husband made another hole in it and put in a copper tube twisted into a spiral. Then he welded a piece of pipe onto the hole that was already there, welding it shut so we had a still. It's come in really handy lots of times: when we buried my husband, when we sent our son off to the army and for celebrating weddings.

Copper pipe

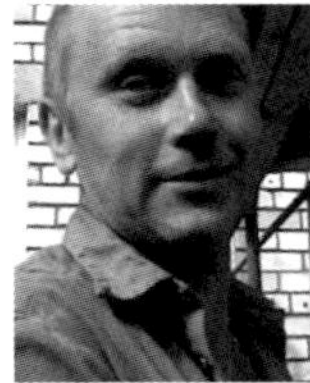

**Sergei Debov**                                                    Ivanovo, 1993

This is just an ordinary handle that we invented ten years ago when I got a sauna. Mum's very big – it's hard for her to bend down. Well, we all have something wrong with us. She said, 'I need you to put a handle on the wall, a metal handle.' A metal handle gets hot in a sauna, but this one never gets hot, nothing happens to it. The door could do with something a bit better of course, but it's a very convenient handle. I've got handles like it everywhere. It's from an ordinary old container – you cut it off and nail it on. This is the door into the house, but the whole business started with the sauna. Once I had made a handle like this for the sauna, I started putting them all over. In winter you can take hold of them with your bare hand, and they feel warm. I've got all sorts of containers – I'm a car mechanic, after all. They don't last for ever, of course, but then I can just go and cut out a new one – the whole thing only takes five minutes! It's perfect because it's made to fit the hand. Before, I used to have an old copper handle here. My father built the house, forty years ago. In Soviet times it never entered anyone's head to filch door handles, even copper ones. But as soon as perestroika started and people were allowed to collect non-ferrous metal, then it all began: they cut out all the aluminium wire – the electric wiring. They cut it while it was still live, not even the danger of getting killed stopped them. And with no electricity – well, you know. The first thing they did was cut and rip everything off, including my door handle. So after I'd made the one for mum, I nailed one on the door too. Then I got to like it – I only change them now and then. My neighbours have borrowed the idea – they're all putting them up too.

Plastic container, nails, screws

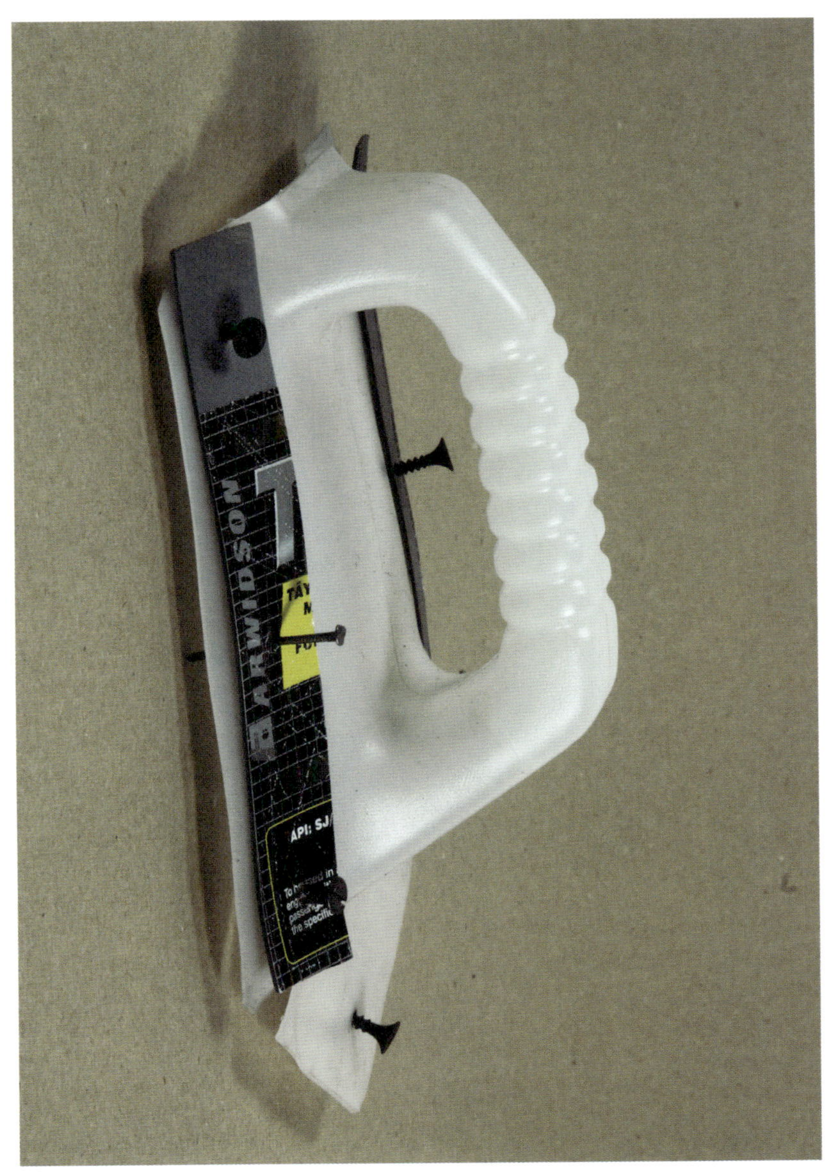

ARWIDSON
TÄY
M
FU
API: SJ/
To be used in
eng
passing
the specific

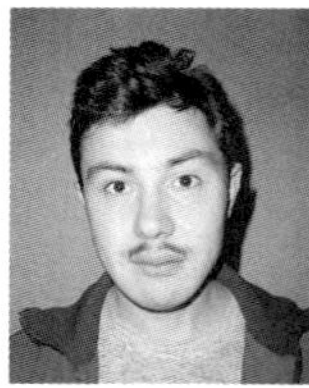

**Oleg Baichurin**                                         Saransk, 1989

I used this when I was studying. I lived in halls of residence with a lot of people. Because of this we had to boil water for tea very quickly, but we had an electric cooker which boiled water very slowly. So we kind of thought up this home-made water boiler. We found a cable with a plug from a kettle, or took it from a small heater and then took two completely ordinary razor blades. We joined them together with matches so that there was a gap between the razor blades. After we fastened the blades together with the matches, we joined the two ends of the wires. And so you lower this thing, this water boiler, into the water, into a 3-litre jar and plug it in and the water boils very quickly. A 3-litre jar boils in about two to three minutes. It's like the simplest way to boil water.

How did we come up with it? Well, in physics there's a law relating to the properties of conductors. Water is a conductor and using a current between plastic is a common method of boiling water. Standard kettles that you can buy in shops are based on this, and everyone uses them because they are convenient. But in 1987 or 1988 it was difficult to buy a kettle, so for us, that water boiler was a real luxury. There were lots of people, all wanting tea. It was quite a powerful conductor and the cable didn't heat up. The first time we left just a small gap, but the water started to bubble, the wires started to buzz and the cable started to burn so we then decided to leave a gap of 2 or 3 centimetres.

Razor blades, matches, cable, plug

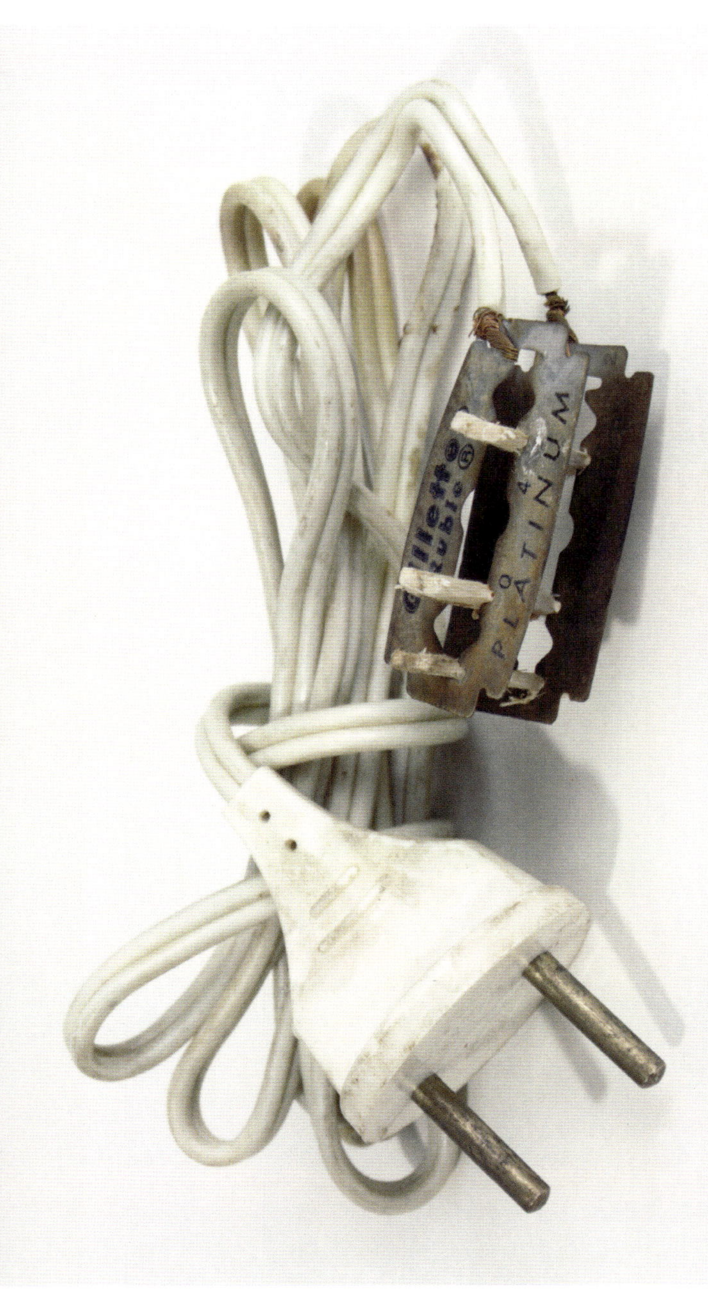


Gillette
Super
PLATINUM

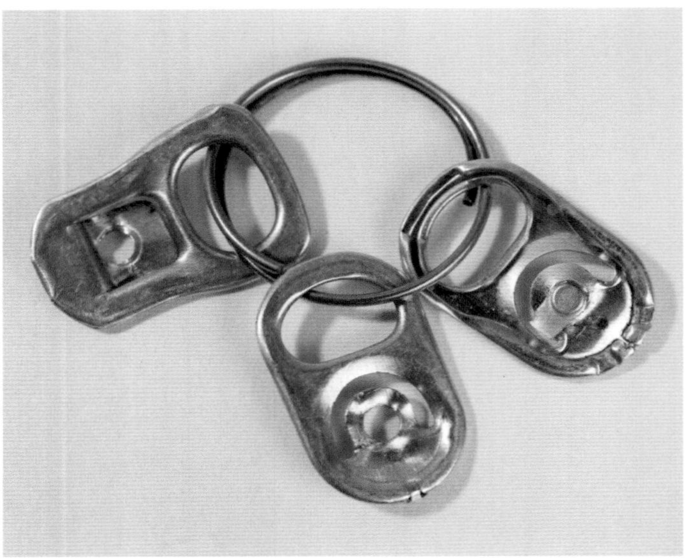

## Oleg Baichurin

Moscow, 1996–8

I was living in Saransk, Mordovia, and working in a factory. They didn't pay us very much and they paid us late, in groceries or the factory's products. Anyway, we didn't get much money in our hands. My friends went to Moscow to earn some real money – all the young people went and I decided to go too. When I got there I stayed with relatives and looked for work, so I had to phone businesses, friends and relations. In Saransk the public phones were free, but in Moscow the phones worked on tokens that you had to pay for and I didn't have much money. Then my nephews told me that instead of tokens you could use the ring-pulls from ordinary beer or soft-drink cans. First I picked up a few ring-pulls in the street and put them in a phone, but nothing happened, then I tried another and it worked – you just have to thump it on the top right corner. The old phones worked on weight so you had to listen for the moment when the ring-pull lands on the lever and hit it at just the right time. I saved a lot of money that way. Of course, I probably wouldn't have tried experimenting with the ring-pulls if I'd had any money. I used to tear them off cans or collect them from beside the phones – they left them there when they emptied the money out of the phone box. They've started putting up new phones now, ones that work with cards, but we'll come up with something.

Aluminium ring-pulls

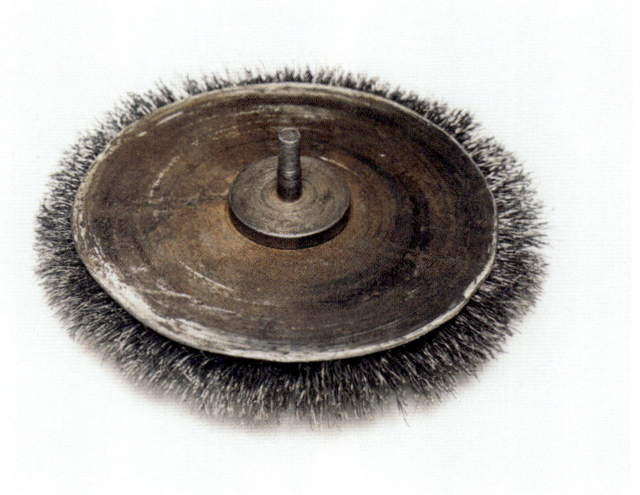

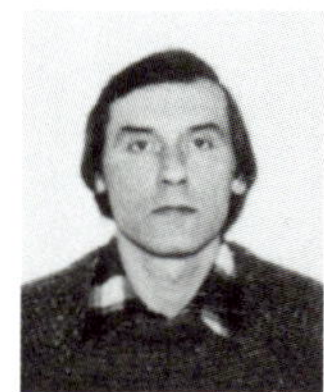

**Aleksandr Klyotskin**                    Moscow, 1996

Well, this is an attachment for an electric drill that cleans the rust off metal surfaces. I had this industrial disc with bristles and I made metal cover plates to shorten the length of them, making them stiffer and increasing the working life of the disc. The discs were cut out by hand with shears, fitted onto the attachment, turned on a lathe and the rough spots smoothed with an abrasive disc. I got the metal rod from the dump, sawed it by hand. I needed to repair an old car – the seams needed to be cleaned down after the welding work. Basically I needed to be able to get the disc into difficult places, effectively clean off the car's sills, arches and wings to remove the rust before putting on the undercoat and paint. On the industrial ones they make, the bristles are either too long or they come out, and the disc doesn't reach very far, or else it's not rigid at all. And so I reckon my design turned out quite well really. This disc has lasted me for three cars now.

Steel plates, industrial brush, threaded axle, nut

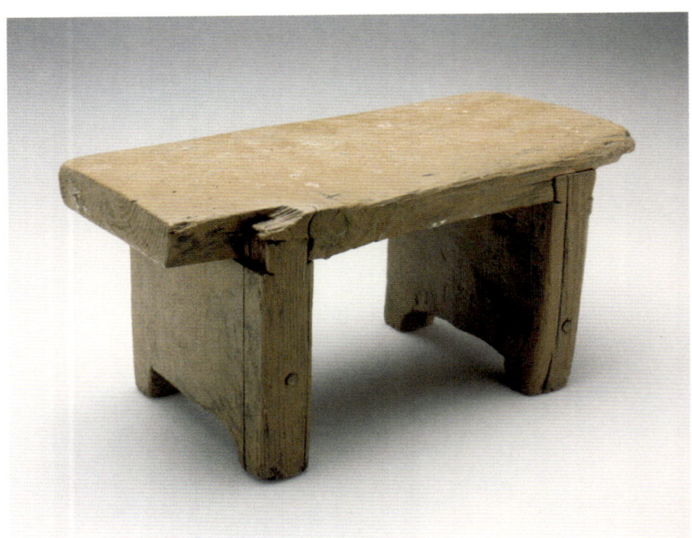

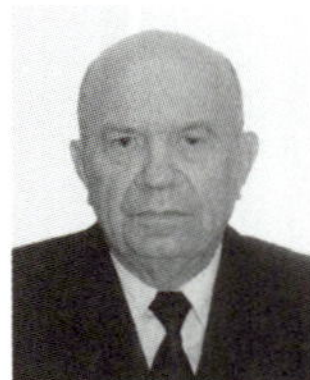

**Viktor Plotnikov**                    Moscow, c.1993

I was sitting on the balcony with nothing to put my tools and what have you on. Then I had an idea – what I needed was a little bench. I'd been planning to make a little bench for the bathroom for ages, so that my wife doesn't have to bend down too far when she's doing the laundry. The material mostly comes from the rubbish tips, and sometimes there are broken crates at work – so I take stuff from there as well. In general, if it's just lying around, I'll take it. We needed a little bench to sit down on, so as not to have to sit on the floor or reach up for something. The materials were waste – rough wood. The joint – they thought that up a thousand years before my time. The locker in the kitchen isn't convenient, but if you just put a little bench down there you can work away. We've got this bookshelf in the hallway and bending down to the bottom shelf is awkward – it's better to sit down when you're looking for something. The little bench is more for sitting on, not putting your feet on.

Planks, glue, paint

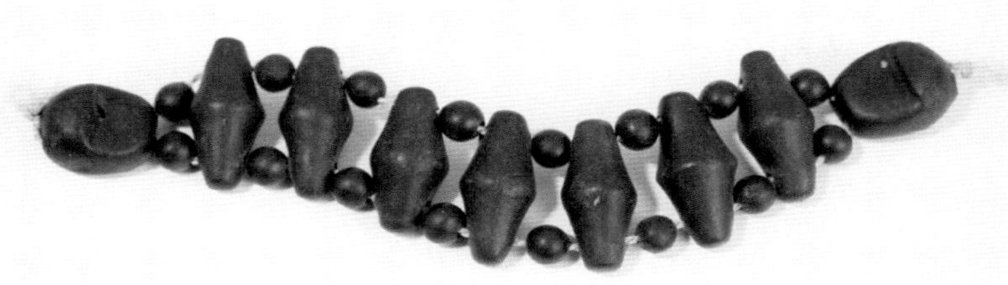

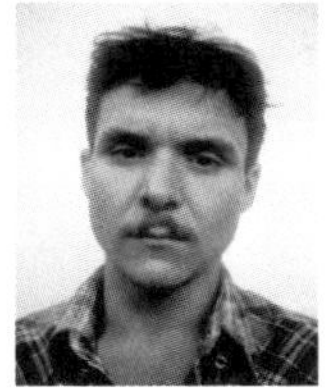

**Denis**                                                          Salavat, 1991

Between 1990 and 1992 I was serving in the army in Bashkiria, in the town of Salavat. In 1991 I was in hospital in Salavat and there was this young guy there who taught me how to make rosary beads out of bread. He said they make beads like that in the prisons – that's typical of prison culture. Some time later I was working at a brick factory where convicts were also working and I actually saw them with these rosary beads. You take the soft crumb of white bread, knead it with your fingers, spit into it and knead it again. Then you add the ash from four packets of 'Prima' or 'Belomor' cigarettes. Knead it all together, spit in it again, and it all turns into this black lump. For the beads, you mould them, prick a hole through with a match and slip the thread though it. They are finished off at the sides with special end pieces and dents for the fingers making them easier to count. Then they are dried for four days in the shade – not the sun. They turn really hard, like stone. There wasn't anything much to do in the hospital, so I made myself some as well. When you count them it calms your nerves. You can meditate with them as well. The time passes quicker – you don't even notice it.

White bread, cigarette ash, spittle, thread

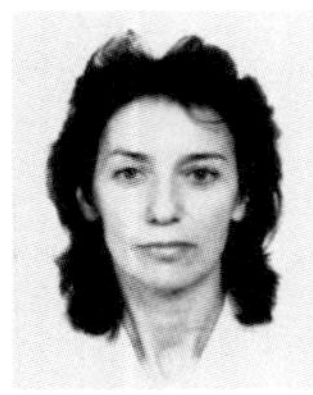

**Natasha**                                                              Ivanovo, 2003

This is a contraption that goes back to my childhood. It was my chemistry teacher's invention, not mine. She was a really impressive woman. Paradoxically, I've completely forgotten her name, even though I remember lots of details about her: her manicure, her lovely clothes... Anyway, she came up with this idea – she took an empty lipstick case and made a sort of chalk lipstick. She put a piece of chalk in it and moved it up as she used it. She used to do a lot of writing on the blackboard, and when the lesson ended, she closed the little case and put in on her desk. It was all very elegant, and it suited her style. That was about 1985 or 1986. I never saw anyone else with one like it. You can easily sharpen the chalk with a metal ruler or even with a nail file you might carry in your handbag. It's easy to put the chalk in, but none of the other teachers I work with does it. I don't know why. I think it's very convenient. Of course, male teachers don't need this, but women teachers have to set an example, they have to be tidy, look neat and beautiful. It's not good if your hands are dirty, if you get chalk on your clothes – that just won't do. And I've never seen sticks of chalk that come with wrappers, or in cases.

Lipstick case, chalk

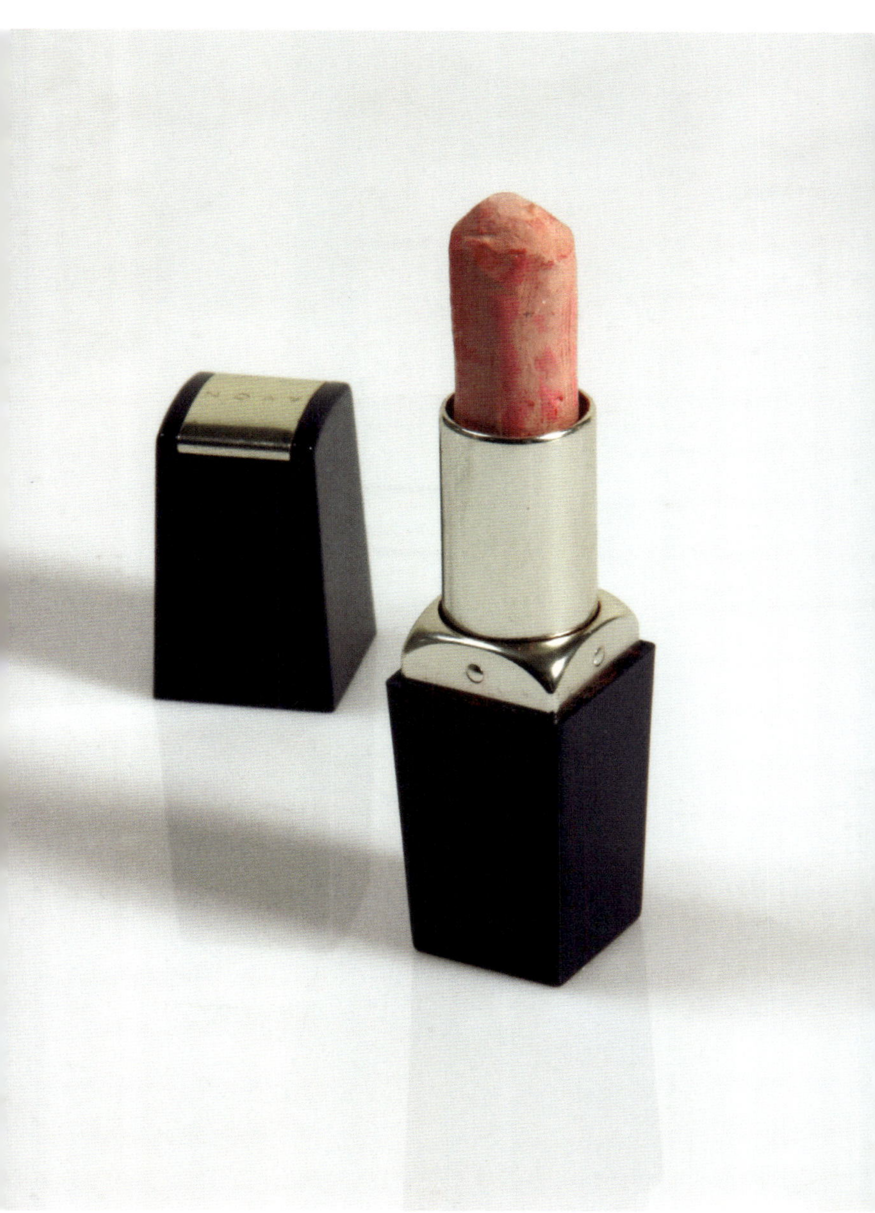

# Afterword

Vladimir Arkhipov

In the Russian language the word for 'creative work' (tvorchestvo) shares a root with the word for 'Creator' (Tvorets). The word for 'art' (iskusstvo) shares a root with the word for 'Tempter' (Iskusitel). Formerly, when artists still believed in God, they 'Created'. Today, when most artists do not believe in anything, they make art. There is no creation left in art. So what is an honest artist to do? I have found a partial answer to that question. Since I require a viewer and I am doomed to self-conscious aesthetic reflection, I cannot be absolutely honest and sincere. But I know that every day hundreds of millions of people discover their connection with God in some way when they create. The act of creation has no need of justification. It is self-sufficient. The most interesting visual traces left by creation are those that have not been subject to conscious aesthetic assessment by their creators. All that is required is to find them and present them in a skilful manner. The right of choice is mine. I spent a long time searching for and selecting a modern folk phenomenon (which as yet has no name), as an example: millions of people throughout the world create unique everyday items for themselves. I interview them, take photographs, show their things in exhibitions. In this way, I combine their creative work with my art.

Selected exhibitions include:
*Items of Pride and Shame*
Perm Museum of Contemporary Art, Perm, Russia 2021
*Russian Contemporary Art Triennial*
The Garage Museum, Moscow, Russia 2017
*Post Folk Archive*
Bonnefantenmuseum, Maastricht, Netherlands 2014
*Ostalgia*
New Museum of Contemporary Art, New York, USA 2011
*Berlin-Moscow/Moscow-Berlin 1950–2000*
State Tretyakov Gallery, Moscow, Russia 2004
*Post-Folk Archive*
Ikon Gallery, Birmingham, United Kingdom 2002

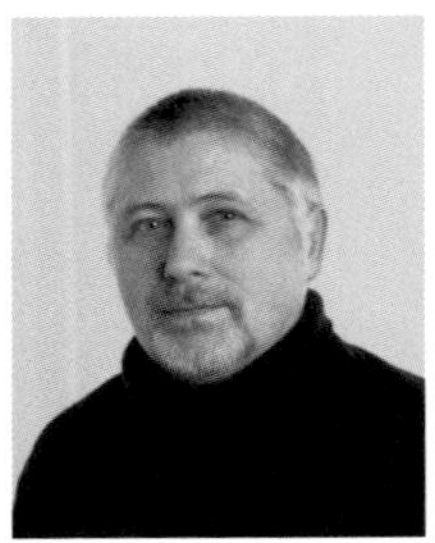

Vladimir Arkhipov was born in Ryazan in 1961. After graduating from the State Radio Institute he worked as an engineer for five years. A self-educated artist, in 1994 he began collecting and exhibiting home-made objects and in 1996, studied visual anthropology under Valery Podoroga at the Russian State University for the Humanities. Alongside an audio and video archive, he has created a worldwide database of these objects. He is currently working on the concept and methodology of The Museum of Other Things.

otherthingsmuseum.com
youtube.com/user/artVladimirArkhipov/playlists

Published in 2006
Reprinted in 2022

FUEL Design & Publishing
33 Fournier Street
London E1 6QE

fuel-design.com



Printed in China

Distributed by Thames & Hudson / D.A.P.
ISBN 978-1-9162184-7-5

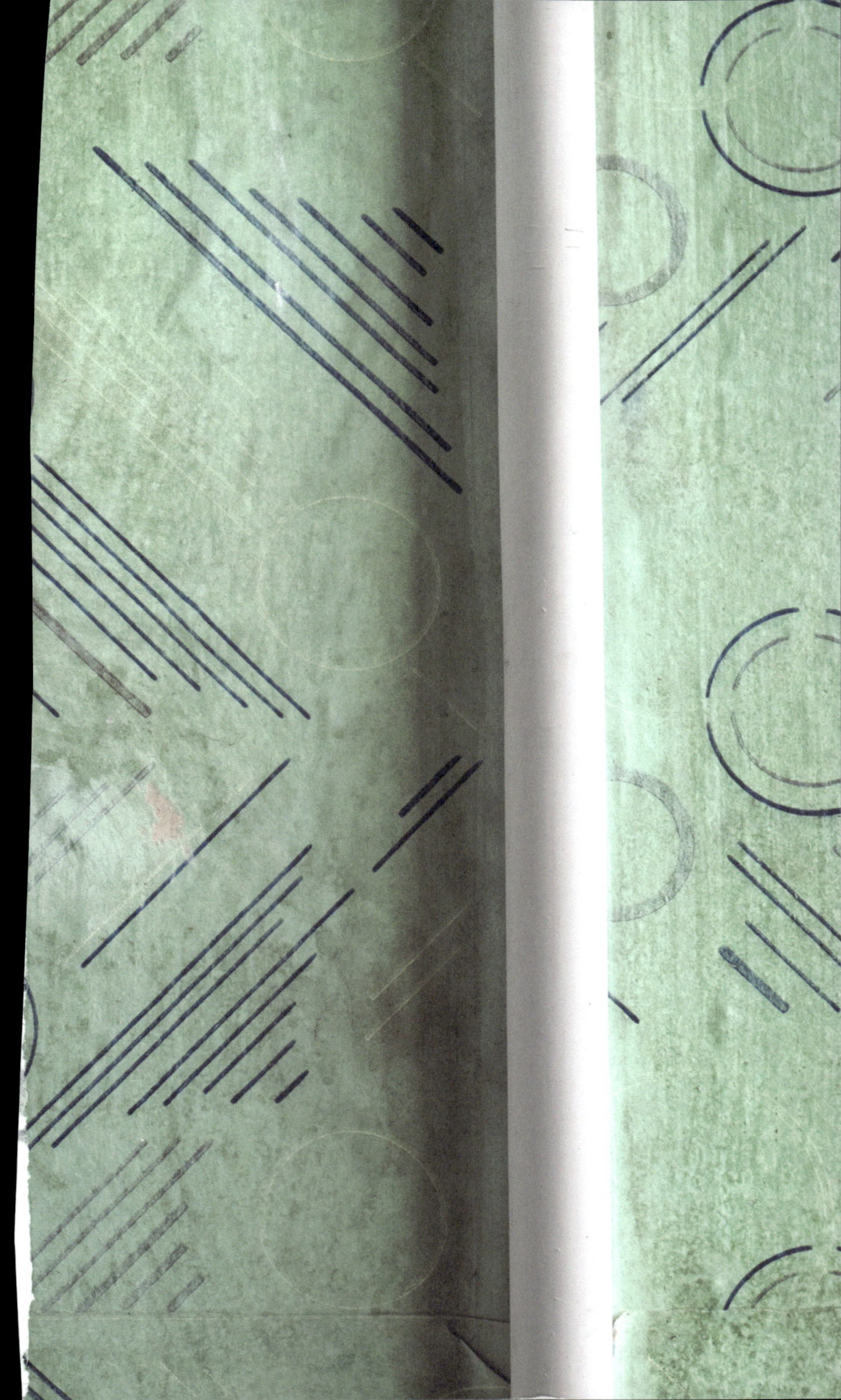

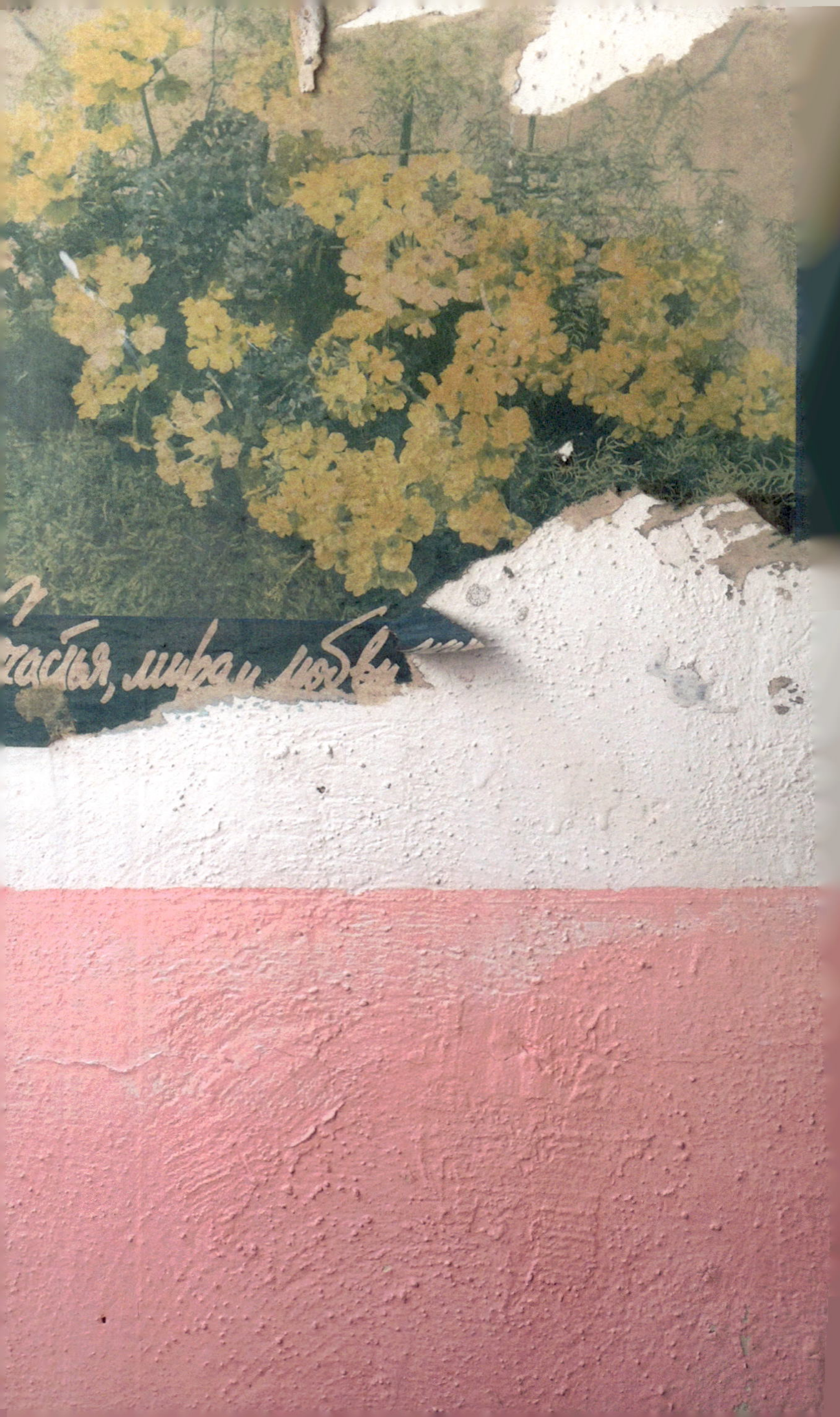

счастья, мира и любви